THE FUTURE
OF
CAPITALISM

With the compliments of

ALSO BY LESTER C. THUROW

Poverty and Discrimination (1969)

Investment in Human Capital (1970)

The Impact of Taxes on the American Economy (1971)

Generating Inequality: Mechanisms of Distribution in the U.S. Economy (1975)

The Zero-Sum Society (1980)

Dangerous Currents: The State of Economics (1983)

The Management Challenge: Japanese Views (1983)

The Zero-Sum Solution (1985)

Head to Head: The Coming Economic Battle Among Japan, Europe, and America (1992)

THE FUTURE

OF

CAPITALISM

HOW TODAY'S ECONOMIC FORCES

SHAPE TOMORROW'S WORLD

Lester C. Thurow

William Morrow and Company, Inc.
New York

Thurow, Lester C.
    The future of capitalism : how today's economic forces shape tomorrow's world / Lester C. Thurow.
        p. cm.
    Includes bibliographical references and index.
    ISBN 0-688-12969-2 (hardcover)
    1. Economic forecasting. 2. Capitalism—Forecasting.
3. Technological innovations—Economic aspects—Forecasting.
4. Skilled labor—Forecasting. 5. International economic relations—
Forecasting. 6. United States—Economic conditions—1993–
7. Twenty-first century—Forecasts. I. Title.
HB3730.T55   1996
330.12'2—dc20   95–42443
                                                                      CIP

Printed in the United States of America

2   3   4   5   6   7   8   9   10

BOOK DESIGN BY REBECCA AIDLIN

*To all those who are willing to invest
in the distant future
and to O.T.W.*

Acknowledgments

The central thrust of this book was presented as the Castle Lectures in Ethics, Politics, and Economics at Yale in 1995/96. The Castle Lectures are designed to promote interdisciplinary reflection on the moral foundations of society and government.

A variety of groups too large to individually mention helped hone my arguments with their critiques over the past two years.

I benefited from the help of a good group of MIT student commentators, research assistants, and fact checkers—Cherng Chao, Edith Chan, Pansy Lin, Jill Woodworth, Madeline Zavodny.

Contents

We are like a big fish that has been pulled from the water and is flopping wildly to find its way back in. In such a condition the fish never asks where the next flip or flop will bring it. It senses only that its present position is intolerable and that something else must be tried.

—Anonymous Chinese saying,
quoted by Perry Link in *China in Transformation*,
Daedalus (Spring 1993)

Chapter 1

New Game, New Rules,
New Strategies

Since the onset of the industrial revolution, when success came to be defined as rising material standards of living, no economic system other than capitalism has been made to work anywhere. No one knows how to run successful economies on any other principles. The market, and the market alone, rules. No one doubts it. Capitalism alone taps into modern beliefs about individuality and exploits what some would consider the baser human motives, greed and self-interest, to produce rising standards of living. When it comes to catering to the wants and desires of every individual, no matter how trivial those wants seem to others, no system does it even half so well. Capitalism's nineteenth- and twentieth-century competitors—fascism, socialism, and communism—are all gone.

Yet even as the competition fades into the history books, something also seems to be shaking the foundations of capitalism. It, too, seems to be like that Chinese fish flipping and flopping to find its way back into a stream that has moved.

In the decade of the 1960s the world economy grew at the rate of 5.0 percent per year after correcting for inflation.[1] In the 1970s, growth dropped to 3.6 percent per year. In the 1980s there was a further deceleration to 2.8 percent per year, and in the first half of the 1990s the world could manage a growth rate of just 2.0 percent per year.[2] In two decades capitalism lost 60 percent of its momentum.

In all of Western Europe not one net new job was created from 1973 to 1994.[3] Over the same time period the United States generated thirty-eight million net new jobs even though it has one third fewer people. Europe's unemployment rates, which had been about half those found in the United States throughout the 1950s and 1960s, by the mid-1990s had risen to be twice those of the United States (10.8 percent versus 5.4 percent in March 1995).[4] If Europeans who have exited from the workforce but who are of normal working age were included in the statistics, European unemployment is at least 20 percent.

The Japanese stock market falls from 38,916 on the Nikkei Index in December 1989 to 14,309 on August 18, 1992—a bigger decline in real terms than the fall in the American stock market between 1929 and 1932.[5] That crash along with a similar crash in property values leads to a Japanese recession that goes on seemingly without end. In 1994, Japanese industrial production was 3 percent below that of 1992.[6] Each year forecasters predict that growth will resume the next. In mid-1995 those who in mid-1994 were predicting growth in 1995 were facing a Japanese economy with no growth and predicting growth in 1996. At some point the forecasters have to be right but meanwhile the world's second largest capitalist economy is stuck—unable to restart its economic engines.

In the United States, after correcting for inflation, the real per capita gross domestic product (GDP) rises 36 percent from 1973 to mid-1995 yet the real hourly wages of nonsupervisory workers (those who don't boss anyone else—a vast majority of the workforce) decline 14 percent.[7] In the decade of the 1980s, all of the earnings gains went to the top 20 percent of the workforce and an amazing 64 percent accrued to the top 1 percent.[8] How far can inequality rise before the system cracks?

In the summer of 1994, Mexico was a country that had done everything right—balanced its budget, privatized more than one thousand state-owned companies, chopped government regulations, joined NAFTA, and agreed to cut tariffs and quotas dramatically. Private capital poured in. President Carlos Salinas was a hero with his picture on the cover of every business magazine. Six months later Mexico is in ruins. By April 1995, 500,000 Mexican workers had lost their jobs with another 250,000 expected to shortly join them.[9] Average purchasing power was on its way to a 30 percent decline. President Salinas was again on the cover of every magazine—but as an exile, accused of being incompetent and/or corrupt, possibly in bed with the drug dealers, and who had lost his chance to head the World Trade Organization. Why didn't the policies work? The policies were precisely those most recommended for leaders who wish to run market economies.

The intellectual discourse surrounding such events has the characteristics of the Indian parable wherein a dozen blind men are each feeling some part of the elephant—the tail, the trunk, the tusks, the legs, the ears, the back, the sides. Each thinks that he is feeling a different animal and when they report back on what they have felt, they describe very different animals. The real elephant never emerges in their analysis.

The eternal verities of capitalism—growth, full employment, financial stability, rising real wages—seem to be vanishing just as the enemies of capitalism vanish. Something within capitalism has changed to be causing these results. Something has to be changed to alter these unacceptable results if capitalism is to survive. But what is "it"? And "how" can "it" be changed?

To understand the underlying elephant it is necessary to examine the forces that are changing the very structure of the economic world in which we live. What are the fundamental forces? How do they interact with each other? Where will those forces push events? How will they change the nature of the economic game and what it takes to be a winner? Projecting current trends forward is always wrong. Such projections miss the turning points in human events.

As with the Chinese fish in the quotation at the beginning of this book, mad flipping and flopping is as likely to get humans farther away from the safety of an environment where they know how to function as it is to get them closer. To make it to safety, the new environment in which we suddenly find ourselves must be understood.

The causes are to be found in the interactions of new technologies and new ideologies. They are the forces driving the economic system in new directions. Together they are producing a new economic game with new rules requiring new strategies to win.

The "how" is mysterious. How does a system that believes it takes competition to make the firms within capitalism efficient, adapt to a changing environment and maintain its efficiency if the system of capitalism itself has no competition? Perhaps with all of its competitors driven off the economic playing fields, capitalism has lost its ability to adapt to new circumstances?

Those who govern the existing system, no matter how left-wing and revolutionary their political ideologies, are social conservatives. The system has chosen them to rule and therefore it must be the "right" system. Without any outside or inside threats to the existing system, all changes lower the probabilities that they will continue to rule in the future. Since they know that they govern by virtue of today's rules, they instinctively oppose change—different people might govern if the rules were different. Nowhere is this principle more vividly seen than in the old Communist world. The second and third generations of leadership were still ideological Communists, but had become the most socially conservative elements in their societies. Social systems build up defenses against change like the body builds up defenses against diseases.[10]

Historically, outside military threats, inside social unrest, and alternative ideologies have been used as justifications for overcoming the vested interests in the status quo. They are what have allowed capitalism to survive and thrive. The rich were smarter than Marx believed. They understood that their own long survival depended upon eliminating revolutionary conditions—and they did. An aristocratic conservative in Germany, Bismarck, invented public old age pensions and health care in the 1880s. The son of a British duke, Winston Churchill, instigated the first large-scale public unemployment insurance system in 1911.[11] A patrician President, Franklin Roosevelt, designed the social welfare state that saved capitalism after it collapsed in America. None of these things would have happened if capitalism had not been threatened.

There have been other periods when the dominant social systems had no competitors—ancient Egypt, imperial Rome, the Dark Ages, Japan until Admiral Perry arrived, the Middle Kingdom of China. In all of these situations the dominant social system lost its ability to adapt. As technology and ideologies changed, none of them could keep it together—or put it back together.

Socialism was invented shortly after capitalism as a remedy to the visible nineteenth-century defects of capitalism—widening inequalities, rising unemployment, a growing workforce of castoffs. To cure those defects, socialists believed, it would be possible under socialism to build a new human being—a "social individual," who would be "the foundation stone of production and wealth."[12]

Communism failed because in practice no one succeeded in creating that new human being. It proved impossible to motivate most human beings to work hard for social objectives for very long. In the 1920s and 1930s the Soviets could be motivated to build socialism. In the 1940s they could be motivated to defeat Hitler. In the 1950s and 1960s they could be motivated to rebuild from the destruction of fascism. As late as the 1950s, the USSR seemed to work—its growth rates exceeded those in the United States. But seventy years after the experiment began, the Soviets could no longer be motivated to work to build socialism and the system collapsed. In the contest between individual values and social values, individual values won.

But during the contest the outcome was not so certain. On December 8, 1941, when the United States entered World War II, the United States and Great Britain were essentially the only capitalistic countries left on the face of the earth and Britain was on the edge of a military defeat.[13] All of the rest of the world were fascist, Communist, or third world feudal colonies. The financial crises of the 1920s and the Great Depression of the 1930s had brought capitalism to the edge of extinction. The capitalism that now seems irresistible could, with just a few missteps, have vanished.

Effectively, the second way, communism, and what the Europeans call the third way, the social welfare state, have ceased to be viable alternatives. While the social welfare state did not collapse as communism did, it has essentially gone broke. Even in countries such as Sweden where the social welfare state has had its greatest support, it is in retreat. "Survival of the fittest" capitalism stands alone. There is no alternative. In office, political parties on the Left (the French or Spanish socialists) adopt exactly the same policies as the parties on the Right (the British or German conservatives).

As the second world collapsed, the third world splintered. Within it there are now clear winners (the little tigers of Hong Kong, Singapore, Taiwan, and South Korea), potential winners (Thailand or Malaysia), those rapidly integrating with global capitalism (China)—and the losers (Africa).[14] The third world is gone just as much as the second world is gone.

As we watch, the world's economic topography alters.

THE UNDERLYING FORCES

To understand the dynamics of this new economic world, it is useful to borrow two concepts from the physical sciences—plate tectonics from geology and punctuated equilibrium from biology. In geology the visible earthquakes and volcanoes are caused by the invisible movement of the continental plates floating on the earth's molten inner core. Mexico's economic crisis was as unexpected and violent as any volcanic explosion. Corporate downsizings rock human foundations (expectations about their economic futures) as profoundly as any earthquake. But no one can understand volcanoes or earthquakes by looking at them. The geophysicist must probe deeper to look at the forces generated below the surface of the earth by the continental plates. So too no one can understand what happened to Mexico by looking at the clumsy mistakes made by policy makers in Mexico City. Those suddenly in the middle of an economic earthquake cannot tell you why it is happening any more than those in the middle of a real earthquake can.

But plate tectonics also causes the slower, almost imperceptible changes that fundamentally alter the earth's surface within what are for geology short periods of time. In continental plate tectonics what seems static, the surface of the earth, is in reality in constant flux. The Indian plate pushes under the Eurasian plate and what is by weight and volume the world's largest mountain massif, Nanga Parbat, in the Himalayas, rises more than two feet every hundred years.[15] Relatively quickly something significant happens—Nanga Parbat becomes the world's tallest, as well as the world's largest, mountain.

So too with economic plate tectonics, the economic surface of the earth, the distribution of income and wealth, seems static, but in a relatively short period of time what was barely noticeable in any given year (a less than 1 percent per year decline in the real wages of non-supervisory workers for more than twenty years) radically alters the distribution of purchasing power. By the turn of the century the real wages for nonsupervisory workers will be back to where they were at mid-century, fifty years earlier, despite the fact that the real per capita GDP more than doubled over the same period of time.

Beneath the fundamental remaking of the economic surface of the earth that is now under way and the more spectacular economic earthquakes and volcanoes that are so visible are the movements of five economic plates. Five economic plates whose forces are just as irresistible as those of geology.

To understand what those forces are doing and what must be done to adjust to them, it is necessary to borrow the concept of "punctuated equilibrium" from evolutionary biology.[16] Normally evolution proceeds at a pace so slow that it is not noticeable on a human time scale. The top-of-the-food-chain, survival-of-the-fittest species usually only become more dominant—bigger and stronger. But occasionally something occurs that biologists know as "punctuated equilibrium." The environment suddenly changes and what has been the dominant species rapidly dies out to be replaced by some other species. Evolution takes a quantum leap. Natural selection, which normally works on the margins, suddenly alters the core of the system.

The best-known example is, of course, the dinosaurs. They dominated the surface of the earth for 130 million years, but then suddenly all of them became extinct (or birds?).[17] Recent theories point to a comet hitting the surface of the earth near the Yucatán Peninsula with such force that it caused sulfuric volcanoes to erupt on the other side of the earth.[18] A persistent cloud of sulfuric dust destroyed the environment that made the dinosaurs possible. For reasons that are still not clear, mammals could cope with this new environment and they became the earth's dominant species. But whatever happened, it happened quickly, and profoundly changed who would dominate—and who would become extinct.

Periods of punctuated equilibrium are equally visible in human history. Although they came almost two thousand years later, Napoleon's armies could move no faster than those of Julius Caesar—both depended upon horses and carts. But seventy years after Napoleon's death, steam trains could reach speeds of over 112 miles per hour.[19] The industrial revolution was well under way and the economic era of agriculture, thousands of years old, was in less than a century replaced by the industrial age. A survival-of-the-fittest social system, feudalism, that had lasted for hundreds of years was quickly replaced by capitalism.

Biological, social, or economic systems enter periods of punctuated equilibrium with slowly evolving but firmly established structures. They emerge from periods of punctuated equilibrium with radically different structures that once again begin slowly evolving. The characteristics needed to be a winner on one side of a period of punctuated equilibrium are very different from the characteristics needed to be a winner on the other side. During periods of punctuated equilibrium everything is in flux, disequilibrium becomes the norm, and uncertainty reigns![20]

Today the world is in a period of punctuated equilibrium—which is being caused by the simultaneous movements of five economic plates. In the end a new game with new rules requiring new strategies will emerge. Some of today's players will adapt and learn how to win in this new game. They will be those who understand the movement of the economic tectonic plates. They will become the top-of-the-food-chain, "fittest" individuals, business firms, or nations. Historically, they will come to be seen as the economic equivalent of the mammals.

THE FIVE ECONOMIC TECTONIC PLATES

The End of Communism

With the end of communism the one third of humanity and the one quarter of the landmass of the world that used to be controlled by that system will be joining the old capitalistic world. Those formerly living under communism will live in a world with a very different set of criteria for success and failure but those already living under capitalism will find that digesting this mass of humanity and geography profoundly alters the shape of their economic world.

A Technological Shift to an Era Dominated by Man-made Brainpower Industries

In the industrial societies of the nineteenth and twentieth centuries, most industries had natural, God-given homes geographically. Those homes were determined by the location of natural resources and the possession of capital. Coal could only be mined where coal existed; great seaports had to have good natural harbors. Labor-intensive products were made in poor countries; capital-intensive products were made in rich countries. In contrast, man-made brainpower industries don't have natural predetermined homes. They are geographically free—capable of being located anywhere on the face of the earth. The economically dominant will be able to create, mobilize, and organize the brainpower that determines their location.

A Demography Never Before Seen

The world's population is growing, moving, and getting older. Population is booming in the world's poorest countries. The push of miserable conditions at home and the pull of higher standards of living abroad are leading tens of millions of people to move from poor countries to rich countries just when unskilled labor is not needed in the wealthy industrial world. The world is also developing a new class of human beings—a very large group of elderly, relatively affluent people, most of whom do not work, and who are dependent upon government social welfare payments for much of their income.

A Global Economy

Shifts in technology, transportation, and communications are creating a world where anything can be made anywhere on the face of the earth and sold everywhere else on the face of the earth. National economies fade away. A substantial disconnect arises between global business firms with a worldview and national governments that focus on the welfare of "their" voters. Countries splinter, regional trading blocs grow, the global economy becomes ever more interconnected.

An Era Where There Is No Dominant Economic, Political, or Military Power

The rules for the world's trading system have always been written and enforced by its dominant economies—Great Britain in the nineteenth century and the United States in the twentieth century. But the twenty-first century will have no dominant power able to design, organize, and enforce the rules of the economic game. The unipolar economic world dominated by the United States is over, a multipolar world has arrived, but how is the economic game to be designed, organized, and maintained in a multipolar world?

THE ECONOMIC MAGMA

In geology, movements in the continental plates are driven by currents in the earth's molten inner core, its magma. Similarly, the five economic plates that determine the shape of our economic world float on a fluid mixture of technology and ideology. Changes within and interactions between these two forces create the currents that drive the economic plates into each other.

In the last period of punctuated equilibrium, when capitalism emerged from feudalism, changes were needed in both technology and ideology before capitalism could emerge. Technologically, capitalism needed an inanimate power source to which large amounts of equipment could be attached. When the only available power sources were either human or animal, the amount of capital equipment that could be attached to either was too limited to allow the creation of capitalism. Leonardo da Vinci, for example, had many wonderful inventions on paper—but none of them could be built without a source of power that was beyond his imagination.

The steam engine was the missing link. With it enormous amounts of capital equipment could be used at one location (textile mills) or in integrated, geographically dispersed, operations (the railroads). Steam railroads made the creation of national markets possible, and steam-driven factories made it possible to build companies of a scale that could serve those national markets. With the steam engine and the large amounts of equipment that could be attached to it, production could reach a level where economies of scale became possible. Output could rise proportionally faster than input. Higher productivity led to higher wages and profits, which led to more purchases of existing goods and the ability to indulge oneself in new luxuries that quickly became necessities. The accumulation of capital, and hence the ownership of capital, was central in harnessing the productive power of mechanical energy.

Electricity and the internal combustion engine eventually replaced steam as the primary energy source—making possible more decentralized forms of production—but they in no fundamental way changed the system. They were just more efficient.

Because of steam power a system of feudalism where those who owned the land made the important decisions was replaced by a system of capitalism where those who owned the plant and equipment made the important decisions. Capitalism gave decision-making power to the owners of capital precisely because they controlled the key ingredient in the new system—the power source. They were the generals in command of capitalism. They hired and fired the troops (labor), they promoted and demoted their junior officers (managers), they decided where the battles (production) would take place geographically, they decided where they would attack and where they would retreat (the markets they would attempt to conquer, the markets they would ignore), and they picked those weapons (technologies) that would bring them victory (profits). Labor was not the decision maker in either feudalism or capitalism, since land was the key strategic ingredient in feudalism and mechanical energy was the key strategic ingredient in capitalism. Over the course of the nineteenth century, the "robber barons" of capitalism replaced the feudal barons of the old system. Capitalism gave decision-making power to the owners of capital precisely because they controlled the key ingredient in the new system—capital.

But capitalism also needed changes in ideology. In the Middle Ages avarice was the worst of all sins and the merchant could never be pleasing to God.[21] Capitalism needed a world where avarice was a virtue and the merchant could be most pleasing to God. The individual needed to believe that he or she had not just the right, but the duty, to make as much money as possible. The idea that maximizing personal consumption is central to individual welfare is less than two hundred years old.[22] Without this belief the incentive structure of capitalism has no meaning and economic growth has no purpose.[23]

In periods of punctuated equilibrium, ideologies and technologies, new and old, do not match. Before good economic combustion can be reestablished, the two must again become compatible or consistent. This is a complicated process, since what is possible depends heavily on what we believe. Beliefs filter experiences, condition visions of reality, and alter the technologies that will be deployed. But new technologies alter beliefs as well as offering new choices.

Old, well-established social systems usually have to have a visible failure before it is possible for them to adapt to a new environment. Without visible failure most minds are closed most of the time. Failure opens up the windows of the mind to thinking about new ways of doing things. To act after a crisis has arisen, however, usually means that the needed changes are much more painful than they would have been if the new environment had been understood and the necessary adaptations made before the crisis arrived.

Societies flourish when beliefs and technologies are congruent; decline when the inevitable changes in beliefs and technologies become incongruent. This reality can be seen by looking at the history of successful societies in the past—many of them built on very different values and operating very different technologies from those that exist today. But they all needed this congruence if they were to succeed.

Agriculture began in the Nile River Valley, since early man did not know how to plow the earth and had not yet learned the need for fertilizer—he was missing two key technologies.[24] But on the Nile, with its annual floods and inundations of mud, plowing and fertilization were unnecessary.[25] One had only to seed. The soft new mud automatically eliminated the need for plowing and fertilization. The technologies naturally existed for a successful agricultural economy to flourish.

But if that new agricultural economy was to develop and replace a nomadic herding culture, it needed the right values—an ideology that persuaded large numbers of human beings to collectively build and maintain the communal dikes that would hold the mud and water on the banks of the Nile and not let it flow back into the river. For this was a land with almost no rainfall. Enormous discipline would be necessary to run the irrigation systems necessary to grow crops.

Probably because of the consistency of the weather and the flow of the Nile, the ancient Egyptians developed an ideology very different from ours. The focus of life was on death. A belief in a life after death more real than life itself led them to develop the social discipline to make investments in the future that dwarf all those that came after them. The pharaohs lived in mud palaces but were buried in monumental stone edifices. The proportion of Egyptian time and resources devoted to building those pyramids given the technologies with which they worked are beyond our comprehension.[26] When the Nile Valley was under water during the annual flood, the entire workforce would be mobilized for half of the year to build monuments that are still wondrous given modern technologies (the Great Pyramid of Giza is higher than St. Peter's in Rome).[27] For a lifetime pharaohs would carefully hoard possessions to carry with them on their journey into eternal life. Average people struggled to build for themselves small tombs to help them make the same journey into eternal life as the pharaoh would make from his magnificent tomb.[28]

Collective needs were more important than the individual—there was no personal self-examination or opinions as far as we know.[29] Their ideology of being interested in the distant future and being uninterested in the individual was as important to their long-term success as the mud of the river Nile.

In contrast, success came to the Romans not because of technology but because of their ideology. As stated by one of their contemporaries, the military observer Vegetius: "The Romans were less prolific than the Gauls, shorter than the Germans, weaker than the Spanish, not as rich or astute as the Africans, inferior to the Greeks in technology and in reason applied to human affairs. What they had was the ability to get organized and a vocation for domination."[30]

A unique set of values led to armies with unparalleled discipline that obeyed orders when others didn't.[31] Their communications, command, and control system was superb.[32] The Romans won wars although they never had any military technologies that their enemies did not have. They were uninterested in technological advancement, made few improvements in fifteen hundred years, and often rejected those advances that did appear (a Roman emperor deliberately rejected a mechanical device for moving stone columns).[33]

Their social organization resulted in the building of bridges, roads, and aqueducts that still stand. Nine hundred years after the Via Appia was built, the historian Procopius called it one of the greatest sights in the world and noted that none of its stones had broken or worn thin despite hundreds of years without maintenance.[34] The economic results of this ideology included a transportation system that could bring grain to Rome from all around the Mediterranean to service a city of more than a million people with horses and carts.[35] Agriculturally, they had the structures necessary to mine fertilizers and annually spread them on their fields. The average Roman enjoyed material standards of living that would not again be seen again until the onset of the industrial age in the eighteenth century. Rank and file Romans never reached the helpless insignificance that would afflict common Europeans during the Dark Ages.[36]

Organization paid off. It built an empire that included one hundred million people and stretched almost three thousand miles from east to west and twenty-two hundred miles from north to south.[37]

But Rome did not accomplish this with our beliefs. The Romans had no belief in the rights of each individual regardless of whether they were free or slave (and many were slaves). Even the free were not equal—all were assigned to classes or orders.[38] The individual counted for little and there was no sense of "self that could serve as a bulwark against judgments imposed from the outside by the community."[39] They did not honor the dissenters. Their religion discouraged individualism but encouraged a sense of belonging to the community—the exact opposite of what ours does.[40]

The Romans condemned the "vulgar and ignoble" commercial values that now lie at the heart of capitalism.[41] A free man could not work for wages since that was to be subject to another man's orders and equivalent to being a slave.[42] In Cicero's words "wage labor was sordid and unworthy of a free man."[43] In Rome itself half of the population received free or subsidized grain. There was a "just" price, that was not a market price.[44] By law and tradition, Roman senators could not be businessmen. To the extent that they engaged in business, they had to hide it—often using their slaves to conduct their business affairs. Roman prestige was not determined by their income or their role in the economy but by their military success.

Military conquests often led to great wealth but that wealth was converted into *dignitas* not by personal consumption but by giving gifts (usually a public building with their name on it) to the citizens of their city. Leaders did not build palaces for themselves; that was for oriental despots.[45] The prestige of giving gifts to the public was so high that in Rome only the emperor himself was allowed to build public buildings. Being rich and enjoying a high standard of living was not the goal. To the Roman the collectivity of a never-ending empire was more important than their own personal standards of living.[46]

In Aristotle's eyes, the "magnificent man was the gift-giving man"—not the man who accumulated.[47] Gifts were a moral duty. But it was not our concept of charity to the needy. The gift was designed to glorify the empire and the giver. The gift emphasized the fact that the giver was a public man.[48] To put one's name on a building was to give one immortality.[49] As a consequence, the homes of the Caesars were simple compared with what they built for the public.[50]

A model of the imperial city of Rome reveals a very different balance between public and private buildings than that which we would see in the model of any modern city. Proportionally, there was much more public space and much less private space.[51] Public buildings dominate.[52] In our societies the opposite is true—the private is dominant and the public is secondary. For them the private was negative; the public was good.[53] The rich did not have running water, but the public baths did.[54] What Cicero said about the Romans, "the Roman people hate private luxury, they love public magnificence," can be said about no current society.[55] They did not build an empire with our values.

On the other side of the globe, China invented all of the technologies necessary to have the industrial revolution hundreds of years before it occurred in Europe. At least eight hundred years before they were to occur in Europe, China had invented blast furnaces and piston bellows for making steel; gunpowder and the cannon for military conquest; the compass and rudder for world exploration; paper, movable type, and the printing press for disseminating knowledge; suspension bridges; porcelain; the wheeled metal plow, the horse collar, a rotary threshing machine and a mechanical seeder for improving agricultural yields; a drill that enabled them to get energy from natural gas; and the decimal system, negative numbers, and the concept of zero to analyze what they were doing. Even the lowly wheelbarrow and the match were used centuries earlier in China.[56]

In the fifteenth century, China would have been the candidate if historians had been asked to pick who was about to conquer and colonize the rest of the world militarily and to pull ahead of it economically by converting from an agricultural to an industrial base. Europe, the actual conqueror, was composed of a group of squabbling little principalities, far behind China technologically, with none of its integrated political and social organizations.

But it did not happen. China did not have the right ideologies. The

Chinese rejected, did not use, and forgot the very technologies that could have given them world dominance. New technology was perceived as a threat, not an opportunity. Innovation was prohibited. The canonical texts, those inspired by Confucius, contained the solution to every problem.

Choices are rarely straightforward and rational. There are always a multiplicity of competing ideas about the "proper" way to organize work. Even within business firms embedded in the same national cultures, technological choices are heavily influenced by the internal power politics, values, history, and culture of individual firms.[57] New technologies affect performance but they also affect status, self-assessment, influence, power, and authority. History matters.

MAJOR FAULT LINES

As we shall see in later chapters, in an era of man-made brainpower industries, capitalism is going to need some very long-run communal investments in research and development, education, and infrastructure. Yet when capitalism's normal decision-making processes are used, capitalism never looks more than eight to ten years into the future and usually looks only three to four years ahead. The problem is simply put. Capitalism desperately needs what its own internal logic says it does not have to do.

To some extent this has always been true, but the problem has also been compounded by the end of the cold war, an ideology of radical individualism, and an era of government budget deficits where governments are no longer making long-term investments. The proper role of government in capitalistic societies in an era of man-made brain power industries, is to represent the interest of the future to the present, but today's governments are doing precisely the opposite. They are lowering investments in the future to raise consumption in the present.

With brainpower as the only source of strategic competitive advantage, firms should be integrating their skilled workforce ever more tightly into their organizations. But with corporate downsizing, they are doing precisely the opposite. Workers at all skill levels are being told that their corporation has no loyalty to them—and implicitly that they should have no loyalty to it. With such values, how are man-made brainpower firms to hold on to, and enhance, their only strategic asset?

How is a capitalistic system to function in a brainpower era when brainpower cannot be owned? Most firms that now have this characteristic (law firms, accounting firms, investment banks) are not run by absentee outside capitalistic owners. They hire, pay, promote, make decisions, and select leaders in a very different manner from the General Motors or General Electrics of this world. When firms dominated by brainpower try to bring in absentee capitalistic owners, it doesn't work. The "rainmakers" (those who bring in the money) simply take their skills elsewhere. The capitalist can give them nothing that they need.

How are nation-states to enforce their rules and regulations when businesses can move (often electronically) to some other place on the face of the globe where those regulations do not apply? How are international organizations designed to function in a unipolar world with a dominant power to function in a multipolar world without a dominant power?

As we shall see, if there is one rule of international economics, it is that no country can run a large trade deficit forever. Trade deficits need to be financed and it is simply impossible to borrow enough to keep up with compound interest. Yet all of world trade, especially that on the Pacific Rim, depends upon most of this world being able to run trade surpluses with the United States that will allow them to pay for their trade deficits with Japan. When the lending to America stops, and it will stop, what happens to current world trade flows?

To flourish, human societies need a vision of something better. By definition utopias cannot be built, but they provide elements that can be built into our current, less than perfect economic systems to allow them to adapt to new circumstances. For the past 150 years socialism and the social welfare state have provided this source of new ideas. Elements were taken from each and built into the structure of capitalism. But socialism is dead and the social welfare state has both gone broke and in many countries reached a natural stopping point. Where are the visions of better human societies to come from? If they don't exist, what happens to our current societies? Do they lose the ability that all human societies need most—the ability to adopt and adapt?

Democracy believes in "one man, one vote" (equality of political power), while capitalism believes in letting the market rule (in practice, great inequalities in economic power). In the twentieth century this ideological conflict between the egalitarian foundations of democracy and the inegalitarian reality of capitalism has been finessed by the grafting of social investments and the social welfare state onto capitalism and democracy. A state-funded social safety net would protect the vulnerable (the old, the sick, the unemployed, the poor) from economic extinction, and social investments in education would narrow the earnings gaps that markets would otherwise generate. But social investments such as education are being crowded out of government budgets to pay for pension and health benefits for the elderly. The ideology of inclusion is withering away, to be replaced by a revival of survival-of-the-fittest capitalism.

The losers, those who are left out and cannot make the system work, retreat into religious fundamentalism, where a world of certainty replaces a world of uncertainty. But the values of religious fundamentalism are completely inconsistent with the needs of twenty-first century capitalism. One wants to repress deviant activities while the other needs those deviant activities to determine what the new survival-of-the-fittest characteristics will be.

AN EPOCH OF PUNCTUATED EQUILIBRIUM

When technology and ideology don't smoothly mix, the economic magma fluxes. Tectonic plates are violently thrust into each other—volcanoes erupt, earthquakes shatter the earth's crust, mountains rise, valleys fall. What has been a top-of-the-food-chain, survival-of-the-fittest species madly flips and flops its way into extinction trying to get back into a stream that is no longer there. The banks of the river move; water flows in new directions. A period of punctuated equilibrium comes into existence.

The economic surface of the earth, the distribution of income and wealth, is now being fundamentally remade. The economic losers are spewed out in a social volcano called religious fundamentalism. An economic earthquake shatters the Mexican economy. China's economy rises; Japan's economy falls. World growth slows dramatically. Real wages fall for most Americans. Europe cannot create jobs for its young.

Old successful business strategies (focused on the wants of the middle class) fail. No one knows what the consumer is going to want to buy, and not buy, using electronic shopping. Chief executive officers of major corporations lose their jobs at rates never before seen. A period of economic punctuated equilibrium comes into existence.

A brand-new world with brand-new opportunities has arrived. While the economic plates cannot be pushed back to re-create the old environment, their irresistible movements can be understood, and our actions and institutions modified to allow us to thrive.

This book is an attempt to understand the movement of the economic plates that lie below the visible surface of our economic earth so that it will be possible for those who understand what is happening to them to chart a new direction that enables them to survive and thrive. Periods of punctuated equilibrium offer many new, as yet unexplored territories. They are exciting times. In normal times, when almost everything that can be explored has been explored, the topology is not so interesting.

Perhaps the best way to think of what lies ahead is to imagine that you are Columbus. There is a fortune to be made in the East Indies and you believe that you have a new, better way to get there—by sailing west rather than walking east. Like Columbus, you have a map but like his, half of the territory on it is marked "terra incognita." The world to the west is to a substantial extent unknown, but a ship still has to be built to survive storms of unknown ferocity; equipped with sails that will speed it to its not so clear destination, and provisioned with the right amounts of water and food for a journey of unknown length.

What will be the dynamics of the new world into which we are about to sail?

Chapter 2

Mapping the Economic Surface of the Earth

Economically, the distribution of income and wealth is the equivalent of the surface of the earth. It drives our economic weather. In capitalistic economies the distribution of spending power determines what will be produced, who will be paid, and who will use the economy's goods and services. Without spending power, individuals in a very real sense simply don't exist. For most individuals, spending power depends upon current and past earnings. Among males twenty-four to forty-four years of age, for example, earnings account for 93 percent of income.[1] "Work" is the name of the economic game.

But when it comes to work and earnings, the economic surface of the earth is being transformed at speeds never before seen. A brandnew, very different topography is emerging.

ALMOST EVERYWHERE: SURGING INEQUALITY

Not surprisingly, during the Great Depression income differences narrowed. Capitalistic wealth essentially vanished as the business community went broke. Everyone's income and wealth fell, but those at the top simply had farther to fall than those at the bottom. Many of those at the bottom could still move back to live with relatives on the family farm where they could provide themselves with a subsistence standard of living. Equally unsurprising, during World War II, while twelve million Americans were fighting and dying for their country (an inherently egalitarian activity), government wage and price controls were deliberately used to narrow earnings differentials.

What is surprising is that when price and wage controls were removed after World War II, and when the economy returned to prosperity, it did not return to the wider earnings differentials of the 1920s. Stability reigned in the 1950s and the 1960s. Those of us teaching income distribution economics at that time had to struggle to explain why the distribution of earnings did not change even though the economy was changing in remarkable ways.

But suddenly in 1968, much like a sudden surge in a long-immobile glacier, inequality started to rise.[2] Over the next two decades that surge in inequality spread and intensified so that by the early 1990s, both between and within groups, inequalities were rapidly rising in every industrial, occupational, educational, demographic (age, sex, race), and geographic group. Among males, the group most sharply affected, earnings inequalities doubled in two decades.[3]

In the decade of the 1980s, all of the gains in male earnings went to the top 20 percent of the workforce and an amazing 64 percent accrued to the top 1 percent.[4] If incomes rather than earnings are examined, the top 1 percent gets even more—90 percent of total income gains.[5] The pay of the average Fortune 500 CEO goes from 35 to 157 times that of the average production worker.[6] CEO salaries tripled in France, Italy, and Britain and more than doubled in Germany between 1984 and 1992.[7] What emerged has been aptly described as the "winner take all" society.[8]

Female earnings followed male earnings with a ten- to fifteen-year lag. Initially, in the 1970s the distribution of female earnings had been much more equal than that of men. The earnings of women with a college education were not much higher than those of women who only graduated from high school. Women simply did not have access to the high-wage jobs open to college-educated men. By the 1990s at least some of those jobs were open to women and the female distribution of earnings was starting to look like the much more unequal male distribution of earnings.

Despite the effort of millions of wives who went to work to compensate for the earnings losses of their husbands, relentlessly, year after year, the income share of the top quintile (20 percent) of households rose and the income share of the bottom quintile declined.[9] In the end, top-to-bottom inequalities rose by a third.[10] In no year were the changes large, but like the inexorable rise of Nanga Parbat, the cumulative effects were large. By 1993, America was setting all-time records with the top quintile of households having 13.4 times as much income as the bottom quintile.[11]

Mysteriously, most of the widening dispersion among earnings is being produced within what are supposed to be homogeneous groups of workers. The central statistical fact is not widening earnings gaps between the skilled and the unskilled or between the educated and the uneducated, but widening earnings gaps among the skilled, among the unskilled, among the uneducated, and among the educated. By age, 85 percent of the rise in inequality occurred among those of the same age rather than between those of different ages. By education level, 69 percent of the rise in inequality occurred among those with the same education, rather than between those of different education levels. By industry, 89 percent of the increase in inequality occurred among those in the same industry rather than between different industries.[12]

Changes in physical wealth mirrored those in earnings and income. The share of total net worth of the top one-half of 1 percent of the population rose from 26 to 31 percent in just six years between 1983 and 1989. By the early 1990s the share of wealth held by the top 1 percent of the population (more than 40 percent) was essentially double what it had been in the mid-1970s and was back to where it had been in the late 1920s before the introduction of progressive taxation.[13]

FOR MANY: FALLING REAL WAGES

In 1973, inflation-corrected real wages began to fall for males. Here again real-wage reduction gradually spread across the workforce until by the early 1990s male real wages were falling for all ages, industries, occupations, and every educational group including those with post-graduate degrees.[14] Average median earnings for males working year-round full-time fell 11 percent (from $34,048 to $30,407 in 1993 dollars) between 1973 and 1993 even though the real per capita GDP was rising 29 percent over the same period of time.[15] Year-round full-time white males did even worse—experiencing a 14 percent decline.[16] Male college graduates between forty-five and fifty-four years of age in their peak earning years suffered an almost unbelievable one-third reduction in median earnings.[17] While detailed data are not yet available, in 1994 and early 1995 the pace of decline was accelerating with wages falling at a 2.3 percent per year rate.[18]

In the last two decades, only the top quintile of the workforce has experienced real-wage gains (see Table 2.1). The farther down the distribution, the larger the declines become—a 10 percent reduction for the fourth quintile and a 23 percent reduction for the bottom quintile.

Table 2.1
CHANGES IN REAL WAGES AND INCOMES
1973–1992

Quintiles	Males Year-Round Full-Time Workers (Wages)	Household (Incomes)
Bottom	−23%	−3%
Two	−21%	−3%
Three	−15%	−0.5%
Four	−10%	+6%
Top	+10%	+16%

SOURCE: U.S. Bureau of the Census, *Current Population Reports, Consumer Income* (Washington, D.C.: Government Printing Office, 1973, 1992), pp. 137, 148.

Declines in earning capacity have been particularly sharp for the young.[19] Despite increases in average educational attainment, those twenty-five to thirty-four years of age took a 25 percent reduction in their real earnings. For year-round full-time male workers eighteen to twenty-four years of age (mostly high school graduates), the percentage earning less than $12,195 (1990s dollars) rose from 18 percent in 1979 to 40 percent in 1989.[20] Real starting wages were lower and the young were simply not getting the advancements that they could have expected in the past.

What has happened cannot be explained as a diversion of cash income into fringe benefits.[21] From 1979 to 1989 the percentage of the workforce with private pensions declined from 50 to 43 percent, and the percentage of those with health insurance declined from 69 to 61 percent.[22] While the top quintile of wage earners' employer-paid health care coverage fell only marginally, the lowest quintile took very substantial cuts.[23] From 1978 to 1993 the gap in pension coverage between male high school dropouts and those with college degrees nearly tripled.[24]

At no other time since data have been collected have American median real male wages consistently fallen for a two-decade period of time. Never before have a majority of American workers suffered real-wage reductions while the real per capita GDP was advancing.[25] Something very different was at work in the American economy.

Real-wage reductions began later for women than for men, but by 1992 real wages were falling for all female workers except those with four or more years of university education.[26] With male wages falling consistently and female wages rising for most of the 1970s and 1980s, mean annual earnings for year-round full-time female workers rose from 41 percent to 72 percent those of men from 1968 to 1993.[27] But that was of little solace to female workers. They wanted their earnings to catch up with those of males, but they did not want it to happen by having their husbands' earnings fall.

President John F. Kennedy was fond of talking about a "rising tide raising all boats," but by the early 1970s what had traditionally been true was no longer true. The economic tides could rise yet most boats could sink. From 1973 to 1994, America's real per capita GDP rose 33 percent, yet real hourly wages fell 14 percent and real weekly wages 19 percent for nonsupervisory workers (those males and females who do not boss anyone else).[28] By the end of 1994 real wages were back to where they had been in the late 1950s. With current trends, by the turn of the century real wages will be below where they were in 1950. Half a century with no real-wage gains for the average nonsupervisory worker. It has never before happened in America.

These wage patterns have now existed for more than two decades and are not related to the phases of the business cycles. Take any set of measurements from the top of a boom to the top of the next boom or from the bottom of a recession to the bottom of the next recession over these two decades and the same patterns emerge. While the real per capita GDP has risen in eighteen out of the past twenty years, real weekly wages have fallen relentlessly in fifteen out of those same twenty years.[29]

Historically, the remedy for low wages has always been more education. Today that no longer looks very attractive for males. With earnings for high school graduates falling faster than earnings for college graduates, the college–high school earnings gap is increasing, and as a consequence measured returns to education are rising. But when real wages are falling for both male high school and male college graduates, investing in education doesn't get the individual graduate off the down escalator and onto the up escalator. It merely prevents the individual from being even farther down on a descending escalator that is carrying everyone with it. Educational investments become a defensive necessity.

As can be seen in the data on household incomes in Table 2.1, the American female came to the rescue of the American male in the 1970s and 1980s.[30] Despite sharp cuts in male earnings, real incomes fell only marginally for the bottom 60 percent of the households between 1973 and 1992. Household incomes were buffered by a 32 percent rise in female real annual earnings.[31] About one third of this increase was due to higher wage rates and two thirds to more hours of work per year. As far as the bottom 80 percent of households was concerned, wives worked more outside of the home and their increased earnings compensated, or more than compensated in the case of the fourth quintile, for their husbands' reduced earnings.[32] By the mid-1990s more than half of all employed women (note that the statistic includes households without males) were providing at least half of their household's income.[33] But despite all of this extra effort, real median household incomes peaked in 1989 and by 1993 they were 7 percent below where they had been [34]

Looking forward, wives are unlikely to be able to offset their husbands' falling real earnings. Wives, especially those married to husbands in the bottom 60 percent of the earnings distribution, are already working full-time and now have little extra time to increase work effort.[35] In recent years female real-wage rates, as we have seen, have also been falling for all but college-educated women. In the future, falling male earnings are apt to be mirrored in falling household incomes.

DOWNSIZING THE CORPORATION

In the late 1980s and early 1990s, two waves of corporate downsizing swept across the economy eliminating about 2.5 million good jobs.[36] Announced major corporate downsizings rose from 300,000 in 1990 to 550,000 in 1991 and then fell back to 400,000 in 1992.[37] This first wave of reductions was not surprising since layoffs are a traditional American response to a recession. But two things were different. Instead of temporary layoffs, permanent reductions in force were announced. Instead of being concentrated on blue-collar workers, white-collar workers and managers were laid off in large numbers.[38] In the 1980–81 recession three blue-collar workers were laid off for every one white-collar worker.[39] In the 1990–91 recession the ratio was down to two to one.[40] At the end of the 1980s, in a nonrecessionary period, 35 percent of those being laid off were managers, 31 percent were clerical workers, 8 percent were from sales, and only 19 percent were blue-collar workers.[41]

But then a second wave of downsizings struck—a wave that clearly had nothing to do with the 1991–92 recession, since it occurred among firms with high and rising profits after the recession was over. Announced downsizings soared to 600,000 in 1993, set a one-month all-time record of 104,000 in January of 1994 and were down only slightly to 516,000 jobs for the year as a whole.[42] And the beat goes on. In 1995 downsizing will approach 600,000.[43] At the same time, corporations were making the highest profits they had made in more than twenty-five years.[44]

Such dramatic reductions in force create an economic puzzle. How can efficient, profitable firms announce that they will continue to serve their existing customers, yet in a short period of time reduce their workforces by 10 to 30 percent?[45] In competitive markets how could profitable firms have gotten as inefficient and grossly fat as these statistics seem to indicate they had gotten? What happened cannot be attributed to abnormally high productivity growth in those firms that were downsizing, since it wasn't higher than in those firms that were not downsizing.[46]

One answer is that the downsizings were not as large as they seemed. Some downsizing was simply a shift to outside suppliers. If additions to suppliers' workforces had been included in the statistics, the downsizings would have been much less dramatic. To some extent downsizing was a technique for reducing wages without having to cope with the sociology of an unhappy workforce that had just had their wages reduced. If wages had been directly reduced at the major firms, labor's willingness to cooperate in generating higher productivity would probably have vanished. To prevent that from happening, high-wage workers were fired at major firms and lower-wage replacements were added to the payrolls of smaller supplier firms. Downsizing with outsourcing allowed the search for soft productivity gains (a workforce with better motivation and higher levels of cooperation) to continue while simultaneously reducing real wages.

A sudden shift in technology (presumably modern telecommunications and new computer technologies allowing firms to operate with a very different workforce structure than in the past) has been suggested, but this explanation simply does not fit the facts: These technologies did not just suddenly appear. They had been gradually permeating the workplace for thirty years. It is difficult to believe that their effects lay dormant for decades—and then suddenly popped up.

By getting rid of traditional hierarchy, pushing decisions down to the lowest possible level, and working in teams, firms may have discovered that old output levels can be produced with many fewer workers—reports of such breakthroughs certainly exist, with the dramatic changes at the Chrysler Corporation being perhaps the best example. But if true, it indicates that the corporate drive for efficiency is a very "sometimes" thing. Such changes could have been and should have been made long ago.

The second wave of downsizings can also be seen as the sudden imposition of a new tougher social contract between owners and workers. In the old implicit post–World War II social contract, major employers paid what economists came to call efficiency wages. Wages were higher than they would have had to be to acquire a workforce with the right skills, because above-market wages gave workers an incentive to voluntarily cooperate with their employer, an incentive to work hard, and an incentive not to quit—taking their skills with them to some other employer. Without the political threat of socialism or the economic threat of powerful unions, maybe efficiency wages just aren't needed anymore. In the future the motivation for cooperation and effort is not going to be above-market efficiency wages but "fear"—the fear of being fired into an economy of falling real wages.

Whatever the cause, downsizings have destroyed the old implicit post–World War II social contract wherein everyone received annual wage increases, temporary cyclical layoffs were limited to blue-collar workers, and white-collar workers and managers could expect lifetime employment if their firms remained profitable and their individual performances were satisfactory. In today's brave new world some workers and managers will end up having lifetime employment but very few managers or workers will be offered an up-front guarantee.

While downsizings began in the United States, they have now spread to Europe and are threatening Japan. In the first four months of 1994, 180,000 downsizings were announced in Germany—an economy one quarter as large as the United States.[47] In 1995 major firms such as the Deutsche Bank announced 20 percent downsizings—the elimination of more than 10,000 jobs in Germany alone—while at the same time announcing that they had made profits of $1.75 billion in the first half of the year.[48] Overall Germany expects to lose 500,000 jobs in major sectors such as the automobile, machine tool, electrical, and chemical industries.[49] Italy has already lost 200,000 jobs. France's biggest tire maker announces that it had cut its workforce at its major French factory in half in a three-year period while at the same time making more tires than ever.[50]

In the United States those downsized take a major economic blow. In the first wave of downsizings 12 percent ended up exiting the labor force entirely and 17 percent remained unemployed two years later. Of the 71 percent who are reemployed, 31 percent took a wage reduction of 25 percent or more, 32 percent have had their wages reduced by 1 to 25 percent, and only 37 percent have found employment at no loss in wages.[51] If a downsized worker has fifteen or more years of seniority, lives in a low-growth region, and is forced to switch industries, he or she typically loses more than 50 percent of his or her previous wage.[52] Those over fifty-five simply are thrown out of the workforce.

In studies of RJR Nabisco's layoffs, 72 percent eventually found work but at wages averaging only 47 percent of what they had previously been paid.[53] In this second wave even those who kept their jobs often found that to do so they had to take large wage cuts. The largest retail clothing chain in Boston cut the wages of all of its clerks 40 percent in 1993 despite the fact that it was profitable.[54] The Bridgestone/Firestone Rubber Company suffered a long strike to compel its workforce to accept lower wages and a longer day and to tie all future wage increases to increases in productivity.[55]

In the process of downsizing, American firms are developing a contingent workforce composed of involuntary part-timers, temporary workers, limited-term contract workers, and previously laid off "self-employed" consultants who work for wages far below what they had previously been receiving. Even in a world-class company, such as Hewlett-Packard, 8 percent of the workforce is now employed in a contingent status.[56]

With contingent workers, companies get lower labor costs and greater deployment flexibility. Contingent workers receive lower wages, less fringes, fewer paid holidays, and must accept greater economic risks and uncertainty. Over the last decade three quarters of the increase in part-time work has been involuntary. For part-timers the probability of having pensions or health benefits is less than a third those of full-time workers, their skills-adjusted wages are much lower, and most of the jobs open to them are dead-end jobs.[57] Male temps make half what they would if they were regular workers.[58]

A LUMPEN PROLETARIAT

Most advanced industrial economies are also producing what Marx would recognize as a lumpen proletariat—those whose potential productivity is so low that they are not wanted by the private economy at any wage rate that would come close to allowing them to support themselves in anything like the normal standard of living. Today we know them as the homeless—a floating group that is now estimated to involve about 600,000 people on any given night and 7 million over a five-year period of time in the United States.[59]

Homelessness began in the United States in the late 1970s. Initially the rest of the industrial world saw "homelessness" as a phenomenon peculiar to an inadequate American social safety net, but homelessness has now spread throughout the industrial world.[60] France estimates that it has 600,000 to 800,000 homeless.[61] People can be seen sleeping on the streets of almost every major city in the wealthy industrial world—even in the park across from the Imperial Hotel in Tokyo as one goes jogging around the emperor's palace.

While there is some overlap with the homeless, there are 5.8 million males who are the right age to be in the workforce and who in the past used to be in the workforce; who are not in school, are not old enough to have retired; who exist but have no obvious means of economic support; who have either been dropped from, or have dropped out of, the normal working economy in the United States.[62] This is social disengagement on a massive scale. One can argue about the precise connections between this group and crime, but it is hard to construct a scenario where it leads to anything positive.[63] There are now more men in prison or on probation in the United States than unemployed men.[64] Forty percent of homeless unmarried men have been in jail. Nothing can make those into good numbers.

There are a variety of causes. Closing mental hospitals without building the promised halfway houses and support groups explains perhaps one third of the problem.[65] Something had to happen when New York reduced its mental hospital population from ninety-three thousand in the 1950s to nine thousand in the mid-1990s.[66] Urban renewal led to the destruction of low-cost housing. Families no longer take care of their own. But the biggest cause is the economy. It simply does not need, want, or know how to use a large group of its citizens.

President Clinton got it right when he talked about the problem:

> ... the castoffs and the drop-outs who were left out of the boom of the 1980s and who now are living in a world apart. They don't vote, don't work, don't report crimes, don't necessarily send their children to school, and sometimes don't even have a telephone to receive calls. And in the vacuum in which they live, it is unclear whether society holds any claim on them or power to censure them.[67]

ECONOMIC VIABILITY OF THE FAMILY

When goods become more expensive, individuals buy less. Children and families are no exception. Family structures are disintegrating worldwide.[68] Only Japan defies the trend toward more divorce and more children born out of wedlock.[69] Elsewhere, births to unmarried mothers have soared. Worldwide, from 1960 to 1992 births among unmarried mothers twenty to twenty-four years of age almost doubled and among those fifteen to nineteen years of age quadrupled.[70] The United States is far from being the world's leader in this category, ranking sixth.[71] Divorce rates are rising in the developed and under-developed world—as are female-headed households. In Beijing the divorce rate rose from 12 to 24 percent in just four years from 1990 to 1994.[72] Female-headed households, or households where females provide 50 percent or more of total income, are becoming the norm everywhere.

With males less able to be the principal provider, with children needing ever more expensive educations for ever longer periods of time, and with fewer and fewer opportunities for young children to supplement family incomes with part-time or seasonal jobs (as they used to do when extended families lived on the farm), the costs of supporting a family are rising sharply just as the family's earning ability is falling. From the perspective of economic analysis, children are high-priced consumption goods that are rapidly becoming more expensive.

In America, 32 percent of all men twenty-five to thirty-four years of age earn less than the amount necessary to keep a family of four above the poverty line. Mother has to go to work if the family wants to have an acceptable standard of living.[73] Yet wives are given a double message: Go to work and make the money the family needs but stay at home and take care of the children. She goes into the paid labor force to rescue the family's economic position but still ends up doing twice as much housework as her husband.[74] She feels stressed because she is stressed.

Economics is of course not solely responsible for these changes. Individual fulfillment now ranks higher than family in public opinion polls.[75] "Competitive individualism" is growing at the expense of "family solidarity."[76] The "I" consumption culture drives out the "we" investment culture.

The response quite naturally is to form fewer families and to have smaller numbers of children. In the United States the percentage of families with dependent children is down from 47 percent of the total in 1950 to 34 percent in 1992. When children do exist, parents spend less time with them—40 percent less than they did thirty years ago.[77] With mother at work more than two million children under the age of thirteen are left completely without adult supervision both before and after school.[78] Effectively, no one ends up taking care of the children, but they have to be left alone since paying for day care would use up most of mother's wages and negate the purpose of going to work in the first place.

In an agricultural world where the family worked as a unit, children had real economic value at a very early age, especially during planting and harvesting times. The elderly could both take care of the young children and do a little work. For everyone the extended family was the social welfare system if they became sick, disabled, or old. One supported the family and left it only reluctantly since it was difficult to survive without it.

Today members support the family less, since it is now much less necessary to their own successful economic survival. People do not work as a family. Often they seldom see each other, given different work and education schedules. Once grown and often living thousands of miles apart, they lose track of each other. Living away from each other, the extended family has been blown apart. The family is no longer the social welfare system. The state has replaced it and the family will not resume these duties even if the state were to withdraw. In the language of capitalism children have ceased to be "profit centers" and have become "cost centers." Children still need parents but parents don't need children.[79]

Men end up having strong economic incentive to bail out of family relations and responsibilities. When men leave their families, their real standard of living rises 73 percent—although that of the family left behind falls 42 percent.[80] Among families with dependent children 25 percent don't have a male present.[81] Whether it is by fathering a family without being willing to be a father, by divorce and being unwilling to pay alimony or child support, or by being a guest worker from the third world and after a short time failing to send payments to the family back home, men are opting out.[82] Today's societies are failing to make men into fathers.[83] Men can only see their own welfare as coming ahead of or behind that of their families.[84] Yet where are the pressures for the social values that support the sacrifices necessary to support a family to arise? Current values call for choices rather than bonds. Nature makes mothers but societies have to make fathers.

On the other side of the equation, in the United States women get welfare only if no man is present in the home. Children's economic standards of living are often higher as wards of the state in foster care than they would be if they stayed in their disintegrating families. Single mothers can be made to work, but work unfortunately costs the state more than just sending welfare checks.[85] They have to have equipment, supervision, and work with others who have complementary skills if they are going to become economically viable. Wages have to be high enough to cover the additional costs (day care, transportation) of going to work. Their current productivity doesn't justify the private wages that would cover the necessary costs of going to work and society simply isn't willing to pay what it would cost to make them viable.

Historically, the single parent has been the norm in no society, but patriarchal linear life is now economically over. Family values are under attack, not by government programs that discourage family formation (although there are some) and not by media presentations that disparage families (although there are some), but by the economic system itself. It simply won't allow families to exist in the old-fashioned way with a father who generates most of the earnings and a mother who does most of the nurturing. The one-earner middle-class family is extinct.

Social arrangements are not determined by economics—there are many possibilities at any point in time—but whatever the arrangements, they have to be consistent with economic realities. Traditional family arrangements aren't. As a consequence the family is an institution both in flux and under pressure.[86] The issue is not one of "character development" but of hard-nosed economic self-interest or more precisely putting one's own self-interest second to that of the family.[87]

Basic questions about how the family should be organized have been put in play by economic reality. Changes within capitalism are making the family and the market less and less compatible.

THE MIDDLE CLASS

Since the lowest-paid workers have never had privately provided pensions or health care plans, they cannot lose them. Since they neither expected nor received promotions and never believed that their real wages would rise over their lifetimes, their expectations cannot be shattered. Politically, the lumpen proletariat don't matter. They don't cause revolutions; they are inert. In the United States the poor don't even vote.

What matters is the expectations of the middle class. Disappointed middle-class expectations cause revolutions, and the middle class is now being told that their old expectations are out of date.[88] Fewer of them are going to be able to own their own homes.[89] They are going to live in a very different world where inequality rises and where real wages fall for most of them. The era of annual wage increases is over; they cannot expect rising standards of living over their lifetimes or for their children.

The middle class is scared and should be scared. It does not have inherited wealth and must depend upon society for economic security, but that is exactly what they are not going to get.[90] Government is retreating from its provision of economic security and corporations are treating them as hired "gunslingers" with fewer and fewer of the fringe benefits that guarantee security.

The rich will pay for private security guards out of their higher incomes while the middle class gets by with unsafe streets, bad schools, uncollected garbage, and deteriorating transportation.[91] As the conservative analyst Kevin Phillips so aptly puts it, the "middle class is a social outlook rather than a definite level of material comfort," but fewer and fewer individuals will have that social outlook, for in the long run that outlook must find some validation in reality.[92]

Reality is slowly seeping in and changing perceptions. In 1964 only 29 percent of the population said the country was run for the rich, but by 1992, 80 percent were saying that they thought the country was run for the rich.[93] And looking at the economic results of who got what over the previous twenty years, who could say that they were wrong.

DIFFERENT SOCIAL SYSTEMS, DIFFERENT SURFACE MANIFESTATIONS

What began in America is now clearly spreading to the rest of the first world. In the early 1980s the United Kingdom started to experience the rising inequality that had begun ten years earlier in the United States. While average incomes rose more than one third from 1979 to 1993, the income of the bottom 10 percent fell 17 percent.[94] A decade later the same trends started to emerge on the European continent.[95] In the early 1990s the wage gap between the top and bottom deciles of the labor force was rising in 12 of the 17 OECD countries that keep such records—on average increasing from 7.5-to-1 in 1969 to 11-to-1 in 1992.[96]

Small real-wage reductions were even beginning to appear in such unlikely places as Germany.[97] Finnish wages fell in four of the first five years of the 1990s.[98] As a symbol of the times right after Christmas in 1994, the French division of IBM announced a 7.7 percent reduction in money wages.[99] Employees were given a choice between wage reductions or permanent reductions in force and 95 percent of the fourteen thousand employees affected voted for the wage reductions. Their French unions were not even consulted.

But something was happening in Europe even before real wages started to fall. In Europe social legislation and institutional realities diverted the same tectonic pressures that were producing falling wages in the United States into rising unemployment.[100] European social legislation makes it very expensive, and almost impossible, to fire workers. Since workers could not be fired, they didn't have to accept the "give-backs" and real-wage reductions that were forced upon American workers. As a result, continental European wages and fringe benefits rose while those in the United States were falling. By the mid-1990s most of Western Europe had wages far above those in the United States. Germany topped the charts with an hourly wage rate of more than $30 if fringe benefits were included and about $17 if they were excluded.[101] Including social costs, manufacturing labor costs in Germany are more than two thirds higher than those in the United States.[102]

But if it is expensive or impossible to fire labor, profit-maximizing business firms will not hire. Throughout the 1950s and 1960s, European economies operated with unemployment rates about half those found in the United States. But at about the same time that falling real wages began in the United States, unemployment started to rise in Europe.[103] By the mid-1990s, Europe's unemployment rates had risen to be twice those found in the United States (10.8 percent versus 5.4 percent in March 1995)—and in some countries such as Spain (23.2 percent), Ireland (14.3 percent) and Finland (16.8 percent) three to four times as high.[104]

Southern Europeans argue that their reported unemployment rates are not really as bad as they look, since many workers are really employed in the black economy (the economy where taxes are not paid and government labor regulations are ignored) but report themselves as unemployed in the white (legal) economy. Unemployment rates in northern Europe, however, are clearly worse than those reported. With very generous disability systems, many of these countries such as the Netherlands have enormous numbers of potential workers (about 15 percent) officially outside of the labor force because they are receiving government disability payments.[105] Very few are really disabled and unable to work. If they were counted as unemployed, which they really are, measured unemployment would be much higher.[106]

While there are factors at work other than the social welfare system, Europe ends up with a much lower participation rate. Overall, among those of working age 77 percent work in the United States, but only 67 percent work in Europe.[107] If this extra 10 percentage points difference reflects people who would like to work and who would be working if they lived in the United States, then Europe's real comparable unemployment rate would be about four times that of the United States.

Europe's unemployed also have remained unemployed for long periods of time—so long that they might be better seen as permanent castoffs from the production process than as unemployed. In France, 39 percent of the unemployed are unemployed for more than one year;

in Germany long-term unemployed account for 46 percent of total unemployment; and in Ireland this number soars to 60 percent.[108] In contrast, only 11 percent of Americans are unemployed for more than one year.[109]

Unemployment is also highly concentrated among the young. In some European countries more than 60 percent of the young people who have left school are unemployed. In the long run that creates a workforce that does not receive the training that it should be getting and a generation of young people without work experience. What that will do to skills and work habits in the long run remains to be seen, but it is hard to sketch out a scenario where persistent unemployment among those eighteen to twenty-five years of age yields positive benefits.[110] Perverse expectations about how the world works are set up and in the long run such expectations have to be much more costly than paying for the social welfare system that now keeps the young pacified.

The European problem is not created by job losses. In the 1980s the United States lost 2 percent of its jobs every month while Europe was losing only 0.4 percent of its jobs.[111] The problem is created by a lack of job expansion. While Western Europe reported no net new jobs from 1973 to 1994, the United States generated 38 million net new jobs.[112]

The causes are straightforward. Anti-inflationary policies lead to restrictive monetary policies that deliberately produced high unemployment. As the long-term unemployed come to have a smaller and smaller effect on wage increases (without work experience and skill development they are less and less competitive with those who have been working), ever higher levels of unemployment were necessary to obtain the same anti-inflationary effects.[113] With generous unemployment insurance benefits, workers were slow to take new jobs and refused to take jobs at lower wages.[114]

In France the minimum wage for thirty-nine hours of work is $1,215 per month with another 40 percent required in social charges.[115] The social legislation creating such wages and other social practices has produced European economies with a very compressed distribution of earnings whereby the lowest decile of the workforce earns 80 percent more than the lowest decile of the workforce in the

United States.[116] As a consequence a whole set of low-wage industries and services that exist and expand in the United States cannot exist or expand in Europe.[117]

When Asians write about the European welfare system for those of working age, they write with incredulity.[118] They just cannot believe it. Five weeks' vacation! One month Christmas bonus! Eighty percent of wages replaced when on unemployment insurance! Their disbelief is one of the reasons why the system cannot continue. Firms can move to the Far East and avoid all of those European fringe benefit costs.

With both average and minimum wages high, European firms invested in the capital equipment necessary to raise efficiency and survive paying the wages they have to pay, but they have no interest in expanding employment in Europe. Total costs are simply too high relative to those being paid in the rest of the world.[119] If a business needs to expand, there are more profitable, lower-wage places to do so. In 1994, Germans invested more than 26 billion marks abroad while foreigners were investing only 1.5 billion marks in Germany.[120] Swedish manufacturing firms raised their output 16 percent in Sweden while at the same time raising their output 180 percent in the rest of the world.[121] By moving some of their production to Alabama and South Carolina, Mercedes and BMW will halve their German labor costs. They also let it be known that they hope that this fact would be duly noted by their unionized German labor force.[122]

Yet at the same time, Germany has been remarkably successful at running its economy with very high social welfare charges. In key industries like machine tools, it has been able to maintain its market share while the United States, with much lower social charges, was losing more than one third of its market share.[123] As long as such success was occurring in some sectors, why should German workers accept across-the-board wage cuts? The crisis that makes people willing to change was not yet at hand.

Continental Europe essentially managed to protect the wages of those who remained employed (nine countries in Western Europe had wages substantially above those in the United States in 1994 and another two were at parity although no European country has productivity levels equal to those of the United States) but at an enormous cost in higher unemployment and lost jobs.[124] Instead of spreading real-wage reductions across the workforce, wages were reduced to zero for the unemployed. Instead of sharing earnings reductions as was done in America, those Europeans with jobs shared their income with the unemployed in the form of paying higher taxes to finance a very generous system of unemployment insurance. If European and American wage payments are averaged across the employed and the unemployed, real-wage reductions start at about the same time and are roughly similar in size—same tectonic forces, different surface manifestation, similar bottom-line results.

Incipient cracks can now be seen in this system.[125] The European Commission regularly issues reports urging changes in the European system of social welfare payments, minimum wages, regulations governing part-time work, unemployment insurance, union powers, and store opening laws to permit greater labor force "flexibility." While no official wants to say it out loud, "flexibility" is simply a code word for "falling wages."[126] If "flexibility" were to occur, there is every reason to believe that the European wage structure would move rather rapidly toward the American pattern. When the United Kingdom abolished its Wage Councils, 40 percent of the workforce ended up working below the old minimum wages.[127]

In the more communitarian form of capitalism practiced in Japan, neither the falling real wages of America nor the rising unemployment of Europe is yet visible. With its guarantee of lifetime employment, Japan essentially has a system of private unemployment insurance. As a consequence Japanese companies have built up enormous numbers of idle workers on their private payrolls. Even the Japanese admit that many of those workers have nothing to do. If those supported on this system of private unemployment insurance were added to those officially recognized as unemployed, about 10 percent of the Japanese labor force would be unemployed—a number not far below that for the EEC as a whole.[128]

While the Japanese social system has protected its workers from the forces afflicting workers elsewhere in the industrial world, a steep price has been paid in terms of profitability. Japanese firms traditionally earn fewer profits than firms elsewhere, but in the first four years of the 1990s, the Japanese have essentially run a "profit-free" economy. Those firms with profits were counterbalanced by those firms with losses. Even in the Japanese variant of capitalism, that cannot go on forever. In the Japanese business press there is now lots of talk about the need to reduce wages to remain competitive and examples of firms that have for the first time moved to offshore production bases to lower their wage costs.[129]

INDUCED CHANGES IN ECONOMIC STRUCTURE

Capitalism is very good following changes in incomes. When the distribution of income is altered, who sells what to whom quickly adjusts. Marketing and production shift to focus on the groups that have been gaining purchasing power and away from those that have been losing purchasing power.

That shift is already visible in retailing. The middle-class stores (Sears, Macy's, Gimbels, etc.) have all had economic problems (gone out of business, lost market share) in the past fifteen years while the upscale stores (Bloomingdale's) and the downscale stores (Wal-Mart) have all been doing very well. Those well positioned to take advantage of the shifts in the distribution of spending power won in the world of retailing in the 1980s and early 1990s. Those with such strong middle-class brand names, Sears being the best example, that it was virtually impossible to move upscale or downscale were in deep trouble.

This shift has occurred not because there just happened by accident to be idiots managing all of the middle-class stores while geniuses were managing at either end of the spectrum. Customers with middle-class incomes were becoming fewer in number—a few moving upscale as their incomes rose but most moving downscale as their incomes fell. Sometimes in the advertising world this shift is called "the end of the Marlboro man."[130]

In the decades ahead it is the stores such as Wal-Mart that should be expected to have problems. To do as well as Wal-Mart has done, they have to be good, their competition has to be bad, and the fundamental forces of the economy have to be with them. Wal-Mart's market is the bottom 60 percent of families and with both male and female real earnings now falling for those families, the purchasing power of their current customers has to decline. No one can sell more to those who have less. If a retailer's market share is already very large among this class of consumers (the Wal-Mart case), it is going to be very difficult to offset falling per capita sales with a rising market share.

If per capita incomes are up yet wages are down, someone has to be getting all of that extra income. As we shall see in detail in Chapter 5, that someone is the elderly. The income share of the elderly has doubled in the last two decades. It is they who are the big economic winners. It is they who in the future will be driving the economic system.

The shift in purchasing power toward the elderly already lies behind the great economic success of the cruise line industry. Cruising is a perfect vacation for the elderly who have a lot of time, whose mobility is often impaired, and who may have days when they don't feel well while on vacation. New product development in other industries will similarly increasingly shift to focus on older citizens. Electronic home shopping is a good example.

Technically every retail store in America could close down today and everything could be bought electronically tomorrow. What will be purchased electronically depends upon what Americans want to buy in a social experience and what Americans just want to buy. Sensing this, shopping malls are now busy installing food courts, entertainment areas, benches for resting and visiting, and in other ways encouraging people to come spend the day. Ultimately the young may want a social experience with their shopping while the elderly with limited mobility may be anxious to buy their tomatoes over their televisions. The market for electronic shopping may not be computer nerds but the elderly. But that means having equipment and procedures where the elderly feel comfortable.

The biggest visible changes will probably be seen in television programming. Traditionally advertisers have wanted programs that would appeal to eighteen- to twenty-five-year-olds. Without yet having family responsibilities, having large discretionary income that is expected to grow rapidly, and not having formed their buying habits, they have been the advertisers' optimal target. But none of the old assumptions are now true. With sharply falling real incomes, the young have much less discretionary income than in the past and no prospects that their incomes will rapidly rise in the future. The young still have more malleable consumer preferences, but it does no good to alter the preferences of those having little discretionary income with which to satisfy their new tastes.

The difficulties in discarding old "truths" in order to respond to new "truths" can be seen in the fact that television executives are still looking for those demographics for eighteen- to twenty-five-year-olds—even though this is clearly the wave of the past.[131] But they will eventually learn. As discretionary income moves from the young to the old, advertising will follow it. The television programming that today focuses on the young will be refocused on the old. Marketers will learn that while it is difficult to make the elderly into their customers, once sold the elderly don't quickly leave to try someone else's products. If they are already your customers, the difficulties of changing their preferences become an asset and not a liability.

CONCLUSIONS

The conclusions are simple. No country not experiencing a revolution or a military defeat with a subsequent occupation has probably ever had as rapid or as widespread an increase in inequality as has occurred in the United States in the past two decades. Never before have Americans seen the current pattern of real-wage reductions in the face of a rising per capita GDP. In the next six chapters we will discuss why.

Chapter 3

Plate One: The End of Communism

The earthquake that ended communism sent 1.9 billion people tumbling into the capitalistic world.

ECONOMIC GEOGRAPHY

For the one third of humanity who lived within the old Communist world, the economics of everyday life will change profoundly. They will be given opportunities to make their own decisions that were never open to them in the past, but they will be asked to take risks (be unemployed, have their incomes go down as well as up) and undertake activities (search for bargains or apartments, start new businesses) that they have never had to do in the past. They will get the chance to become rich but will have taken from them some of the good things of life (high-quality, readily available, free child care; large subsidies for the performing arts; free education) that they had come to expect. Without the huge subsidies of communism, the Bolshoi Ballet may never again be as good.

But within the old capitalistic world everyday economic life will change just as profoundly. Industries are, and will be, geographically on the move. Things used to be said that were never true. "Saudi Arabia is the world's biggest producer of oil." It never was. The USSR was always the biggest producer of oil (19 percent of world production in 1987) but it could be ignored since its oil fueled the Communist world and only a small amount ended up in the old capitalistic world.[1]

Today one cannot even think about the oil business without considering the oil supplies that will flow from the countries that used to make up the old Soviet Union. The Caspian Sea may eventually become more important than the Persian Gulf. Off the north coast of Siberia there may be something even bigger. The new supplies of the old Communist world have effectively destroyed the monopoly power to set prices that OPEC and the Persian Gulf countries used to enjoy. For those in the oil business where one invests in wells and pipelines, whom one must negotiate with and what one expects about the future price of oil are fundamentally different now that communism is gone.

But what is true in the oil business is equally true elsewhere. In 1993, 1.6 million metric tons of aluminum left the old Soviet Union for the old capitalistic world.[2] All across the capitalistic world people were closing down smelters or asking their governments for protection. The Norwegian smelter might have been more efficient than the Russian smelter, but it was the Norwegian smelter that was slated to shut down. The Russians had no capitalists who had to be paid, used fully depreciated equipment, and had nothing else that they could do. What looked like a very nice dollar price to the Russian looked like a money-losing dollar price to the Norwegian.

In 1994, Russian aluminum exports were limited by quotas imposed by the old capitalistic governments and it was the size of Russian nickel exports that surprised everyone.[3] Soviet titanium used to go into corrosion-resistant Soviet nuclear submarines. Today it can be found in Russian-made titanium ice screws and carabiners at your local American mountain climbing store—a very low-value usage for what used to be a very expensive military metal.[4] In 1995 the issue was wool. In just eighteen months wool exports soared from 9 million kilograms to 186 million kilograms—devastating the old capitalist producers, in places such as Australia, because it was sold at only one quarter of the normal price.[5]

Who in the nineteenth century was the world's largest producer and exporter of grain products? It was not the United States, Canada, Argentina, or Australia—today's big exporters. It was imperial Russia—the Ukraine and the area around it. The Ukraine is potentially the best place on earth for growing grain. Good soil and good rainfall coexist with what is the world's best natural transportation system—a lot of rivers that flow south into the Black Sea, so that grain can be exported with cheap water transportation and does not have to bear the cost of those thousands of kilometers, lengthy, expensive rail journeys, that exist in the other major grain-producing countries.

The Ukraine does not yet have its act together, but what happens when it does? John Deere and Fiat, the two largest makers of farm machinery, will set up credit companies like the General Motors Acceptance Corporation to lend money to those who own the land to allow them to buy machinery. In return they will receive grain to sell on world markets. Those sales will drive millions of less productive grain farmers out of business all around the world.

In the United States it is clear who goes out of business. Go to the 98th meridian, remembering that about one third of Kansas is east of the 98th meridian, and draw a line from the Canadian border to the Gulf of Mexico; then swing west to the Rocky Mountains. Every grain farmer in that part of the United States goes out of business. The soil is worse, the rainfall is worse, and the transportation system is much, much worse than what is found in the Ukraine. It won't happen tomorrow, but it will happen.

The real threat to French grain farmers comes not from America, but from Eastern Europe. The French will learn to eat their croissant made from Ukrainian wheat or they will turn around and find two million Ukrainians living in Paris. What is true for agriculture is true elsewhere. Western Europeans will learn to buy the products that Eastern Europe can make (closing down their own production facilities for making those products) or Eastern Europeans by the millions will move west in search of higher wages.

The old USSR was a high-science society capable of building the most sophisticated military weapons—with more than twice as many space launches as the United States. Those engineers and scientists have not disappeared. Already there are American companies that have organized engineering groups in St. Petersburg and Moscow that can be managed electronically from California or Massachusetts. Russian physicists are perfectly capable of teaching at American universities and they now apply for teaching jobs by the dozens when such positions are advertised. Why should anyone pay an American physics Ph.D. $75,000 per year when a Nobel Prize winner can be employed in the old Soviet Union for $100 per month? Scientific wages have already started to respond to what is effectively a new cheap source of very highly skilled labor.

Every social system has some things it does well and some things it does badly. Communism ran bad economies but good school systems. It believed in universal education and attempted to implement that ideal. In many countries it was building on educational foundations that were already very strong (for example, Hungary) and in many others (China, for one) it was grafted onto a culture (Confucian) with strong existing beliefs in the importance of education. Take any Communist country and it will be better educated than its neighbors. Cuba is better educated than Latin America. China is better educated than India. When it comes to formal skills that can be learned in schools, Eastern Europe is probably better educated than Western Europe. The citizens of the old Communist world don't yet have the concrete job skills or the knowledge of how one plays the capitalistic game found in western Europe, but they will learn.

Suppose one gave a comprehensive examination to all high school graduates in America to test their educational qualifications and then gave that same examination to everyone in the old Communist world (1.9 billion people). How many of the latter would pass that exam with test scores higher than those achieved by the average American high school graduate? The answer is essentially "infinity"—hundreds of millions of people know more than the average American.

Why should anyone pay an American high school graduate $20,000 per year, when it is possible to get a better-educated Chinese for $35 per month who will work hard twenty-nine days each month and eleven hours per day in China? If one drives east from Germany, one quickly reaches countries with educational standards equal to that of Germany but where wages are only 5 to 10 percent as high.[6]

The effective worldwide capitalistic supply of educated labor has been vastly expanded and that new supply is going to have large impacts on the wages of the educated in the old capitalistic world—a shock that lies ahead of, not behind, us.

While the old Soviet Union will have its biggest impacts on natural resource industries and scientific labor, China will have its biggest impacts on the manufacturing that uses low- and mid-range skill. Where production skills can be quickly taught to smart, relatively well-educated, ambitious, hardworking workers, China will be an immediate player in the world economy as it already is in industries such as textiles, shoes, and electronic parts. A lot of the world's low- and mid-skill manufacturing will move to China. This affects jobs in the wealthy industrial world but it also affects jobs in the mid-wage developing world. The leather shoe industry located in southern Brazil and northern Argentina is already under heavy competitive pressure from China.[7]

Viewed from the cosmos, all of the world will benefit from China's development. Up close it will look threatening.

CHINA

China is on the move economically (growing at the rate of more than 10 percent per year for more than fifteen years) and the old capitalistic world will have to transform itself quickly if it is not to have a bad case of indigestion as it absorbs 1.2 billion Chinese into the global economy. Given the importance of the more than one fifth of humanity who live in China, it is worth examining more closely.[8]

While no one is more of a China optimist than I, given the overoptimism that often appears in the business press, it is important to start with a dose of reality. Past growth rates are not as good as they look, and the future will not be as good as the past. Published growth rates exaggerate Chinese success. Local officials in China get bonuses depending upon the growth rate of their regions, and those same local officials are in charge of collecting economic statistics. It would take a saint not to exaggerate one's own success and local Chinese officials are not saints. Periodically, Beijing punishes some local official for exaggerating his area's economic performance just to keep the whole system quasi-honest, but the published statistics should still be discounted a bit for statistical exaggeration.[9]

In any country if inflation is underestimated, output will be overestimated, since real output is simply a measurement of the economy's monetary output from which inflation has been subtracted. While the underestimation of inflation and the resulting overestimation of output isn't consistent from year to year, in recent years it seems to have been large. Just making an inflation correction for industrial production lowers official estimates of GDP growth from 13.4 percent to 9.0 percent in 1994 and from 11.8 percent to 7.0 percent in 1993.[10] Similar corrections for agriculture and services would cause further reductions in measured GDP gains.

Communism invested in a lot of projects that are simply in the wrong places making the wrong things—things that people don't want at costs that would dictate losses in a capitalistic society. Many of these projects are now losing massive amounts of money and only survive with public subsidies. Since firms need to make profits in market economies, these projects have no long-term future. About one third of these state industries will eventually have to be shut down.[11] When they are, they will become a subtraction from the statistics of economic growth. The potential shutdowns are not limited to the firms that now lose money. Under communism many things (transportation, raw materials, energy, to name a few) were free or heavily subsidized by the state. When China completes its movement to the market, many of the inputs that industries buy will rise dramatically in price and what looks like profitable firms will quickly become unprofitable ones that must be shut down.

Part of the bad performance in Eastern Europe is due to a lot of shutdowns, subtractions from economic growth, having already been made. In China most of those subtractions lie ahead. When they are made, growth will slow down.

Services weren't valued by those who did central planning under communism and weren't counted as output in communistic statistics.[12] As a result, services were grossly underprovided and what services were provided were not counted. Count what was always there, let the private sector provide the services that communism would not let them provide, and there will be a one-time boom in service production with almost no required investment. But these past deficiencies in communism will eventually be eliminated and the growth in services will eventually begin to require investment if it is to continue. When that happens, growth will slow down.

There is also a central statistical mystery that flows from rural China. With 73 percent of Chinese employment in agriculture, it is difficult to have a rapid national rate of growth unless agriculture is advancing reasonably rapidly.[13] In the first ten or fifteen years of the movement to the market, agriculture boomed. Abolishing the communes improved the incentive structure and led to a big jump in agricultural output with no investments in irrigation, fertilizer, machinery, pesticides, or transportation. But those easy gains could not continue forever. Sooner or later the inefficiencies of Communist agriculture would be eliminated and further gains would depend upon investments in needed inputs. In agriculture this moment of truth has already arrived. In the last five to ten years, agricultural output has stagnated, by the admission of Beijing (rural incomes have fallen from 58 to 38 percent of urban incomes), yet there has been no slowdown in published national growth rates.[14] As a result, published growth rates should probably be thought of as urban growth rates and not total growth rates.

Housing took only 1 percent of household incomes when communism was economically alive and well. Rents did not even pay for heat much less construction and upkeep. But under communism, wages were essentially adjusted downward to reflect the existence of that free housing. When housing and other goods and services are repriced and begin to be sold at market prices, wages will have to rise to compensate. The necessary upward wage adjustment means that labor will not be as cheap in China as it now looks. As wages rise to cover real living costs, China will quickly cease to offer the world's lowest-cost labor. Firms simply looking for low-cost labor will locate elsewhere. China will have to move upscale in technology to justify those higher wages— a process that is much harder and much slower than simply attracting outsiders looking for low wages.

With the inefficiencies of the communes eliminated and with large income gaps now emerging between rural and urban areas to keep the 80 percent of the Chinese who live in rural areas from moving to urban areas (as many as fifty million people may already have moved), massive investments in fertilizers, pesticides, machinery, transportation, communications, and electrification will have to be made to raise rural productivity and incomes. That investment can only come from the investment funds now used to support light manufacturing in coastal locations, and when it occurs measured growth will have to slow down.

These investments in rural areas simply have to be made if social peace is to be maintained. What the farmer gets is what the urban dweller pays minus transportation and distribution costs. These are now so high that they often take most of the value of the farmer's production. For many the costs are so high that it does not even pay the farmer to send his crops to be sold. He is forced to remain a subsistence peasant unconnected with the monetary economy.

The rapid growth of the last two decades is to some extent a measure of the inefficiencies of communism rather than indicative of the long-term growth potential of Chinese capitalism. The Communists made massive investments that did not pay off because of a poor incentive structure. While some of these projects cannot be rescued, others can. Correct communism's inefficiencies with better incentive systems and the investments of the past can often be made to pay big returns with very little new investment. A hotel building that long existed if given good management and good services becomes a real hotel. In essence, the effect is a little like repairing the bridges on the Rhine River after the war. A single bridge repair allows a lot of previously existing investment to go back into production.

Inefficient Communist factories can be made to run at much higher output levels by simply using better management techniques. Costs are low because the factories are already there. But eventually the existing factories that can be rehabilitated are running at peak efficiency and the amount of investment necessary to support any particular growth rate soars.

Initially growth could be allowed to occur along the coast where little infrastructure was needed, especially along that part of the coast that could use the infrastructure of Hong Kong. But China is a big continental country. More than one billion Chinese cannot be allowed to move to the coast—as will happen if infrastructure investments are not made and incomes rise on the coast and stagnate in the interior. China must make massive investments in new infrastructure to roll the economic boom to the center and west of the country.

Because of its history China has less infrastructure (communications, transportation, electrification) than even smaller, poorer countries like India. China is three times as large as India yet has 20 percent fewer miles of railways.[15] In India the British Army built railroads in the nineteenth century so that it could efficiently garrison the country. China had the disadvantage of being a quasi-colony where none of the countries (Britain, France, Russia, Germany, Japan, the United States) involved in its quasi-colonization took responsibility for building its national infrastructure.

In addition, because of his experiences in fighting the Japanese during World War II, Chairman Mao believed in regional self-sufficiency and did not build the heavy infrastructure that was built in other Communist countries such as the Soviet Union. China is unique when it comes to its lack of modern infrastructure. What has to be done is enormous.

What can only be described as regional economic warlords make this problem more difficult and costly than it ought to be. Regional officials attempt to monopolize economic growth for their areas by being unwilling to spend their money on cooperative regional infrastructure projects that would in the long run lower the costs for everyone. While China needs more ports and airports, it already has ports and airports that are grossly underutilized because they were built in the wrong places. The best example is the four new airports that have been, or are being, built in the Hong Kong area. One airport with high-speed rail connections to the major towns in the area would have been both cheaper and would have provided an areawide transportation grid. But it did not happen. What is going to emerge is a lot of debt and a lot of unused capacity located at the wrong places. China cannot afford to spend money on duplicative facilities or poorly located facilities.

Looking forward, China will have to take some of the investment funds that are now going into rapid payoffs in light manufacturing and use them to make long-term investments in infrastructure and agriculture. When that happens, growth slows down.

For all of these reasons, China's growth rate will be substantially lower in the future than it has been in the past. When thinking about sustainable growth rates, subtract at least 4 percentage points from current published figures.

Popular articles also grossly exaggerate how rapidly China will make it into the developed world. Start with China's per capita GDP as measured by international currency values of about $370, or its per capita GDP of about $1,600 measured by what it would cost in America to buy what the average Chinese does buy (what is known to economists as a purchasing power parity calculation).[16] Japan has a per capita GDP of about $38,000 if it is evaluated at 100 yen to the dollar. Assume that Japan grows at 3 percent per year (almost 1 percentage point below what it has achieved in the past 100 years), and assume that China grows at 6 percent per year (more than 50 percent better than any large country has ever done although over a 100-year period of time). Plug these starting per capita GDPs and these assumed future growth rates for the two countries into a hand calculator, let the program on compound interest grind the numbers out to 2100 (104 years from now), and China still has a per capita GDP less than 20 percent that of Japan starting with the $370 number and less than 70 percent that of Japan starting with the $1,600 number.

China will of course have a bigger GDP than Japan when its per capita income is only one tenth as high, since Japan has 123 million people and China has 1.2 billion people. China will be a great power politically and militarily in the twenty-first century. But it already is probably the world's second military superpower after the United States. Military power depends upon absolute size. To be a world economic player one must have a high per capita GDP and be technologically sophisticated. India has a bigger total GDP than the Netherlands but the Netherlands is a world player (has effects on others) while India is not. Most of the large Indian GDP is food and other simple necessities locally grown and locally eaten. Beginning from where China is now, it will take more than a century to make it into the developed world. It took Japan that long and no one has ever done it faster.

In the very long run China may not make it into the developed world—although I would place my personal bets that it will. To do so takes successful decade after successful decade of good economic performance. Latin America is littered with countries that have had a couple of good decades economically and then collapsed. Skeptics can legitimately point to a history of Chinese instability that precludes the economic performance of a marathon runner. Perhaps it is like much of Latin America, an economic sprinter who will collapse before it reaches the finish line. I don't believe so, but no one can demonstrate that this outcome is impossible. But China will not implode as the USSR did or as a recent U.S. government intelligence estimate predicted.[17] Thousands of years of holding together as a unified country mean a lot when it comes to predicting future disintegration.

None of this is to fundamentally downgrade China's current performance. It has been sensational. Its problems (rural tensions are clearly rising, too many people are removing to the cities, the boom isn't moving westward fast enough) reflect its success.

This leads to an interesting question. Why is China moving so quickly and easily toward a market economy while the rest of the

Communist world is having so much trouble doing so? There are four principal reasons for the Chinese success relative to the failures that are found in middle and Eastern Europe.

First, the Chinese have also proved that it is possible for a society that is still very poor to voluntarily save and hence invest a high percentage of its GDP—nearly 40 percent.[18] That means that foreign investment is important, but not essential. Because of its high internal savings rates, if China were subject to capital flight Mexican-style it would not affect China the way that it affected Mexico in late 1994. With or without foreign investment the resources to build the future are available. Foreign technology and management are essential; foreign funds are not.

Second, China has an effective government that can design strategies and, once those strategies have been agreed upon, can make and enforce decisions. The transition from communism to capitalism is difficult and it cannot be made without an effective government. In Eastern Europe where government has essentially collapsed and where citizens distrust all governmental activities, "the market has met its match."[19] Economies plunged downward for many years and only now seem to have hit bottom and to be slowly moving upward.

In the late 1970s, China began its reforms in the countryside by abolishing the communes and giving every peasant family their share of the land—the family responsibility system. Technically the peasants were given a fifteen-year lease for annual crops and a fifty-year lease for tree crops with the right to transfer (sell) land leases in 1988.[20] But in reality every peasant knows that the land is permanently theirs and it isn't going to be taken back by the state. With better incentives in the following six years from 1978 to 1984, rural China's agricultural output rose by two thirds.[21] Privatizing urban industries when the food stores are full, as they are in China, is simply very different from trying to privatize urban industries when the food stores are empty as they are in the old USSR.

To this day the privatization of agriculture has yet to occur in the agricultural areas of the old Soviet Union. Their ideology just won't let them do it. Officially the collective farms have been abolished, but nothing has been put in their place. The leaders of the agricultural cooperatives don't want to lose their jobs and they ignore directives from Moscow. Very murky property laws lead to a situation where no one knows who owns the land and, as a result, 40 percent of harvested grain rots in the fields. Fearing urban unrest, the government holds grain prices down to levels that make it unattractive to farm. The result in 1995 was the worst grain harvest in thirty years—worse than when communism was alive and well.[22] But it should also be said, in all fairness, that privatizing agriculture is inherently much easier in China after only thirty years of communism than it is in Russia after seventy-five years of communism. There are still peasants in China who remember how to run private farms. There are no such people in the old Soviet Union.

In the industrial area, China initially limited its experiments with markets to special economic zones rather than trying to implement the market in some economic big bang that would cover the entire country. The Chinese strategy was to move forward gradually with success feeding upon success. The privatization of agriculture led to the privatization of services, which led to the privatization of small-scale retailing, which led to the privatization of small-scale manufacturing. The export sector was freed before the import sector. As the special economic zones expanded, the scope of the market expanded.

The privatization of the housing stock is now under way. But why would anyone buy their apartment if they now pay only 1 percent of their income for their current apartment? On day number one there is the same lousy apartment, but now the new owner must pay for heat, maintenance, and taxes. Under capitalism, housing costs 30 or 40 percent of family income. In housing, the market cannot be used to move to the market.

Being able to make effective decisions, the Chinese government has essentially told its citizens that they *will* buy their current homes. Not long ago I met with a group of foreign service officials who had been ordered to buy their current apartments. They were allowed to do so at about one third of construction costs (a great deal from a capitalistic point of view), but their disposable income left for the purchase of other consumer goods would be severely reduced as a result. They did not like having to buy, but bought because they had no choice if they did not want to lose their jobs.

To succeed, market economies need to know who owns what. Under communism the state owned everything. The market economic game has to begin with an initial distribution of income and wealth.

Governments have to be able to make and enforce decisions—giving or selling whatever they please to whomever they want.

While the Chinese way of doing this is less than a perfect process, the Chinese government is capable of making such decisions.[23] Governments in much of Eastern Europe are not. There, privatization has too often been basically a process of spontaneous self-combustion whereby the strong (usually the old Communists) simply grab what used to be state assets for themselves. This unsanctioned privatization process creates the feeling that everyone and everything is corrupt. The wealthy are not those who can organize new production, but those who are best at seizing property that used to belong to the state—the public. The market quickly comes to be seen as unfair, and political support for official privatization falls. Much of Russian crime is what might be called private privatization.

Communism and the Confucian culture also reinforced each other's interest in education. Relative to other big developing countries such as India, Indonesia, or Brazil, China is both better educated and more broadly educated. Teaching modern production skills to those with a good basic education is simply much easier than teaching the illiterate.

China's third great advantage is its overseas Chinese. Management functions are very different under communism and capitalism. Under communism managers were essentially quasi-militaristic economic officers. There was a central economic plan, the battle plan, established in Moscow or Beijing. Managers were told what to make and were sent the necessary materials, components, people, and money for wages. They were told when a flatcar would arrive to take what they had produced to some unknown location and how they would be punished (court-martialed) if their production was not ready. Managers never bought anything, never sold anything, never negotiated with anyone, never studied market information, never worried about profits and losses, and never talked to a customer. They were army colonels in an economic army doing what their generals told them to do.

What is the American success rate in turning Army colonels into business people? Precisely zero. Business requires a completely different mentality. In Russia the system is using the old army colonels and it doesn't work. In China the old army colonels were essentially replaced by overseas Chinese who know how to play the capitalistic game since they were raised in capitalistic economies. Factory managers are often overseas Chinese and headquarters functions can be performed in Hong Kong or by those (the Taiwanese) who funnel their money or talent through Hong Kong. These overseas Chinese (living in Hong Kong, Taiwan, the Americas, Southeast Asia, Singapore) bring money and technology, but what they really bring that is of greatest value is the knowledge and contacts necessary to play the capitalistic game.

The trust generated by family relationships in turn lets them teach the Chinese of the People's Republic of China how the game is played much faster than would be possible if PRC Chinese had to learn from the Americans, Europeans, or Japanese and weren't sure what to believe or disbelieve.

China's fourth great advantage springs from the fact that while only 18 percent of Chinese employment was in large state enterprises, Russia had 93 percent of its employees in state enterprises. China has some very big facilities (Beijing Iron and Steel with sixty-two thousand employees), often given to them by the Soviets, but they are a smaller part of the national economy and the national economy can be allowed to grow around them before they must be shut down.[24] China can postpone dealing with this very difficult problem. Russia cannot. At the same time, China had 72 percent of its employment in collective farms while the USSR had only 6 percent.[25] It is much easier to move an economy of small-scale holdings to the market than it is to move an economy of large-scale holdings.

The idiosyncrasies of its founding Communist fathers played a role in this key difference. Stalin learned his economics in the 1920s when the secret of capitalism was supposedly to be found in vertical integration and gigantic economies of scale. In the 1920s, Ford's Rouge plant in Detroit was held up for emulation everywhere—iron ore and coal coming in one end of the plant, 112,000 people working in the facility, and cars coming out the other end of the plant.[26] Stalin fell in love with such facilities and 77 percent of all the products made in the old Soviet Union, a country of 280 million people, were made in one and only one giant factory.[27]

Capitalists quickly learned that such plants didn't work. But how is an economy composed of such plants to be privatized? Everyone knows that under capitalism they should be closed down. If they did work and were transferred to anyone, that person would have a private monopoly. Single monopolistic producers don't lead to competitive market economies. Even worse, now that the USSR is fifteen different countries, each one of them has too much of what it produces, not enough of what the other fourteen produce, and no way to trade with each other. In the USSR physical problems embedded in concrete and equipment make it very difficult to build a market economy.

In contrast, Chairman Mao essentially learned his economics fighting the Japanese Army during World War II. He noticed that if China had nothing vital to be destroyed or conquered, China was too big to be conquered. The Japanese could put one Japanese soldier in every Chinese village and half of the villages of China would still have no Japanese soldiers. His military experience led him to stress local self-sufficiency. Every area produced everything—watches, bicycles, food. Backyard steel mills were part of this strategy. The resulting diseconomies of scale were large; they may even have approached the efficiency losses incurred with Stalin's giganticism, but they led to an economy of small-scale enterprise that is relatively easy to privatize.

While it certainly is not an advantage to be poorer, being so China has been willing to psychologically admit that it is not a first world country and must copy to catch up. Much of Eastern Europe has refused to psychologically admit that it has something to learn managerially and technologically from the first world.

Uncertainties certainly exist. How does China roll the boom west into the interior of the country and how does it create rural prosperity? While Deng Xiaoping is not yet dead, he is clearly out of the decision-making loop, and power relationships are being reoriented—seemingly without disturbing economic growth. In the early 1990s, China was growing rapidly while most of the rest of the industrial world was in the midst of a recession or a period of slow growth. This magnified China's position on the world's economic stage in a way that exaggerated both its importance and its accomplishments. Measured by market exchange rates, China accounts for just 1 percent of world GDP. China's growth will slow down, growth in the rest of the world has already accelerated and will accelerate further, Japan's seemingly endless recession will end, but China will remain a major story in the restructuring of the earth's economic surface.

Those studying real earthquakes go to China. It simply has more earthquakes than any other place on the face of the globe. Those interested in economic earthquakes might be given the same advice.

THE END OF IMPORT SUBSTITUTION AND QUASI-SOCIALISM IN THE THIRD WORLD

Lord Keynes once observed that "practical men who believe themselves to be quite exempt from any intellectual influence are usually the slave of some defunct economist."[28] In the third world the slave master was Raul Prebish, who headed the Economic Commission for Latin America in the 1950s. He argued that the road to development should be built with import substitution and quasi-socialism. Place high tariffs and quotas on what was imported from the developed world, establish government-sponsored corporations to make what had formerly been imported, substitute local production for imports since a market for the products already existed, and growth could occur.

It was a plausible theory—accepted almost everywhere in the third world. The fact that the old colonial masters were those whose imports would be cut off and that revolutionary communism seemed to be growing more rapidly than capitalism in the 1950s did not hurt the rapid acceptance of the theory, either. Unfortunately, quasi-socialistic import substitution did not work anywhere it was tried. Quasi-private-public business firms simply lived behind their high quotas and tariffs, enjoyed government subsidies, made a lot of money, lived well, and never worried about matching the efficiency of the developed world.

In the 1970s and 1980s there were four developing countries that essentially rejected this strategy and became export oriented. With the exception of Hong Kong, their business firms were protected in their home markets where tariffs, quotas, and administrative guidance kept out competing first world products, but this protection was given only if they were at the same time exporting and matching the efficiency of the developed world. It was believed that what these firms had to do to survive in world markets—become efficient—would eventually be brought back to their domestic activities. Those beliefs proved to be true. Today those same four formerly poor countries have per capita

GDPs that have effectively taken them out of the third world: Hong Kong, per capita income in 1993 $18,000–$20,000; Singapore, per capita income in 1993 $16,000–$17,000; Taiwan, per capita income in 1993 $10,000–$11,000; and South Korea, per capita income in 1993 $8,000–$9,000.[29]

It is important to understand that the success of these small countries on the Pacific Rim plus the collapse of communism and socialism has caused an intellectual revolution in the third world. NAFTA, for example, would not have been possible without that revolution. For decades the Mexicans tried to isolate themselves from the U.S. economy. They had strict limits on the employment of both American managers and American capital in Mexico. Today the Mexicans want to play the world game. But so does everyone else in the third world.

Some countries (Indonesia, Malaysia) are junking their past ideologies faster than others (India, Egypt), but all are junking their beliefs in import substitution and quasi-socialism. Everyone wants to be export oriented. Instead of having sixty-five million people in four countries playing the export game, there will be three billion people everywhere in the third world anxious to play the export game. Whatever the degree of competition from low-wage third world countries at the end of the twentieth century, up the intensity level manyfold as we move forward into the twenty-first century. Some of that low-wage competition is also going to focus on high-skill jobs. Texas Instruments designs its most sophisticated computer chips in India. Motorola has equipment design centers in both India and China.[30]

THE MIDDLE EAST

Everywhere economic geography is in flux. Consider the Middle East if peace should exist—thirty million low-wage workers in Egypt, technology in Israel, the Palestinians are the best educated of the Arabs, wealthy consumers and investors in the Persian Gulf region. It won't happen tomorrow, but within a decade or two a very interesting economy could exist in this part of the world.

In some industries such as tourism it could happen much faster. Imagine a tour starting with the ancient antiquities of Egypt, going on to the religious shrines of the Holy Land, visiting Petra in Jordan (the

Indiana Jones Roman city at the bottom of the canyon), followed by the world's best beaches and scuba diving in the Red Sea. One does not need too much peace in the Middle East in order to be safer there than one is in Florida—and millions of people will alter their vacation plans.

Similarly, consider peace in the Caucasus Mountain region. The Caucasus Mountains dominate the Alps when it comes to skiing—they are higher, have more snow, better weather, and an unspoiled environment. Once the skier is on an airplane, why stop at the Alps—go an hour or two more. Austrian companies are already offering heli-skiing in the Caucasus Mountains that is impacting the number of Europeans heli-skiing in Canada.

There is also a greater Turkish common market waiting to be built among the mostly Turkish-speaking peoples living at the intersection of Europe, the Middle East, and central Asia. It may not come into existence, but then again, it might.

POLITICAL GEOGRAPHY

Political borders are important to economics, since they mark the line across which tariffs are collected, quotas set, different legal and tax systems applied, social investments made, and administrative guidance given. During the cold war the USSR and the United States could agree on one thing: It was dangerous to permit changes in national borders, since the two great powers were too apt to be drawn into the resultant boundary disputes between their clients. Whichever side felt itself losing in the boundary dispute would demand aid from its great power ally and that aid would be very difficult to deny if alliance solidarity was to be preserved. And if one great power gave aid, the other would certainly have to match it. By experience both great powers learned that whenever someone tried to move boundaries by force (whether in Cuba, South Korea, Vietnam, Afghanistan), the resulting bipolar power disputes came close to getting out of hand. Wherever boundaries could not be agreed upon (as in South Korea and Germany), both sides had to maintain large armies at those borders to stabilize the situation. Neither superpower could afford to let its clients be pushed around by the clients of the rival bloc, but both superpowers knew that if they were drawn into local border disputes by their clients there was too great a chance that the missiles would start flying between Washington and Moscow.

With the end of colonialism the names on the map of the world often changed after World War II, but borders hardly ever changed. With the end of communism the borders as well as the names are changing. Some of these new countries have not existed as nation-states for half or three quarters of a century (for example, Poland), some have had very short histories (the Baltic republics whose modern existence was only between World War I and World War II), some have not existed for hundreds of years (the Ukraine and the Muslim republics of central Asia conquered by Russia in the seventeenth and eighteenth centuries; the countries of Caucasia, which have not been independent since before the Ottoman Empire), and some have effectively never before existed (Belarus). Some of these countries will be established in peace (the Czech Republic, Slovakia, and Slovenia) and some will appear or disappear in the context of war (Georgia, Azerbaijan, Armenia, Croatia, Serbia, Bosnia, Macedonia). New nations whose names are hardly known (Chechenya) will continue to split off or attempt to split off from old nations (Russia). Some of today's new nations won't remain nations long (Belarus?).

Within the old Communist world new countries and new governments are being built from the wreckage of communism. Nation building is never easy. Rules have yet to be written; traditions have yet to be established. Political power bases are initially fluid and unstable. Turbulence and chaos are to be expected.

Powerful ideologies and ruthless revolutionary leaders were necessary to hold together today's warring ethnic groups in middle and Eastern Europe. Communism was such an ideology. Stalin was such a leader—a Georgian ruling Russians. It did not make any difference to which ethnic group you belonged, his or someone else's; all were repressed. Tito was equally tough—a Croat ruling Serbs using a Serbian army. With the demise of the ideology of communism and the deaths of those hard revolutionary leaders, the ethnic groups of Eastern Europe and central Asia find that they can no longer live together. It is as if they had suddenly come out of an ice age, thawed, and begun fighting again with the intervening decades of peace not remembered.

But with the end of the cold war, borders are also going to be changing outside of the old Communist world. Every border in Africa is essentially in the wrong place—the place where the British and French armies just happened to meet. The existing borders make no sense geographically, ethnically, linguistically, historically, or economically. Somalia and Rwanda are but the initial geopolitical rumblings from Africa. If one looks at the implicit American permission given to the Turks to invade the Kurdish part of Iraq, which is being protected from the Iraqi Army by the American Air Force, while at the same time the Iranian Kurds are encouraged to rebel against the government in Tehran, both the complexity and absurdity of what is happening are dramatically evident.

India has never been one country except when unified by an outside invader (the Moguls or the British). It is a subcontinent of many religions, many languages, many ethnic groups, and many skin colors. British India has already split into three countries (Pakistan, India, and Bangladesh) and more will appear. Nationalistic unrest is not limited to the Sikhs or Kashmirs. One of the unifiers of India, the belief in socialism and the need for central planning from New Delhi, has melted away with the end of communism. Bombay and the region around it have a population that would make it one of the world's larger countries without the rest of India. What does New Delhi bring to the economic table now that central planning is believed to be a hindrance rather than a help?

The ideology of small ethnic groups is not limited to the second or the third world. The Labor party promises devolution (separate parliaments) for Wales and Scotland in the United Kingdom. The Northern League talks about dividing Italy into a North and a South. The Basques and Catalans want more political independence in Spain. The Bretons and Corsicans grumble in France. North America has its Quebec. Puerto Rico doesn't know what it wants to do.

If one talks to Quebecers it is clear that a profound change in attitudes has occurred. In the last surge of nationalism two or three decades ago, there was an underlying worry that economies of scale were central to economic success. Quebecers would have to take a sharp reduction in their standards of living if they were to become independent and separate from English-speaking Canada. They voted 60 to 40 against leaving Canada. Today that belief no longer exists. In the most recent election they voted 50.4 to 49.6 for staying in Canada, but among those whose native language was French the vote was 60 to 40 for leaving Canada.³¹ Only the solid pro-Canada vote of the 18 percent who do not have French as their mother tongue kept Quebec in Canada.

Potentially small countries have noticed that some of the wealthiest countries in the world (for example, Switzerland, Austria, Norway, Sweden) and some of the fastest-growing countries in the world (Singapore, Hong Kong, Taiwan) are small—often nothing more than city-states. What others have done, they can do. What they see others doing, they want to do. As long as Quebec is allowed to remain within NAFTA, Quebecers believe, and they are right, they can gain whatever economies of scale there are to gain and maintain their standards of living without having to be politically associated with English-speaking Canada. Most of Quebec's exports go to the United States, and not the rest of Canada, anyway.

At the same time, the need to bargain for access rights in world markets has caused precisely those groups that do not want to live with their immediate neighbors to want to join larger regional economic units such as the European Common Market or the North American Free Trade Agreement. They see these larger regional groupings as economic insurance policies guaranteeing their participation in the world economy. Being partially ruled from a far distance by those they hardly know is simply much better than being totally ruled by those they know only too well near them.

A powerful dynamic is under way. Economics is pushing nations to disintegrate and regions to integrate simultaneously. Events and institutions in one part of the world push events and institutions in another. If the European Common Market did not exist, no one would have proposed the North American Free Trade Agreement. If these two agreements did not exist, no one would be talking about a trading group on the Pacific Rim.

The geopolitical changes seen on the face of a map in the seven years since the Berlin wall fell are startling—but they are merely the beginning, not the end, of a fundamental redrawing of the political lines on the face of the earth.

NO COMPETITORS

Capitalism and democracy now live in a unique period where effectively they have no viable competitors for the allegiance of the minds of their citizens. It has been called the "end of history."

Militarily, there are no systematic threats to the world's major capitalistic democracies. No one has the power to invade and conquer any of them. There is no credible military threat to the United States that even the American military can imagine when justifying their budgets. They have to retreat to making arguments about defending places, like the Baltic Republics, where it is not clear who threatens them—and where it is equally clear that no matter what happens, the United States is not going to defend them.

Politically, authoritarian dictatorships still exist and will continue to exist, but they are not buttressed by an ideology (the utopian visions of Nazism or communism) that can command the voluntary allegiance of anyone or by the historical traditions of feudalism (an aristocracy that was accepted by the public). They have no promised land to promise.

For much of the nineteenth and all of the twentieth centuries, capitalism faced off against socialism on the inside and communism on the outside. But those ideologies now have no future except in the history books. Capitalism stands alone.

Chapter 4

Plate Two: An Era of Man-made Brainpower Industries

THE DISAPPEARANCE OF CLASSICAL COMPARATIVE ADVANTAGE

The classical theory of comparative advantage was developed to explain the geographic location of industry in the nineteenth and twentieth centuries. In the theory of comparative advantage, location of production depended upon two factors—natural resource endowments and factor proportions (the relative abundance of capital and labor).[1] Those with good soil, climate, and rainfall specialize in agricultural production; those with oil supply oil. Countries that were capital-rich (lots of capital per worker) made capital-intensive products, while countries that were labor-rich (little capital per worker) made labor-intensive products.

In the nineteenth and for most of the twentieth century, the theory of comparative advantage explained what needed to be explained. The United States grew cotton in the South because the climate and soil were right; it made cloth in New England because New England had the water power to drive, and the capital to finance, textile mills. New York was the biggest city in America since it had the best natural harbor on the East Coast and the capital to build a water connection (the Erie Canal) to the Midwest. Pittsburgh was the iron and steel capital, since given the location of America's coal, iron ore, rivers, and lakes, it was the cost-minimizing place to be. In an age of railroads, Chicago was destined to be America's transportation capital and hog butcher to the world. Texas was oil, and the availability of electricity dictated that aluminum be made on the Columbia River in the state of Washington.

Consider this list of the twelve largest companies in America on January 1, 1900: the American Cotton Oil Company, American Steel, American Sugar Refining Company, Continental Tobacco, Federal Steel, General Electric, National Lead, Pacific Mail, People's Gas, Tennessee Coal and Iron, U.S. Leather, and U.S. Rubber.[2] Ten of the twelve companies were natural resource companies. The economy at the turn of the century was a natural resource economy.

But something else is interesting about that list. Bits and pieces of each of these companies exist inside other companies, but only one of those companies, General Electric, is alive today. Eleven of the twelve could not make it to the next century as separate entities. The moral of the story is clear. Capitalism is a process of creative destruction whereby dynamic new small companies are continually replacing old large ones that have not been able to adjust to new conditions.

The same picture was true outside of the United States. Before World War I more than one million workers toiled in the coal mines of Great Britain—6 percent of the total workforce.[3] Coal was king. It was the motive force that powered the world. Today less than thirty thousand workers toil in those same coal mines.

In 1917 manufacturing was on the rise but thirteen of the twenty largest industrial enterprises ranked by assets were still natural-resource-based companies: United States Steel, Standard Oil, Bethlehem Steel, Armour and Company, Swift and Company, Midvale Steel and Ordnance, International Harvester, E. I. du Pont de Nemours and Company, United States Rubber, Phelps Dodge, General Electric, Anaconda Copper, American Smelting and Refining, Singer Sewing Machine Company, Ford Motor Company, Westinghouse, American Tobacco, Jones and Laughlin Steel, Union Carbide, and Weyerhaeuser.[4]

In the late nineteenth and early twentieth centuries, those with natural resources, such as Argentina and Chile, were rich while those without natural resources, such as Japan, were destined to be poor.[5] Everyone who became rich in the nineteenth and twentieth centuries had natural resources.

Once a country became rich, it tended to stay rich. Having a higher income, it saved more; saving more it invested more; investing more it worked with more plant and equipment; working with more capital its productivity was higher; and having higher productivity it could pay higher wages. For those who grew rich, there was a virtuous cycle leading them to more riches. As they became rich, they shifted to cap-ital-intensive products that generated even higher levels of labor pro-ductivity and even higher wages.

In contrast, consider the list made in 1990 by the Ministry of In-ternational Trade and Industry in Japan speculating as to what would be the most rapidly growing industries in the 1990s and the early part of the twenty-first century: microelectronics, biotechnology, the new material science industries, telecommunications, civilian aircraft man-ufacturing, machine tools and robots, and computers (hardware and software).[6] All of them are man-made brainpower industries that could be located anywhere on the face of the earth. Where they will be lo-cated depends upon who organizes the brainpower to capture them.

Natural resource endowments have fallen out of the competitive equation. Modern products simply use fewer natural resources. Bridges and cars have fewer tons of steel embedded in them, and devices such as the computer use almost no natural resources. Modern transporta-tion costs have created a world where resources can be cheaply moved to wherever they are needed. Japan is a good example, having the world's dominant steel industry yet having no coal and no iron ore. That could not have happened in the nineteenth century or for most of the twentieth century.

After correcting for general inflation, natural resource prices have fallen almost 60 percent from the mid-1970s to the mid-1990s.[7] Bet on another 60 percent fall in the next twenty-five years. Raw materials are going to be pouring out of the old Communist world but, even more important, the world is on the edge of a material science revo-lution that will be turning out made-to-order designer materials. Bio-technology is going to be speeding up the green revolution in agriculture. Few will become rich in the twenty-first century based sim-ply on their possession of raw materials.

Capital availability has also fallen out of the competitive equation. With the development of a world capital market, everyone essentially borrows in New York, London, or Tokyo. Today an entrepreneur in Bangkok can build a plant as capital-intensive as any in the United States, Germany, or Japan despite his living in a country with a per capita income less than one tenth that of those three countries. Effec-tively, there simply is no such thing as a capital-rich or a capital-poor country when it comes to investment. Capital-intensive products are not automatically made in rich countries. Workers in rich countries won't automatically work with more capital, have higher levels of productivity, or enjoy higher wages.

In an era of man-made brainpower industries capital/labor ratios cease to be meaningful variables, since the whole distinction between capital and labor collapses. Skills and knowledge, human capital, are created by the same investment funds that create physical capital. Raw labor (the willingness to sacrifice leisure) still exists, but it has become much less important in the production process and can, in any case, be bought very cheaply when there is an entire globe of poor under-employed workers to draw upon.

Today knowledge and skills now stand alone as the only source of comparative advantage. They have become the key ingredient in the late twentieth century's location of economic activity. Silicon Valley and Route 128 are where they are simply because that is where the brainpower is. They have nothing else going for them.

With the invention of science-based industries in the twentieth century—the first being the chemical engineering industries of Germany—the deliberate invention of new products became important. Those who invented new products would produce those products during the initial, high-profitability, high-wage, stages of their life cycle. Eventually production would move into the third world but by then the product would have become a labor-intensive, low-wage commodity with low profitability. Textiles were the classic example. They fueled the industrial revolution in both Great Britain and the United States but are today a standard third-world-manufactured product.

But what came to be called "the product cycle" no longer exists. The art of reverse engineering along with the growth of multinational companies interested in employing their technologies wherever production costs are lowest has led to a world where new product technologies flow around the world almost as fast as capital and natural resources. Proprietary new product technologies aren't necessarily employed where they are invented or by those who financed them.

Think of the video camera and recorder (invented by Americans), the fax (invented by Americans), and the CD player (invented by the Dutch). When it comes to sales, employment, and profits, all have become Japanese products despite the Japanese not inventing any of them. Product invention, if a country is also not the world's low-cost producer, gives one very little economic advantage. Technology has never been more important, but what matters more is being the leader in process technologies and what matters less is being the leader in new product technologies.

Being the low-cost producer is partly a matter of wages, but to a much greater extent it is a matter of becoming the masters of process technologies, having the skills and knowing how to put new things together, and the ability to manage the production processes. To be masters of process technologies a successful business must be managed so that there is a seamless web among invention, design, manufacturing, sales, logistics, and services that competitors cannot match. The secret of being the best is found, not in being either labor- or capital-intensive, or even in being management-intensive, but in having the skills base throughout the organization that allows it to be the low-cost integrator of all of these activities.

The classical theory of comparative advantage is often taught as if everyone benefits from trade. Technically that is not true. The total income of every country that takes advantage of comparative advantage grows, but there will be individuals within each country who lose. What the theory holds is that those who gain from international trade receive enough extra income from their activities that they could compensate those who lose when international trade commences. If that compensation isn't actually paid (and it almost never is), then those who lose are quite rational to oppose international trade.

But in the classical theory the losses usually will be quite small. First, full employment is assumed to exist. Free trade does not push anyone into unemployment. Second, transition costs are assumed to be zero. There is no region-, industry-, or firm-specific physical or human capital that is destroyed when workers are forced to shift between regions, industries, or firms. Third, returns are assumed to be everywhere equal. Each industry has the same rate of return on human or physical capital. Each firm and industry pays the same wage rate for a worker's being willing to give up an hour of leisure. As a consequence, being forced to shift jobs doesn't change wages very much, if at all.

In the classical theory of comparative advantage, there is no role for government in determining the location of industry. There was a "right" place to do everything given by natural resource endowments and factor proportions. If everything was done in the "right" place, the world would maximize its total production. Wise governments know that any attempt to alter private location decisions would simply burden the economy with the inefficiency costs of having economic activities located in the "wrong" places.

This set of beliefs led to what are now the immortal words attributed to the chairman of President George Bush's Council of Economic Advisers, Michael Boskin: "It doesn't make any difference whether a country makes potato chips or computer chips."[8]

But none of these assumptions is of course true. Trade can cause unemployment. Those who lose their jobs when imports expand often remain unemployed for long periods of time. Theoretically, governments could stimulate their economies to prevent higher unemployment but they often don't. There are transition costs in moving people between regions, industries, or firms. Empirically, wages and rates of return on capital do not equalize in even rather long periods of time.

In 1992 average American wages ranged from $20.68 per hour in cigarette manufacturing and $19.70 per hour in malt beverage manufacturing to $5.94 in women's dress manufacturing and $5.29 in eating and drinking establishments.[9] If fringe benefits are included, these differentials expand by one fourth.[10] Average rates of return on common equity ranged from 27 percent in pharmaceuticals to minus 26 percent in building materials in 1992.[11] Looking at returns by firm rather than industry, the differences are even larger.

Such differences persist over long periods of time. Real-world economies are dynamic and never settle down into an equilibrium world of equal wages or equal rates of return. Pharmaceuticals have become a hot political issue precisely because they have yielded the highest rate of return on capital for essentially the entire post–World War II period. Petroleum has paid wages above the mean (plus 29 percent) and household services wages below the mean (minus 36 percent) consistently.

Wages don't just depend upon individual productivity. Ph.D. university-based economists playing on the American team make a lot more money than their equivalents who play on the British team. Their knowledge is not less than ours, but they generate less revenue with their activities because of the productivity of the other team members with whom they work. The value of any individual's knowledge depends upon the smartness with which it is used in the entire system—

the knowledge absorption abilities of both the buyers and other suppliers.

These realities do not change the conclusion that there are net benefits from international trade, but they do mean that the aggregate losses and the number of losers can be very large. If the winners actually compensated the losers, the winners could lose most of their gains. Losers are often very numerous and lose large amounts of their income. Fighting hard to prevent such losses is not irrational.

Another layer of complexity is added when man-made brainpower industries that depend upon research and development and human skills dominate the system. Investors don't just respond to a fixed set of investment opportunities. Research and development investments create a set of industrial possibilities. Countries don't have the same set of investment opportunities.

The industries of the future have to be invented. They don't just exist. In the era ahead countries have to make the investments in knowledge and skills that will create a set of man-made brainpower industries that will allow their citizens to have high-wages and a high standard of living. By way of contrast, natural resource industries were essentially a birthright. One was born in a country with a lot of natural resources or one wasn't. Man-made brainpower industries are not a birthright. No country acquires these industries without effort and without making the investments necessary to create them.

The theory of comparative advantage still holds but a country's comparative advantage is created by what it does—more precisely by what investments it makes. If a country has not generated the necessary skill base, Ph.D.s in microbiology, it cannot have a biotechnology industry.

American observers often worry about the excessive growth of the service sector with its lower than average wages. While understandable these are not the right worries. Historically, our statistical data have divided industries into agriculture, mining, construction, manufacturing, and services, where services is a heterogeneous category that includes everything not counted in the other four categories. Services is simply too heterogeneous to be an interesting category. On average, the services industries pay wages one third less than those in manufacturing, but some service industries, such as finance or medicine, pay the highest wages in the economy.

The real issue is not the growth of services but whether the economy is making a successful transition from low-wage, low-skill industries (some of which exist in each of our standard statistical categories) to high-wage, high-skill industries (some of which exist in each of our standard statistical categories). Two of the largest twelve companies in America in 1900 (Pacific Mail and People's Gas) were service companies and two of the industries that the Japanese identified as most desirable ninety years later (telecommunications and computer software) were also service industries. Success or failure depends upon whether a country is making a successful transition to the man-made brainpower industries of the future—not on the size of any particular sector.

In an era of man-made brainpower industries, the global economy is a dynamic one always in transition. There aren't lengthy periods of time without technical change where competition can equalize wages and rates of return on capital investment so that all activities are equally lucrative, so that it doesn't matter what one does. While there certainly are long-run market forces equalizing returns, specific firms and industries maintain above-average wages and above-average returns on capital for long periods of time. They do so by moving from product to product within technological families so fast that there is almost no chance for those not in the industry to enter it quickly enough (it takes time to develop the necessary brainpower and skills) to drive down above-average returns on these new activities. As others enter, they are in fact phasing out these new activities to replace them with other, even newer, higher-return activities.

Cost barriers to entry are high and the time necessary to catch up with market leaders is lengthy. To catch up with the American aircraft manufacturing industry, for example, Europe's Airbus Industries required more than two decades and more than $26 billion in public funds.[12]

The economist's concept of equilibrium is useful, since it identifies the long-run direction of economic forces, but it is not a useful concept for describing economic reality at any moment in time. At every instant of time the economy is operating in a period of short-run dynamic disequilibrium, moving toward equilibrium, but with dynamic change coming so fast relative to the time lags that would be necessary to reach equilibrium that periods of short-run disequilibrium never have a chance to become periods of long-run equilibrium.

During such periods of disequilibrium there are often very high wages to be earned and very high rates of return on capital investment to be had. By keeping one generation ahead in making microprocessors, Intel's profits were 23 percent of sales and its net return on assets 17 percent despite having to set almost $500 million aside to cover the costs of correcting a flaw in the Pentium chip.[13] Keeping one jump ahead in software, Microsoft's net income was running at 24 percent of sales in 1995.[14] These above equilibrium returns made Bill Gates into America's wealthiest person with $15 billion in net worth before he was forty.[15]

Such returns will not last forever (in economics they are known as disequilibrium quasi-rents), but they can last for many years—Intel's profits have run far above average for more than a decade. These profit opportunities are the modern equivalent of finding El Dorado—the city of gold. They are very nice to have while they last and they generate permanent wealth that doesn't disappear after the gold mine has yielded its last ounce of gold. Of such events are personal and national fortunes made.

If a firm or a country wants to stay at the leading edge of technology so that it can continue to generate high-disequilibrium wages and profits, it must be a participant in the evolutionary progress of man-made brainpower industries so that it is in the right position to take advantage of the technical and economic revolutions that occasionally arise. The costs of being forced out of such industries are not just the costs of having to move people and capital from one industry or geographic location to another, or of the lower wages that laid-off workers will receive upon reemployment. In the short and medium term the real costs are the lost high wages and profits that one could have had if one had stayed at the leading edge of the wave of new technologies. In the long run the costs are those of getting shut out of future developments and not being able to be a player in new high-wage, high-profit opportunities that will arise. Countries that have not made random access memory chips won't make microprocessors.

If natural resources have ceased to dominate economic activity in a world of man-made brainpower industries, if factor proportions have dissolved in a world of global capital markets and worldwide logistics, if new product introductions come so fast that there is never time enough for equilibrium to develop in labor or capital markets, if transition costs are very large, if high and persistent unemployment is a worldwide fact of life, then the real world is far removed from the classical theory of comparative advantage. Trade still yields great net benefits, but how those benefits are distributed, who receives the benefits and the losses, becomes a much more complicated problem.

SKILLS: THE ONLY SOURCE OF LONG-RUN SUSTAINABLE COMPETITIVE ADVANTAGE

With everything else dropping out of the competitive equation, knowledge has become the only source of long-run sustainable competitive advantage, but knowledge can only be employed through the skills of individuals. As with everything else, knowledge and skills will move around the world—but slower than anything else. Education and training take a long time to complete, and many of the relevant skills are not those taught in formal educational institutions but the process skills that can only be learned in a production environment. The theory of semiconductor design is relatively easy to learn. Actually building semiconductors to the tolerances that are required (less than half a micron) is very difficult.

Today's transportation and communications technologies mean that skilled workers in the first world can effectively work together with the unskilled in the third world. Skilled components can be made in the first world and then shipped to the third world to be assembled with low-skill components that have been made there. Putting the first world's skilled together with the lower-waged third world's unskilled cuts costs, allows profits to rise, and permits some of the first world's skilled workers to have higher wages than they would have if they were still working with the higher-waged unskilled workers of the first world.

Research and design skills can be electronically brought in from the first world. What sells can be quickly communicated to the third world factory and retailers know that the speed of delivery won't be significantly affected by where production occurs. Instant communications and rapid transportation means that markets can be effectively served from production points on the other side of the globe.

Multinational companies are central in this process, since their decisions as to where they will develop and keep technological leadership is central to where most of the very good jobs will be located.[16] Multinational firms will decide to locate their high-wage leadership skills in the United States not because they happen to be American firms but only if America offers them the lowest costs of developing these technological leadership skills. The countries offering companies the lowest costs of developing technological leadership will be the countries that invest the most in research and development, education, and the infrastructure (telecommunications systems, etc.) necessary to exploit leadership positions. National wealth will go to those countries that build the constellations of skills that reinforce each other.

Organizations with global skills will have to be built and managed. Those with the skills to put the necessary worldwide webs of skill together are apt to be the highest paid of the knowledge workers—the elite of the elite.

In the past, first world workers with third world skills could earn premium wages simply because they lived in the first world. There they worked with more equipment, better technology, and more skilled co-workers than those with third world skills who lived in the third world. These complementary factors effectively raised their productivity and wages above what they would have been if they had been working in the third world. But that premium is gone. Today they will be paid based on their own skills—not based upon the skills of their neighbors. Put bluntly, in the economy of the future those with third world skills will earn third world wages even if they live in the first world. Unskilled labor will simply be bought wherever in the world it is cheapest.

If one looks at the breakthrough firms of the early 1990s, it is clear that there is a lot of productivity to be gotten by tearing down traditional functional walls between areas such as R&D, design, manufacturing, or sales and by pushing decision making much farther down into the organization to cut out layers of management hierarchy. But all of those actions require a much better educated and skilled workforce at the bottom. Those down at the bottom of the organization have to be capable of understanding the firm's strategy so well that, because of their intimate local knowledge, they will make decisions better than the decisions that the "boss" would have made under the previous system.

If the person on the unloading dock runs a computerized inventory control system wherein he logs delivered materials right into his hand-held computer and the computer instantly prints out a check that is given to the truck driver to be taken back to his firm (eliminating the need for large white-collar accounting offices that process purchases), the person on the unloading dock ceases to be someone who just moves boxes. He or she has to have a very different skill set.

Factory operatives and laborers used to be high school graduates or even high school dropouts. Today 16 percent of them have some college education and 5 percent have graduated from college. Among precision production and craft workers 32 percent have been to or graduated from college.[17] Among new hires those percentages are much higher.

In an era of man-made brainpower industries, individual, corporate, and national economic success will all require both new and much more extensive skill sets than have been required in the past. By themselves skills don't guarantee success. They have to be put together in successful organizations. But without skills there are no successful organizations.

The hallmark of the industrial revolution has been the slow replacement of the unskilled by the skilled. But for most of its duration, public investments in education have raised the supply of skills at least as fast, and perhaps faster, than the market demanded. That did not occur by accident. Mass universal compulsory public education was invented by the textile mill magnates of New England, who needed better-educated workers in their factories. Their motives were partly altruistic and partly economic. They were willing to pay taxes to help finance that education, but they did not want to pay the entire cost. They wanted the help of other taxpayers.

By nature the education investments of democratic governments tend to be egalitarian. Historically, those investments of government have allowed the unskilled to gradually become skilled—first by free grade schools, then free high schools, and finally free (the GI Bill—$91 billion in grants and $103 billion in loans in today's dollars), low-cost (public), or subsidized (private scholarships) university educations.[18] Without government investments in education, education would undoubtedly have remained the preserve of the rich as it has in every country where the investments have not been made. Government investments in education created the middle class.

Ahead lies a period not of slow evolution but of punctuated equilibrium when the skill sets required in the economy will be radically different from those needed in the past. This rising need can be seen in the recent studies showing rates of return on skill investments to be more than twice those of investments in plant and equipment.[19] But support for public egalitarian skill investment is being slashed—loans are replacing private scholarships, tuitions are rising sharply in public universities as taxpayer funds are withdrawn, federal loans replace what used to be federal scholarships, and public educational spending is being cut more than proportionally at both state and federal levels whenever budget reductions are made.

The necessary supply of skills will undoubtedly arise in the era ahead, but those additional supplies need not come, and probably will not come, from the unskilled workers who currently live in the first world. With the ability to make anything anywhere in the world and sell it anywhere else in the world, business firms can "cherry pick" the skilled or those easy (cheap) to skill wherever they exist in the world. Some third world countries are now making massive investment in basic education. American firms don't have to hire an American high school graduate if that graduate is not world-class. His or her educational defects are not their problem. Investing to give the necessary market skills to a well-educated Chinese high school graduate may well look like a much more attractive (less costly) investment than having to retrain an American high school dropout or a poorly trained high school graduate. As the data on falling wages indicate, the unskilled in the first world are on their way to becoming marginalized.

In a global economy what economists know as "the theory of factor price equalization" holds that an American worker who does not work with more natural resources than a South Korean (and none can, since there is now a world market for raw material to which everyone has equal access), who does not work with more capital than a South Korean (and none can, since there is a global capital market where everyone borrows in New York, London, and Tokyo), who does not work with more skilled complementary workers than a South Korean (and none can, since multinational companies can send knowledge and skills to wherever they are needed around the world), and who does not work with better technology than a South Korean (and few will, since reverse engineering has become an international art form whereby new product technologies move around the world very fast, South Korea is making R&D investment at rates higher than those of many developed nations, and multinational companies will use their new technologies in South Korea if that is the cheapest place to do so) will find that at each skill level he or she has to work for wages commensurate with the pay found for that skill level in South Korea. Adjusted for skills, South Korean wages will rise and American wages will fall until they equal each other. At that point, factor price equalization will have occurred.

Until the early 1970s a truly global economy did not exist and unskilled Americans were awarded a wage premium simply because they were Americans. They would automatically work with more raw materials, employ more capital-intensive processes, have workmen with more skills, and use better technology than would workers in South Korea. But this premium is vanishing—and will ultimately disappear entirely.

None of the brainpower industries listed by the Japanese has a natural home. Where these seven industries will be located depends upon who organizes the brainpower to capture them. Organizing brainpower means not just building an R&D system that will put a nation on the leading edge of technology in each of these seven areas, but organizing a top-to-bottom workforce that has the brainpower necessary to be masters of the new production and distribution technologies that will allow them to be the world's low-cost producers in each of these seven areas.

In today's global economic game, technology strategies have become central. Americans will face others with strategies for conquering the key strategic industries of tomorrow. Europe's Airbus Industries is the best current example of this reality. In 1994 it received more orders for new planes than Boeing. What is the American answer to Airbus Industries? Whatever arguments Americans advance to prove that Europe has "wasted" too much of its money in developing the Airbus, it exists and isn't going away. America will have to develop defensive industrial policies to deal with situations where the rest of the world targets one of America's key industries—even if Americans decide not to have offensive industrial policies. But what is true in sports is equally true in economics: If one plays defense all of the time and is never on offense, one never wins.

A technology strategy does not mean that a government has to pick winners and losers. The European Common Market picks what it thinks are hot technologies and then announces that it has matching funds in programs such as JESSI, ESPIRIT, or EUREKA, where if at least three companies from two different countries come through the door with a good project and half the money, these private funds will be matched with government money. Government is not picking winners and losers, but it is expanding time horizons and the scale of operations and making it cheaper for firms to play tomorrow's game.

A country's technology policy is its industrial strategy. It determines where that country will play the game. Technological investments conversely require an industrial strategy. What is strategic and what is not?

To make the right R&D investments, America must analyze its skill and technological strengths and weaknesses, as well as those of its principal competitors. It has to understand where the keys to achieving economic success are located. Is leadership in the telecommunications industry of tomorrow to be gotten by strengthening America's laboratory leadership in key technologies or in building a fiber optics test bed such as the one that is now being built in eastern Germany?

BRAINPOWER TECHNOLOGIES AND THE NATURE OF THE FIRM

New communications technologies such as cheap, high-quality video conferencing are transforming, and will continue to transform, the internal communications, command, and control functions (what the military calls C^3) of the business world. When reporting has to be person-to-person, how many people can physically report to any one other person—twenty? thirty? Whatever the number, divide that number into the total number of people in a firm to determine the levels of hierarchy necessary. When those reporting to each other had to be located together so that they could physically meet, the necessities of communications, command, and control dictated many levels of management and the existence of a large corporate headquarters.

In an era of electronic interactions, however, the issues of who reports to whom, how many people report to each supervisor, and where the reporters and the reportees are located are not determined by physical necessities. Learning the corporate gossip (who's up and who's down) and finding a godfather to help advance your career (traditionally probably the two most important reasons for wanting to have an office at the corporate headquarters) don't require a physical location at corporate headquarters anymore. Geographically fluid C^3 systems replaced fixed C^3 systems.

As JoAnne Yates, a professor at MIT, has demonstrated in her excellent book on corporate communications, to a surprising extent the C^3 systems of the modern corporation are still directly modeled on the patterns set by the nineteenth-century railroads.[20] They were the first firms that needed communications, command, and control systems that could operate across large geographic areas. They also had a peculiar problem. Being invented before the telegraph, trains were the fastest known method of communication. How was one to coordinate two things, often on a single track where they could run into each other, when the things to be coordinated were faster than any other method of communication?

The answer was a hierarchical organization run by the timetable, the rule book, and the stopwatch. Downward coordination through written rules and orders; upward communication of experience by reporting progress in meetings. The system was designed to optimize the detailed transmission of orders down through the corporate hierarchy, since orders down were more important than information up if trains were to be safely run.

To a surprising extent our modern corporations are still run along the same lines even though they have very different problems and very different methods of communication.

Almost by definition hierarchical chains of command are poor transmitters of information up through the organization. Amorphous information tends to get lost as it moves up from one person to another. Underlings don't like to tell their bosses bad news (one almost always gets blamed) and bosses don't like to feel that they are simply information-transmission belts upward from their underlings. Deliberately vague reports of potential disasters become ever more vague as they move up the organization.

Giving orders to subordinates that can be made to look as if they come directly from you, and not your boss, is very different from telling one's bosses what your subordinates told you when he will hold you responsible for the failures being reported. Information only flows up a chain of command when one is delivering very good news or when something has gone very wrong and cannot be hidden.

Modern communications systems make today's corporate organizations relics of the past. What is the best way to organize a modern corporation? It probably has not yet been invented. Business is in a period of stripping out layers of management (some of them will probably be put back in) and experimenting with different reporting and information systems. But what we do know is that a very different communications, command, and control system will lead to very different forms of business organization.

If knowledge is power, and it is, the possessors of knowledge are going to be radically different in the future, and with that difference will flow changes in power relationships. This is already visible in retailing, where the bar codes and the knowledge that goes with them have shifted economic power from national manufacturing companies with famous brand names to retailers who control shelf space and know what is or is not selling much better and faster than those who make the products.

Best practice currently calls for breaking down divisions into functional areas such as marketing, manufacturing, R&D, and design and pushing decisions down the hierarchy as far as possible. While that requires very different workers at the bottom, people smart enough to make the right decisions, it also requires very different people at the top, those who can communicate the companies' strategies so well that those at the bottom will make the decisions that those at the top would have made if they had had all of the information possessed by those at the bottom.

Walk into any office building today and count the number of offices with no one in them—idle space, computers not turned on (9 percent in active use), telephones unused.[21] The normal occupant is away doing something else—meetings, travel, selling, whatever. With today's technology all of this idle space and equipment is unnecessary. Employees could walk into their company building, sit down at the first vacant desk, plug in their personal telephone number, call up their computer's files, order the flat-screen TV set on the wall to show pictures of their family, and instantly be in business in their own personal offices. The problems are not technological—all of the necessary technology exists—but learning what will and will not work sociologically. One's office is one's cave. Just ordering people to give up their personal offices would cause a revolution. The winners will be those who find a way to change the sociology to make the temporary office seem as if it is a personal physical cave to which the worker can retreat. They will cut office overheads by startling amounts and be the new cost leaders.

While no one knows for certain the shape of the business organization of the future, we do know with certainty that the business organization of the future will be very different.

VALUES IN AN ELECTRONICALLY INTERCONNECTED GLOBAL VILLAGE

The same new technologies are producing a world where values and economics reverberate back and forth with each other creating something brand-new. Human culture and human values are for the first time being shaped by a profit-maximizing electronic media. Never before have societies left it almost completely to the commercial marketplace to determine their values and their role models. Both in its depth (the amount of time spent watching it) and breadth (the percentage of the human population who watch it), TV creates a permeating cultural force that has never before been seen. Movies are the modern art form. The head of the Boston Pops resigns to write and play background music for movies because he believes that is where the mass audience is to be found.

TV and the movies have replaced the family in generating values.[22] The average American teenager watches twenty-one hours of TV per week while spending five minutes per week alone with his or her father and twenty minutes alone with his or her mother.[23] By the time the teenage years have arrived, he or she will have seen eighteen thousand murders.[24] The average American over the age of eighteen watches TV not much less than the average teenager—eighteen hours per week—and is probably equally under its influence.[25] One can argue about the exact extent to which TV violence causes real violence and what happens when the number of TV murders per hour doubles, but no one can doubt that values are heavily influenced by what we see on TV.[26] Perhaps it isn't surprising that the total murder rate is down while that among the young is up.

While on a safari across the Saudi Arabian desert in early 1995, my oldest son and I came across some bedouin camel herders with an encampment of tents, miles from the nearest roads and electrical lines, but with a satellite dish pointed at the heavens and an electrical generator to power it. They were watching on TV what you and I watch on TV. That is the modern world.

The world of written communications, the world that has existed since the onset of widespread literacy, stresses linear logical arguments that move from one point to the next with each point logically building on the last point. Emotional appeals are certainly possible, but they are harder to make on a piece of white paper than face-to-face. A visual-verbal media in many ways moves us back to a world of illiteracy. What counts is the emotive visual appeal to feelings or fears and not the logical appeal to abstract rigorous thought.

Logical appeals can be made on the electronic media, but it is a far better medium for stirring emotions than for transmitting logical information. One has to learn to read. It requires work, time, and investment. One does not have to learn to watch the TV set. It requires no effort. That difference is a big difference. As the vocabularies of those on TV shrink, as they are, the vocabularies of those who watch TV shrink along with them. Moving from the written word to a visual-verbal media is going to change the very ways we think and make decisions. The famous speakers and speeches of ancient Greece and Rome are no more. Neither are those famous American speakers and speeches. The great debates between Webster and Calhoun over slavery or the Gettysburg Address are simply impossible today.

Writing replaced oratory slowly since writing's full impact required the existence of widespread literacy and that only slowly happened over thousands of years after writing had been invented. The electronic media will have effects as powerful as those of writing, but they will come much more rapidly since one does not have to "learn" how to watch TV or the movies. The new medium is more verbal and more emotive, but it is also not the direct face-to-face environment of the illiterate village, either. This is a verbal and emotive environment not controlled by the village elders and families but a verbal one controlled by those who want to make money—something very different.

In the United States negative political advertisements neatly illustrate the clash between rational thought and emotion. The public says that they dislike negative political advertising. They believe it corrupts the political process and it leaves them cynical about all politicians. But negative political advertisements work—they win elections for those who use them. What the public logically rejects, it emotively accepts. Not surprisingly, politicians use what moves the public to change their voting behavior and don't listen to what the public tells them about their thoughts. Yet both are real. Negative advertising can both work (win elections) and can at the same time create cynical citizens who believe that every politician is corrupt and ripping off the system.

With the television cameras there to record Gorbachev's visit, Tiananmen Square lingers on in the world's memory. Cut off from the world of television coverage, the horrors of Cambodia and Burma did not exist until they were made into movies—*The Killing Fields* and *Beyond Rangoon*. Bosnia could never be completely ignored by the world's leaders, since it has never disappeared from the TV screens.

In a TV culture what one believes to be true is often more important that what is actually true when it comes to understanding and predicting human actions. Nothing makes this power more evident than the fact that in recent years murder rates have been falling in America's cities (in some cities such as New York dramatically), and in some cases (Boston, for one) are now as low as they were thirty years ago, yet the reporting on murder has convinced almost everyone that murders are dramatically rising.[27] Feelings that a crime wave is under way caused demands to arise for the authorities to do something tangible. By referendum, California in 1994 passed its three-strikes-and-you're-out prison-sentencing reform. What is seen on TV is more real than reality.[28] That unreal "reality" has led to such a concern about crime that California's unversity budgets are being shrunk to expand prison budgets. Yet, viewing the situation rationally, there are no old perpetrators of street crimes. A three-strikes-and-you're-out law is essentially a pension system for old criminals. Student numbers shrink; prison populations soar. By 1995, California's prison budgets were double those of its universities, with state expenditures per person in prison four times as high as expenditures per person in its universities.[29]

In movies such as *Jefferson in Paris* or *Pocahontas,* people lose track of what is historically real and what is theater.[30] Did Jefferson have a black mistress? How old was Pocahontas? Were American Indians natural environmentalists? Since everyone knows that what these movies portray will come to be seen as historical facts, even if they aren't, and even if the makers are not even pretending to represent historical facts, they become controversial.[31]

The media becomes a secular religion essentially replacing shared history, national cultures, real religions, families, and friends as the dominant force creating our mental pictures of reality. But the media are not Rasputin with a covert or overt political agenda. It is not left or right. It has no overarching ideology or agenda.

One can denounce it as Republican presidential candidate Bob Dole did ("We have reached the point where our popular culture threatens to undermine our character as a nation [producing] nightmares of depravity"), but the denunciations are irrelevant because the media are not controlled by any one individual or group of individuals.[32] The media simply provide whatever sells—whatever maximizes profits. If right-wing radio talk show hosts get high ratings, they will be the ones on the air. If left-wing radio talk show hosts got higher ratings, the right-wing hosts would be off the air.

What sells is excitement. The same citizens who applaud Senator Dole's attack on the values portrayed in popular movies and music buy both. If they didn't buy what they say they don't like, it would not be produced. It is simply not exciting to watch Senator Dole's role models and values of the past.

What sells is speed and instant gratification—TV shows have to be completed in thirty to sixty minutes, movies in two hours; both have to move very quickly from episode to episode. Individual consumption is glorified (as in *The Lifestyles of the Rich and Famous*) as the only focus for private ambition—individual fulfillment the only legitimate goal. For the TV hero, death and all real limitations are abolished; there is no duty or sacrifice, no role for the community, no common good; all behavior is depicted as legitimate; feelings, not actions, are supposed to demonstrate values. Emote, don't think. Communicate, but don't commit. Be cynical, since all heroes will ultimately be shown to be fools. "Freedom from" does not imply an "obligation to." All social organizations, including government, are voluntary and they exist only to give the individual the means to pursue his or her own private ends. When the viewer doesn't like it (whatever *it* is), the media message is, he/she should exit and drop out.[33]

Under the pressure of a medium that does not believe the willingness to wait has any value, the percentage of those who believe in the value of hard work fell from 60 to 44 percent in just ten years.[34] The destruction of the past and the elimination of the social mechanisms that link one's experience with those of earlier generations is an "eerie phenomenon" of the late twentieth century.[35]

In today's world the neighbor most often invited into your home is not a real neighbor. It is a TV family far wealthier than the real average American family (about four times as wealthy), which leaves the real American family with a very misleading, exaggerated notion of how wealthy the average American really is. Comparing themselves with that mythical family, everyone ends up with feelings of relative deprivation.

In the media world no one with the exception of cops and drug dealers ever works. The TV world is a world of consumption without production. Nothing has to be done in the past to generate consumption in the present; nothing must be done in the present to guarantee consumption in the future. Investment in the future simply does not occur. Yet capitalistic economies need investments in the future if they are to survive.

Capitalistic culture and TV culture fit together nicely since both are interested in making money. Yet their values are not congruent. One has to have some focus on the future; the other sees no future that requires sacrifice.[36] One can only change the content of the media by persuading the citizenry that something that is now regarded as dull is exciting, and that is very hard to do. It is hard even to imagine how one would make an exciting TV show about individuals patiently not consuming so that they can invest in the future.

At mid-century, books were written (for example George Orwell's *1984* and Aldous Huxley's *Brave New World*) about how modern communication technologies would permit authoritarian thought control, but they got it exactly backward. Modern electronic technologies promote radical individualism, and mass culture controls national! leaders much more than national leaders control the mass culture. The electronic media is changing values and those values will in turn change the nature of our society.

The wired village will inevitably lead the world in the direction of more direct rather than representative democracies. One can argue that representatives have more time to think about the issues; but those in favor of direct democracy can respond that they are also much more subject to lobbyists. And if one looks at places such as Switzerland or California with a tradition of direct democracy, it is difficult to argue that they are a worse form of government. But it is a different form of government. Like or dislike it, direct democracy is on the way. What the technology permits, our ideology will require.[37] Why should voters filter their beliefs through elected representatives if that is no longer a physical necessity?

What is expected to be our most rapidly growing, profitable industry, an as-yet-unnamed industry at the intersection of telephones, television, computers and media arts, is having an enormous influence on how old activities (for example, home shopping) are done, the new activities (video games) upon which the consumer is willing to spend his or her money, but most importantly on the values that are brought into both our consumption and production activities.

Chapter 5

Plate Three: Demography—Growing, Moving, Getting Older

GROWING

Sir Thomas Malthus was wrong about European population growth rates in the nineteenth century. Even as he spoke about the starvation that was inevitable given the then current population growth rates, those rates were slowing down dramatically. One hundred and fifty years later, by the end of the twentieth century much of the developed world was below ZPG (zero population growth). After World War II, the third world, however, was on exactly the reverse track.[1] Their population growth rates moved from low to high as death rates, especially in the first year of life, fell dramatically as a result of modern medicine and public health measures (clean water, vaccinations, antibiotics). Populations exploded.

India, for example, began from a position of rough equality between its birth rate and death rate at about 45 per thousand in 1941. Death rates plunged to 9.9 per 1,000 in 1991, birth rates fell, but only to 29 per 1,000. The net result is a population growth rate stuck at about 2 percent for the last four decades in a country that is likely to become the world's most populous country early in the twenty-first century.[2]

The World Bank projects an increase in the world's population from the current 5.7 billion to 8.5 billion by 2030.[3] What is frightening about the World Bank's forecast is not so much the 50 percent increase, an extra 2.8 billion people, but that 2 billion of those people will be born in countries where daily earnings are less than $2. These countries are simply not going to be able to make the investments that are necessary to make water available to feed their populations, much less educate them and give them the tools that they will need to earn their living. If one adds in problems like AIDS (Zimbabwe is estimated to have an infection rate of 20–25 percent), it is not hard to envision disaster.[4]

The direct issue is not food but water. With water, food can be grown on lands where it is not now grown.[5] Just as surely without water, food production falls. Currently, eighty poor countries with 40 percent of the world's population already have water shortages that could cripple agriculture.[6] But to say that the issue is water is to misstate the real issue, which is not water per se but affordable water. With enough money, oceans can be desalinated and food can be grown where it is not now being grown, as Saudi Arabia does. But the costs of desalinization and the infrastructure (pipes and pumping stations) necessary to get the water to where it is needed are enormous.[7] If an analysis was made of the energy it took to grow food in the middle of the Saudi Arabian desert, more energy would be used up in getting fresh water to the fields than was generated by the food grown on those fields. Only very wealthy countries, such as those in the Persian Gulf region, can even dream of making such investments—and even there it does not make sense. What are by other standards wealthy places such as Hong Kong have mothballed their desalinization plants as too expensive even for drinking water.

If population growth rates in poor countries do not decrease—and there is little that those living outside such countries with rapid population growth rates can do to make a slowdown occur—it is easy to sketch out a very Malthusian future for parts of the world in the twenty-first century. Populations simply keep rising until they meet the limits of malnutrition. Tropical Africa will be the first to hit those limits. Its population is rising dramatically, food supplies lag far behind, and per capita incomes are lower than they were in the mid-1960s, when many of these countries were receiving their independence.

In the 1970s falling population growth rates led to a false optimism about the world's population. The decline was real but all of it was located in China. Its size (1.2 billion people) and its birth control policy (one child per family) had a dramatic effect on the world's population growth rate. China's policies are still in place but further declines now depend upon developments outside of China. At the moment, the slowdowns and speedups in population growth rates in different countries essentially offset each other.[8]

Human populations at their maximum can grow at about 4 percent per year (some of today's growth rates are not too far away from this limit), yet over the past century no country's economic growth rate has averaged better than 3.6 percent per year. If the United States population had growth at 3.5 percent per year over the past century, its per capita income today would be lower than it was during the Civil War, since over the past one hundred years its economic growth rate averaged only 3.1 percent per year.

Simple mathematics demands that population growth be less than economic growth if real per capita incomes are to rise. With population growth averaging 3 percent in the Middle East and Africa and 2 percent in south Asia and Latin America, these regions can have substantial real growth rates yet make no progress at raising per capita income.[9]

In addition, people are the ultimate source of environmental pollution and degradation. As the number of people grows, the quality of the earth's environment can only fall. Environmental projects are merely holding actions that slow the rate of decline. Over the course of its lifetime an American baby born in 1990 produced 1 million kilograms of atmospheric waste, 10 million kilograms of liquid waste, and 1 million kilograms of solid waste. To have the average American standard of living, he or she needed to consume 700,000 kilograms of minerals, 24 billion BTUs of energy (4,000 barrels of oil) 25,000 kilograms of plant foods, and 28,000 kilograms of animal products (the slaughter of 2,000 animals).[10]

While one can debate whether third world starvation will occur, there is no debate about what population growth rates imply for the economic success of those in the third world who do not have their population growth under control. No country has succeeded in making it into the developed world without a century of 1 percent or less population growth. The reasons are simple. Before per capita incomes can grow, new people have to be equipped with the productive resources that would allow them to generate the existing average income.

To become an average American, existing Americans must equip new Americans with about $250,000 worth of investment per person in education, infrastructure, plant and equipment, housing, and food until that new American is old enough to work. With a 4 percent population growth rate (an extra 10.5 million people each year), Americans would need to invest $2.7 trillion per year just to keep per capita incomes from falling, yet America's total GDP is only $7 trillion. A little less than forty percent of what is produced in America would have to be devoted to making new Americans into average Americans. Given what existing Americans need and/or want for their own personal consumption, there simply would not be enough money left over to invest in the activities necessary to raise the standard of living of existing Americans.

Put bluntly, people who are born in poor countries with rapid rates of population growth are going to die in poor countries. No amount of inside organization or outside aid can overwhelm a high population growth rate. Whatever one believes about the world's ability to provide enough food, huge income gaps will emerge not just with the first world but between those parts of the third world that have their populations under control and those that do not.

While regional disasters can be expected if current trends are projected into the future, it is also important to note that population forecasts are very uncertain. Whatever factors are suggested as to why people have bigger or smaller families, counterexamples can be found somewhere in the world. Conventional wisdom says that populations that are modernizing, urbanizing, wealthy, and becoming more educated experience declining population growth rates.[11] Persian Gulf countries have all of these characteristics yet they also have some of the fastest population growth rates in the world.

MOVING

While there is a great deal of uncertainty about the world's future population growth, there is complete certainty about the massive population movements that are now taking place from the third world to first world countries. In the 1980s, 7.9 million people legally moved into the United States and 7.3 million people legally moved into the rest of the first world.[12] In 1992 there were estimated to be 3.4 million illegal aliens (about 2 million of whom had come in the 1980s) living in the United States.[13] In the 1990s immigration accelerated and by 1995, 9 percent of all Americans had been born abroad, with a very uneven spread among the states—including 25 percent of all Californians not native-born.[14] Within the third world, millions of people are moving from somewhat poorer to somewhat richer countries—more than 2 million per year in Asia alone.[15] In addition, there are 23 million refugees in the world. Overall, about 100 million live outside of the country where they were born.[16]

Nothing compares with what is now happening except the mass migrations of the late nineteenth and early twentieth centuries, but those migrations (about 650,000 people per year were coming to the United States) were very different.[17] Some of the individuals who moved were poor (Americans tend to exaggerate the number who were really poor) but most were middle- or lower-middle-class families moving from rich countries (England, Germany, Italy) to empty countries (the United States, Argentina, etc.). Those empty countries needed both people and unskilled labor. Today's industrial countries need neither. Those who migrate are certainly energetic, and often smart, but before they can become useful citizens in the developed world, they will need massive investments in their skills.

Undoubtedly an immigration policy could be designed that would contribute to American economic growth rather than be a drain upon it. Individuals could be admitted based on their skills and the funds they were willing to invest in America.[18] Those who needed social services, such as education, could be excluded. Only the skilled young could be admitted to keep the ratio of tax-paying workers to pension-collecting retirees higher than it otherwise would be.[19] But such a growth-oriented immigration policy would have to be adopted and enforced. Neither seems possible. None of America's recent immigration policies has focused on growth, and none of them has been enforced.

The motive for migration is partly the pull of being able to earn higher incomes in the first world and partly the push of miserable conditions in the third world. If actual population growth rates follow World Bank predictions, the push factors will be enormous. The impact of what falling standards of living will do to migration can be seen in the movements between Mexico and the United States in the aftermath of the Mexican financial crisis and the resulting sharp cuts in Mexican living standards in late 1994. In the first quarter of 1995 the number of people seeking U.S. citizenship doubled, and the Mexican border patrol made 1.4 million arrests—up 30 percent from the previous year—and for everyone arrested, a minimum of two people get across the border without being arrested.[20]

But even if the World Bank's dire population forecasts are wrong, the pull factors are going to lead to population movements more massive than any the world has ever seen. The reasons are simple. Transportation costs have dropped enormously.[21] Even relatively poor people can afford an airline ticket to the other side of the world. While there used to be only one border where people could walk from a low-income third world country to a high-income first world country (that between Mexico and the United States), with the end of communism there are now many places with huge economic gaps (for example, Eastern to Western Europe, China to Japan) between peoples with very different incomes who live very close together.

More important, for the first time in human history, the electronic media have produced a world where those in even the most primitive villages on the face of the globe regularly see on their village TV sets the standards of living of those who live in the most affluent parts of the globe. The way of life portrayed on TV and the standard of living of the average TV family are often far above those of the average American family, but people watching them on the village TV set think that what they see exists for the average American. Living in poverty and watching those wealthy people on TV, a poor villager would be crazy not to try to move! Even Japan with its unmatched social controls is now believed to have more than one million illegal guest workers.[22]

Consider a poor Mexican villager. California is not far away with a per capita income twenty times as high as Mexico's. What is the worst that can happen if he attempts to walk across the border? He is caught, put on a bus, and sent home. His tired feet get a rest. If he keeps trying, eventually he will succeed. California isn't going to throw him in jail. It costs too much. And in any case, if one looks at space per person, food, TV, exercise equipment, etc., the standard of living in a California jail is higher than that of a poor Mexican village.

What is happening between Mexico and the United States is mirrored by North Africa and Europe. Birth rates are up, pushing people out. Income gaps are huge, pulling people north. As in the United States, there is often a lot of hostility directed at the large numbers coming in to France, Spain, and Italy.[23]

The movement from poor to rich is very different from the movement from rich to empty. Historically, the average immigrant in the United States has been better educated than the average native-born American, and their children stayed in school longer. Within fifteen years their family incomes had caught up with those of native-born Americans, and within thirty years their incomes were higher than those of native-born Americans. They always used welfare less than the natives.[24]

But today's immigration is more complex. With respect to education, immigrants over twenty-five years of age are bimodal relative to those born in the United States. They are both 42 percent more likely to have a bachelor's degree than native-born Americans and 112 percent more likely not to have finished high school.[25] While there is enormous variance, today's immigrant on average has less education, is more likely to drop out of high school, and has an income that does not seem to be catching up with those of native-born Americans (see Table 5.1).

Adjusting for education, recent immigrants are starting out at much lower wages than earlier immigrants.[26] Today's economy has very little demand for raw unskilled labor. Many of today's immigrants are undoubtedly very good people (bright, energetic, hardworking), but they will be of little value economically unless they are educated and trained. Who is going to pay for the necessary education to make them into productive, self-sufficient people? If one looks at the California initiative that passed in the November 1994 election (Proposition 187), it is clear that native-born Americans do not want to pay for the education of immigrants. But if they aren't willing to pay, who will pay? If the answer is no one, then America has implicitly made the decision to build a third world society inside its first world society. Depriving immigrants of education will not persuade them to go home. They won't get educated at home either.

Past immigrants did not move into a society with a social welfare system. Today's do.[27] While people do not move just to receive welfare, welfare lowers the risk of moving. Immigration is tough. About one third of the thirty million foreigners who came to the United States between the Civil War and World War I went home.[28] Immediately after World War II, immigrants were less likely to use the welfare system than native-born Americans, but today they are more likely to

Table 5.1
SOCIOECONOMIC CHARACTERISTICS OF IMMIGRANTS AND NATIVES

	1970	1990
Natives		
Education (years)	11.5	13.2
% Receiving Welfare	6.0%	7.4%
Immigrants		
Education	10.7	11.6
% Receiving Welfare	5.9%	9.1%
Wage Differential with Native-born	+0.9%	−15.2%
Recent Immigrants (less than 5 years in U.S.)		
Education	11.1	11.9
% Receiving Welfare	5.5%	8.3%
Wage Differential with Native-born	−16.6%	−31.7%

SOURCE: George J. Borjas, "The Economic Benefits of Immigration," *Journal of Economic Perspectives*, Spring 1995, p. 4.

be on welfare, and if on welfare, cost more per person than native-born Americans (see Table 5.1). The net result is a per capita cost about twice as high as that for native-born Americans.[29]

Big differences in welfare usage exist across immigrant groups. Some groups are doing very well economically and others very poorly. Seventy-seven percent of the Laotians and Cambodians in California are on welfare. The seven states with the most illegal aliens spend nearly $4 billion on their health care, education, and incarceration while getting less than $2 billion in taxes paid by the illegals.[30] The Republican "Contract with America" pledges to cut off all aid to legal immigrants as well as illegal immigrants if they are less than seventy-five years of age.[31] But how the side-by-side existence of those with third world incomes denied government aid yet paying taxes and those with first world incomes getting government aid but not paying taxes is going to work sociologically and politically is not at all clear.

All across the developed world, anti-immigration movements are growing like mushrooms. In the first round of the French presidential elections in 1995, Jean-Marie Le Pen, the far right candidate, got 22 percent of the blue-collar vote, strong support in affluent areas, and 15 percent overall on a platform that called for expelling France's three million immigrants.[32]

Massive population movements are under way. While they probably could not be stopped, they could be contained if Americans were willing to do a number of things that they are not now willing to do: have a national identity card with stiff penalties for anyone who hires someone without that card; check randomly and repeatedly everyone's identity card to ensure that they are in the country legally; quickly deport anyone without the necessary card. Identity cards could be regularly required at the security checkpoints that we now have to pass at airports and in most other forms of transportation. On the highways some toll booths could randomly be used as identity card checkpoints, and high-voltage electrified fences could be built at borders such as the Mexican-American one. Short of such policies, those who want to migrate cannot be stopped.

GROWING OLDER

The really explosive part of the volcano pushed up by demography, however, lies in the aging of the world's population. A new class of people is being created. For the first time in human history, our societies will have a very large group of economically inactive elderly, affluent voters who require expensive social services such as health care and who depend upon government for much of their income. They are bringing down the social welfare state, destroying government finances, and threatening the investments that all societies need to make to have a successful future.

Back in 1900, 4 percent of America's population was over sixty-five years of age. Those over sixty-five now account for 13 percent of the population.[33] After 2013 the number of elderly will grow very fast in America, since the baby boom generation, the first of whom were born in 1947, will reach sixty-five and start to retire. Where there are now 4.5 workers working to pay for every pension, in 2030 there will be only 1.7 workers available to be taxed to pay for every pension.[34]

In many rich and poor countries the percentage of the population over the age of sixty-five will double by 2025.[35] In Japan in 2025 the elderly are expected to account for 26 percent of the population. In the United States, projection of the proportion of the population that will be elderly depends heavily on what is assumed-amount immigration—a source of young people—but the elderly will be at least 20 percent of the population.[36]

The United States faces what might be called the "double forty whammy." On average, those over sixty-five receive slightly more than 40 percent (41 percent to be precise) of their income from government.[37] And slightly less than 40 percent (38 percent to be precise) of the elderly receive 80 percent or more of their income from government. (Sixty-two percent get 50 percent or more.) In contrast, only 35 percent receive money from private pensions.[38]

This enormous transfer of resources has made the elderly into one-issue voters (whether government increases or decreases their monthly pension payments or health care benefits). In democracies, one-issue voters have a disproportionate impact on the political process, since they don't split their votes because of conflicting interests in other issues.

Already the needs and demands of the elderly have shaken the social welfare state to its foundations, causing it for all practical purposes to go broke. If one adds payments to the elderly to interest on the national debt, remembering that today's budget deficits are being produced by our unwillingness to pay for today's expenditures on the elderly, interest plus entitlements are swallowing government budgets. Project the numbers forward and government simply goes broke. It will have promised its elderly more than it can collect in taxes from those who are working.

Today the welfare state plus interest payments (most accumulated in recent years to make payments to the elderly) take 60 percent of total tax revenue. (Excluding interest on the national debt, half of the federal budget goes to the elderly.[39]) By 2003 they will take 75 percent and by 2013 they will take 100 percent if current laws remain unchanged.[40] In Western Europe today's programs for the elderly will take 50 percent of the GDP by 2030. In Eastern Europe the problems are even worse, since the Communists were even more generous with their promises to the elderly. Poland gives more of its GDP to its elderly (21 percent) than any other country on earth.[41]

Everything else is being cut in government budgets to make room for the elderly. Leaving the elderly aside, domestic spending has fallen from 10 to 7 percent of the GDP in the last twenty years in the United States.[42] In the Organization for Economic Cooperation and Development (OECD), the association of developed nations as a whole, five times as much money is spent on social expenditures on those over sixty-five per capita as on those from fifteen to sixty-four years of age.[43] Most important, expenditures on the elderly are squeezing government investments in infrastructure, education, and research and development out of the budget—down from 24 to 15 percent of the federal budget in twenty years.[44]

Spending on the elderly is not an issue of equity or deprivation. In 1970 the percentage of the elderly in poverty was higher than for any other part of the population. Now there are fewer poor people among the elderly than any other group in the population. For many in the United States, real standards of living actually rise with retirement. The savings from not working are bigger than their reduction in earnings.[45]

Adjusting for household size, capital gains, taxes (state and federal), noncash benefits such as health insurance and school lunches, and imputed returns on equity in owner-occupied housing, the elderly have a per capita income a whopping 67 percent above that of the population as a whole.[46] Looking at cash income alone in the 1960s, the average seventy-year-old was spending only 60 percent as much as a thirty-year-old. Today that seventy-year-old is spending 20 percent more.[47] Government spending on the elderly by itself now gives the elderly per capita incomes equal to 60 percent of the American average.[48] In Germany and France, transfers to the elderly give them incomes equal to 80 percent of the average.[49]

The elderly are also much wealthier than those who are not elderly.[50] Those sixty-five to seventy-four years of age have $222,000 in net worth vis-à-vis $66,000 for those aged thirty-five to forty-four.[51]

The elderly obviously don't want their benefits cut. The alternative is raising taxes, but that is also a very unattractive option. Today's 15 percent social security tax rate would have to be boosted to 40 percent by 2029 to provide the benefits that have been promised.[52] Moving out farther and assuming no changes in current laws, future payroll tax rates can rise as high as 94 percent if one is pessimistic about controlling health care spending on the elderly.[53] What is called generational accounting leads to some very disturbing future tax rates. The tax system implodes.

Over the past twenty-five years many of our entitlement programs have implicitly been paid for by cutting defense spending from peak Vietnam War levels. But even with the end of the cold war and a willingness to cut military budgets (and the new Republican majority say they are not willing to have further defense cutbacks), there is not much room left for such shifts. Defense spending is now down to less than 4 percent of GDP, and even if America were willing to take defense spending down to zero, the day of reckoning for the social welfare state would only be postponed by a few years.

Pensions are a matter of benefits and numbers. Health care for the elderly is also a matter of technology. New, more costly technologies constantly escalate per capita costs. While per capita costs differ greatly across countries, in the last decade health spending as a fraction of the GDP has escalated right across the OECD with only Sweden and Ireland bucking the trends.[54]

Expenditures on the elderly have fundamentally altered our fiscal systems. In the 1960s government generated what was then called the fiscal dividend. However large its current deficit, if government simply did nothing—passed no new laws—within a few years it would be producing a budget surplus. With economic growth, tax revenue grew faster than government expenditures. Today the exact opposite is true. Even with rapid economic growth and no new programs, government spending rises faster than tax revenues because of entitlements for the growing population of the elderly. If government does nothing, deficits expand rapidly.

All of President Clinton's budget cutting and tax increases in his first two years in office only brought a small amount of breathing space. By 1996 the deficit will again be rapidly rising even if no new spending programs are passed. What is faced by President Clinton is faced by every government. Even Sweden, which is in many ways the inventor of the social welfare state, and is still the place where it enjoys some of its greatest political support, is having to cut back.[55]

Instead of a fiscal dividend, governments all around the world now confront structural fiscal deficits that cannot be cured by economic growth. If one looks at the Group of Seven (the world's largest economies) in 1993, the structural deficits that would exist even if their economies were operating at full employment ranged from 3 percent of GDP in Germany, the United States, France, and Canada to 5 percent in Great Britain and more than 7 percent in Italy.[56] Only Japan was better off, with a structural deficit of less than 1 percent, but Japan faces the fastest-growing elderly population in the industrial world and today's small Japanese structural deficit is going to rapidly become tomorrow's large structural budget deficit.

Across the OECD between 1974 and 1994, government debt has risen from 35 to 71 percent of GDP and that does not count the unfunded pension and health care liabilities that lie ahead.[57] In 1995 only one of the OECD countries, oil-rich Norway, was expected to run a budget surplus.[58]

Technically, in the United States the elderly can argue that the pension part of their benefit package does not contribute to government debts, since the pension part of social security, but not the health care part, is running a surplus—tax revenues from earmarked taxes exceeds expenditures. But that is an illusion. To evaluate the impact of government budgets, it is necessary to look at total revenue and total expenditures as a whole. If governments are running a deficit in their overall budgets, the fact that one part of the budget has a surplus because there is an accounting convention that earmarks more taxes than this sector of the budget needs is irrelevant. Whatever the earmarking, governments are net dissavers and that is what affects the economy. What matters is what is driving the expenditure side of the budget. The driver is the elderly.

The problem of running up debts to pay for the elderly is straightforward. Just to make the arithmetic, simply suppose that taxes collect 30 percent of GDP and suppose that market interest rates are 10 percent. When government debt reaches 300 percent of GDP, all of government revenue has to be used to make interest payments on outstanding debt and nothing is left for anything else. Belgium, Italy, and Canada already can see this limit ahead of them (see Table 5.2).

In Belgium public debt is 142 percent of GDP and unfunded pension liabilities another 165 percent of GDP (see Table 5.2). While it does not pay interest on its unfunded pension liabilities, if it did (and it should if they are not to break future governments' budgets), with a 10 percent interest rate it would need to collect 30.7 percent of the GDP in taxes just to pay interest on its debts. In addition, it collects 10 percent of GDP from the young to pay pensions to the elderly. Add in something for health care and Belgium would need to collect taxes approaching 50 percent of the GDP just to finance interest payments and the elderly.[59] Not surprisingly, these expenses have driven investment activities out of the Belgium budget. R&D is running far below normal European levels and is only one third that of the United States.

While all of our economic resources are not going to be given to the elderly (there are other things such as police and fire departments that simply have to be financed), no one knows how the growth of entitlements for the elderly can be held in check in democratic societies. Even when they are only 13 percent of the population, they are so powerful that no political party wants to tangle with them.

House Majority Leader Newt Gingrich's Contract with America does more than explicitly exclude the elderly from its cutbacks. It promises to spend more on the elderly by raising the amount of income that can be earned before social security benefits are cut and to reduce the taxes paid on social security benefits by high-income individuals.[60]

A conservative French finance minister, Alain Madelin, was forced to resign just for suggesting that public employees be forced to contribute more to their own retirement.[61]

Long before they are a technical majority of the population, the elderly will be unstoppable politically, since those under age eighteen legally cannot vote and those between eighteen and thirty tend not to vote. Democracy is going to meet its ultimate test when it has to confront the economic demands of the elderly. Can democratic governments cut benefits for a group of voters that will be close to being a majority?

Today it cannot. President Clinton appointed a panel to recommend changes in the system but it could only report back that it could "not agree on any specific proposals to slow the growth of Social Security, Medicare, or other government benefit programs," even though it

Table 5.2
DEBT AS PERCENT OF GDP

Country	Gross Debt	Unfunded Pension Liabilities in 1990	Total
United States	85	66	151
Japan	79	218	297
Italy	123	233	356
Germany	53	160	213
France	56	216	272
Canada	96	250	346
United Kingdom	52	186	238
Belgium	142	165	307

SOURCE: OECD. Cited in "Public Sector Finances," *The Economist*, July 8, 1995, p. 115.

could agree that the current programs would raise the government deficit eightfold by 2030 if nothing was done.[62]

Democracy is not yet a survival-of-the-fittest species. In terms of letting everyone vote, it is less than one hundred years old. It is going to meet the ultimate test in the elderly. Can it cut the benefits that go to a majority of its voters? If the answer is no, democracy has no long-run future. Other investments have to be made that will not and cannot be made unless those benefits are under control.

The political problems are not created entirely by the political power of the ever more numerous elderly. Means-tested benefits (benefits that decrease as income and wealth increase) would result in dramatic cost savings, but it is not just the elderly with above-average incomes and wealth who are opposed to it. All of us will eventually become old and all of us, especially the near elderly, would rather use our own money for the luxuries of life and let the government pay for our necessities when we are old. Less generous programs are ultimately less generous programs for *us* and not just for *them*.

Even for the young not yet worried about retirement, the shift toward making the elderly pay more of their own bills is not without a downside. The shift means that the young may have to pay, or feel the guilt associated with not paying, for some of the costs of taking care of their parents if their parents don't budget their income appropriately. More dire, for those with parents who have assets, making the elderly pay means smaller inheritances.[63] One will not inherit the house or the stock portfolio that one expected to inherit if it was sold to pay medical bills or provide the equivalent of a monthly pension. The young would rather not lose their inheritances.

The political message is simple. Targeting benefit to low-income elderly families reduces costs and improves economic efficiency (gets the money to those who need it most), but it quickly loses political support.

A balanced budget amendment is often offered as a solution. But it isn't. A balanced budget amendment can be passed but it has no meaning unless politicians are willing and able to cut back on the entitlements for the elderly. If those who make the laws don't want to obey the spirit of a law, they can always avoid doing so. They can simply spend more than incoming revenues and justify it with some of the fine print that has to accompany any balanced budget amendment.

Any balanced budget amendment has to have some exceptions and some implementation provisions. How are revenues and expenditures to be forecast? What happens if an unexpected recession occurs? What happens if a major war breaks out? How are expenditures to be counted—do the expenditures of government corporations such as the postal service count? Do asset sales count as revenues? Do major infrastructure investments count as current expenditures? How are loan guarantees to be counted? All of these "details" make it possible for any government that does not want to obey a balanced budget amendment to avoid obeying it. If spending is to be cut, in the end those who have been elected have to cut it.

The problem of the elderly is not just a government problem. Private firms face the same dilemma in private pension and health programs for the elderly.[64] In the private sector, health care programs are universally underfunded and pension programs are often less than fully funded. In the United States there is a 20 percent shortfall in private pension plans, yet 75 percent of the companies with underfunded programs are financially healthy companies. Older companies such as the auto companies with a lot of retirees and generous pension and health plans for those retirees would have little or no corporate equity if these obligations were fully reflected on their books.

The elderly are not the big dissavers that they are sometimes portrayed to be (spending all of their accumulated wealth so that they die on the day when their assets run out), but they quite understandably are not big savers for the future. The results can be seen in savings rates. In OECD countries gross savings rates have fallen from 24 percent to 19 percent of GDP between 1977 and 1992.[65]

Much of the decline in personal savings rates in the United States, from about 9 percent in the decades after World War II to 3 percent in the 1990s, can be attributed to the elderly or those about to be elderly.[66] The near elderly, being more confident about public and private employers providing pensions, are saving less than they used to right before retirement, and the elderly who know that they have monthly pension checks and health coverage are spending more during retirement. Savings rates fall just when, as we shall see in Chapter 14, man-made brainpower industries will require a significant increase in savings.

If one is looking for a group in need, it is not the elderly. The group with the highest proportion now in poverty is children under the age of eighteen. Yet government spends nine times as much per person on the elderly (those who do vote) as it does on the young (those who don't vote).[67] Precisely the group that most needs investments if there is to be a successful American economy in the future is the group that is getting the least. How are they to pay taxes to support the elderly if they don't have the skills to earn their own incomes?

In the years ahead, class warfare is apt to be redefined to mean not the poor against the rich but the young against the old. As a young Frenchwoman said during a strike to protest government laws that would have lowered the wages of the young, "We have no future! That's why we're out here."[68] In America this conflict is already clear. The elderly systematically vote against education levies when they have a chance.[69] The elderly establish segregated restricted retirement communities for themselves where the young are not allowed to live so that they do not have to pay for schools.

The most dramatic recent example of impending social conflict occurred in Kalkaska, Michigan, a retirement haven, where elderly voters essentially robbed the school budget to pay for other things such as snow plowing and then refused to vote the funds to allow the schools to finish the school year. Schools closed months early and some of Michigan's schoolchildren missed much of a year's schooling.[70] While the elderly are probably still interested in their own grandchildren, they no longer live in the same communities with their grandchildren. Each of those elderly Kalkaska voters could vote against educating someone else's grandchildren yet convince themselves that somehow voters elsewhere in America would treat their grandchildren differently.

The implicit post–World War II social contract has been that parents will take care of children but that society, the taxpayer, will take care of parents. Both parts of that bargain are collapsing. More and more parents are not taking care of children, and the taxpayer is going to have to retreat from his promise to take care of the elderly.

REFORMING THE SOCIAL WELFARE SYSTEM

What has to be done is as economically clear as how to do it is politically opaque. Single-issue politics where large voting groups fight over income redistribution is what democracies do worst.[71] By always being willing to exempt the elderly from budget cuts, those who know politics best, our elected politicians, have already decided that the problem is politically impossible to solve. But the problem has to be solved, since 100 percent of any society's tax revenue cannot be given to the elderly.

No society, no matter how it pays for it, can afford to let ever larger fractions of its population live in idleness for ever longer periods of time. Societies can guarantee a fixed number of years in retirement (ten years, fifteen years, twenty years), but no one can any longer guarantee retirement at some fixed age such as sixty-five as life expectancy lengthens. There is also no reason why any social welfare system should transfer so many resources to a group that it ends up with above-average incomes. That leads to the social absurdity of the poorer members of society paying taxes to subsidize the richer.

The answer to what must be done has to begin with some explicit goals. How much of a person's preretirement income should be replaced with a system of compulsory government pensions? The mirror image of that question is, how much should someone be expected to save if they wish to have a retirement standard of living equal to their preretirement standard of living? Just to motivate the thought processes, let me suggest a possible set of goals.

The maximum benefit should be a public pension that would guarantee a retired couple no more than two thirds of the median earnings of the average workingman and average workingwoman (jointly $23,876 in 1992) since the average couple supports a family of three.[72] The minimum benefit should be a pension that ensures that all elderly families have an income at least equal to the poverty line.

Whatever a family's preretirement earnings, it would be guaranteed a poverty-line pension. Above this level, families should get a pension equal to half of their preretirement earnings in the ten years before retirement. When a family's preretirement earnings reached twice the national average, they would be guaranteed a pension equal to two-thirds the earnings of the average working man and woman. Earnings more than this would not yield higher pensions. With the exception of the working poor, everyone would be expected to save if they wish to have an income equal to that of their preretirement earnings.

The age of retirement is easy to calculate. How much taxes are people willing to pay? What essential services have to be provided and what essential investments have to be made? Subtracting the latter two numbers from the first yields the funds available to support the social welfare system. Make another subtraction for everything else other than spending on the elderly that has to be done in the social welfare system. Take the resulting funds, the annual income needed in retirement to have a per capita income equal to that of the nonelderly, the number of elderly, and it is easy to calculate the maximum number of years that the average elderly person can be supported in retirement. Subtract this number from average life expectancy at age sixty-five (now seventeen years) and one has the retirement age society can afford.

The age of retirement has to be raised and early retirement eliminated. When Bismarck set the retirement age at sixty-five in the German pension system in 1891, the average German lived to be less than forty-five.[73] Today that would be roughly equivalent to saying that there is a government pension for all those over the age of ninety-five. If this were the actual rule, there wouldn't be any problem.

Raising the retirement age will not be popular. While sixty-five used to be the age at which the largest number of people retired, it is now sixty-two and falling.[74] Already by age sixty-one labor force participation rates are about 10 percentage points lower than they were at age fifty-five. Yet no one can finance a system where life expectancy rises and the age of retirement falls.

Pundits can talk about letting people voluntarily take care of themselves when they are elderly, but there is a simple reality—too many won't. At retirement, sixteen million Americans have no voluntary savings and nothing but their pensions to sustain them.[75] The average American family has only $1,000 in accumulated net financial assets, and to finance a future pension income equal to what today's retirees receive they would be required to save a sum equal to eleven times their own current income.[76] Those with thirty years of their working life left would be required to save one third of their pretax incomes each and every year for the next thirty years to reach this goal.

Those fifty-four to sixty-five years of age and just about to retire have less than $7,000 in net financial assets and are in even worse shape.[77] Many of course have some equity in their homes, but with home equity loans, housing equity is not building up nearly as fast as it did in the past. Including home equity, the 50th percentile household of those fifty-one to sixty-one years of age have only $99,350 in accumulated assets.[78] Current consumption would have to be cut back drastically for the current generation of near elderly if they were to self-finance their own retirement.

When Americans get a chance to rob their pension plans, they do so. Thirty-eight percent of workers who change jobs and have a chance to take money out of their pension plans take the money and run.[79] Workers in general and lower-paid workers in particular don't take advantage of tax-free opportunities to save. The baby boom generation systematically uses home equity loans—an activity that will dramatically lower their postretirement resources, since they end up consuming whatever capital gains they do have on their homes before retirement—

to raise their current consumption.[80] Today's baby boomers are saving only one third of what they need to in order to have the standard of living in retirement that their parents currently enjoy.[81] Three out of four Americans expect a crisis when they retire, since they have saved little or nothing.[82] They are right that there will be a crisis.

There is a fundamental reality that Americans don't save unless they are forced to save.

Employers are getting out of the pension business. They have cut their pension contributions in half (from $1,039 to $506 per worker) between 1980 and 1991 and this trend will only accelerate.[83] Jurisdictions requiring employer-financed pension plans will only find employers relocating elsewhere.

History will record that Lee Kuan Yew got it right in Singapore with his Provident Fund (self-financed social welfare benefits), while Bismarck got it wrong in Germany with his social welfare system of intergenerational transfers. In Singapore every person must contribute 20 percent of their wages to a personal savings account where it is matched by 20 percent from employers. The account's investments are half managed by the individual and half managed by the government and can only be used for health care, education, housing, and one's old age. Taxes are not levied on the young to pay for the old. The old live on what they have been forced to save and the additional saving that they have voluntarily done.

But once a system of intergenerational transfers exists, it is only possible to move to self-financing very slowly. The problem is simple. The big winner in a system of intergenerational transfers is the first generation. They receive benefits when they are old without having had to pay anything into the system when they were young. The system did not exist when they were young. They get but did not pay. The big loser is the last generation. They pay into the fund for their entire lifetimes but there are no young people behind them to pay benefits to them. They pay but do not get.

Today's retirees are essentially the first generation and they are the big winners in social security. While no one will be the last generation in terms of humankind, if the generations are very different in size or benefit levels have expanded dramatically, the smaller and later generations (today's baby-dearth generation born after 1963) will to some extent be the last generation having to pay for the much larger generation (the baby boom generation born between 1947 and 1963) ahead of them.

While those born in 1900 received a real, inflation-adjusted, 12 percent rate of return on their social security contributions (far more than they would have gotten in private capital markets), those born in 1975 will earn less than a 2 percent real rate of return.[84] In Sweden the generation that retired in the 1960s got six times as much as they paid into the system but the generations that will retire after 2010 are expected to get less than 80 percent of what they paid in.[85] That is simply unfair, yet most of the elderly have convinced themselves that they have "paid for" their current benefits and are not on welfare. They have "earned" what they get.

Nothing could be further from the truth. The average elderly male now is repaid all of his social security tax payments plus interest in less than four years.[86] After that he is on welfare in exactly the same sense that a welfare mother is on welfare.

While more saving for retirement should be encouraged, such actions cannot solve the current problem. They in fact compound it. If today's workers are essentially forced ("encouraged") to save for their own old age, but if nothing is done to cut the costs of the current system for those who are already elderly, today's workers must simultaneously finance both today's elderly and their own old age. They have their economic burdens essentially doubled. As a result, the shift from a system of intergenerational transfers to self-financing can occur only very slowly—one would have to think about a fifty- to seventy-five-year period of time. The shift to more self-financing should be slowly made in the long run, but doing so will not change what needs to be done in the medium term.

Whatever is done has to be announced far in advance, so that families can plan for their retirement. No one can change their retirement plans quickly. Retirement benefits and ages have to be known fifteen to twenty years in advance. New laws have to be written not so much to cut current benefits but to cut the increases in the benefit stream that are programmed into current laws. Only very gradually will the elderly have to pay more out of their own savings. But benefits do need to be selectively cut to bring the per capita income of the elderly back into balance with that of the nonelderly. There is simply no justification for a social welfare system that taxes those with lower incomes (the young) to give it to people with higher incomes (the elderly). There is no need to return to the "bad old days" when the elderly had much less than the nonelderly, but there is also no need to continue to finance a world where the per capita income of the elderly exceeds that of the nonelderly by large amounts.

While the direct means testing of benefits may be impossible since it undercuts the political viability of the system, the elderly have to pay income taxes that are consistent with their incomes. In the United States a couple with one child earning $30,000 pays $2,449 in federal income taxes. An elderly couple needing to support only two with an equally large income of $30,000 income (40 percent of it coming from social security) pays only $791 in taxes.[87] Equally wealthy elderly should pay equal taxes.

Since pensions and health care benefits are consumption activities, the right way to pay for pensions and health care benefits for the elderly is not a payroll tax on work but a consumption tax—a value-added tax—on other forms of consumption. If pensions are not to squeeze out investment, they must be set up in such a way that they squeeze out other forms of consumption. A progressive consumption tax also means that the elderly continue to help pay for their pensions after they cease working unless they are willing to contribute to society by savings.

Using the payroll tax to finance benefits for the elderly creates what economists know as the tax wedge. When employers look at workers, they see expensive workers—labor compensation, which includes wages, private fringe benefits, and public payroll taxes, is high. When workers look at those same jobs, they see low-wage jobs, because the only part of that compensation package that is relevant to them is take-home wages. The rest of it either goes to others (the elderly) or yields benefits in a distant future that are completely discounted.

Both sides essentially bail out of the tax-paying economic system. The employer moves his operations to some other part of the world where private fringe benefits and public social benefits don't exist. From offshore production bases the employer continues to sell his products in the old home market, but he no longer makes his products or pays his taxes in his home market. By doing this, he lowers costs and raises profits. The employee seeks to do the same. He seeks to get whatever social welfare benefits are available (unemployment insurance, disability payments) and moves into the illegal black economy where taxes are not paid and where cash wages are often higher than after-tax wages in the legal white economy, because the employers do not have to pay for public or private fringe benefits.

Because both sides have quit paying the taxes that are necessary to finance the social welfare system, the costs of the welfare system rise for those who are left in it, and their incentives to bail out increase. In the long run, a payroll-tax-financed system of social welfare spending is simply not viable.

Whatever is done, the sooner it is done the easier it is to do. Bringing the system into balance now leads to fewer debts tomorrow. Lower interest payments mean that fewer taxes need to be collected to finance the system. Politically, the same interest in speed exists. The electoral power of the elderly can only grow as they become more numerous. The longer the elderly are addicted to government pensions, the harder it is going to be to stop that addiction. What humans have always had quickly seems a right and not a privilege. Such a shift in attitudes is already clearly visible.

But the elderly are not the entire social welfare problem. In Sweden two thirds of the population gets some kind of a regular check from the government.[88] In northern Europe it is clear that there is something that might be called a "second generation" problem. When welfare systems were first established, the existing ethos limited usage so that people didn't use the system unless they badly needed to. Such attitudes still exist (even today there are millions of people in the United States who are legally entitled to be on welfare, who would have higher family incomes if they went on welfare, but who would feel ashamed to be on welfare and do not apply for benefits to which they are entitled) but to a much lesser extent. But over time such inhibitions died away and what was initially regarded as a system only to be used in case of dire need became an entitlement to be used whenever it was convenient to do so.

These same inhibitions, however, allowed the politicians of a few decades ago to think that the long-run costs of the systems they were designing were much lower than they actually were. Since few people used the system in the first generation, costs were low, and the system could be made more generous because benefit hikes could be easily afforded. Over time the systems were expanded to the point that benefits often yielded wage-replacement rates of more than 90 percent (107 percent for pensioners in Greece, 100 percent for being an invalid in Germany, 124 percent for maternity benefits in Portugal, 97 percent for disability benefits in Belgium), so that when work expenses were subtracted, large numbers of people were actually better off not working.[89] But what was cheap in the first generation became expensive in the second generation as more and more people got used to using the system.[90]

This process can be seen very clearly in the Scandinavian systems of disability payments and sick pay. Every society has people who become sick or disabled, permanently or temporarily, and cannot work. What is to happen to them? Scandinavia designed a social welfare system where the disabled received payments equal to 90 percent of the wages they would have gotten if they had been able to work. Over the decades the generosity of the laws governing disability changed very little but attitudes toward those laws changed enormously. Something that was once self-limited to those severely ill or in dire need began to be used by millions of basically healthy workers to give themselves nineteen extra vacation days per year or an early disability retirement pension.[91]

Costs soared while tax payments dropped. What was once an economically viable privilege becomes an economically unviable entitlement. Scandinavian systems that have been in effect for a long time now have to be scaled back to keep costs under control. When the systems were scaled back, absenteeism fell dramatically by two thirds.[92] But the benefits for those truly in need, of course, also dropped.

With all of the talk about paying less taxes, one would think that Americans wanted fewer social benefits. It is important to remember that nothing could be further from the truth. The elderly want their benefits. They are not alone. Rather than paying privately for health, flood, hurricane, or earthquake insurance, middle-class voters want government to provide the necessary insurance. But when government does pay, those who bought private flood or earthquake insurance become suckers—paying privately for their own coverage and publicly through taxes for someone else's coverage. Every flood or earthquake for which the government offers disaster relief reduces the number of those who in the future will buy the private coverage that makes them ineligible for public benefits. They are not stupid. In the flood-prone zones of the Midwest, only 7 percent now carry flood insurance.[93] The same attitudes can be seen in health insurance. More than 50 percent of those who were covered under Medicaid cut back on their private insurance as a result.[94]

Rather than being interested in insurance policies that only pay for catastrophic unusual occurrences—the unexpected huge costs that few can afford and no one expects—the public wants first-dollar coverage. It wants government or corporations to pay for the unusual risks, but also to pay for the everyday expected expenses that most should, and could, easily pay for themselves.

The increasing unwillingness to live with risk in our modern societies probably comes from the shift out of agriculture. In an agricultural world, annual incomes rise and fall dramatically depending upon the weather. People have no choice but to live in a world with a lot of uncertainty about their annual incomes. Having to live with big risks that cannot be eliminated makes living with the little risks of life seem natural. But in an industrial world everything seems more controllable. There may be uncertainties but they are uncertainties created by other humans and at least in principle are avoidable. Not having to live with unavoidable big risks to their incomes makes humans less willing to live with the little unavoidable risks of life.

Fatalism and "caveat emptor" are gone and have been replaced by the social insurance state.[95] The result is an enormous mismatch between redistribution wants and the willingness to pay taxes to pay for those wants.

CONCLUSIONS

The demographic plate profoundly changes the nature of the capitalistic system. Millions of low-wage unskilled immigrants have to have an impact on the wages of millions of higher-wage unskilled native-born Americans just as the wages of millions of well-educated workers who live in what used to be the second world have to have an impact on the wages of better-educated Americans. In a capitalistic system of supply and demand, it could not be otherwise.

A big increase in the number of elderly people has to profoundly change the nature of the system. Not expecting to live too much longer and no longer working, they simply are not, and should not be, interested in investments in the future. But investments have to be made if the young are to be economically viable and generate the income necessary to finance the pensions and health care of the elderly. One cannot tax what does not exist. Nothing should be more important to the old than the economic success of the young.

We have met the financial "enemy" and he is the elderly "us" in both the public and the private sector.

Chapter 6

Plate Four: A Global Economy

For the first time in human history, anything can be made anywhere and sold everywhere. In capitalistic economies that means making each component and performing each activity at the place on the globe where it can be most cheaply done and selling the resulting products or services wherever prices and profits are highest. Minimizing costs and maximizing revenues is what profit maximization, the heart of capitalism, is all about. Sentimental attachment to some geographic part of the world is not part of the system.

Technologically, transportation and communication costs have fallen dramatically and the speed with which both can be done has risen exponentially. This has made possible completely new systems of communications, command, and control within the business sector. Research and design groups can be coordinated in different parts of the world; components can be made wherever in the world it is cheapest to do so and shipped to assembly points that minimize total costs. Assembled products can be quickly shipped to wherever they are needed with just-in-time air freight delivery systems. Sales can be global. From 1964 to 1992, first world production was up 9 percent, but exports were up 12 percent, and cross-border lending was up 23 percent.[1]

But ideologies were just as important as technologies in the development of a global economy. When the capitalistic global economy began its development in the immediate aftermath of World War II, the new technologies that are now thought to be essential to a global economy did not yet exist. Ideology sent the capitalistic world off in a global direction that was later reinforced by technology. The technologies to expand and reconfigure a global economy that would come later would still have been developed but historic ideologies would certainly have delayed their usage—and may have prevented it entirely.

Technology accelerated the development of today's global economy, but social attitudes and the government actions that flowed from those attitudes created the global economy.

The United States in particular with its history of isolationism could easily have become after World War II the modern equivalent of China's Middle Kingdom. It was wealthy; it was militarily dominant; it had the protection of large oceans to the east and west, and large, friendly, militarily weak neighbors to the north and south. Economically, it did not need the rest of the world for anything. It would have been very easy for the United States to fall back into its historic isolationism. Even after communism arose as the enemy, there were important political leaders who wanted it to do so.

In the McCarthy era, Americans made communism into an inside threat and during the cold war Americans saw communism as an outside military threat, but the reality was that communism was never either an inside political threat to "take over" in America or an outside military force that directly threatened to conquer America. There were inside political threats and outside military threats elsewhere in the world (Italy, France, West Germany, South Korea), but they were only indirect threats to America if America decided it wanted to be the global leader of an anti-Communist military bloc. If it wanted to retreat into isolation, it was not directly threatened by communism. In the end it was probably the indirect threat global communism posed for global capitalism that tipped the balance away from isolationism to internationalism.

But it is not just in the United States that the post–World War II world would have been very different without the threat of communism. If Europe had had no inside challenges from socialism and no outside military threats from communism, Europe would have had both the internal cohesion and the economic resources to regain and maintain its prewar colonial empires. Even facing external communism and internal socialism, countries like France and Great Britain retreated from their colonial empires with great reluctance, under military pressure, and facing enormous U.S. pressure—a pressure that would not have existed if the United States had not believed that colonialism was inconsistent with fighting communism. The British-French invasion of Egypt to retake the Suez Canal and their subsequent retreat under American pressure dramatically symbolizes both what they would have liked to do and their inability to do it without American support. Without American support, they simply had to retreat from their colonies. Without the threat of communism, colonialism would have lasted much longer than it did.

The outside threat, communism, was a one-world ideology. It was an "ecumenical," not a national event.[2] In Marx's vision a universal Communist ideology would sweep away national politics and create a unified global social system with worldwide egalitarian standards of living. In his eyes nationalism was one of the key enemies of communism. Attachments to nations would have to be crushed and replaced with one-world communism. "Like the early Christians, most pre-1914 socialists were believers in the great apocalyptic change which would abolish all that was evil and bring about a society without unhappiness, oppression, inequality and injustice."[3] There was even serious talk in the late 1940s when communism had just extended its grip to Eastern Europe and China of everyone formally joining the Soviet Union and creating one big Communist country that would eventually expand to include everyone on the face of the globe.

In the aftermath of Sputnik when Khrushchev was pounding his shoe on his desk at the United Nations, when the Soviet Union was believed to be economically growing faster than the United States, when China was the model for development in the third world, and when communism had just come to the Western Hemisphere in Cuba, the global threat to capitalism was taken very seriously. One-country capitalistic responses clearly weren't good enough. Something global had to be put in place to "contain" global communism.

While the Communist world did not become a single country, the existence of a competitive ideology preaching a global approach forced the capitalistic economies into a defensive, you-have-to-be-one-to-fight-one global mentality. Worldwide military alliances were needed. Economic growth outside of the United States became more important to the United States than economic growth within the United States, since the United States needed wealthy partners who could afford to share the military manpower burdens that were necessary to contain communism more than it needed to raise its already very high standards of living.

Some of the GATT–Bretton Woods system (the World Bank, the International Monetary Fund [IMF], "most favored nation" [MFN] trading rules) was designed before the Iron Curtain came down, but its eventual shape (a series of trading rounds dismantling tariffs and quotas, U.S. leadership and management, the United States as a global economic locomotive, and an open American market where everyone could sell their goods) was formed in the "heat" of the cold war. Having America as a large, open, rich market was particularly important, since it is far easier to become rich by selling things to wealthy people than by selling to poor people. Since there was only one large group of rich people on the face of the earth after World War II, access to the U.S. market was a prize worth winning. The United States could use that ability to grant or deny access to its market to tie people elsewhere in the world into the American system.

If one looks at the countries that have become rich since World War II, all of them have gone through a period of time when their exports focused on the American market. In the 1960s, 35 percent of Japan's exports were coming to America and in the 1980s, 48 percent of the Asian dragons' (Hong Kong, Taiwan, South Korea, and Singapore) exports were coming to the United States.[4] China is doing the same in the 1990s. In the last ten years more than 50 percent of its increase in exports have come to the United States.

Although the Marshall Plan was not formally part of the GATT–Bretton Woods system, the same forces brought it into existence.[5] It brought huge amounts of aid to the formerly wealthy war-torn countries that fought World War II. Both old enemies (Germany, Japan, Italy) and old allies (Great Britain, France, the Netherlands) had to be rapidly rebuilt to preserve capitalism and to allow them to afford to support the large military establishments necessary to contain communism.

Foreign aid was for the poor what the Marshall Plan was for the rich. Prior to World War II the term "foreign aid" did not exist. The purpose of third world colonies was to make colonial powers rich—not the reverse. In the context of the cold war, foreign aid was designed to give third world nations an incentive to try capitalistic development at a time when many believed that socialistic development was the only viable route into the first world.

In the development of the GATT–Bretton Woods system, the Marshall Plan, and foreign aid, there was always a mixture of motives but the mix gradually came to be dominated by anticommunism. Economic aid and open markets were given to keep countries within the U.S. orbit of influence and outside the orbit of Soviet influence. It would be nice to say that the aid went only to those who believed in democracy and capitalism but it would not be true. Aid went to those who agreed to stay out of the Communist orbit regardless of whether they were dictatorships or whether they believed in market economies. Foreign aid was often defended as a cheap way to buy anti-Communist troops.

With communism dead, the threats that were instrumental in producing a global capitalistic economy are over. But historic paths make a difference. Whether a global economy would have been built without the presence of a Communist threat can be debated, but that debate does not change today's reality that a global economy exists. Stopping its development might not have been hard at the beginning, but dismantling it now would be very difficult—most likely impossible. A global economy now shapes everyone's view of the world and alters how each of us thinks. Everyone faces a new reality. Everyone is mutually interdependent and linked in very different patterns of supply and demand than might otherwise have existed. Powerful institutions (world banks, multinational firms, international institutions) are in place with a vested interest in maintaining themselves and their environment. Getting rid of the existing world economy would require some painful structural readjustments. Export industries would have to be shrunk. Import-competing industries would have to be expanded. Huge economic losses would be forced on those who earn their living as exporters or importers in the existing global economy. Not being able to take advantage of the comparative advantage inherent in foreign trade, the prices of some products (for example, oil) would rise dramatically and those who buy such products would find themselves with much reduced real incomes. In a very real sense the global economy has become physically embodied in our ports, airports, and telecommunications systems. But most important, it is embodied in our mind-sets.

REGIONAL TRADING BLOCS

Jumping from national economies to a one-world economy is a leap too big to make. As a result regional trading blocs are emerging as natural stepping-stones in an evolutionary process toward a truly global economy. Those blocs, however, lead to some contradictory trends. The blocs are moving to freer trade within each bloc, but at the same time more government management of trade is developing between the blocs. An index of world free trade may well go up (more free trade within the blocs overwhelms more managed trade between the blocs) at the same time that an index of managed trade also rises.

In a world of regional trading blocs, selling one's products if a country is not part of one of the trading groups is going to become increasingly difficult for developing countries. Market access will be a privilege that has to be earned and not a right that is bestowed automatically. Most developing countries will have to negotiate access to the world's wealthy markets. What happens to the countries that no one wants in their trading groups and that aren't important enough to demand access?

A few third world countries will have automatic entry. Mexico already has such entry with NAFTA. Europe's strategic interests and fears of massive migration leave it no choice but to find some associative arrangements for Eastern Europe and for North Africa.[6] Economic failure to either the east or the south would certainly lead to uncontrolled migration into the European Community and perhaps wars on their borders. Those asked to join will be asked because they bring something to the table—usually geography. But some will be left out. Who wants the marginalized economic losers of the world (say, Africa south of the Sahara) on their team?

No one in the post–World War II world has gotten rich without easy access to the wealthy markets of the first world—almost always America's markets, since Japan consumes very little of the third world's manufactured products and Europe does only slightly better. To acquire access, every country in Latin America wants to join NAFTA. Probably even Castro would apply to join if he thought there was any chance that he would be admitted. All of middle and much of Eastern Europe wants to join the European Community. The Russians are too proud to ask, but they would love to be asked to join the European Community.

Regionalization is going to be a messy process—two steps forward, one step to the side, and often one step, or even two steps, backward. Nations do not give up power gracefully. Although their momentum is irreversible, regional trading groups, the wave of the future, are often going to look more like the wave of the past—as they did in early 1995.

Of the three major trading regions existing in early 1995, economically NAFTA was probably in the worst state. To prevent Mexico's financial collapse, the United States had to undertake enormous financial commitments. Those commitments were politically unpopular, weakened the dollar, and the resulting Mexican recession and cuts in imports were eventually expected to cost the United States 1.3 million jobs.[7] In Mexico itself the austerity package imposed by the United States and the International Monetary Fund was expected to cost 750,000 jobs and cut real purchasing power by one third for the average Mexican family.[8]

Canada was not in the headlines but its fundamentals were even weaker than those in Mexico. Proportionally, its budget deficit was three times that of the United States and interest on its federal debt absorbed 40 percent of its total spending.[9] Despite a large trade surplus with the United States, the Canadian current account deficit was proportionally twice that of the United States and the value of the Canadian dollar was falling even faster than that of the American dollar.[10] Effectively, the United States was having to borrow large amounts of money on world capital markets to relend to Canada to prevent it from becoming another Mexico.

NAFTA's problems are not surprising. Historically, the survival rate of free trade areas is very low. EFTA, the European Free Trade Area, collapsed in the face of the European Common Market. Free trade areas have never lasted very long. America's initial efforts to establish what was essentially a free trade area, the Articles of Confederation, failed and had to be replaced eight years later with the current United States Constitution establishing a single country with a full common market of reciprocal obligations. Unless NAFTA is supported by a bigger vision, even if only political union at some very distant date, its chances of long-run survival are not good.

The reasons are straightforward. Free trade areas level down with falling wages and prices, while common markets use social investments to level up. For many free trade is painful. Their firms and their jobs disappear. Not surprisingly, they fight the establishment of free trade areas vigorously. Those who benefit from free trade tend to be more numerous but their gains are usually very small relative to their total incomes. As a result, they aren't as much of a political force even though they may be more numerous.

It makes a lot of difference to governments that are trying to persuade their voters to undergo painful restructurings if they can point to big benefits—social investments that are tangible, certain, and occur regularly. In the European Community the Spanish have had to face up to German competition and to allow German ownership of their business firms—but in return they have gotten funds from those same Germans to make very large infrastructure investments.

To persuade one's citizens to undergo painful restructurings also requires a vision greater than that provided by economics alone. Common markets have a vision of something larger. Free trade areas don't. Initially the European Community was seen as a vehicle for ending wars between Germany and France. Without a noneconomic vision to sell, no one is willing to suffer the short-run pain that economic free trade requires to arrive at the long-run gains. Knowing that being willing to make such structural adjustments will lead some future average American to be better off has never made any actual Americans willing to undergo cuts in their own personal incomes today.

Periodically the governments of the Americas meet to discuss the Free Trade Areas of the Americas (FTAA) that would include all of the countries of the Americas. But they can only agree that they will do something, no one knows what, by 2005. If the whole effort was serious, the countries of Latin America would be allowed to join NAFTA one at a time when they had met some previously established set of entry criteria rather than trying to organize something entirely new.[11]

The European Community has a political vision and it is a common market, but it suffers from some very difficult foreign policy problems.

Bosnia lies in the heart of the Community, right between Greece and Italy. Initially, Bosnia was going to be the place where Europe proved it could have a unified foreign policy. In the summer of 1991, Jacques Delors, head of the European Community, asked the American government to stand aside. "We do not interfere in American affairs; we trust that America will not interfere in European affairs."[12] President Bush acquiesced and deliberately stood aside. Probably to prove to the Europeans that they could not run Europe without America's leadership. President Bush proved to be correct, but what neither he nor they knew was that after standing aside until it was proven that Europe could not solve Europe's problems, the problems would become much harder to solve and getting America reinvolved would prove to be very difficult. Bosnia is now a European problem that Europe will have to solve with only peripheral American help, even though the United States brokered a peace agreement in late 1995. If it can't, European unity will have suffered a major setback and a sequence of new Bosnias will probably emerge.

Western Europe's biggest economic failing is not its obvious problems—a double-digit unemployment rate that only seems to get worse or repeated currency runs on first one and then another EC member. Its biggest failing is that it should be to middle and Eastern Europe what the overseas Chinese are to China—but it isn't. It should be exporting investment equipment and sophisticated consumer goods to the old Communist countries of Eastern Europe while restructuring to import light manufactured products and agricultural commodities from those same countries. But thus far it lacks the imagination and leadership. Perhaps now that east Germany is on the way up economically, the Germans will have the time, money, self-interest, and imagination to be the overseas Chinese of Eastern Europe.

Businesses blame governments for not giving a clear direction, and governments cite the evident chaos and lack of governmental system in middle and Eastern Europe, but the chaos and uncertainty in Eastern Europe is no greater than it is in the People's Republic of China. On the Pacific Rim it was not governments but businesses that took the lead. Governments, such as that in Taiwan, often opposed business investments in Communist China.

But the vision of a greater European union still remains and should not be forgotten. The Maastricht treaty has been signed and an inner group has promised to have a common currency by 1999. In the end they will do so not so much because they want to but because not doing so is too painful for both those inside the common currency area and those left outside. The outsiders who do not meet the convergence criteria (a set of conditions, such as maximum government deficits and debts, that have been set as conditions necessary for membership) become second-class citizens starved for capital, forced to pay higher interest rates, and subject to speculative attacks. Those inside have to fear the competitive devaluations forced on those left outside.[13] Insiders lose export markets to outsiders who have to devalue.

In the end three of the four countries that voted upon whether they should join the EU in 1994 did so by big majorities. On March 26, 1995, seven European nations dropped their border controls on each other.[14] Despite the problems, the European Community is moving forward. The British are of course still the British. There are votes to be gotten by making "the case against Europe" in a vituperative way where Jean Monnet, one of the post–World War II architects of the Common Market, is described as "a French brandy salesman turned international bureaucrat." A British conservative government rips itself up over the issue.[15] But in the end they will go along because they have no choice. Left out of Europe, the British have no economic future.

The Pacific Rim looks better if one is very selective about where one looks and ignores places such as the Philippines, Laos, Cambodia, Vietnam, and Burma. Parts of the region are growing rapidly. But those parts represent only 4 percent of the world's GDP, while another part, Japan, represents 16 percent of the world's GDP and is shrinking. A 7 percent growth rate outside of Japan can be completely offset by a 1.8 percent decline in Japan. As a result, the entire Pacific Rim (including Japan) has grown much more slowly than the United States in the first half of the 1990s.[16]

In 1994 in Bogor, Indonesia, eighteen Pacific Rim countries, including the United States, Canada, and Australia, promised to create a free trade area by 2020 (to be called APEC—Asia-Pacific Economic Cooperation). But what should grab everyone's attention is the year, 2020. Whenever politicians promise to do something in the distant future, but take no actions to get there in the present, they are committing fraud.[17] To say 2020 is equivalent to saying that there will be no free trade area in your and my lifetime. Most of those making that promise will be dead before 2020 and none of them will still be in office. Meeting one year later, the leaders of these same countries could not agree even on a basic road map because of the "group's diversity." Put bluntly by one of the participants, "there is no consensus."[18]

On the Pacific Rim the fundamentals for a trading bloc just do not exist. Like NAFTA no one has a bigger vision of political unification. Countries are at very different stages of economic development and they need (want) very different trading regimes. The rich want free trade in services; the poor want protection.

To include America in the group is to include the ultimate Trojan horse. It has no interest in a cohesive trading group in Asia. It has its own NAFTA and too many European connections. Divide and rule is the name of the game. But America cannot be excluded, since unlike both the European Community and NAFTA, each country's best trading partner is not found within the region if the United States is excluded. Everyone's biggest market is the United States. Without access to that market they would all fail. Everyone is squeezed between the American market they need and the Japanese funds they want.[19]

The European Common Market was fortunate to begin with three countries (Germany, France, and Italy) approximately equal in population and not too different in stages of economic development, and a relatively small number of countries. No one country could dominate. Consensus was possible. NAFTA was the opposite. It combined the world's largest economy with two much smaller economies and it was always clear who would be making most of the decisions. Canada wasn't even consulted when President Bush asked Mexico to join.

But how is group voting power to be distributed in a Pacific Rim trading bloc? The Pacific Rim has one country that is an economic giant, Japan, but a military pygmy, which as a country has very little interest in the problems of those elsewhere in the world, even those in Asia. The region also has one country (China) that is a population giant, probably the second military power in the world already, growing rapidly, but still with an economy less than 7 percent the size of Japan's. How do the two split decision-making powers? Who leads; who follows? Given these giants, what voting powers go to the other countries? The rest are all small economically, politically, militarily, or in terms of population. Together they have neither the population or military power of China nor the economic muscle of Japan. If one adds in the United States, allocating voting power becomes completely impossible. Until there are real answers to such questions, APEC should be seen for the mirage it is. Its purpose is to make the citizens of these countries feel that something is happening (they too are moving to regionalization) when it isn't.

Comparing what is happening now, five years after my previous book, *Head to Head: The Coming Economic Battle Among Japan, Europe and America*, was written, Japan looks much weaker. In 1991 no one would have believed that it could get completely bogged down in a recession with no strategy except time and good luck for escaping. No one would have believed that its financial markets would crash and wipe out more than one third of its wealth. Nor would they have believed that the political system could essentially implode in political scandals leaving Japan unable to formulate political, military, or economic policies. At the same time, any society that is as well educated as Japan, as hardworking as Japan, and that invests as much as Japan still has the important fundamental long-run assets for success.

The United States looks stronger than it did at the beginning of the decade. American auto manufacturers and semiconductor makers once again have the world's largest market shares. No one would have predicted that they would ever again take the number one position away from Japan. Competition and ruthless downsizing have had positive effects. The fat has been stripped out of the system, but it is not yet clear that Americans are now willing to create economic muscle on top of their lean frame. The United States has done nothing to correct its low savings and investment rates. If anything the situation is worse, with sharp cutbacks in government investments in education, infrastructure, and research. Nor has it done anything to upgrade the education of those who do not attend universities. Building a first world economy on top of a massive third world workforce does not create the strongest of economic foundations.

Europe's problems are political. It may rip itself up with ethnic conflicts. Those conflicts, however, do not seem to threaten regional integration. If anything they strengthen it, since the microcountries that are created all want to join a bigger economic union. Policy makers have to be willing to reengineer their countries so that growth can occur at rates that produce jobs and falling unemployment. Today they talk of doing so but they have yet to act.

At the end of *Head to Head*, I stated, not that Europe would win the competition to be the leading industrial area of the world in the twenty-first century, but that it held a position from which it could win, regardless of what the other players did, if it played its current position on the chessboard correctly. I still believe that to be true— although I may be the last Euro-optimist on the face of the globe.

GLOBAL CHALLENGES TO NATIONAL ECONOMIC POLICIES

A global economy creates a fundamental disconnect between national political institutions and their policies to control economic events and the international economic forces that have to be controlled. Instead of a world where national policies guide economic forces, a global economy gives rise to a world in which extranational geoeconomic forces dictate national economic policies. With internationalization, national governments lose many of their traditional levers of economic control.

After World War II when the American government attempted to regulate dollar-denominated securities to better control its money supply, the Eurodollar market promptly developed in London. Dollar-denominated securities were traded in London rather than New York since American authorities could not regulate these trades because they weren't done on American territory and British regulations did not apply to trades denominated in dollars—not pounds. British authorities could have extended their regulations to dollar-denominated securities but they had no interest in doing so. These financial instruments did not affect British monetary policies and their trading brought a lot of jobs to London. British authorities also knew that if London attempted to regulate dollar-denominated securities their trading would just move elsewhere.

As the financial capital of Europe's strongest economy, Frankfurt should have become the European financial capital, but the German authorities insisted upon regulating financial trading and that insistence was the second ingredient in London's success in becoming Europe's financial capital. Without American and German regulatory policies, London would have become just another regional financial capital in Europe.

More recently the Japanese government tried to prevent the trading of some of the modern complex financial derivatives that depended upon the value of the Nikkei Index in Tokyo. As a result, that trading simply moved to Singapore, where it had exactly the same effects on the Japanese stock market as if it were done in Tokyo. This was dramatically brought home to the world when a single trader for Barings Securities in Singapore was able to place a $29 billion bet on the Nikkei Index and lose $1.4 billion when the index did not trade with the ranges that he expected.

As a result of the banking crash of 1932, the American government passed laws making it illegal for American commercial banks to engage in investment banking activities. The government did not want investment banking losses to cause commercial depositors to lose their checking and savings accounts. Today this simply means that Citibank, America's second largest bank, undertakes its investment banking operations from its London offices, where it is not subject to American regulation. America has lost the resulting jobs and gained nothing in terms of risk reduction since Citibank's London activities could just as easily as those in New York bring down Citibank.

Or consider antitrust issues. Whose regulations apply to whom and where? Royal Dutch Airlines (KLM) was allowed to buy a controlling interest in Northwest Airlines, and British Air can, if it wants, exercise an option to take control of U.S. Air, even though it is clear that if these two airlines were American they would not have been allowed to buy either Northwest Airlines or U.S. Air under U.S. antitrust laws. They were treated differently since they were "foreign." Yet we have a world air travel market where "foreign" has little meaning to the traveler. Antitrust laws should be made to apply equally to all. Not doing so leads to the absurdity that American airlines are discriminated against in their own home markets by their own government. Making the world even more complicated, those foreign headquarters firms that are exempted from American antitrust laws could have had Americans as their dominant shareholders.

Costly German regulations on biotechnology (the German public seems to think that biotech will create a horrible Frankenstein monster) have simply led the German chemical and drug companies to do their biotech research in America—much of it in Boston. What should have been German research jobs are in America, and when production starts, those jobs may also be in America—and not Germany.

The era of national government regulation of business is simply over. Activities go to where they are unregulated and often that relocation can happen without anyone physically moving. Insurance and financial activities are electronically performed in Bermuda or the Bahamas, while almost all of those doing the activities are still sitting in their offices in New York or London.

Europe has tried very hard to offer workers protection from recessionary layoffs and downsizing by making it time-consuming and very expensive to fire existing workers. While it was possible to make firing workers so expensive that few firms would incur the required costs, those same regulations led to a European economy where no one is willing to hire new workers and face the financial costs of firing them in the next cyclical downturn. European firms have moved their expansionary activities to other parts of the world where it is not so costly to hire and fire people. Mercedes-Benz and BMW moved to the American Alabama and South Carolina—not by accident the places in America with the fewest government regulations and the lowest social charges. European employment stagnates and over time unemployment rises to higher levels than it would have if firms had been allowed to freely hire and fire.

Remembering the financial disasters caused by uncontrolled capital flows before the war, every government with the exception of the United States after World War II instituted controls on the flows of capital into and out of their countries. Many of those controls were still in place as late as the 1970s. Controls were possible, since an Italian who wanted to move money into Switzerland illegally had to put money into his backpack and walk across the Alps. At least in principle, governments knew how to stop such activities. But with both the technologies and the financial institutions to move money using a personal computer, it is difficult to imagine the enforcement of capital controls. Laws could be passed but they would not be enforceable.

Since capitalistic economic activity naturally migrates to the places with the fewest regulations and the lowest social charges, national governments are now competing with each other for economic activity much as American states compete with each other to persuade business firms to locate in their state. In a global economy if a country is a high-tax, high-spending society, say Sweden, business will simply move to low-tax, low-spending societies, say those in east Asia, to avoid taxes and Sweden will be left without the tax revenue necessary to finance the level of services that its voters might want.

Government expenditure programs that benefit business such as those that finance training or infrastructure can still be defended (the benefits the business firms derive from having them may be bigger than the costs they incur paying for them), but consumption benefits that go directly to citizens become harder and harder to finance with business taxation. By locating in America, Mercedes and BMW reduce the amount that they pay to finance the German public pension system.

The European Community is now trying to harmonize its regulations, taxes, and social expenditures so that firms don't make their location decisions based upon which country within the European Community regulates the least or taxes the most. But tax harmonizing brings with it an implicit harmonization of spending levels, since total tax burdens must be basically similar. The Maastricht treaty provisions for creating a common currency increase this pressure by requiring convergence in government budget and debt policies. In the end national governments lose much of their power.

In a global market all of the pressures are to harmonize down— much as we see American states competing to induce business firms to locate in their jurisdictions by giving them special tax breaks. The jurisdictions with low taxes or few regulations are under no pressure to change; the jurisdictions with many regulations or high taxes are under a lot of pressure to change.

World regulation is not about to replace national regulation. No one can agree on who should regulate, what should be regulated, or how it should be regulated. Whatever might be agreed upon, it would have little meaning, since someone would always have an incentive not to adopt those agreed-upon regulations. If that someone didn't agree, that form of economic activity would simply move to their jurisdiction and add to their economic success. They could intellectually agree that certain regulations would help the world economy yet not adopt or enforce those regulations in their jurisdiction because refusing to do so would raise the incomes of their citizens.

Many today would argue that international pressures to regulate less and tax less are good pressures, not bad pressures. Yet it is well to remember that most of our current system of business regulation arose in two real-world experiences—the "robber barons" era of the last half of the nineteenth century and the financial collapses and Great Depression of the 1920s and 1930s. Those who were alive then saw something that needed to be regulated. Without regulations, perhaps we too will again see something that needs to be regulated.

But the era of national economic regulation is ending and the era of global economic regulation is not yet here. For at least a while capitalism is going to be tried with much less government regulation.

GLOBAL CHALLENGES TO INTERNATIONAL ORGANIZATIONS

With the addition of the second world to capitalism and the decision of much of the third world to play the global capitalistic game, the global economy is both bigger and more of a reality than it ever has been, but there is also no system of rules to guide that economy. The existing trading system—the GATT–Bretton Woods system—was designed for the unipolar world that existed in the aftermath of World War II and not today's multipolar world. It will have to be redesigned for the new multipolar realities, including regional trading blocks.[20]

The heart of the GATT–Bretton Woods system is what is known as MFN—most favored nation. MFN means that every country will give to all countries whatever the best deal is that it gives to its most favored trading partner—its most favored nation. But that is exactly what no one is now willing to do. Germany does not give to the United States the deal that it gives to France. France is in the European Common Market; the United States is not. The United States does not give to Brazil the deal that it gives to Mexico. Mexico is in NAFTA; Brazil is not. The club still exists but the club no longer has a set of principles that tells it what to do.

If one wants to be legalistic, one can argue that the original GATT rules probably permit the European Common Market but not NAFTA. There is a special provision in the treaty that allows customs unions when the ultimate goal of that customs union is political integration. From this perspective the European Common Market would legally qualify, since at least some of the countries involved are talking about creating a single country and they have signed a treaty to create a single currency. But NAFTA in no sense qualifies. It is simply a free trade area with not even vague plans for eventual political union. But even if the European Common Market is legal under the rules, it destroys the rules since it is such a large exception to MFN.

The GATT–Bretton Woods system has also come to the end of the line economically. It took not quite a decade to negotiate the latest trading round, the Uruguay round signed in Marrakech in 1994, but if one examines what was agreed upon, what was signed is an empty document. Press releases could state that tariffs were reduced on industrial goods by almost 40 percent, but beneath those statistics lay a decline from 4.7 to 3 percent. The difference between two such small numbers makes no difference to world trade.[21] The World Bank, the IMF, and the GATT predict that what was agreed upon in Geneva will raise the world GDP by $140 to $274 billion by 2002.[22] That sounds impressive until one asks the size of the denominator. The world GDP is about $30,000. Even the maximum gain, a $274 billion increase spread over nine years, means that there will be a little less than a 1 percent increase in the world GDP. These gains are so small that they are within rounding error—no one will ever know whether they really existed or not.

It was nice, maybe even important, that the world's governments could put their name on a piece of paper, but there was nothing in that piece of paper. Lowering tariffs and reducing quotas (what trading rounds do) has simply reached a point of diminishing returns. There aren't many quotas or tariffs left to cut. There are a host of real things that need to be done. A new system of trading rules has to be developed to govern the behavior of regional blocs. What are they allowed and not allowed to do to each other? But how are those rules to be written and enforced? In a multipolar world without a dominant economic focal point, who manages the system? Who is the lender of last resort stopping financial panics and capital outflows from bringing the system down? Who provides the open, easily accessible markets for those who wish to develop?

If the rest of third world or the second world is to develop using export strategies, the rest of the rich world will have to import more. But why are they suddenly going to be willing to do so? France is the world's fourth biggest economy, yet bananas are its largest third world import. It doesn't buy manufactured third world exports such as textiles. Japan is as closed to third-world-manufactured imports as it is to American imports. With only 23 percent of the world's GDP, the United States cannot continue to be the export market for everyone who now wishes to develop. If today's poor must get rich by selling to each other (i.e., selling to other poor people), they are going to get rich very slowly—if at all.

Within the developed world the issue of cultural protection will be central. The American press often makes fun of French efforts to protect French culture—keeping English words out of the French language, fighting to limit the importation of American movies and TV programs, and trying to stop the spread of the Internet because it is an English-language electronic highway. All can be made to look ridiculous rather easily. But the only really ridiculous feature of the French argument is that France is economically the fourth largest country on the globe and is the owner of a powerful long-lasting culture that is in no real sense threatened by an Anglo-Saxon media culture.

Small countries if they wish to preserve their national heritage have something serious to worry about. One can legitimately argue that protecting one's culture is a matter of life and death for human societies.[23] The issue has been dramatically posed by the then head of the European Common Market, Jacques Delors: "I would simply like to pose a question to our American friends: Do we have the right to exist? Have we the right to preserve our traditions, our heritage, our languages? . . . Does the defense of freedom include the effort of each country to use the audio visual sphere to ensure the protection of its identity?"[24]

But there is no easy way to draw the line between economics and culture. Eighty percent of the movies shown in Europe are American but only 1 percent of the movies shown in America are European.[25] The French market for French films has halved in a decade and in 1994 the top five movies in France were all American.[26] That certainly is a cultural invasion. Movies are cultural, but they, not airplanes, are America's biggest economic export. The industry that is developing at the intersection of TV, telephones, computers, and the visual arts is the fastest-growing industry in the world. The United States cannot afford to be limited to 40 percent of the European market (a French proposal), the world's largest market, in what is its most important export industry. If America were to agree to that rule for Europe, one minute later every country in the world would have a similar rule and America's largest export industry would be destroyed. In the end, the Europeans did not adopt the compulsory 40 percent rule but agreed to allow individual countries to limit foreign programming if they wished.

If such arguments are legitimate, they can be used to protect almost anything. Americans could argue, for example, that the auto is part of their national culture (it certainly is) and that they therefore have the right on cultural grounds to keep out Japanese or European cars. Consider professional sports—are they culture or economics? At the time of the World Cup matches in the United States in 1994, I posed that question to Mr. Bengeman, the minister of industries in the European Common Market. He argued that soccer was culture; his assistant argued that soccer was economics. The truth of course is that it is both and no line can be drawn. Affluence and electronics have turned culture into the biggest of big businesses.

Wherever that line should be drawn and whatever small countries would like to do, the world is probably past the point of no return when it comes to limiting the importation of the global electronic culture in which everyone lives. With satellites and cheap satellite dishes not under the control of governments, it is not clear how the French government could stop the French from watching the programs that they wanted to watch. Presumably it could engage in electronic jamming as the Soviets did during the cold war to prevent imported programming from entering France, but to even mention the possibility is to highlight its absurdity.

For the developed world, selling intellectual property at the highest possible prices is central. For the underdeveloped world, buying (getting it free is even better) intellectual property at the lowest possible prices is central. What are the right rules for the protection of intellectual property rights? Over 90 percent of the videos, CDs, and computer software used in China are pirated. American companies lose billions. But copying to catch up is what everyone has to do if they want to join the first world. Remember those textile mills that the Americans copied from the British.

In a world of brainpower industries, there have to be effective incentives to develop new ideas. Patents and copyrights are always in an internal tension between maximizing the incentives to invent that call for very long, strictly enforced monopoly rights and the incentives to spread knowledge that would call for making copying easy and free. Both are necessary for maximizing national and world GDPs.

A global economy encourages free riding. Why should a country pay for basic research and development if its firms can use whatever new technologies are developed elsewhere in the world? Let other taxpayers pay. Be a free rider. Being smart, governments are targeting more and more of their R&D money on development and less and less on basic research to create the jobs and high wages that get themselves reelected. Yet if everyone follows this strategy and no one invests in R&D, new industries aren't developed.

Economically, one can make a convincing argument that the world should have a global science foundation patterned on the American National Science Foundation to pay for basic research and that development costs should be left to private companies. But neither part of that equation is acceptable politically. Who should pay how much and where should the research be done? Both are unanswerable political questions. Even in the United States, now that the cold war is over and the rationale for R&D spending has to be economic rather than military, there are more pressures to spread federal R&D dollars among the states in a more egalitarian way rather than directing the funds to those who can do the best research.

The issue is not just one for governments. Multinational firms become a big issue. The R&D of multinational companies tends to get done at home (87 percent was in 1991) but most of the jobs are gained where the R&D is used.[27] As firms move the output of R&D more rapidly around the world, there will be more and more government reluctance to help pay for it and greater feelings that national firms are traitors to their fellow citizens—burying research costs in the prices of what they sell but using it to raise someone else's income.

The world clearly needs a new trading system that is in correspondence with today's multipolar reality, a system that can address today's issues of cultural exports and intellectual property rights, but it doesn't have that new trading system. In theory the new World Trade Organization (WTO) set up at Marrakech is supposed to develop those new rules, but it is an empty organization with no leadership and a voting procedure (one country, one vote) that guarantees that it cannot design the new system. Any international organization with 117 members in which Mauritius has as much voting power as the United States or China is not an organization that is going to be able to come to any conclusions.[28] The Uruguay GATT round took years beyond its announced deadlines before a consensus could be reached on what was basically an empty agreement. New rules will be much tougher to negotiate and the world cannot wait decades for them to be set.

The global economy will not wait for the right conference to occur. In the absence of that conference the rules for the new world order are right now being written in Brussels. The Common Market is now the world's largest market, and those who control the conditions of entry into the world's largest market have always written the rules for world trade. That is why Great Britain wrote the rules for world trade in the nineteenth century and the United States wrote them in the twentieth century. An illustration of this new reality can be seen in the "ISO 9000" quality control standards that most of the world's manufacturing firms are trying to achieve. To sell high-precision products on world markets, you must be ISO 9000–certified. ISO 9000 is a European standard that is being applied to the rest of the world. Twenty years ago if there had been such a standard, it would have been drafted in the United States and then imposed on the rest of the world—not drafted in Europe and then imposed on the United States.

To some extent the Common Market will write the rules for world trade simply because it is the only international group now in the rules-writing business. It must write the rules for those inside the European community and tell those outside how they can gain entry. Whatever it writes for outsiders will be copied by others as their rules governing outsiders since they aren't in the business of international rule writing.

While the issues in the GATT–Bretton Woods trading system are crucial, the other institutions of the post–World War II system, the

International Monetary Fund (IMF) and the World Bank, are similarly in flux. Both are floundering in search of a role. The IMF was initially designed to provide temporary balance of payments loans to wealthy industrial countries, yet no major industrial country has borrowed from it in the last two decades. By default it has become the lender of last resort to the third world, but it does not have the resources to stem capital outflows when they occur in places such as Mexico. Its current functions are necessary, but if one were designing an institution to fill its current role, no one would design an institution that looks like the current IMF. The growth of world capital markets and their ability to move massive amounts of money in and out of third world countries, if nothing else, means that the IMF needs to be structured very differently with a lot more funds at its disposal.[29]

The World Bank was designed to finance public infrastructure. The third world still needs to build public sector infrastructure so that the private sector can operate efficiently, but public sector infrastructure lending often effectively ends up supporting something other than public infrastructure. Money is fundable. If the World Bank finances a good project, it is likely that the country would undertake the project in any case, and as a result the World Bank's loan has freed up the country's own resources to spend on whatever it likes. That doesn't happen if the World Bank only funds projects that countries would not otherwise undertake, but if it does so, it finances marginal projects with high failure rates that make the World Bank look stupid.

Since much of the third world believed in socialism until very recently, what they did with their own resources when they were freed up by a World Bank loan (often supporting quasi-public corporations that competed with private corporations) was not to the liking of many politicians or taxpayers—especially conservative American politicians. In response to this criticism the World Bank now has a private sector lending window. But if the lending is to be to the private sector, why does one need a public sector bank? Private sector international banks would be glad to finance any good private sector lending opportunities.

Here again as with the IMF there are real problems in the third world that need first world help, but the institution that needs to be designed to play this role would probably not look like today's World Bank.

DEMOCRACY, THE NATION-STATE, AND A WORLD ECONOMY

While the world is not negotiating a global common market, the whole world essentially has the same needs to coordinate and harmonize that exist in the European Community. In Europe ideology is pushing economics; in the world, economics is pushing ideology. But whatever the direction of forces, the place to which one gets pushed is the same.

Cooperative policies are needed to make the global economy work, but cooperation will require the surrender of a lot of national sovereignty. A cooperative Keynesian locomotive sharply limits government's freedom to act independently in the economic sphere. Interest rates and budget balances have to be agreed upon collectively for some set of countries. Microeconomic systems of government regulations have to be harmonized. Once agreed upon, they cannot be unilaterally altered. What is required to make "cooperation" work is not all that different from what is required to make a formal common market work.

To make a global economy work requires giving up a substantial degree of national sovereignty, but the political Left and Right are both correct when they argue that this is undemocratic. It is undemocratic rule by foreigners or, even worse, rule by international bureaucrats. It could only be democratic if there were an elected democratic world government, yet the Left and the Right would both be the first ones to object to any such government.

As a result, for some period of time the world economy game will be played in an environment where the rules are in flux—and not clearly known. Even when they have been written and are known, it is not clear who will enforce them. Levels of uncertainty escalate enormously in periods of punctuated equilibrium.

Chapter 7

Plate Five: A Multipolar World with No Dominant Power

American post–World War II leadership of global capitalism flowed naturally from America's military position at the end of World War II. In a very real sense the American economy was the world economy. Everyone had to buy from or sell to Americans, since they were the only people with money to spend and had almost two thirds of the world's industrial production capacity.[1] Because the United States had developed atomic weapons and was the only non-Communist economy capable of supporting a large military establishment, there could be no other military leader.

But America's precise economic role flowed out of the particular sequence of events that followed the war. Much as people expected the transition from communism to capitalism to be painless and rapid after the Berlin Wall came down and the USSR imploded, so too people expected economic recovery from World War II to be painless and rapid. It wasn't. The end of the war did not bring quick recoveries among either old allies or newly conquered enemies. The problem was simple. Among both old allies and old enemies, foreign exchange reserves had been exhausted buying the supplies necessary to fight World War II. Not being destroyed by the war, America was the only place left where the equipment could be purchased to repair war-torn economies. To earn the funds necessary to buy the equipment required to rebuild, other countries had to sell something to Americans. But until that new equipment was up and running, nobody had anything to sell that Americans wanted to buy. The system was in gridlock. There was simply no way for foreigners to get the money necessary to buy the equipment that had to be bought if civilian production was to resume.

The answer was a government jump start called the Marshall Plan.

The United States would give its old allies and former enemies the financial resources they needed to finance the purchases of the equipment that was necessary to rebuild war-torn factories. The Marshall Plan worked, but it needs to be remembered that it was initiated in 1948, three years after the war was over.[2] It took a substantial period of time for the realization to sink in that capitalistic self-combustion was not going to happen spontaneously. The repeated economic crises and inability of the economy of Great Britain, America's closest wartime ally, to recover after the war was probably the key event that persuaded American leadership that something had to be done.[3]

Initially the Marshall Plan was offered to the USSR and Eastern Europe, but Marshal Stalin turned the offer down. His announced goal was to build a global Communist economy that would compete with, and eventually overwhelm, capitalism.

The Marshall Plan involved large amounts of money. Payments amounted to 2 percent of the American GDP.[4] On the receiving end, that amounted to 10 percent of the recipients' GDPs. Today a 2 percent of GDP transfer would amount to about $140 billion per year in economic aid. In contrast, America now gives only $8.7 billion in economic and humanitarian aid and $5.3 billion in military aid—0.3 percent of GDP.[5] Even more important than the money was the American commitment to a multiyear solution and the rest of the world's knowledge that the U.S. was fundamentally behind them for the long-run pull back to prosperity.

America's motives were partly altruistic and partly generated by its fears of communism. Over time, if one looks at the rhetoric with which actions were politically defended, fears of communism rose in importance and altruism fell in importance. In the end internationalism was sold in a country of historic isolationism (the United States) as anti-communism. Fifty years later the anti-Communist rhetoric used to sell American internationalism has come to haunt those who still believe in American internationalism. If communism is gone, why should Americans have an international perspective? The Republican "Contract with America" does not contain a single word about international economics, foreign trade, or foreign investment.[6] Perhaps the Contract with America does not call for isolationism, but it certainly calls for a significant American retreat from world leadership.

American leadership of the non-Communist bloc in the immediate aftermath of World War II was a simple necessity, since it was the only large undamaged industrial economy left standing and only it had the military power to resist the expansion of global communism. If a country wanted to stay out of the Communist bloc, it had little choice but to join the American bloc and accept American leadership. Since everyone with the exception of Canada in North America and a few neutrals in Europe (Sweden and Switzerland) needed American aid, the post–World War II capitalistic economy had American leadership built into its very warp and woof. The post–World War II capitalistic economy was designed to swirl around the United States just as much as the post–World War II Communist economy was designed to swirl around the old USSR. Within the non-Communist bloc, no major capitalistic power, not even France, ever became as independent as China was eventually to become within the Communist bloc. Whenever allies threatened to not follow American leadership, the threat of communism could be used to hold the global system together.[7]

If the Marshall Plan was the starter motor, the GATT–Bretton Woods system was the engine of postwar economic growth. Not surprisingly, it echoed what worked for America in its domestic markets. With the United States as its manager, it was an Anglo-Saxon rule-driven, legalistic system. Rules rather than government administrative guidance (the systems used in both Japan and France) were at its center. Economic locomotive power came from the United States. It would provide a large affluent open market to which exporting was easy. Its monetary and fiscal policies would short-circuit recessions and promote vigorous growth.

The United States focused on the alliance's geopolitical military needs (Japan was an unsinkable aircraft carrier on the northern Asian Rim, the plains of northern Europe were where the Russian Army had to be stopped—and it would have been a political and military disaster if either had fallen into the Communist orbit) and let its private companies and its economy take care of themselves.

Being much wealthier and not needing to worry about its balance of payments, it did not have to demand reciprocal rights in other markets. The Japanese could limit American access to the Japanese market and prevent Americans from buying majority ownership in Japanese companies while at the same time getting unlimited access to the U.S. market and the right to buy anything they wanted in America. The

Japanese government could, and did, act as a monopsonistic buyer of technology, pushing down the price of acquiring technology and insisting that licenses be given to everyone—and not just a few "partner" companies. Instead of invoking its antitrust laws and power, America looked the other way.

American companies did not have the American government in their corner because they did not need the American government in their corner. If anything, foreign companies needed U.S. government help in exporting to the American market so that their countries could earn the foreign exchange that they needed to defend themselves from communism. Some of the practices keeping American companies out of Japan, such as those the U.S. auto companies are now trying to change, were actually invented by General MacArthur and his staff.

When the inevitable cyclical downturns of capitalism came, it was an American responsibility to be the unilateral global Keynesian locomotive. Easier monetary policies (lower interest rates) and expansionary fiscal policies (lower taxes or higher spending) were used to speed up the American economy during global recessions. As growth picked up in U.S. markets, exports into America from the rest of the world would automatically rise, starting a recovery elsewhere in the world. As late as the 1982–83 recovery from the 1980–81 recession, most of the economic speedup in both Europe and Japan could be traced to more exports to the U.S. markets.

The explicit goal of the post–World War II system was to create an environment where other countries could become as rich as the United States. It happened. Exact measures of how many countries are richer than the United States in terms of per capita GDP depend upon whether the evaluation is made using market exchange rates or purchasing power parities to convert different GDPs into some common measure, but by either measure there are now a substantial number of countries that are effectively equally wealthy and on both measures a few that are much wealthier.

Both calculations reflect part of the truth. Purchasing power parity (PPP) calculations measure how rich Americans are vis-à-vis the rest of the world when everyone is spending their money at home. They measure the local costs of buying an identical basket of goods and services in different countries and ask what the exchange rate would have to be to make the amount of income that would be needed to buy those two baskets the same. (Since people in different countries don't buy exactly the same basket of goods and services, exact measures of PPP differ depending upon what basket of goods and services is being used.)

Market exchange rate calculations of per capita GDPs indicate how rich people are when they spend their money abroad. If an average American takes his dollar income to Japan and exchanges it for yen, how much would he be able to buy relative to what the average Japanese buys? Conversely, if the average Japanese took her yen income to America and exchanged it for dollars, how much would she be able to buy?

Japan is the country where there is the biggest difference between the two measures. Using the U.S. per capita GDP of $25,847 in 1994 as a base, Japan has a purchasing power parity per capita GDP just 79 percent that of the United States ($20,526).[8] Yet when evaluated at exchange rates, it had a per capita GDP 80 percent larger ($46,583) when the yen was at 80 to the dollar.[9] When the market was placing a value of 80 yen to the dollar, the OECD's purchasing power parity calculations were indicating that exchange rates ought to be between 180 and 225 yen to the dollar.[10] As a result, the Japanese are affluent at home but very rich when traveling abroad.

As the world recovered from the destruction of World War II and parts of the rest of the world caught up with the United States economically, the American fraction of the world's GDP obviously had to fall. Instead of representing more than 50 percent of world GDP as it was as late as 1960, the United States now represents slightly less than 25 percent of world GDP if market exchange rates are used to make the calculations.[11] It was inevitable that U.S. leadership was gradually going to wane as its economy grew smaller relative to the rest of the world. The first twenty-five years after World War II were unique in the degree of economic weakness found in the rest of the industrial world. This period reflected not American superiority but the destruction of World War II.

In addition to representing a smaller part of the world's GDP, the United States is now the world's second largest market, with the European Common Market holding the first position. Given several equally wealthy and one larger economy, it is not surprising that the rest of the world is less willing to follow American economic leadership at exactly the time that the United States is less willing to offer leadership. The rest of the capitalistic world simply does not need the United States as much as it did in the past. It is now much easier to say no.

THE IMPLOSION OF THE USSR

With the USSR imploding into fifteen different countries, with Russia's military withdrawal eastward thousands of kilometers from central Europe, and the inability of the Russian Army to even police their vastly reduced domains in places like Chechenya, there simply is no Communist military threat that forces capitalistic countries to huddle together under the U.S. military umbrella. Other countries don't need U.S. military protection.

At the height of the cold war in Europe, NATO was seen as an alliance for keeping the Russians out, the Americans in, and the Germans down. But why keep the Americans in if the Russians are gone and the Germans are up—unified and by far the strongest economic and military power in Europe. Whatever one believes about the possibilities that Russia will eventually regain its balance and become a military power, and hence threat, that remote possibility is decades in the future. It would take decades to build an economy that could support a large modern army and decades to rebuild a military force that has completely disintegrated. The Russian military bear may not be extinct, but it is clearly near extinction, and would require a very long time to again become a formidable force.

In the Far East, defense budgets are growing very rapidly. North Korea neatly illustrates the problems of U.S. leadership. Given the possession of plutonium, nuclear weapons are easy to make. Systems for delivering nuclear bombs to distant targets, however, are very difficult and expensive to produce. Realistically, a North Korean bomb only threatens China, Russia, Japan, and South Korea. If those countries don't want to take actions to deal with a possible North Korean bomb, why should Americans undertake that responsibility? A North Korean bomb does not threaten America. During the cold war both the Soviet Union and the United States would have cracked down on North Korea, since both knew that if North Korea dropped a bomb on South

Korea the probability of thousands of missiles flying between the United States and the Soviet Union was simply too high to tolerate.

The flipping and flopping in American foreign policy in the Korean peninsula should come as no surprise given the death of the Soviet empire. There simply isn't a straightforward American national interest at stake. What replaces "containment" as the central core of American policy? A reflexive American leadership wants to be seen to be leading but is not willing to put in the military and diplomatic effort with either the North Koreans or the neighboring countries that should be directly concerned to solve the problem. The problem was simply diplomatically declared "solved" when it clearly was not.

While explicit threats (America won't militarily protect you if you don't go along with it on economic issues) were never made during the cold war, they did not have to be. Without being told, everyone knew that they could only diverge from American leadership so far without getting into trouble. But those implicit constraints on disagreeing with U.S. leadership are over. As a result, the United States cannot implicitly use its military power to bolster its leadership.

Looking at raw military power, it may be true that no country has ever had so much military power vis-à-vis any conceivable enemy or even the whole rest of the world as the United States has in the mid-1990s. America is the only military superpower with nuclear weapons, sophisticated delivery systems, and global logistical capabilities. With its satellite technology and its ability to interrupt the communications systems of any or all of its enemies and friends, no one could conceivably believe that they could inflict serious damage on the United States itself without knowing that the United States could erase them and their country from the face of the globe.

But all of that military power is essentially unusable and irrelevant in the era ahead. President Bush had a strategy for maintaining U.S. leadership. America would become the policeman for the world. He intervened in the Persian Gulf to show how the United States could lead and what it could do with its modern weapons. He did not intervene in Bosnia to show the Europeans that they still needed U.S. leadership. Both lessons were vividly true—but irrelevant. Being a world policeman requires a country to be willing to use force and when forces are used some of those forces will die or at least have to be risked. When the great powers cannot even police the tiny warlords of Somalia, since a few deaths would have been required, something has changed dramatically.

Given America's isolationist history, President Bush's vision of America being a world policeman was probably always unrealistic, but TV makes that role impossible. Logically, it makes no difference whether one learns about his country's soldiers dying in the local newspaper or on the local TV news programs. But visually and emotively, it is very different. People care a lot more about deaths when soldiers are dying in real time on the TV than they ever did when those deaths appeared in their newspapers.[12] The result has been to severely limit governments' ability to deploy their troops—even in conflicts where death rates will be very low and even though every one of those troops are volunteers who presumably signed up for a career in the armed forces because they wanted to be in a risky profession. Even the Russians in Chechenya found that fighting a war on TV is very different from fighting a war in the newspapers.[13] Russian mothers did not like watching their sons die any more than American mothers want to watch their sons die.

TV no longer reflects reality, it is reality. If starving Somalian children are on TV, the world wants to do something about it. If they aren't on TV, they don't exist and nothing is done. At the time when the world's media forced an intervention in Somalia, there were many places on the globe with more chaos and more starving children. Today the chaos is just as bad in Somalia but the media are gone—and so are the U.S. and UN troops. The results are schizophrenic. The public wants their government to do something in Somalia, but does not want to see any of their troops injured.

Bosnia is another example. It is not Vietnam (a country of 100 million people covering more than two thousand miles north to south). It is a very small country with 4 million people. If more than 500,000 NATO troops were there, as they were in the Persian Gulf War, there would be a NATO soldier under every tree in Bosnia. Yet no one wanted to commit troops until ethnic cleansing and exhaustion had run their course.

Recognizing the political fallout from casualties, the military high command has been on the side of those who do not want to do anything in Bosnia. But if deaths are intolerable, the leadership of the American military will have to face up to the reality that the American voter will eventually come to understand that he is paying for a large defense establishment that will never be used. A large army, navy, and air force may be necessary if the United States is going to be a world leader and at least occasionally use its military power, but if the military's only job is defeating those who directly threaten America, then America needs only a very small army, navy, and air force. There are no current external threats to America and any such threat would take an enormous time-consuming military buildup on someone's part. As that buildup occurred, the United States would have plenty of time to rebuild its military establishment after any sharp cutbacks. Unknown distant future threats are not a reason for spending so much money on the military now. America certainly has military power, but it is completely unable to use it unless someone directly threatens the United States and no one does.

Attitudes and speech patterns remain in place long after they no longer reflect reality. No matter how many speeches are made proclaiming that it won't happen, NATO will fade away as an important American-led military alliance. With the Soviet Union gone, Europe's problems and perspectives are not America's problems and perspectives. The American taxpayers simply aren't going to pay for the defense of those richer than themselves from an enemy that cannot be specified or imagined. On the other side, Europe doesn't want the shock of a rapid American withdrawal, but it no longer wants Americans running European military and foreign policies.

AMERICA'S TRADE DEFICIT

Theoretically, trade surpluses and deficits should have little or nothing to do with global leadership. The American economy is doing very well. In the first half of the 1990s, it was the fastest-growing economy in the industrial world. Its trade deficit is a very small tail on a very big economic dog. Technically, America's trade deficit is not a constraint on anything it might want to do. But the reality is otherwise. The unwillingness of the United States to do anything about its trade deficit in the long run substantially undercuts its ability to exercise global leadership.

Because the United States has allowed a system to develop where it directly runs a large trade deficit with Japan and allows the rest of the world to finance their large trade deficits with Japan by running trade surpluses with the United States, the foreign exchange markets systematically trade dollars for foreign currencies at rates that grossly undervalue the dollar if one looks at measures of purchasing power parity. Since Americans pay for their excess of imports over exports with dollars, large supplies of dollars flow into the world's financial markets that are not counterbalanced by demands for dollars, and this surplus of dollars has to push the dollar down. In the long run the dollar must continually fall until the current account deficit has been eliminated.

While a falling dollar does not affect American living standards very much (a 5 percent fall in the value of the dollar raises consumer prices only 0.2 percent), a lower-valued dollar makes it much more expensive for the United States to engage in international activities. Dollars have less international purchasing power and more dollars have to be spent. To some extent influence is bought, and buying influence becomes more expensive for Americans. America's political and military power simply costs much more if it is to be exercised.[14] As it becomes more expensive, Americans buy less. An undervalued falling dollar basically leads to less American influence than there ought to be, given America's efficiency and productivity.

With a falling dollar, from the perspective of the American taxpayer, it looks like he or she is having to pay more taxes to finance America's external activities. He is subsidizing the world and paying for activities (American troops in Europe or Japan, dealing with North Korean atomic weapons) that benefit those with per capita income as high or higher than his. He is living in a world where he loses more jobs to imports than he gains through exports. He is a sucker.

Having to ask Germany and Japan to pay for the Persian Gulf War makes Americans into hired mercenaries even if we don't like to think of ourselves in those terms. America's place as the world's largest giver of foreign aid is lost to Japan, not because Japan has increased its foreign aid budget, but simply because the value of the yen has risen vis-à-vis the dollar.[15] Japan effortlessly supplants the United States when it comes to buying influence with foreign aid in the third world.

The same loss of power occurs in the private sector. With a falling dollar, fewer foreigners want to hold dollar assets and that lowers the power and influence of American banks. Foreign investments become much more expensive for American corporations, and American investments become much cheaper for foreign corporations. When it comes to who can afford to buy whose assets, the balance of power tips away from Americans.

Because of the intractability of Japan's surpluses with the United States and the rest of the world (the American deficit cannot disappear unless the Japanese surplus disappears), a falling dollar has done little or nothing to correct America's trade deficit. Given this reality, there is only one direction in which the dollar can move in the long run, down, even if purchasing power parity calculations would indicate that it is already grossly undervalued.

At some point a falling dollar has to lead the rest of the world to quit holding dollars as foreign exchange reserves (anyone holding dollars is going to get back much less than they initially put into dollars), quit pricing their foreign trade in dollars (profits go down as the selling price for one's goods declines with the falling dollar), quit investing in America (American assets are cheap but they are becoming cheaper and those who buy now will take large capital losses), and demand repayment of their existing loans as they come due. All of these reactions undercut both America's willingness and its ability to be a global leader.

If the European currency unit (now called the ECU but in the future to be called the Euro) had been in place as the currency of a unified Europe in the winter of 1994 and spring of 1995, it would probably have replaced the dollar as the reserve currency of choice in world trade. In the aftermath of the Mexican crisis, people wanted out of dollars since they were taking enormous losses on their dollar-denominated investments and transactions but there was no place to go. No individual European currency is large enough to offer the necessary degree of liquidity and Japan's closed markets make it impossible to earn the yen that firms or governments would need if the yen were to become the reserve currency.

From the point of view of preserving world leadership, one can make a strong case that Americans should do what is necessary at home and abroad to preserve the value of the dollar and to maintain its role as the world's reserve currency of choice.[16] If the dollar loses its position as the world's reserve currency, America loses much of its freedom of action. America could run out of foreign exchange reserves in exactly the same sense that Mexico ran out in late 1994 and find the rest of the world dictating its internal economic policies just as the rest of the world dictated Mexico's domestic policies in 1995. But Americans aren't going to act.

In the rest of the world, governments adopt painful policies to stop currency values from falling, since there are enormous domestic public pressures to act. But in the United States there are no pressures to act.

In the rest of the world a falling currency means possible bankruptcy for private companies or public authorities whose loans are denominated in foreign currencies. If the Mexican peso falls 50 percent in value, peso earnings have to double to pay interest and repay principal or the firm goes broke. Not surprisingly, those who are about to go broke pressure their government to protect the value of its currency—to protect the existence of their investments and their personal wealth. In the American case, with dollar-denominated loans those who suffer losses when the dollar plunges are not the American borrowers but the foreign lenders whose loans are now worth much less when evaluated in their own currencies—but they don't vote in America.

In the rest of the world inflation accelerates when currency values fall. Import prices rise and since imports are a large fraction of consumption, the consumer price index rises right along with imports. That reduces the real purchasing power of wages. Workers ask for higher wages in compensation for higher import prices, but if they get higher wages that just further accelerates the rate of inflation. Real incomes have to be reduced, since those with falling currency values (higher import prices) have less claim on the goods and services produced by the rest of the world. Foreign citizens demand action to stop their currencies from falling to protect the real value of their purchasing power and to stop inflation.

But something very different happens in the United States. Since foreign firms are unwilling to give up their large American sales when their currencies rise, they hold dollar prices constant to preserve their American sales. Essentially they are willing to accept lower profits when evaluated in their home currencies as a necessary cost of protecting their American sales. For Japanese auto manufacturers, losing $1,000 per car but more than covering marginal costs may be much better than losing three million American car sales and having to start very painful structural readjustments. As a result, import prices rise relatively little even when the dollar plunges.

While the real-trade-weighted value of the dollar fell 33 percent in the decade from 1984 to 1994, the prices of imports rose only 11 percent. Since America imports about 12 percent of its GDP, imports added only 1.2 percentage points of inflation to the 28 points of inflation (as measured by the implicit price deflator for the GDP) that occurred over this time period.[17] If those imports had been made in domestic industries (where the average price increase over the decade was 31 percent), those same products would have added 3.7 percentage points to the overall inflation rate and the American inflation rate would have been 2.5 percentage points higher than it was. As a result, imports were holding down, not pushing up, domestic prices despite the falling value of the dollar.

Since a falling dollar does not cause American inflation rates to accelerate, those who think that they lose when inflation accelerates have no interest in lobbying for a strong dollar. They have much more to lose from the higher interest rates necessary to stop the dollar from falling than they have to gain from a stronger dollar. And voters certainly have no abstract interest in paying the higher taxes or in getting fewer public services—both of which would be necessary to balance the budget—that the austerity programs demanded by the rest of the world would require.

Since domestic economic necessity cannot be invoked to justify defending the dollar, to do so, an American administration would have to persuade the American public that world leadership was at stake and that preserving world leadership justified the painful policies that would cut American standards of living. Some leaders would have to make the argument that the surplus of imports over exports that the American consumer now enjoys is not worth the price that Americans will eventually have to pay. In the end, the resulting debts will have to be paid by selling off America's assets cheap (America's capitalistic inheritance if you will) and by having less influence and less leadership in both the public and private sectors in the world economy. But politically, this argument would be very difficult to make since Americans have come to believe that world leadership is their "birthright," as it were, and they are not sure that they want to be world leaders anyway.

A NEW WORLD TRADING SYSTEM

The GATT–Bretton Woods trading system was an American-dominated system that swirled around America. But that system has come to the end of its natural life. There simply aren't many more formal tariffs and quotas on industrial goods to dismantle.[18] The system could be expanded to include agricultural products (a declining sector), but the service trade, the world's growth sector, is not inhibited by formal tariffs and quotas. Restrictions exist but they are deeply embedded in legal systems, government actions, and business practices that are not easily amenable to systemwide prohibitions such as those that force tariff reductions.

What matters now are issues like sales of movies in Europe, intellectual property rights in China, the persistent trade surpluses of Japan—none of which GATT is capable of solving. Each of these three issues required bilateral negotiations in the year immediately after the Uruguay round was negotiated, signed, and ratified precisely because the Uruguay round did not deal with any of the larger issues. Most important, GATT did not deal with the issue of building a new set of rules to govern world trade in today's multipolar world of regional trading blocs.

By the very realities of what it needs to do, any new trading system will inevitably reduce the U.S. role in the world economy, since many of America's dominant positions, such as large allocations of voting rights in institutions like the World Bank or the IMF, were given to it after World War II when it possessed a much bigger fraction of the world GDP than it does now. In any new system, the United States will have fewer voting rights and less influence. Once negotiations on a new trading system opened and it became clear to the American public how much of its former power and current leadership position it would lose, the public would be very unlikely to support whatever new arrangements were agreed upon. The decline in relative power that these new agreements would reflect has already occurred, but they would be the equivalent of putting America's relative decline up in neon lights.

The single-polar world that lies at the heart of the old system is gone and a multipolar world has emerged. A paper organization, the World Trade Organization (WTO), has been created to draw up the rules for this new multipolar economy, but by its very nature the WTO (an organization where each country has one vote) is incapable of writing the new rules necessary for a multipolar world. Effectively, there is no world trading system for the United States to manage even if it were willing to do so. And the United States could not create a new system even if it wanted to. Unlike the Bretton Woods period (1944), it cannot force everyone to come to the table, sit them down, rap them on the knuckles, and make them agree to an American-designed trading system that would fit today's realities.

The Mexican financial crisis in late 1994 and early 1995 illustrates the problems. Since Mexico was America's neighbor and NAFTA partner, President Clinton had no choice but to design and lead a rescue plan through the new Republican Congress. He then designed a new plan that relied much more heavily on funds from the IMF. America's old European allies refused to vote for the plan. Both the first proposal and the final plan brought speculative attacks on the dollar. The international financial community was essentially willing to bet its money that the United States was not capable of rescuing Mexico. The king was dead, but there was no new king.

THE END OF AMERICAN INTERNATIONALISM?

Since internationalism was sold as anticommunism in the United States, the demise of communism permits the rise of what might be called the new American isolationism.[19] The new isolationism is not a dramatic sudden shift from the patterns of the 1980s back to the patterns of the 1930s but a slow withdrawal from international responsibilities, where at each stage of the withdrawal there will be vigorous denials that any withdrawal is occurring. But much as the impact of plate tectonics on the surface of the earth cannot be seen as it is occurring, if one looks backward a few years one sees dramatically different American responses to similar events.

Nothing could be a better illustration of this reality than the contrast between the American response in the Persian Gulf and its response to the war in Bosnia. If Saddam Hussein had just held off a few years and were invading Kuwait now, no one would be doing anything. With the collapse of the USSR, Persian Gulf oil is no longer essential—certainly not to America. Bosnia would be demanding attention; two interventions could not be accomplished simultaneously. Commentators would quickly point out that protecting a medieval Middle Eastern kingdom in a country carved out of Iraq by British colonial masters was a very strange cause for risking American lives.

That gradual shift in attitudes was first seen in the 1992 presidential debates between Bill Clinton and George Bush. President Clinton insisted that he would be a domestic President. President Bush promised to continue being an international President. Bush lost. His demonstrated international success in the Persian Gulf War just a few months earlier bought him nothing when it came voting time in November of 1992.

After being elected in 1994, the new Republican Congress started off by announcing that it was against many of the international institutions that lie at the heart of today's global system. Payments were to be eliminated for new UN peacekeeping operations and funding from old operations was to be cut from 31 to 20 percent.[20] No American troops were to be placed under "foreign" command.[21] These proposals would essentially end UN peacekeeping missions. No American funds were to be given to multilateral banks such as the World Bank or the Asian Development Bank. The Arms Control and Disarmament Agency and the Agency for International Development were to be terminated along with the Voice of America and Radio Marti. Aid to Russia and the other ex-Soviet republics as well as to Turkey, Greece, Cyprus, and Ireland was to be phased out over a five-year period of time.

Military spending is to be raised on a "Star Wars" antimissile defense system to protect America from "rogue dictatorships like North Korea" (a very unlikely event since intercontinental missiles are much harder to build than nuclear weapons), yet no American troops are to engage in peacekeeping missions—the only kind of military activity that is likely to occur.[22] Most of the techniques used by America to exercise leadership since World War II would be eliminated.[23] Aid to Turkey, Greece, and Cyprus, for example, was part of our effort to keep the eastern end of the Mediterranean peaceful and bring about a settlement of the Cyprus dispute between Greece and Turkey (both members of NATO). While verbally maintaining that Congress is still interested in global U.S. leadership, the American military budget is to be reshaped for the twenty-first century version of an isolationistic America in the Contract with America. A few rogue Republicans joined with the Democrats to vote down the Star Wars proposal, but it remains to be seen what will happen when funds are actually appropriated. Without the use of troops or money, there is a much reduced leadership role for the United States in the twenty-first century.

One of the 1996 Republican presidential contenders, Pat Buchanan, even talks about "a New World Order to restore our sovereignty."[24] What the rest of the world would see as their expanding legitimate influence on world decisions in the era ahead, he sees as America giving up its rightful decision-making ability to others.

None of this, of course, stopped those same Republicans from complaining when America's European allies insisted on giving one of the jobs traditionally held by an American, the head of UNESCO, to a European. Rhetorically, the age of American leadership is not over. To court the twenty-three million American voters of middle and Eastern European origin, both Republicans and Democrats talk about expanding NATO to include countries such as Poland but then vote to cut the infrastructure investments (bases, communications systems) that are necessary to maintain NATO. It is very clear that no one would vote to spend the $20 to $50 billion that it would cost to expand NATO coverage eastward.[25] The new Republican Congress would certainly vote against stationing more U.S. troops in Eastern Europe.

The threat to American leadership can be seen in the Middle Eastern peace process. President Clinton promised to cancel $275 million in Jordanian debt to persuade Jordan to sign a peace treaty with Israel. The Republican Congress initially threatened to reduce this to $50 million—a more than fivefold reduction.[26] Clinton was also clearly told by the Congress not to attempt to buy Syria's cooperation in the peace process. Buying peace in the Middle East was okay when there was a threat from the USSR to intervene and America was competing with the USSR for Arab allegiance, but peace was not worth buying now that the threat of communism has disappeared. Why should non-Jewish American taxpayers be generous in paying for peace between Israel and Arabs? Let them fight if they wish, the Russians won't jump in, and whatever happens, it won't affect America anyway. But in the process America will also have lost its ability to be a leader for peace in the Middle East.

Leadership implies burdens as well as power. One of those burdens is a lesser ability than countries that are not world leaders to focus on one's narrow short-term economic self-interest. If a country is so weak, or feels so weak, that it has to focus exclusively on its own short-run self-interest, it cannot be a global leader. Factually, America is not so weak; it could rather easily rebuild itself to become a high-investment society, but psychologically it seems to feel so weak that it cannot act domestically or internationally.

In the mid-1990s the United States stands where the United Kingdom stood at the end of World War I. It is no longer willing, or maybe no longer able, to do what it once did. Unlike then, there is now no country in the wings capable of taking over, if only it would. The United States' post–World War II role was partly determined by its economic size and its military power, but only partly. Its language is the world's business language, its system of higher education is open to foreigners, and its mass media dominate the world—all of these underlay its leadership.[27] Looking forward, no other country or set of countries has anything close to the necessary set of ingredients to be a global leader.

If Europe was really one country with a unified foreign policy, it might be able take over the post–World War II role of the United States. The ECU or as it is now to be known, Euro, could, for example, replace the dollar. But it isn't. For at least the next half century, Europe will not be a world leader, since it will have to concentrate on consummating its own unification. European unification, including adding middle and Eastern Europe into the European Community, will take all of its funds, all of its public attention, and all of its leadership time. Military problems in its own backyard, such as Bosnia, will prevent it from having any interest in military problems farther away—such as atomic weapons in North Korea.

As the second largest economy in the world, Japan is a candidate for global leadership, but Japan has no global military capability and more important, no political interest in much of the world. It is not going to wrestle with the Bosnian problem, the Rwanda problem, or even problems such as North Korea in its immediate neighborhood. But even if these realities did not exist, it still could not be a global leader without fundamentally reshaping its economy and society. A global leader has to have an economy and a society that outsiders can both understand and penetrate. Japan is neither.

To be a reserve currency, for example, the rest of the world has to be able to run trade surpluses with the reserve currency country so that they can accumulate the currency reserves that they need. In the case of the yen, Japan can force economically weaker countries that trade with it to accept debt in yen terms (it has done so in much of east Asia), but the percentage of debts denominated in yen should not be confused with the yen becoming the reserve currency of choice. It cannot be a currency of choice until other countries can voluntarily accumulate yen reserves, and that cannot happen unless those countries are able to run trade surpluses with Japan.

In the spring of 1995 both China and Indonesia were complaining about the imbalances between their yen-denominated debt and their dollar-denominated sales.[28] In Indonesia's case 40 percent of its $90 billion in debt was yen-denominated, its yen obligations rose $350 billion for every 1 percent rise in the value of the yen, but most of its sales were to the United States and denominated in dollars. Standards of living would have to go down in Indonesia to pay those larger Japanese debts. Countries such as Indonesia can be forced to accept yen-denominated debt, but they will not voluntarily choose to have their trade denominated in yen until most of their sales are in yen.

In the latter years of the Roman Empire, Germans often commanded Roman armies. Just as imperial Rome had to have a system for making talented people from its conquered territories into Roman citizens, so any global leader has to have a system for making talented foreigners into the equivalent of citizens. If one looks at American immigration policies, American universities, or American business firms, they absorb talented foreigners very easily.

Japan is precisely the opposite. It is the country in the world where it is hardest to become a Japanese citizen, hardest to get into a good Japanese university as a regular student, and hardest for foreigners to become CEOs of Japanese companies. All of Japanese society would have to be rebuilt before Japan could become a global leader.

At the same time, Japan's practices make leadership impossible for anyone else. The inability of foreigners to successfully export into Japan or to own successful firms in Japan effectively makes it impossible for anyone else to lead. If the United States is not big enough to carry the trade deficit that the Japanese surplus requires, who else can?

HOLDING THE SYSTEM TOGETHER
WITHOUT A LEADER

Social systems are held together by a number of forces. Common language and religion are two of those forces, but they are not enough—witness the Mideast, where the Arabs speak the same language, have the same religion, belong to the same ethnic group yet are divided into numerous warring countries. In China, by way of contrast, the world's largest group of homogeneous people have stayed together as one society for four thousand years with the help of a unifying ideology (the Confucian system) that preaches integration and not individualism. Both the Christian and Muslim religions, which stress the personal ties between God and man, are too individualistic to hold societies together by themselves. In both Christian and Muslim societies, warring with those of the same religion is even more common than warring with those of a different religion.

A powerful outside conqueror can hold antithetical groups together. The outside threat of communism unified the countries inside the American bloc. Some were democracies; some weren't. Some believed in market economies; some didn't. Some were rich; some were poor. What they all had in common was a desire to stay outside of the orbit of communism. But without a unifying ideology, once the outside threat goes away unity quickly disappears.

To last for very long any social system needs to be buttressed by a powerful integrating ideology. The Romans were building a "great" empire; the ancient Egyptians were searching for eternal life. All such ideologies postulate some goal bigger than either the individual or the local ethnic group to which the individual belongs. Communism was such an ideology for a short period of time. It lasted for a much shorter time than any of these other older ideologies, probably because it postulated an earthly goal—a higher material standard of living—that was easily checkable and upon which it could not deliver.

When both outside threats and the unifying ideologies disappear, the next step is to find unity by directing anger against some set of despised insiders. Yugoslavia illustrates the phenomenon. With communism dead and with no external threat from the old USSR, they could afford to start fighting among themselves. America's version of ethnic cleansing, Proposition 187 in California, targets immigrants, legal and illegal, who are to be denied government services.[29] They are the despised group. The Contract with America targets the poor—whom it claims are poor because they are lazy. More than half of the $9.4 billion in budget cuts passing the House ($5.7 billion to be precise) came from low-income housing programs alone.[30] They are the despised group.

Unfortunately, neither capitalism nor democracy is a unifying ideology. Both are process ideologies that assert that if one follows the recommended processes one will be better off than if one does not. They have no "common good," no common goals, toward which everyone is collectively working. Both stress the individual and not the group. Workers are expected to maximize their own incomes—quitting whenever wages are higher somewhere else. Firms are expected to maximize their own profits—firing workers whenever it will raise profits. Voters are expected to vote their self-interest. Neither imposes an obligation to worry about the welfare of the other.

When anyone talks about societies being organic wholes, something more than the statistical summation of their individual members' wants and achievements, both capitalists and democrats assert that there is no such thing. In both, individual freedom dominates community obligations. All political or economic transactions are voluntary. If an individual does not want to vote, or buy something, that is his or her right. If citizens want to be greedy and vote their narrow self-interest at the expense of others, that is their right. In the most rigorous expressions of capitalistic ethics, crime is simply another economic activity that happens to have a high price (jail) if one is caught. There is no social obligation to obey the law. There is nothing that one "ought" not to do. Duties and obligations do not exist. Only market transactions exist.

In the past half century the capitalistic world economy has been held together not by the ideology of capitalism but by the fear of communism and the resulting power and leadership of the United States.

What happens when a dominant ideology collapses and is replaced with ethnic nationalism can be clearly seen in the old USSR and Eastern Europe.

In the old capitalistic economy, without leadership we see a similar, if slower, unraveling. Ethnic regionalism (in Scotland, Wales, Quebec; northern versus southern Italy; the Bretons and Corsicans; the Catalans; the Basques) is on the march everywhere. Every failure leads to more failures. NATO is a lesser institution because of its inability to deal with Bosnia. Other restive ethnic groups will now be quicker to resort to arms. Similarly, the inability to quickly contain the Mexican financial crisis means that financial markets will be more aggressive in the future in attacking the IMF or American efforts to contain future instabilities. The dollar is seen as weaker because the countries such as Germany that did not vote for the American IMF plan to rescue Mexico are expected to get even by not spending their money to support the dollar when it is attacked.[31] Whether that unwillingness actually exists doesn't really matter. What matters is that market players think that the dollar won't automatically receive the support from other central banks that it has gotten in the past.

Today there are no threats, no ideologies, and no leaders strong enough to hold the world system together. The net result is the end of communism, the end of the GATT–Bretton Woods system, a world of economic parity, a world where no one can allow their troops to die if their national existence is not at stake, a lack of unifying ideologies, and the unconstrained individuality of democracy and capitalism. A world without unifying ties and global political leadership.

It is easy to bemoan the fact that President Clinton isn't a gutsy give-'em-hell, do-what's-right Harry Truman; that Prime Minister John Major caves in on the moral issues in Bosnia while Prime Minister Margaret Thatcher stiffened President Bush's backbone during the Persian Gulf War; that Prime Minister Helmut Kohl doesn't lead the Germans in playing the role in Eastern Europe that the overseas Chinese play in China; that President Jacques Chirac doesn't have the vision of President Charles de Gaulle; and that the Japanese prime ministers are the invisible men on the world stage. When one sees weak leaders everywhere, it says more about the times than it does about the individuals.[32]

Their lack of leadership reflects neither their character nor their leadership skills, although they may be defective in both. Whatever their personal defects, those defects play only a marginal role. In a period of punctuated equilibrium there are no leaders, since no one clearly understands the threats—or the opportunities of the environment. Everything is in flux with no constant points from which political leverage can be gained.

Surveys of American leaders show that even among the leadership cadres there is no consensus as to what the objectives of American foreign policy should be. With the exception of stemming nuclear proliferation, and even this issue only commands 70 percent support, nothing gets majority support.[33] No one can lead public opinion unless they know how the game is played and what it takes to be a winner—and no one does.

The new electronic information technologies also make it much harder to lead. To rule it is necessary to have a degree of miracle, mystery, and authority, but to be elected one must come into the voter's living room on their TV sets as the average likable man. One of the harsh realities about the electronic media is that it chews up its stars as fast as it creates them. No one has a long half-life as the star of the program. With leaders this means probing into their personal lives to prove that they are not the paragons of virtue that they must pretend to be when elected. It is clear that few of America's past greats could pass moral muster today (Jefferson with a possible black mistress, Benjamin Franklin with a possible teenage lover). Few knew that Franklin Roosevelt could walk only with great difficulty. Everyone knows about every wart on President Clinton.

A lack of leadership causes an ever greater lack of leadership. The more chaotic the world looks, the less the citizens of any one country want their leaders spending their time trying to clean up what looks more and more like a hopeless global mess. Yet if someone is not managing the world trading system and putting pressure on those who are abusing the system, it is clear that the world trading system gradually atrophies and eventually collapses. In a period of punctuated equilibrium with an as yet unclear evolving new environment, potential leaders don't know where to go and followers simply have no reason to follow.

Psychiatrist Ronald Heifetz, a Harvard researcher on leadership, finds that "any constituency that is frightened will fall prey to people with easy answers . . . Leadership means engaging with people in facing up to important problems." But what are the important problems when the world is changing? "Authorities get rewarded for having answers and frequently are not rewarded for saying 'I don't know.'"[34] But who knows when no one genuinely can know? "We look to authorities to maintain the equilibrium of the social group. It's not about arriving. You're involved in an ongoing process of adaptive change."[1] But who is in the group and what adaptations are necessary?

In a period of punctuated equilibrium the survival characteristics of a mammal are wanted, but even today biologists cannot tell precisely what the characteristics were that allowed mammals to survive in the new environment when the dinosaurs disappeared. If the experts don't know looking backward, how can the individual know looking forward?

If one looks at great historical leaders, one sees that they have only arisen when there are potential followers who understand that something has to be done and know approximately what that something is. Consider Winston Churchill—perhaps the greatest leader the British have ever had. Churchill became a leader in World War II. Before that he was a politician with the same leadership skills but without a country that was willing to follow him. He was perpetually in the political wilderness, often tossed out of office. After the war his leadership was quickly rejected, since he wanted to go where the British did not wish to go (preserve the British Empire and resist the social welfare state). He very quickly reverted to being a leader without followers and was defeated despite what everyone acknowledged was his great leadership during the war. Leaders without followers are not leaders. In theory leaders can create followers, but even in normal times the latter is difficult and in periods of punctuated equilibrium it is impossible. Followership almost always creates leadership; leadership only seldom creates followership.

Modern technology has also made it harder to lead. In the past, since no one knew with any accuracy whether the political parade existed and where it was going, ignorance forced a degree of leadership. To have any sense of where the parade was going, one had to organize it and lead it before the parade had formed.

To know where the parade is going today, leaders don't have to be the organizers of the parade. With modern statistical polling and the sophisticated statistical computer analysis, it is possible using public opinion polls and focus groups to look like a leader without having to lead. The pollster (any politician's most important adviser) tells the politician where the public parade is going so that the politician can jump to the front of the parade and look like a leader while he is in fact a follower.

The Republican Contract with America was fashioned in focus groups and no item was left in the contract unless it achieved a favorable rating of 60 percent or higher.[36] Newt Gingrich jumped to the head of the parade and looked like a leader. Yet he was in reality a follower. Given the ease with which it is now possible to look like a real leader without being a real leader, why would anyone want to be a real leader? Real leadership consists of changing the direction of the parade or in getting a new parade organized—something so risky that few want to try. After all, a statesman who isn't reelected isn't a statesman.

The rhetoric of being a world leader is still there. In the words of Newt Gingrich: "Only America can lead the world. America remains the only global, universal civilization in the history of mankind . . . Without a vibrant American civilization, barbarism, violence and dictatorship will increase across the planet."[37] But the reality has melted away.

Our only modern experience of a multipolar world without a dominant leader occurred between the First and Second World Wars. Communist Russia; fascist Germany, Japan, and Italy; and democratic-capitalistic Great Britain, France, and the United States collided in a world without a center of gravity. The results were not happy. Looking at the chaos between World War I and World War II, many would ascribe it to the fact that Britain had quit being the manager of the global system and the United States was not yet willing to assume the responsibilities of global leadership. When the system started falling apart early in the 1920s no one felt that they were responsible for seeing that the disasters of the late 1920s and the 1930s were avoided.

Chapter 8

The Forces Remaking the Economic Surface of the Earth

Having explored each of the five economic plates, we can now understand the tectonic forces that are so dramatically altering the distribution of earnings and wealth. Analysis has to start with the war against inflation. Declared in the mid 1970s; still under way twenty-five years later.

The 1970s and 1980s were inflationary decades. Inflation began with the misfinancing of the Vietnam War, accelerated with the OPEC oil shock and food shocks in the mid-1970s, accelerated and widened because of the use of cost-of-living indexes to adjust wages in labor contracts and prices in supplier contracts, and was then propelled forward by the second OPEC oil shock at the end of the 1970s. While other remedies such as wage and price controls were initially tried, none worked, and eventually all of the world's industrial countries came to the conclusion that the only cure for inflation was to use higher interest rates and tighter fiscal policies (higher taxes or lower expenditures) to deliberately slow growth, to push unemployment up, to force wages down, to keep prices under control.

While the execution of this strategy was sometimes fitful, the strategy has now remained in place for more than two decades. To fight inflation world growth was deliberately slowed from a 5 percent rate in the 1960s to a 2 percent rate in the first half of the 1990s.[1] Today the Federal Reserve Board designs policies to limit American economic growth to a maximum of 2.5 percent or less. Anything more is believed to be inflationary.

Like a real war that has gone on far too long, all of the original reasons for the war—the misfinancing of the Vietnam War, OPEC oil shocks, food shocks, indexed wage and supply contracts, inflationary expectations—are long gone. As the war continues year after year, the negative side effects—falling real wages and rising inequalities—have begun to be more corrosive than the original reasons for joining the battle. As will be seen in Chapter 9, inflation has been conquered. But the combatants against inflation have gotten so focused on "fighting on" that they cannot recognize that they have won.

Slow growth did what it was supposed to do. It pushed unemployment up to rates not seen since the Great Depression. Western Europe has double digit unemployment, with some individual countries above 20 percent. Japan admits to having at least 10 percent of its labor force really unemployed even though they are still being paid by their employers and therefore are not counted in the 3 to 4 percent that are officially unemployed.

In the fall of 1995, America's official unemployment rate was 5.7 percent. But like an iceberg that is mostly invisible below the waterline, those officially unemployed are just a small part of the total number of workers looking for more work. Adding together the officially unemployed (about 7.5 million), those who say they want work but do not meet one or the other of the tests for being actively in the labor force and therefore are not officially counted as unemployed (another 5 to 6 million), and the involuntary part-timers who want full-time work (approximately 4.5 million) yields an effective unemployment rate approaching 14 percent.

There are also 5.8 million males (more than 4 percent of the workforce) who are the right age to be in the workforce (twenty-five to sixty); males who in the past used to be in the workforce; males not in school; males not old enough to have retired; males who are neither employed nor unemployed; males who exist but have no obvious means of economic support; males who have either been dropped from, or have dropped out of, the normal working economy in the United States.[2]

America is also generating an enormous contingent underemployed workforce. There are 8.1 million American workers in temporary jobs, 2 million who work "on call," and 8.3 million self-employed "independent contractors" (many of them are downsized professionals who call themselves consultants because they are too proud to admit that they are unemployed but have few very clients).[3] Together they account for another 14 percent of the workforce.[4]

Most of these workers would rather have normal jobs. What they do, as was so aptly stated in *Fortune* magazine, is create a situation where the "upward pressure on wages is nil because so many of the employed are these 'contingent' workers who have no bargaining power with employers and payroll workers realize they must swim in the same Darwinian ocean."[5]

In addition, 11 million legal and illegal immigrants entered the United States from 1980 to 1993. They were searching for, and found, higher wages in America.[6] Their activities just have to have impacted the employment opportunities and wages for native-born Americans.

These millions of job hunters lead to a human result that everyone can understand. At 5:00 P.M. a mid-sized metal-ceramic firm posts on its bulletin board a notice of job openings for ten entry-level jobs. By 5:00 A.M. it has two thousand people in line waiting to apply for those ten jobs.[7]

This sea of excess labor directly drives wages down and indirectly creates an economic environment where the downward pressures of the other forces (technology, global trade) that will be outlined below are accentuated. This should come as no surprise. If one believes even marginally in the power of supply and demand, surplus labor of this magnitude leads to falling wages. Wages only rise if there are labor shortages. Since slow growth throws the bottom 60 percent of the workforce into unemployment far more than it does the top 20 percent, the earnings of the bottom 60 percent should be expected to fall sharply relative to the top 20 percent in a period of high unemployment.

FACTOR PRICE EQUALIZATION IN A GLOBAL ECONOMY WITH A SKILL-INTENSIVE SHIFT IN TECHNOLOGY

By definition a global economy is one where factors of production—natural resources, capital, technology, and labor—as well as goods and services move around the world. Capitalists make money by moving services, goods, and natural resources from where they are cheap to where they are expensive and from moving the production of goods from where it is expensive to where it is cheap. Technology gets employed wherever it earns the most money. Labor similarly moves to the place where wages are highest. In this process of searching around the globe for the highest returns, wherever they may exist, prices, rents, wages, interest payments, and dividends become more equal. Wages rise in countries with low wages and fall in countries with high wages—a process known to economists as "factor price equalization."

If factor price equalization did not occur, there would be a major economic mystery. How could a global economy be developing, which it surely is, without factor price equalization?[8] Factor price equalization is almost the definition of a world economy. If it did not exist, capitalists would be ignoring opportunities to raise profits. But there is no mystery that needs to be explained. Capitalists aren't missing many opportunities to make more money.

Whatever one believes about the role of factor price equalization in explaining the sharp shifts in the distribution of earnings that has occurred in the last two decades, the pressures of factor price equalization will mount in the future. While only a small part of the third world was export-oriented in the 1980s, most of the third world now all want to play an export-oriented capitalistic game. Only recently have workers in the formerly Communist countries started to compete with workers in the first world for jobs and wages.

In an era of relatively isolated national economies, average first world workers could get wage premiums above those of equal skills in the third world, since they worked with more raw materials, had greater access to capital, used superior technologies, and worked with the first world's large supply of very skilled labor. All of the traditional advantages enjoyed by the unskilled of the first world are gone, or are eroding very rapidly. Better transportation and communications have permitted the development of a global economy where raw materials can be bought by anyone at world prices and cheaply transported to wherever they are needed. Everyone effectively borrows capital on an equal-access basis on world capital markets in New York, London, or Tokyo. When it comes to investment, there are today no rich or poor countries. The art of reverse engineering and the activities of multinational companies lead technologies, especially product technologies, to move around the world very fast. While the complementarities between the skilled and the unskilled still exist, modern communication and transportation technologies have allowed the skilled parts of production processes to be done in first world countries while the unskilled parts are carried out in third world countries. Rich countries can no longer automatically generate higher earnings for their low-skill workers simply by employing more capital, cheaper raw materials, or better technology than their poorer neighbors.

Consider Eastern Europe. Drive one hour east from Germany and you will find wages 5 to 10 percent those of wages in Germany. In Poland, Asea Brown Boveri pays workers $2.58 per hour and in Germany they pay $30.33 per hour. Polish workers are also on the job four hundred hours more per year than those in Germany—reducing the need for training, management, and the overhead costs that go with a higher head count (bookkeeping, health care, etc.). It should come as no surprise that from 1990 to 1994, ABB eliminated 40,000 jobs in North America and Western Europe while adding 21,150 jobs in the formerly Communist countries to the east.[9] ABB was simply doing what capitalists are supposed to do—cost-minimize and profit-maximize. Wages will gradually rise in low-wage countries like Poland but they will also fall in high-wage countries like Germany.

In the special economic zones across the border from Hong Kong, the standard wage for entry-level workers in the metalworking trades is $35 per month where the working month is twenty-nine days and each working day eleven hours long—a net wage rate of 11 cents per hour. China is a special case only in the sense that it will take a long time for the wages of 1.2 billion people to look even remotely like first world wages. The pressures of factor price equalization are not going to quickly dissipate.

When it comes to factor price equalization, economic logic is buttressed by timing. Inequalities started to spread and real wages fall just when imports rose (as a fraction of GDPs in the late 1960s and early 1970s). There is an iron law of wages in a modern global economy: The only wage differentials that can survive in the long run are those justified by the skills that produce higher productivity.

At the same time, technology is moving in a skill-intensive direction. Just-in-time inventories, statistical quality control, pushing decisions down the hierarchy, computer technologies, teamwork, and removal of internal functional barriers all require a much more skilled workforce. In just an eight-year period of time, the coefficient relating mathematical abilities and earnings has tripled for men and doubled for women.[10] While it is impossible to predict the course of future technologies, everything that is now on the drawing boards tells us that the skill-using shift in technology is going to accelerate.

The auto companies that used to hire high school dropouts and high school graduates now want average production workers to have skills, especially math skills, that are associated with those who have gone to junior college in the United States. New technologies have converted what used to be unskilled assembly line jobs into jobs that require a lot more education and skill. The human welder is replaced by a robot and the jobs go to those with the skills necessary to repair robots. The auto industry now hires those with some college education or even college degrees (26 percent of the workforce at the Chrysler Windsor assembly plant have them) for blue-collar assembly jobs.[11]

In the past two decades high-wage jobs have disappeared as American firms lost market share to imports in the auto, steel, and machine tool industries, but they have also disappeared because productivity has grown much faster than demand in these industries.[12] Total employment grew, but all of that growth occurred in the service sector where wages in the United States are on average one third lower than those in manufacturing—and far below those found in industries such as the auto, steel, or machine tool.

In the economics profession there is an argument as to how much of the observed decline in earnings can be traced to factor price equalization and how much can be traced to a skill-intensive shift in production and distribution technologies. Unfortunately, the exact proportions are unknowable, since technology and factor price equalization interact with each other and their impact heavily depends on the tightness or looseness of the labor market in which they are occurring.

Intellectually, it might be nice to know the exact proportions of the observed decline in real wages caused by each of these two factors, but that knowledge does not in the end affect what must be done if the unskilled in the first world are to have first world incomes. They have to have first world skills in either case. It is impossible to hold back either the growth of the world economy or the advancement of technology—and one wouldn't want to even if one could. The advancement in technology is what makes human progress possible and a global economy opens up opportunities for human advancement in the second and third worlds that no one in the first world should want to shut down.

In an era of man-made brainpower industries, if countries do not make the right investments in skills, R&D, infrastructure, and plant and equipment, and if they aren't willing to run macroeconomic policies that produce tight labor markets, they simply will have a lot of people at the bottom of their workforces with very low and falling wages. High wages no longer come automatically for the unskilled who live in rich countries.

Since the broad causes of falling wages are clear and the remedies don't depend upon apportioning the exact blame, anyone not interested in going into the back alleys of economic analysis and economic controversy can jump on to the next chapter. For those who like solving murder mysteries, however, this is one that will challenge your deductive abilities. There are facts not predicted by every theory and facts that are directly contrary to every theory. But solving the mystery also teaches some important lessons about the era ahead.

WHO ALTERED THE WAGE STRUCTURE

In classical factor price equalization, the development of a global economy leads to rising exports of low-skill, labor-intensive products from third world countries. Because labor-intensive goods are cheaper to make in the third world, prices fall for these products, driving the equivalent higher wage, first world import-competing industries out of business. As they close down, they lay off more unskilled than skilled workers, since that is what they employ. Supply and demand then leads the wages of the unskilled to fall relative to those of the skilled.

Since the economic addition of the third world to the first world creates a global economy with much more labor (skilled and unskilled) relative to capital than had previously existed in first world countries alone, each worker (skilled and unskilled) is now working with less capital and the real wages of labor (skilled and unskilled) must fall. Conversely, each unit of capital is working with more labor and the real returns to capital should rise. But here there is a mystery, the returns to capital haven't risen.

In contrast with what would be predicted from classical factor price equalization, however, the source of rapidly rising imports over the past twenty years has been not low-wage third world countries but imports from other first world countries. Trade among OECD countries (the first world) have risen from 38 percent of the total in 1953 to 76 percent in 1990.[13] Imports from third world countries just don't seem large enough or to have risen fast enough to explain the huge changes in earnings that have been observed.

There is also a problem, as we have seen in Chapter 2, in that only a minority of the increase in inequality can be traced to widening wage differentials between different skills. Most of the increase in inequality occurs among those with identical skills.[14] Classical factor price equalization has no explanation for widening within group earnings inequalities.

With the relative wages of the unskilled falling, however, business firms should be employing fewer skilled workers and replacing them with cheaper unskilled workers. Yet using education as a measure of skills, the proportion of skilled workers has universally risen in U.S. industry. This has led many, including the *1994 Economic Report of the President,* to maintain that if skilled workers are becoming relatively more expensive but businesses are still using more of them, factor price equalization cannot be the cause of falling wages.[15] By default, these observers argue, widening wage disparities must therefore be found in a skill-using shift in technology that has led to the demand for a more skilled workforce.[16]

No one doubts that there is such a skill shift. But a skill-intensive technological shift also leaves many of the facts unexplained and faces some facts that are contrary to what it would predict. If a skill intensive shift in technology was at the root of the problem, the real wages for skilled workers should have risen. A skill shift does explain why the wages of the best educated have fallen (among men wages have universally fallen even for those with graduate degrees), why so many are affected (it should be more focused on those directly affected by the new technologies), or why wage differences among those with the same skills should be increasing. Using the same logic as those who argue against the factor price equalization hypothesis, a skill-using technological shift cannot be the source of the problem since there are facts that are not predicted by it and therefore the answer must lie with factor price equalization.

There is of course no reason why factor price equalization and a skill-intensive shift in technology cannot be simultaneously at work. But even working jointly, classical factor price equalization and a skill-intensive technological shift can point to a fact that excuses them as the prime suspects. Neither explains why wages should have become much more unequal among those with the same skills—regardless of whether they are unskilled or skilled.

In searching for the trail of the killer, it is important to remember than in the early 1970s imports were rising rapidly from the rest of the OECD, imports from other OECD countries were large enough to have had big effects on the observed wages in the United States, and the rest of the OECD was then a low-wage area in comparison with the United States. Some of the OECD countries, such as Germany and Japan, by the end of the period paid higher wages, especially when fringe benefits were included, than those found in the United States, but at the beginning they had much lower wages.

Falling real wages began earlier in the United States than elsewhere in the first world precisely because in the 1970s and early 1980s factor price equalization was occurring within the OECD.[17] While the aggregate trade deficit may have been small relative to GDP (3 percent in early 1994), it was very large in the medium-skill industries such as the auto, machine tool, steel, or consumer electronics. With very steep (inelastic) labor supply curves, a moderate fall in the demand curve for medium-skill labor can have a large impact on wages. What looks like a small tail on a very big dog can in fact wag the middle of the dog.

Only at the very end of the period did third world competition begin to play a role in first world wages and only then did the rest of the OECD begin to experience the widening inequalities and falling real wages that had originated much earlier in the United States.[18] Outside of the United States it may be unfair to blame the third world even at the end of the period. Some of the wage pressures that emerged in other OECD countries could easily have been a first world currency market overshoot where wages went above long-run equilibrium values. That is especially true in those countries, such as Germany and Japan, where wages plus fringe benefits went above American levels. When German or Japanese companies set up production facilities in America and pay lower wages than they pay at home, as they did in the late 1980s and early 1990s, they are effectively reversing the downward wage pressures back into their home markets.

While average wages in the rest of the OECD were below those in the United States in the 1970s, there is an even more important difference. The rest of the OECD has a very different skill and pay mix from that found in the United States. At the very top of the workforce, the United States is both the most skilled and by far the highest paid. America's most advanced first world competitors typically employ many fewer university graduates and pay those with university skills much less relative to those with high school skills than is the case in the United States.

If one looks at the skill set of high school graduates who have not completed any university program, these workers will have much higher skills in countries such as Germany or Japan than they do in the United States. Their achievement levels at the end of high school are higher and they receive much better postsecondary skill training— apprenticeships in Germany and elaborate company training in Japan. Before the wage changes of the past two decades, these medium-skill workers in other first world countries had both more skills and lower wages.

At the bottom of the workforce, the United States both pays less and has many more unskilled people who would not meet the performance standards of a European or Japanese high school graduate. Effectively, America has an internal third world labor force that simply does not exist in most of the rest of the OECD.

As a result, it is not possible to unambiguously say whether the United States is more skilled or less skilled or whether American workers are higher paid or lower paid than those in the rest of the OECD. America is uniquely a first world economy with a third world economy inside of it. In the 1970s the United States had more skilled people at the top being paid more, lesser skills but much higher pay in the middle, and very low skills with very low pay at the bottom. American corporations operate with a skill structure very different from that found in Japan or on the European continent. They essentially use more managers and professionals (11.5 percent of the workforce in the United States versus 5.7 percent in West Germany) to deskill the production process.[19] This allows U.S. firms to employ fewer mid-skill workers and more unskilled workers than would be the case in either Germany or Japan.[20] Americans "dumb down" the production process.

German firms operate with fewer managers and professions by "skill-ing up" the bottom of the workforce. Both systems work, just as "sur-vival-of-the-fittest" does not mean that only one species survives on the face of the earth.

Not surprisingly, a more unequal distribution of skills leads to a more unequal distribution of earnings in the United States. If one looks at male heads of households from twenty-five to fifty-four years of age working year-round full-time (see Table 8.1), the differences between the United States and other industrial countries is sharp. In America the top decile earns more relative to the bottom decile, and the middle decile earns more relative to the bottom that occurs in Europe—twice as much as in Germany.

Table 8.1
RELATIVE EARNINGS FOR MALE HEADS OF HOUSEHOLDS 25–54 YEARS OF AGE WORKING YEAR-ROUND FULL-TIME (MID-1980s)

Country	Top to Bottom Decile	Fifth to Bottom Decile	Top to Fifth Decile
United States	7.8	2.8	2.8
Canada	6.1	2.6	2.4
Australia	4.3	2.0	2.1
Germany	3.5	1.6	2.2
Sweden	3.3	1.5	2.2

SOURCE: Lawrence Mishel and Jared Bernstein, *The State of Working America* (Washington, D.C.: Economic Policy Institute/M. E. Sharpe, 1993), p. 429.

Given this reality, it is not surprising that the greatest loss of Amer-ican market share to imports came precisely in those industries (auto, machine tool, steel) that were the biggest employers of overpaid (rel-ative to their intrinsic skills) medium-skill workers. It is precisely this group that also took the biggest wage reductions in the 1970s and 1980s. By the early 1990s this medium-skill group had lower wages than the equivalent workers in most other advanced countries, but those lower wages also more closely corresponded to their relative skills.[21] They had to be paid less since they were less skilled than those doing the same jobs in the rest of the first world.

After World War II, the United States effectively enjoyed substantial economic rents in medium-skill industries that were not justified by their intrinsic skills or unique technologies. Having fully recovered from World War II by the early 1970s, competition with the rest of the industrial world simply eliminated the economic rents that the United States had been enjoying in the middle of its earnings distribution.

Changes in relative prices support this conclusion. The prices of imports, exports, and domestic production have changed in very different ways than would have been expected given classic factor price equalization. In the last two decades import prices have risen slightly faster (4 percent) than export prices—instead of declining as would have been predicted.[22] Given that import prices have risen relative to both domestic prices and export prices, a big increase in imports can only have occurred if there was a massive loss of competitiveness in relatively high-wage, medium-skill industries in the United States, since American producers were losing market share even as their products were becoming cheaper.

Also contradicting the classical factor price equalization assumptions, import-competing industries pay above- and not below-average wages in the United States. Using input-output analysis it is possible to calculate total (direct and indirect) distribution of wages for the exporting sector and the import-competing sector. Those wage distributions can then be compared with the wage distributions of the entire economy. As can be seen in Table 8.2, wages in 1983 in the import-competing sector were both higher (21 percent) and more equal (while 20.4 percent of the entire workforce earned less than $5,000 in 1983, only 12.4 percent of the workforce in import-competing industries did so) than those in the entire economy. But import-competing industries also generate slightly higher wages than those found in the exporting sector (5 percent higher in 1983).[23] If one thinks of the industries in the import-competing sector (the auto, machine tool, steel, and consumer electronics industries) and the industries in the export sector (agriculture, tourist services, wholesale trade), this result is not as surprising as it first seems.[24]

Table 8.2
DISTRIBUTION OF EARNINGS FOR EXPORT- AND IMPORT-COMPETING INDUSTRIES
1983

Annual Earnings	Total Workforce	Export Industries	Import Competing
$ 0–$ 5,000	20.4%	13.1%	12.4%
$ 5,000–$10,000	12.7%	10.5%	10.4%
$10,000–$15,000	13.6%	13.5%	13.4%
$15,000–$20,000	13.2%	14.8%	14.9%
$20,000–$25,000	11.6%	14.1%	14.2%
$25,000–$30,000	9.1%	11.2%	11.3%
$30,000–$40,000	10.6%	13.0%	13.2%
$40,000–$50,000	4.0%	2.2%	2.2%
$60,000–$75,000	1.2%	1.2%	1.3%
$75,000 plus	1.5%	1.4%	1.4%
Median	$16,168	$18,637	$19,583

SOURCE: Lester C. Thurow, "A General Tendency Toward Inequality," *American Economic Review*, May 1986.

Unfortunately, input-output coefficients come both infrequently and late, but given the industries where imports have grown in the 1980s and early 1990s (auto, machine tool, and electronics), it is likely that a 1995 input-output table, if it were to exist, would show an even greater wage premium for the import-competing sector than that which existed in 1983.

The conclusions are simple. Judging by wages the import-competing sector is slightly more skilled than the exporting sector. As a result, when import-competing industries contract, they do not in fact lay off proportionally more unskilled than skilled workers. What they really lay off, we see when we look at the industries where the declines have occurred because of international competition, are a lot of medium-skilled workers.

This reality can be seen if one looks at the wage structure from the perspective of male high school graduates. Relative to male high school graduates, the college wage premium soared from 35 percent to 93 percent between 1973 and 1992. But looking downward the wage premium that high school graduates used to enjoy relative to high school dropouts actually shrank. The wages of high school dropouts rose from 74 to 81 percent of high school graduate wages and the wages of those with less than an eighth grade education were up from 58 to 60 percent of high school wages.[25] This is exactly what one would expect if the pressures of factor price equalization are coming in the medium-skill range and not at the very bottom of the skill pyramid.

OECD factor price equalization explains why the biggest wage reductions are not found among the unskilled but among the medium-skill American males who at the beginning of the 1970s were both less skilled and better paid than their first world compatriots abroad. Something had to give and it did.

OECD factor price equalization and not third world factor price equalization also explains why wages could fall for everyone without a sharp rise in the returns to capital. Since the rest of the industrial world saves and invests much larger fractions of their GDP than the United States, OECD factor price equalization increases the supplies of both capital and medium-skilled workers—and as a consequence the returns to both have to fall in the United States.

Eleven million legal and illegal immigrants (another form of factor price equalization) in a little more than a decade must have had some impact on the wages of those at the bottom of the skill distribution. The confirmation of this is found in the fact that the biggest increase in earnings inequalities occurred in those geographic regions where immigration was highest.[26]

That leaves one piece of evidence (increasing inequalities among groups) that must be explained. To explain the widening distribution of earnings in the United States one has to understand what has happened among those within the same skill sets. To do this, two peculiarities of the labor market must be remembered. First, substitution possibilities are not symmetrical between the skilled and the unskilled labor. Unskilled workers are less than perfect substitutes for skilled workers, because unskilled workers cannot do many things that skilled workers can do, but skilled workers are perfect substitutes for unskilled workers since skilled workers can do anything that unskilled workers can do. This has to be true, unless there is something in the educational process of the skilled that makes them psychologically incapable of doing unskilled work.

Second, if one looks at observationally equivalent workers (those with equal hours of work, education, skills, occupation, industry, and years of experience), there has never been one equilibrium wage but has always been a wide dispersion of wages. For most classifications the dispersion in wages among those who are identical has always been almost as large as the dispersion found in the population at large. The equilibrium wages that are supposed to exist in economic theory (equal pay for equal skills and work) simply don't exist. Only about 10 percent of the variance in individual earnings, for example, can be explained by differences in schooling.[27]

Among humans there is no known distribution of talents that is as unequal as the distribution of earnings. To arrive at the actual distributions, one must postulate a very nonnormal distribution of economic luck or some very complicated interactions between talent and earnings.[28] In the real world, however, wages are attached to jobs, not workers, and workers with equivalent skill levels are spread across a spectrum of jobs in different companies that pay different wages. Individual wages don't just reflect individual skills; they have a team component. Those fortunate enough to work for a high-productivity team (a good firm) are paid more than those with identical skills who work on a low-productivity team (a poor firm). The lucky collect rents.

What matters, in the pungent phraseology of Michael Sattinger, professor of economics at the State University of New York at Albany, "is the distribution of bones" and not the distribution of bone-hunting skills among the dogs.[29] If one throws a distribution of bones to a group of dogs with equal bone-hunting skills, the dogs will not end up with an equal distribution of bones. They can only find the distribution of bones that exists in their economy. Despite their equal bone-hunting skills some will end up with big bones and some with little bones.

In the real world, wages adjust only slowly while entry-level hiring skills are quickly adjusted up or down depending upon the tightness of labor markets. If Ford has 110,000 applications for 1,300 jobs in its new Kentucky plant, why not hire college graduates?[30] On average one gets a better workforce for the same pay. This is in contrast to the textbook model where wages quickly adjust to clear labor markets in the short run, and wage-induced changes in labor supplies slowly clear labor markets in the long run.

In what I have called "the job competition model" in an earlier book, the short-run adjustment process is best seen as a job-filtering system.[31] When unemployment exists or when new supplies of labor come into the system, the most skilled of these unemployed workers essentially take what used to be the best jobs from those immediately below them in the skill distribution. Thus, if more college-educated labor comes into the system, as it has, new college entrants will be forced to take what used to be the best, highest-wage high school jobs. The observed wage distribution for college graduates spreads out (becomes more unequal), and the observed skill level in what used to be high school jobs rises— a college graduate now works where a high school graduate used to work. Average high school wages fall as high school graduates are squeezed out of their best jobs and down the job distribution.

In the 1970s and 1980s, downward wage pressures coming from high unemployment, massive immigration, the loss of international competitiveness in medium-skill industries, and a skill-intensive shift in technology were exacerbated by large increases in the supply of college-educated labor. Medium-skill jobs were becoming scarcer and college workers were taking more of them. An auto industry that used to hire high school graduates for production jobs now hired college-educated workers. Wages didn't change but those who got the high wages paid in the auto industry did change.

When skilled labor is released because of rising imports, skilled workers simply bump down the job distribution, knocking those with lesser skills out of their best jobs. The lowest paid in each skill class moves down to take what had been the best-paid jobs in the skill class below them. The dispersion in the distribution of earnings within each skill class increases as each skill class loses some of what have been its best jobs and gains more of what have been its worst jobs. Average earnings fall for everyone. Changes in relative wages between any two groups depend upon the densities of the distributions over which this bumping occurs.

In the 1970s, college earnings fell relative to high school earnings as college graduates moved down into the upper tail of what had been the best high school jobs. The dispersion of earnings increased among college graduates. High school graduates were retreating economically into a denser part of their earnings distribution, so that the decline in their average earnings was smaller than that for college graduates. Relatively, college wages rose even though real wages were falling for both college and high school graduates.

In the 1980s, immigration soared and medium-skill, high-wage industries lost market share to imports. These economic pressures lowered the central density of the high school male earnings distribution so fast that relative college male earnings rose even though real college wages were falling faster than they had in the 1970s.

OTHER POSSIBLE CAUSES

In addition to the war on inflation, OECD factor price equalization, and a skill-intensive shift in technology, a number of other factors have been suggested as accessories to the murder of the wage structure.

1. Some capitalists certainly plotted to kill America's labor unions. President Reagan's firing of all of America's unionized air traffic controllers legitimized a deliberate strategy of deunionization. In the private sector, consultants were hired who specialized in getting rid of unions, decertification elections were forced, labor laws were altered so that unions were harder to establish and easier to eliminate, and legal requirements to respect union rights were simply ignored—firms simply paid the small fines that labor law violations brought and continued to violate the law. The strategy succeeded in shrinking union membership to slightly more than 10 percent of the private workforce (15 percent of the total workforce). And even where unions still do exist, they have lost much of their power to control wages or negotiate working conditions.

Combined with corporate compensation committees that have escalated CEO salaries from 35 to 157 times those of entry-level workers in the past twenty-five years, one could argue that the capitalists had declared class warfare on labor—and were winning.[32]

Abroad, where there have been no such deliberate efforts to defeat unions, the trends in union membership are mixed. In some countries such as Germany or Japan, little has happened to union membership, but in other countries such as the United Kingdom, it has plunged— the proportion of unionized employees in the United Kingdom has more than halved since 1979 but is still much higher (one third) than what is found in the United States.[33] In the European Union as a whole, union membership starts from a higher level but falls just about as much as it has in the United States.[34]

While the economics literature is inconclusive as to whether unions affect average wages (equally productive companies with and without unions tend to pay the same wages), there is no doubt that unions affect the distribution of wages. Wage distributions are much more equal where unions exist.[35] High school–college wage differentials, for example, have always been smaller in the union sector than in the nonunion sector. As a result, with the demise of unions as a force in the American economy, wage differentials should be expected to rise since these differentials have always been higher in the nonunion sector. In addition, as union fears have waned, the gap between union and nonunion wage has doubled.[36] Higher wages no longer need to be paid in nonunion firms to keep unions out.

Threatening to go abroad to lower wage costs certainly plays a role in lowering wages at home. There are those in Germany who think that the decisions of BMW and Mercedes to build plants in the United States have more to do with negotiating with German trade unions than they have to do with servicing the U.S. auto market.[37] But the same economic pressures exist even when firms have no offshore production sites and no plans to establish them. Everyone has to meet global competition from those abroad who do have lower wages. If higher wages are not sustained by higher productivity, they cannot be defended in a global economy whatever the capitalist might like to do.

America's wage patterns are now emerging in countries where unions are still important, and where no efforts have been made to defeat labor. Deliberate corporate actions to eliminate unions may have speeded up the process, but there is no reason to believe that they have led to long-term results fundamentally different from those found elsewhere.

2. Observed wage reductions may appear worse than they really are if skill inflation has led workers to be recorded as having skills that

they really don't have. Employers know the real skill levels by experience and pay wages appropriate to those real skills rather than the formally reported higher skill levels. A major textile manufacturer, for example, recently tested its high-school-educated labor force and discovered that this workforce in fact operated at a ninth grade equivalency level. What shows up as a reduction in wages for high school graduates may really reflect what are effectively high school dropouts who now get coded in government statistics as high school graduates. Real wages fall because real skills are falling.

3. Deregulation clearly led to some wage reductions. In regulated industries such as trucking and airlines, workers collected some of the rents that accrued from regulation. Truck driver wages and the wages of some airline employees fell dramatically with deregulation. In the case of truck drivers, wages fell three times as fast as elsewhere.[38] The rents that had been built into their wages were transferred back to the consumers buying transportation.[39]

4. In the 1970s as the baby boom generation entered the labor force, capital-labor ratios rose more slowly or even fell. The supplies of labor simply rose faster than the supplies of capital. In such a situation wages must fall, since every worker is working with less capital. In the 1980s this process should have automatically reversed itself, because American demography called for the labor force to grow much more slowly than it had in the 1970s. But the 1980s became a decade of booming immigration and the expected slowdown in labor force growth did not occur. As a consequence, the expected rise in capital-labor ratios did not occur. With less capital per worker, some reduction in wages is to be expected.

5. If one looks at labor's share of GDP over the last two decades, the share going to labor is approximately constant. But the share for wages is down substantially (5 percentage points), while that for pensions is up substantially. While fully funded pension programs simply involve wages being shifted from today to tomorrow, less than fully funded pension programs or health insurance programs where benefits go to current retirees (the usual case) effectively represent wage transfers from those currently employed to those already retired. What shows up in the statistics as fringe benefits is really a private social welfare payment from the young to the old.

LOOKING FORWARD

Since mid-skill wages in the many advanced industrial countries are now above those in the United States, most of the factor price equalization flowing from other first world countries is now behind the United States. But ahead lies the integration of the second world into the first world and a very different third world. The Communist countries did not run effective civilian economies, but they ran excellent education systems. The USSR was a high-science society with more engineers and scientists than any other than the United States. China is capable of quickly generating hundreds of millions of medium-skill workers. The end of communism and the success of the little tigers on the Pacific Rim have led the third world to junk import substitution as a route to economic development and become export oriented. Where a few tens of millions (living in Singapore, Hong Kong, Taiwan, and South Korea) used to be export oriented, third world countries containing billions of people (in Indonesia, India, Pakistan, Mexico) now want to be export oriented. As a result, exports from low-wage third world countries are apt to be much larger in the years ahead. Whatever one believes about the proportion of the observed real-wage declines and increases in wage dispersion that can be blamed on factor price equalization in the past, the proportion is going to be larger in the future.

During the 1970s and 1980s, rising blue-collar productivity, often based on information technologies such as robotics, and rapidly rising imports in medium-skill manufacturing industries reduced the need for factory workers. In contrast, white-collar employment soared despite massive use of information technologies in areas such as accounting and finance. Mysteriously, white-collar productivity grew only slowly or even declined. By the mid-1990s, however, it seems clear, firms have learned how to use information technologies to reduce the number of white-collar and middle management jobs. That is what downsizing is all about. Since most firms now have more white-collar than blue-collar employees (for the whole economy there are three white-collar employees for every one blue-collar employee), firms have to raise white-collar productivity if they are going to become more efficient.

Pressures to reduce employment are clearly moving up the earnings distribution and afflicting ever higher earnings groups. How far wages can be reduced for these upper-level groups remains to be seen. The limits are sociological. When does a sullen noncooperative workforce, especially in the management cadres, raise costs more than what can be gained from wage reductions?

If Europe moves toward the wage flexibility it is talking about, Europe will probably generate some of the service jobs in the late 1990s and early twenty-first century that the United States created in the 1970s and 1980s. That same wage flexibility, however, will allow the forces of factor price equalization and a skill-intensive technology shift to lower real wages. Patterns of wages and employment in Europe and America are apt to converge.

CONCLUSIONS

Those who viewed the economic surface of the earth in 1970 would not recognize the topography of 1995. The changes in the distribution of purchasing power in the next twenty-five years will be even more dramatic. The end of communism (economic plate one) is pushing into the old capitalistic world and offering the old capitalistic world large supplies of cheap, well-educated labor from the second world and indirectly, by destroying belief in import substitution and quasi-socialism, creating huge supplies of very low-wage unskilled third world labor. Migration (economic plate three) is pushing a lot of smart, energetic, but unskilled laborers directly into the first world. New technologies (economic plate two) are generating a skill-using shift in production technologies in both the factory and the office. What needs to be done to offset these forces (massive skill investments) is being resisted by the elderly (economic plate three). A global economy (economic plate four) shoves factor price equalization into capitalism's wage equation and forces wages down. Without a dominant power (economic plate five), there is no economic locomotive for the world's economic train, growth slows down and a context is created where wages can both fall and spread out.

Chapter 9

Inflation: An Extinct Volcano

In the 1970s and 1980s, fighting inflation became the central pre-occupation of the industrial world. Wage and price controls were tried in a number of countries, including the United States, but empirically it seemed to be impossible to control inflation without deliberately creating an environment of slow growth and high unemployment. Inflation was not conquered in this war. The factors that produced inflation in the 1970s and 1980s simply disappeared, and structural changes have occurred to make the economies of the 1990s much more inflation-proof than those of the 1970s and 1980s—just as the economies of the 1960s were much more inflation-proof than those of the 1970s or 1980s.

But as is often the case, beliefs change more slowly than reality. Inflation is gone but inflation fighting still dominates central bank policies.[1] They still believe that the natural rate of unemployment—the rate of unemployment at which inflation starts to accelerate—is so high that they and the fiscal authorities must step on the monetary and fiscal brakes long before tight labor markets can push wages up.

The problem can be seen in the activities of the American Federal Reserve Board in 1994 and 1995. At the beginning of 1994 the Fed saw an economy so inflation-prone that even what was by historical standards a slow recovery from the 1991–92 recession (2.4 percent growth in 1993; 3.5 percent in 1994) represented an overheated economy. Because of this belief, seven times in twelve months, from early 1994 to early 1995, the American Federal Reserve Board boosted short-term interest rates.[2]

Yet every time, the chairman, Alan Greenspan, admitted that the Fed could not point to even a hint of inflation in the current numbers. The Fed could not point to inflation because there was no inflation. The broadest measure of inflation, the implicit price deflator for the gross domestic product, fell from 2.2 percent in 1993 to 2.1 percent in 1994. In the third quarter of 1995 it was running at the rate of 0.6 percent.[3]

Having fallen during the previous recession, the producer's price index for finished consumer goods in December 1994 was below where it had been in April 1993 and annual rates of increase decelerated from 1.2 percent in 1993 to 0.6 percent in 1994. In 1994 labor costs rose at the slowest rate since records have been kept, and the core rate of inflation (the rate of inflation leaving out volatile energy and food prices) was the lowest rate recorded since 1965.

The OECD in its end-of-the-year 1994 report saw no inflation ahead in the United States in 1995.[4] Abroad in the world's second biggest economy, Japan, wholesale prices were 8.5 percent below 1990 levels and were still falling in mid-1995.[5]

Officially, the rate of inflation in the consumer price index (CPI) fell from 3.0 percent in 1993 to 2.6 percent in 1994, but Chairman Greenspan had himself testified to Congress that the CPI exaggerated inflation by as much as 1.5 percentage points, since it underestimates quality improvements in goods (in computers, for example, it has performance rising at only 7 percent per year) and since it both has poor coverage and gives no credit at all for quality improvements in services.[6] It is clear that service inflation is much smaller than reported.[7]

An official government commission, the Boskin Commission, has estimated an upward bias of between 1.0 and 2.4 percentage points in the CPI. This is made up of 0.2 to 0.4 percentage points of bias, because the official index fails to keep up with consumers as they shift to cheaper products; 0.1 to 0.3 percentage points of bias, since the official index fails to keep up with consumers as they shift to cheaper stores; 0.2 to 0.6 percentage points of bias, because the index underestimates quality improvements; 0.2 to 0.7 percentage points of bias, since it lags behind in introducing new products; and a formula bias of 0.3 to 0.4 percentage points, due to the mishandling of products that come into the index at temporarily low prices.[8]

If one is willing to assume that the sectors where quality improvements are hard to measure are in fact improving quality at the same pace as those sectors where quality is easy to measure (and it is hard to think of why they should be radically worse performers), the overmeasurement of inflation may be closer to 3 percentage points.[9]

In addition, health care inflation cannot be controlled with higher interest rates and slower growth. To know what is going on in that part of the economy that is potentially controllable with higher interest rates, health care inflation rates have to be subtracted from the totals. Since health care accounts for 15 percent of GDP and health care prices are rising at a 5 percent annual rate, mathematically another 0.75 percentage points of inflation (almost one third of 1994's total inflation) can be traced to health care.[10] In reality, more than this amount can be traced to health care, since some of health care inflation gets built into the price indexes more than once. If states raise sales taxes to cover the costs of their health care programs, for example, health inflation shows up once as increased costs for health care and once as a sales tax increase in the consumer price index.

If all of these factors are put together, the real rate of inflation outside of the health care sector was undoubtedly very low, perhaps even negative, during the entire period when Alan Greenspan was worrying about inflation. Greenspan could not see any inflation in the indexes because there was no inflation to be seen.

Nor were there any private inflationary expectations at the beginning of 1994. None of the standard private economic forecasting services were suggesting that inflation would accelerate either. The first unexpected increase in interest rates in 1994 imposed hundreds of millions of dollars of losses on some of the world's most sophisticated investors (George Soros, Citibank), who had been betting that interest rates would fall or remain constant. If they had believed that there was any inflation over the horizon, they would not have placed those bets.

Theoretically, there is also no reason why inflation should adversely affect capitalistic growth. Capitalists are smart enough not to suffer from money illusion. Negative effects only appear when inflation gets so high that speculation and inflation avoidance become more profitable than normal business activities and that requires hyperinflation before it occurs. Empirically, there is no evidence that modest rates of inflation hurt growth.[11] Looking at the experience of over one hundred countries for a thirty-year period, a study for the Bank of England found no negative effects on growth for countries that averaged less than a 10 percent per year inflation rate and only very small effects for countries that averaged much more than 10 percent.[12]

An argument can also be made that capitalism works best with something on the order of a 2 percent per year rate of inflation. Anything lower starts to create problems. If prices are falling, one can make money by holding one's money in the proverbial mattress. To stimulate people to take the default risk of lending requires a positive money interest rate of 2 or 3 percent. As a result, if inflation is negative, real interest rates must be high. Real interest rates reached 13 percent in 1933 because prices were falling. Real interest rates cannot be very low unless there is a modest rate of inflation, and without low real interest rates, investment cannot be high.

In a dynamic economy some real wages need to fall to induce labor to move from sunset to sunrise industries. Real-wage reductions are very difficult and disruptive if they have to take the form of lower money wages. Labor rebels. But real-wage reductions are much easier to accomplish if the employer is simply giving wage increases smaller than the rate of inflation.[13] The real reductions can be blamed on the amorphous system rather than on himself.

The same is true for prices. In any economy it is always necessary to change relative prices. If inflation is very low, that can only happen if many sectors experience falling money prices, but capitalism doesn't work very well with falling money prices. With falling prices there is an incentive to postpone. Why buy or invest today when tomorrow everything will be cheaper? In a world of deflation the pressure to act is sharply reduced. Yet action is what causes economic growth. Zero is simply not the right inflationary target in capitalistic societies interested in growth.

When the Fed started raising interest rates in early 1994, it stated that it had to have higher interest rates now to stop inflation twelve to eighteen months into the future because of the time lags in the economic system. Growth in fact accelerated from 3.1 percent in 1993 to 4.1 percent in 1994 and was very close to what was expected at the beginning of the year. By the end of the year neither had the economy slowed down nor had the signs of inflation become more visible than they had been twelve months earlier. By September it was clear that 1994's inflation would be much less than the low rates that were forecast at the beginning of the year.[14] The business press was proclaiming that "the inflationary 'ogre' has been banished—maybe for good, certainly for the foreseeable future."[15] Nor was inflation accelerating in 1995, even though monetary policies did not bring about the expected slowdown in economic growth until the second quarter of that year.

The Federal Reserve Board was chasing ghosts. Inflation was dead but the Fed wasn't willing to admit it.

While the 1970s and the 1980s were inflationary decades, the 1990s and the decades beyond are going to be very different. Inflation died in the crash in asset values that began in the mid-1980s with the collapse of the American savings and loan industry. This was followed by a collapse in property values that rolled around the world. A decade later both purchase prices and rents were still far below their previous peaks. The crash in the Taiwanese stock market was followed by a crash in the Japanese stock market.

While capacity utilization rates were rising in the United States during 1994, in a global economy it is world unemployment and world capacity utilization rates that count—not American rates by themselves. In 1994 the world was awash in excess production capacity. The rest of the industrial world was having a very slow recovery from the earlier recession—at the end of 1994 Japanese growth was strongly negative and European growth only marginally positive.

As we have also seen in detail in the last chapter, globally unemployment rates were at levels not seen since the Great Depression. Labor shortages were not going to be driving up wages for a long time to come.

U.S. measures of capacity and hence capacity utilization are also out-of-date. They don't reflect the outsourcing that has happened. Outsourcing means that effectively firms increase their production capabilities without having to invest themselves. But the capacity increases of their suppliers remain unmeasured, since the capacity indexes assume that nothing has changed in the proportions of value added contributed by component suppliers and original equipment manufacturers (OEMs).[16]

Investments in new information and computer technologies have also made it possible to get more output out of the same capital with fewer people. That is part of what downsizing is all about, yet downsizing is not reflected in official indexes of capacity.

The Fed also doesn't seem to understand that some important structural changes have occurred that make it impossible for inflation to arise from the grave. The addition of the Communist world to the capitalist world and the effective collapse of the OPEC oil cartel in the aftermath of the Persian Gulf War means that a repetition of the energy, food, or raw material shocks of the 1970s are simply impossible in the 1990s. Oil prices are lower in real terms than they were when the first OPEC oil shock happened in the early 1970s, yet exploration and exports from the old Soviet Union have barely begun and Iraq has yet to be brought back into world oil markets.

The real-wage declines that began in the United States are now spreading across the industrial world. The downsizing of big firms with high wages and good fringe benefits continues at an unrelenting pace. If anything, wage reductions are going to be accelerating. The second world and the rest of the third world will join the small parts of the third world that were export oriented in the 1980s. Downward price and wage pressures from these low-cost producers can only accelerate. In 1994 unit labor costs declined by 2.9 percent in manufacturing and rose by only 0.9 percent in nonfarm businesses.[17]

At the same time productivity growth is running at the highest rates seen since the 1960s. In most of the 1970s and 1980s, service productivity was falling, but now it is rising.[18] Services just aren't going to provide an underlying inflationary push as they did earlier. Wages down, productivity up—that simply isn't the recipe for inflation.

All across America large firms are forging new supplier arrangements such as those recently put in place at Chrysler. The number of suppliers is dramatically reduced, suppliers are guaranteed much larger sales, original equipment manufacturers (OEMs) share information and technical expertise with suppliers on design and manufacturing, but suppliers in return commit to annual price reductions in the components they supply to OEMs. The OEMs in turn pass some of those reductions on to their customers to increase market share.

The world is essentially back to the conditions of the 1960s, with much less inflationary-prone economies.[19] Supply elasticities were high then because of the recovery from World War II and the economic integration forced by the cold war. Now supply elasticities are high because of the integration of the second world into the first world and the decision of most of the third world to replace import substitution with export-led growth.

Since World War II, American firms have typically held prices constant, or even raised them, while distributing the fruits of higher productivity in the form of higher wages or higher profits. But under the pressure of international competition, that system is rapidly eroding. In the 1990s many more of those productivity gains are showing up as falling prices and many less are showing up as rising wages.

Knowing that governments have lost their ability to shorten recessions also radically changes expectations. Producers know that they cannot hold prices constant while waiting for a quick recovery from cyclical downturns. The early 1990s demonstrated that no government would come running to the rescue with large fiscal and monetary packages designed to stimulate demand during recessions. Instead, recessions will be allowed to run their course and governments will simply wait for a recovery. If downturns are sharper and longer, business firms will have to reduce prices if they wish to survive those downturns.

There are no ghosts in the attic. Inflation is not about to rise from the dead.

By raising interest rates in 1994 the Fed killed a weak American recovery that had yet to include many Americans and slowed a recovery that was barely visible in the rest of the industrial world. In just two and a half months after the Fed initiated its actions, interest rates on thirty-year Treasury bonds had risen 1.1 percentage points and those on thirty-year fixed rate mortgages had risen 1.3 percentage points. These rates did not soar because there was a sudden upward adjustment in thirty-year inflationary expectations. These numbers reflect the uncertainty, and hence the risk premiums, that investors must demand to protect themselves from a Federal Reserve Board prone to seeing inflation ghosts where they don't exist.

If the battle against inflation is primary, central bankers will be described as the most important economic players in the game. Without it, they run rather unimportant institutions. It is well to remember that in 1931 and 1932 as the United States was plunging into the Great Depression, economic advisers such as Secretary of the Treasury Andrew Mellon were arguing that nothing could be done without risking an outbreak of inflation—despite the fact that prices had fallen 23 percent from 1929 to 1932 and would fall another 4 percent in 1933.[20] The fear of inflation was used as a club to stop the actions that should have been taken. Central banks are prone to see inflationary ghosts since they love to be ghost busters. While no human has ever been hurt by ghosts in real life, ghost busters have often created a lot of real human havoc.

Since growth did not in fact slow down in the year in which Alan Greenspan was raising interest rates, the question Why worry? can be raised. The answer is of course that higher interest rates often act like sticky brakes. The driver pushes down on the brakes and initially nothing happens. So she pushes harder. Suddenly the brakes grab and the car is thrown off the road. And that is exactly what happened in the second quarter of 1995. Growth effectively stopped.

If the economy's maximum noninflationary rate of growth is 2.5 percent (the Fed's announced target), surplus labor is going to be pushing wages down. Even the manufacturers who have to pay those wages think that a 3.5 percent growth rate could be achieved without inflation.[21]

Our societies tolerate high unemployment since only a minority suffer from that unemployment. Most of the movers and shakers in society know that they will not be affected. Politically, high inflation is much more worrying to those in or seeking office, since it seems to reduce everyone's income. Economists can point out that every price increase has to raise someone's income and that the balance between gains and losses seems to indicate that very few are real-income losers as long as inflation is less than 10 percent per year, but all of that analysis is irrelevant. To the voter it does not seem to be true. They merit wage increases but are cheated by price increases.

The high unemployment necessary to fight inflation is one of the factors leading to falling real wages for a large majority of Americans, but this reality is too clouded by other factors and too indirect to be seen as the cause. Political power lies on the side of those who declare a holy war against inflation. Yet those who do so are indirectly advocating lower real wages for most Americans.

The inflationary volcano of the 1970s and 1980s is extinct, but the mind-set produced by its eruptions lives on. As a result, business firms in their planning have to simultaneously plan for a world where there is no inflation, but there will be periodic deliberate recessions designed to fight imaginary inflations.

Labor will continue to live in a world where governments talk about the need to restore real-wage growth but deliberately create labor surpluses to push wages down.[22] As a result, no one should pay attention when they talk about restoring a high-wage economy with growing real incomes. Wages go up when there are labor shortages, not when there are labor surpluses.

Officially, central banks always hold out the prospect that if they just hold down inflation long enough, they will gain anti-inflation "credibility" with the financial markets and rapid noninflationary growth will resume. But it doesn't work. If the German Bundesbank does not by now have "credibility" as an inflation fighter no central bank will ever get this mythical status. Despite its anti-inflation credibility West Germany has had a very slow growth rate—2.3 percent per year from 1981 to 1994.[23] Rapid growth never resumes.

Chapter 10

Japan: The Major Fault Line Across World Trade and the Pacific Rim

Global trade is dominated by a fault line, with Japanese trade surpluses on one side and American trade deficits on the other side. Like real fault lines, this one has long been known—it has existed for more than two decades—and as time passes, the pressures on the fault are building up. The American current account deficit ($145 billion in 1994) and the Japanese current account surplus ($130 billion in 1994) are essentially mirror images of each other. Neither could exist without the other. To talk about either is to talk about the other.

The direct bilateral surplus or deficit between Japan and the United States ($66 billion in 1994) is a symbol of this problem but it is not the problem. The United States could finance a large trade deficit with Japan by running equally large trade surpluses with the rest of the world if the rest of the world could in turn run trade surpluses with Japan so that they could pay for their American trade deficits with the funds earned from their Japanese trade surpluses. The problem is that no one outside of a few raw material producers (or those who restrict Japanese imports) runs trade surpluses with Japan. Everyone else runs large trade deficits with Japan, which they finance by running even larger trade surpluses with the United States.

This is particularly true on the Pacific Rim. In 1993 the Pacific Rim's trade deficit with Japan, $57 billion, was even larger than the U.S. trade deficit with Japan, $50 billion.[1] If the Pacific Rim did not have its American surpluses, it would have to quickly cut back on its purchases from Japan. China (including Hong Kong) is typical. In 1993, China ran a $17 billion trade deficit with Japan, which it paid for with a $20 billion trade surplus with the United States.[2]

Suppose that the United States was to take the advice of the rest of the world and balance its trading accounts. Whatever method it uses (a falling dollar, managed trade, incentives to raise savings), the American trade deficit only disappears if it imports less or exports more. There are no other options. If it imports less, the industries in the rest of the world that sell those imports must shrink. If it exports more, the industries in the rest of the world that compete with American exports must shrink.

Suppose that some combination of greater American exports and fewer American imports leads to a balance in U.S. trade. At that point the rest of the world must, by a process of simple mathematical subtraction, run an aggregate trade deficit of $130 billion with Japan if Japan is to keep its $130 billion surplus. Someone or some combination of someones must carry Japan's surplus as its deficit. Who, or what combination of countries, in the rest of the world could finance such a deficit for more than a very short period of time? If the answer is no one, and it is, the rest of the world would quickly have to quit buying Japanese exports much as Mexico quickly quit buying American products in the aftermath of its foreign exchange crisis. The rest of the world would have no funds with which to buy Japanese goods, and having lost their major export market, the United States, they would not be creditworthy. Japan's trading accounts would quickly come into balance as its export markets vanished.

There is a simple bottom line. Without an American trade deficit, there can be no Japanese trade surplus—no matter how competitive Japanese products are, no matter how much the rest of the world would like to buy them. But any pattern of world trade that depends upon permanent U.S. deficits or foresees permanent Japanese surpluses is simply not viable in the long run.

No country, not even one as big as the United States, can run a trade deficit forever. Money must be borrowed to pay for the deficit, but money must be borrowed to pay interest on the borrowings. Even if the annual deficit does not grow, interest payments grow until they are so large that they cannot be financed. The alternative to borrowing is selling America's assets (land, companies, buildings) to foreigners, but that too is limited since eventually there will be nothing left to sell. At some point world capital markets will quit lending to Americans (the risk of default and the risk of being paid back in currencies of much less value are simply too great) and America will run out of assets foreigners want to buy (the earnings on the remaining assets that might be bought won't cover the required interest costs and compensate buyers for the expected foreign exchange losses that will occur on their holdings).

To illustrate the problem, suppose that a Japanese pension fund buys a $100 U.S. government bond when the exchange rate is 120 yen to the dollar. One year later at an exchange rate of 80 yen to the dollar, what cost the Japanese pension fund 12,000 yen returns only 8,000 yen. The company has lost one third of its investment.

At different times the Japanese have lent the funds (bought U.S. and private bonds) necessary to finance their trade surplus (the American trade deficit) and at different times they have bought assets (the huge property acquisitions of the 1980s) necessary to finance the U.S. trade deficit (the Japanese trade surplus), but they continually have to move funds into the United States if the current pattern of world trade is to persist. The minute the Japanese quit making such investments, the value of the yen soars and the dollar plunges. Even Japanese capitalists cannot engage in such money-losing investments forever.

While the dollar's unique position as the effective reserve currency of the world, America's enormous holdings of assets abroad, and its great wealth at home (there are numerous U.S. assets that the rest of the world would like to buy) mean that America can run a trade deficit for a long period of time, even the United States cannot forever repeal the fundamental rules of economic gravity. No one can run a large trade deficit forever. The United States is very large, it can borrow a lot and sell a lot before it goes broke, but at some point the world's financial markets will clamp down upon it just as they clamped down upon Mexico.

The question is not whether an earthquake will occur. It will. The only question is when, and whether it occurs as one big shock or as a series of smaller shocks that do less damage.

But when conditions have existed for a long period of time and nothing has happened, humans, being human, begin to believe that it is possible to defy economic gravity forever. People begin to act as if the United States can run a trade deficit forever and the patterns of trade they now see can go on forever.

The same willingness to suspend intelligence and disbelief could be seen in the 1970s and 1980s when the Japanese stock market reached price-earnings ratios of more than 100. With such multiples, Japanese companies could have issued shares, effectively borrowing at a below 1 percent interest rate, and invested their borrowings in government bonds yielding 3 percent. Anyone could make an infinite amount of money in such a world. In principle those Japanese P/E ratios could not long exist, since money would be borrowed and profitably re-lent until private borrowing rates exceeded government borrowing rates (private lending is always more risky than public lending, because private companies cannot print the money necessary to repay their loans while governments can). But the Japanese stock market stayed high so long that many came to believe that somehow Japan was different and the rules that applied everywhere else did not apply to it.

Initially many observers said that the values on the Japanese market were crazy. But those values lasted so long that although most of those original observers did not change their fundamental beliefs, they started to sound silly and they eventually shut up. Other analysts then arose to propound theories as to why Japan was different and its high stock market multiples could last forever. In their arguments, land wasn't properly accounted for on Japanese balance sheets, Japanese accounting conventions were different, the Japanese did not want to make money on their investments. But of course it was all nonsense. The Japanese stock market could not forever defy economic gravity and it did eventually crash.

The Japanese stock market fell from 38,916 on the Nikkei Index in December 1989 to 14,309 on August 18, 1992—a bigger fall in real terms than the fall in the American stock market between 1929 and 1932.[3] Even at the onset of the Great Depression, the world had never seen losses of the magnitude suffered in Japan. If one adds together the crash in the stock market (even after some recovery, down 63 percent in 1995), the fall in land (urban residential land down 33 percent, commercial land down 85 percent), housing, and commercial real estate values, and the losses on foreign assets when evaluated in yen (down 50 percent), the net worth of Japanese households has fallen by almost $14,000 billion.[4] Thirty-six percent of the total net worth of all Japanese households has already been wiped out and property prices are still falling—roadside property was depreciating 13 percent per year in mid-1995 and commercial land was down 20 percent in Toyko.[5] The normal rules do, after all, apply to Japan.

Arguments about the American trade deficit are a replay of those heard earlier about the Japanese stock market. Initially there were warnings that it could not go on forever. But now we are at the point where the United States has run a big trade deficit for so long, more than twenty years, that everyone is willing to believe the impossible. Those who said that it could not go on forever have shut up. Like weeds, theories have sprung up as to why the United States is unique— as the world's reserve currency it only borrows in dollars so there is no danger of default, everyone in the world wants an unlimited number of American assets in their portfolios since they are planning to forever stay in dollars and don't care what happens to their wealth evaluated in their home currencies, no one cares whether they lose money on their American investments, etc. But none of these arguments reverse the fundamental truth. They are all nonsense. At some point the United States will lose its ability to finance its trade deficit.

But no one knows, or can know, when. Economics is very good when it comes to assessing fundamental forces and pressures. But it is horrible on timing. Economic theory says nothing about timing. The end will come, it is long overdue if you look at what most economists were saying in the early 1980s, but the fact that it is overdue does not mean that it will happen tomorrow. But nothing repeals the reality that the end will come.

When the end comes, the economic pain in Japan, the United States, and the rest of the world will be extreme. The epicenter of the economic earthquake will be in the United States, but the shock waves will be strongest on the Pacific Rim. In America standards of living will fall, since it will be cut off from the exports it now consumes and will have to start running balance of payments surpluses to pay interest and principal on the debts (now about $1 trillion) it has incurred. Americans will work more (every $60 billion cut in imports leads to 1 million American jobs) yet have a lower standard of living.[6] American firms will quickly gear up to produce more of the goods Americans want to buy, such as cars, but more inputs will be required to achieve the old outputs. The size of the cuts in the standard of living will depend upon the actions of the Federal Reserve. If it is still in a fighting-inflation mode and does not let unemployment fall, the cuts in American living standards will be larger than if it lets today's unemployed and underemployed Americans go back to work.

In Japan, export industries would dramatically shrink. Unless the Japanese government is willing to massively subsidize its export industries, millions will be thrown out of work as companies go bankrupt. If such subsidies are paid, those who work in domestic industries will essentially have to pay much higher taxes (lower their own standard of living) to help maintain the standard of living of those now working in the exporting industries.

The rest of the world will be unable to pay for Japanese imports and they will have to be cut back sharply. To the extent that domestic producers need Japanese components to service local markets, they will not be able to produce even what they can sell at home. Not being able to sell in the United States what they now make for the American market, production will have to be sharply curtailed.

Sales declines will not be limited to the American market. Outside of the United States, sales will also fall since most of those sales are funded indirectly by the funds that these countries earn on their American sales. Many countries that think they have diversified their export base haven't. As a fraction of the total South Korean exports, American sales are down while South Korea's sales to China are up. But if China lost its American trade surplus, South Korea would lose its Chinese sales. In reality, South Korea's export base has not been diversified.

The longer the current situation continues, the larger the eventual structural adjustments that will have to be made. With a $166 billion trade deficit and $1 trillion in international debt, assuming a 10 percent interest rate, $266 billion would have to be cut out of American imports when the end comes. Americans would have to earn rather than borrow the $100 billion that they owe in interest on their international debts and they could no longer finance $166 billion of imports.

Every $60 billion of lost exports in Japan means approximately one million jobs. If its $130 billion trade surplus disappears, Japan loses approximately two million jobs as the rest of the world balances their accounts with Japan. But Japan has to do more than balance its trading accounts. To pay interest on the loans and investments that Japan has made to them, the rest of the world has to run trade surpluses with Japan if they cannot pay for those loans with the American earnings. If Japan has $500 billion in net assets in the rest of the world (outside of the United States), these countries need a $50 billion trade surplus with Japan (assuming a 10 percent interest rate) to fund interest payments on their debts—another one million Japanese jobs lost. The bigger the Japan net asset position, the greater the eventual job loss.

Both countries have enormous incentives to institute adjustment policies before those adjustments are forced upon them by international financial markets. Gradual changes are much less traumatic than sudden changes. For Americans, borrowing huge amounts of money that can only be repaid with large reductions in their future standard of living and selling one's capitalistic inheritance to foreigners isn't any smarter for a country than it would be for an individual. They need to be gradually weaned away from a lifestyle based on borrowed funds. For the Japanese, a gradual adjustment to the long-run realities of economic gravity is much easier than a sudden shock when gravity finally kicks in. Industries find their foreign markets slowly shrinking rather than finding themselves plunging off an economic cliff.

Economically, as long as Japan is willing to keep absorbing losses in its assets held abroad and as long as it is willing to sell exports abroad for less than those same products are sold at home (the Japanese consumer remains willing to subsidize the foreign consumer), there is no economic pressure on Japan to act. And in fact Japan won't act.

Promises to open markets and promises that trade surpluses will shortly disappear have been made too often to be believed. Arguments about whether Japanese markets are really open or closed are easily settled. Are the same products for sale in both markets at the same price (plus or minus transportation costs)? If not, markets are closed, since some capitalist would move goods from the cheaper to the more expensive market until prices come into equilibrium to acquire the riskless profits that are to be made if markets were open.

Since American prices (even of Japanese goods) are far lower than the prices of the same goods in Japan, the Japanese market is closed. The MR2 Toyota sells for $30,435 in Japan and $24,000 in the United States.[7] The U.S. Department of Commerce and MITI found that in the early 1990s Japanese prices were higher for about two thirds of the goods surveyed. The Japanese Economic Planning Agency has found that the price gap between Toyko and New York was widening in the 1990s.[8] Overall, a comparison of purchasing power parity and market-determined exchange rates indicates that the prices of tradable goods are 2.3 to 2.8 times as expensive in Japan as they are in the United States.

Japan's markets are not open, but at the same time there is no reason why Japan should change its habits, culture, or traditional business methods to satisfy American demands. The Japanese way of doing business makes for a more inclusive egalitarian society. The American way leads to a large degree of inequality and the Japanese have every right to reject it. They have a right to defend the Japanese way. At the same time, the United States does not have to accept a big trade deficit simply because the Japanese culture is different.

Given the time horizon of political American trade negotiators (four years at the most) relative to the time horizon of career administrative Japanese trade negotiators, the Japanese can always win bilateral negotiations by simply delaying. Eventually the Americans, wanting to claim a victory before the next election, will agree to a paper formula that allows them to claim a victory while leaving the Japanese trade surplus untouched.[9] Back in Tokyo the Japanese negotiators will quietly toast a victory three months later when most Americans are no longer paying attention to ensure that the Japanese public knows who really "won."[10]

So it was again in the auto dispute of 1995. The Americans embarked on a crusade to open the Japanese auto market with the threat of 100 percent tariffs on Japanese luxury auto exports to the United States if the Japanese did not buy more American parts when building and repairing cars and if Japan did not allow Americans better access to dealerships (in Japan they are owned by the manufacturers and traditionally sell only the cars of one manufacturer) so that the Americans could sell their cars without the cost of setting up a separate dealership network (as the Japanese are able to do when they come to the United States). After months of negotiations a "successful" conclusion was reached, with the Japanese promising to do nothing that they weren't otherwise going to do. Some pledges were made but they were "nonbinding," "nonspecific," and subject to "change." In announcing the agreement the Japanese prime minister, Tomiichi Murayama, crowed that the Americans had "lost" the argument.[11]

Each American president comes into power promising to do something about the Japanese surplus or the American deficit and ends up doing nothing. The Japanese trade surplus and the American deficit at the end of his term of office is bigger than it was when he entered office. President Clinton is a good example of the phenomenon—tough talk, weak negotiations, legalistic Japanese promises, nothing accomplished, the Japanese trade surplus still growing, promises about creating a high-investment society in America but an America with ever lower savings rates and larger trade deficits.

The Japanese prime minister is just as bad, Japanese promises to buy more from the rest of the world being just as empty as American promises to save more. America has negotiated market-opening treaties many times and failed every time. American credibility when it comes to threatening to punish Japan if it fails to open its markets is zero— and the rest of the world's capacity or appetite for doing so is even less.

American trade negotiators do not know enough about Japan to force open the Japanese market. And even if they did, they don't have the power to force Japan to act. If Japan doesn't really want to open, there are always other perfectly legal methods that can be used to discourage foreign sales. If too many cars are being sold, they can simply do what the South Koreans have done—give everyone buying a foreign car a tax audit.[12] Everyone can recount the stories about how Japan managed to keep out this or that product, from companies constructing ice skating rinks to companies selling film. Construction markets, for example in the ice skating rink case, can be legally open but effectively closed by issuing specifications that only Japanese firms can meet.[13] Every company with a dominant world market share reports the same problem. Whatever their market share worldwide, they have a market share in Japan far below what they have anywhere else.[14]

With the exception of raw material producers, Japan runs trade surpluses with everyone. The problem is not what it sells (it sells just about what would be expected from general models of economic behavior) but that it does not buy from the rest of the world what one would expect when the prices of those commodities are much cheaper in the rest of the world. The nature of the problem is easy to see in one set of statistics. Foreign-owned firms produce 17 percent of the U.S. GDP and 24 percent of the German GDP. How much do they produce in Japan? Only 0.2 percent and half of that is by one company—IBM Japan.[15] Often what look like American firms (McDonald's, Disney) are not American-majority foreign-owned in Japan.

If firms can't own, it is very difficult to sell. No one (not Americans, not Europeans, not other east Asians) has significantly penetrated the Japanese market with either exports or domestically built products.

To reduce its trade surplus Japan would have to change its social system and it does not want to do so. Closed markets are a way of life and no one can force open the Japanese market if they do not want to open their markets. The Japanese will open their markets voluntarily or they won't open them. They have many internal incentives to do so. They know that the current pattern of trade is not viable in the long run. They know that their economy is now so big that it cannot forever continue to run as an export-led economy. But no one is capable of making them change.

Because of the stock market and property crash in Japan, Japan has not been able to end what in the rest of the world is remembered as the 1990–91 recession. Japan's recession seems to go on without end. Quarterly growth rates consistently slowed from mid-1990 until late 1992 when they finally went negative. Between then and the end of 1994, quarterly growth rates bounced up and down—three times above zero, three times below zero—but still sharply negative in the last quarter of 1994 (minus 3.4 percent per year) and were minimal in the first two quarters of 1995.[16] When Japan's longest recession since the Great Depression would end, no one could say. By 1995 Japan's industrial production was 3 percent below where it had been in 1992.[17]

Japan's never-ending recession is the product of exactly the same factors that produced the Great Depression in the United States. In the United States in the 1930s, a financial collapse led to an economic collapse. In Japan in the 1990s, a financial collapse led to economic stagnation. Traditional remedies don't work. Japanese interest rates are pushed close to zero (0.35 percent on bank savings accounts) without causing a rebound.[18] In the Great Depression economists knew this phenomenon as "liquidity trap." One set of ineffectual fiscal policies follows another. None is big enough or bold enough to offset the negative effects of the financial collapse. Private sector debt (twice as high relative to the GDP as that of the United States) is simply too large for the private economy to restart its economic engines.[19]

Traditional Japanese methods of restarting economic growth—for example, exporting more—don't work. Japan's economy is simply now so large that even this extra $100 billion in exports gained in the first half of the 1990s wasn't enough to restart economic growth in the aftermath of a recession and a financial collapse. With the value of the yen rising strongly in early 1995, exports could not be expected to rise further and at midyear no one could see a time when vigorous growth would resume. At yen values below 108 yen to the dollar, Japanese capitalism is selling its products abroad below its average costs. At yen values below 80 yen to the dollar, it is selling products below marginal costs.[20] Capitalism does not work with perpetual losses. Something has to change.

Japan needs to build a domestically pulled economy rather than an export-pushed economy if it is to resume growing. It has simply become too big to rely on export-led growth. What it needs is obvious.

Japan has much less housing space per person than other Asian countries that are much poorer than it (South Korea, for example). The Japanese want more space. It is the first thing they buy when stationed abroad. If all of the myriad rules and regulations that make it expensive to build housing in Japan (shade laws, earthquake laws, rice land laws, inheritance tax laws) were swept away, Japan could be riding a housing boom back to prosperity. But if that was done, those who had bought very expensive, very small houses in the past would find the value of those old houses falling. For them, new losses would be piled on top of existing losses. That has to be done if Japan is to prosper in the 1990s, but the Japanese government cannot bring itself to do what it should do, since Japan's political system collapsed owing to earlier political scandals and is now too weak to make the necessary decisions. Japan sits in stagnation waiting for the traditional post–World War II American economy locomotive. But that locomotive is no longer running (see Chapter 11).

When America and Japan talk to each other about solving their deficit and surplus problems before a crisis arises, there is talk but almost no communication. In the words of Seymour Martin Lipset, there is a clash between American beliefs in American exceptionalism and Japanese beliefs in Japanese uniqueness.[21] Both recommend that the other change to become more like them. Yet neither particularly likes the lifestyle of the other.

Neither Japan nor the United States is going to take the actions they should take. Neither has the willingness or perhaps the ability to impose the substantial, but manageable, amounts of current economic pain that would be required to prevent much larger, sudden amounts of pain in the future. Both will wait for the crisis—the day the United States can no longer finance its trade deficit, the day that its American losses are so huge that Japan isn't willing to finance what will be described as the American trade deficit but which is also the Japanese trade surplus.

Since trade deficits can only continue as long as someone is willing to lend the deficit country the money necessary to pay for its trade deficits, the current pattern will essentially continue as long as Japan is willing to lend to the United States the money that the United States needs to pay for its entire trade deficit—a sum about twice that of the bilateral deficit between Japan and the United States, since the rest of the world pays for its Japanese deficits with its American surpluses. Technically, Japan could do so for a long time. The insurmountable problem is not so much the trade deficit but all those outside dollar balances held as reserves by other countries and companies.

At some point, whatever the Japanese do, foreigners outside of Japan will become nervous about the values of their dollar holdings and want to exchange them for assets denominated in yen or marks. At that point Japan basically has to be willing to absorb an enormous number of dollars in a short period of time—a sum many times that of the United States' annual trade deficit. As it absorbs those dollars, the dollar will be declining in value and someone in Japan (the government?) will be absorbing enormous financial losses.

As the dollar loses value (the real, trade-weighted value of the dollar, a measure that corrects for differences in domestic inflation between countries, has fallen 33 percent from 1984 to 1994—43 percent vis-à-vis the German mark and 58 percent vis-à-vis the Japanese yen), it makes less and less sense to use the dollar as a store of value (in early 1995, 60 percent of official foreign exchange reserves and 50 percent of private financial assets were still denominated in dollars) or as a medium of transactions (two thirds of world trade was still denominated in dollars).[22] Anyone denominating their assets in yen or marks rather than in dollars or anyone signing contracts in yen or marks rather than dollars would have been a lot richer than those who used dollars. Capitalists don't forever forgo opportunities to get richer. Whatever the Americans and Japanese do, the rest of the world will at some point flee from the dollar.

When it was the dominant world power in capitalism, America could at least in principle dream of making the system work by forcing other countries to become more American. Such an attitude is of course what lies behind America's trade negotiations with the Japanese over automobiles and with the Chinese over pirated movies, computer software, and CDs. We want them to change to operate their economies more like Americans do. But Americans cannot do that anymore. In both cases American negotiators were ultimately unsuccessful. Nothing has changed in the Japanese auto market. The Chinese publicly agreed to close their plants that were pirating software but shortly thereafter quietly reopened them.[23]

America's only power is to control its own economy. It has something the rest of the world wants very badly—access to the American market—and it can use access to that market as part of its bargaining strength. Americans run only one economy and are smart enough to change only one economy—their own. The correct and only American answer to the problem of closed markets abroad is to set up what I will call the "principle of correspondence." There must be some relationship between what a country sells in America and what it buys from America.

For those with persistent large surpluses such as Japan, this might mean auctioning off import tickets without which Japanese exports could not be sold in the United States. The amount of import tickets sold might, for example, be $10 billion more than the amount that Japan had bought from the United States in the previous year. If Japan buys $100 billion worth of American imports in 1995, it can sell $110 billion worth of exports in 1996. If it buys $200 billion, it can sell $210 billion. The ball is in the Japanese court. Americans aren't going to tell the Japanese how to run Japan (the Japanese decide whether they are going to buy or not buy much cheaper rice from the rest of the world), but we Americans are going to tell them how we plan to run the United States. But such a policy also means cleaning up our own economic act by shifting from a low-investment, high-consumption society to a higher-investment, lower-consumption society.

At some point the current trading system chokes to death its Japanese surpluses, its American deficits, and everyone's failure to penetrate the world's second largest market. While we don't know when or how the U.S. trade deficit will end, it will end. Everyone will know that the end is near when the rest of the world refuses to lend to the United States in dollar terms and demands that their loans be denominated in some foreign currency. If the United States complies with those demands at that time, it will be stupid beyond belief—saddling itself with debts that only grow bigger as the value of the dollar falls.

When the current pattern of structural deficits and surpluses ends, there will be a huge shock to third world development. In the post–World War II period, the United States was the big, wealthy open market that provided the place where export-led growth could start. The pattern made sense. Only the United States and Canada were wealthy areas that did not need to recover from the destruction of World War II. But even after they became wealthy, neither Europe nor Japan has been willing to play this role. Japan imports practically no third-world-manufactured products that it does not reexport, and Europe's imports are highly restricted.

In their turn, Europe, Japan, the four little Asian dragons, and now China have all used the American market to jump-start economic development. Without easy access to wealthy first world markets, economic development is difficult if not impossible in the second and third worlds. Everyone who has made themselves substantially richer since World War II has had access to the U.S. market.

That access is also central to patterns of trade that do not directly involve the United States. On the Pacific Rim countries run big trade deficits with Japan, which they finance out of their trade surpluses with the United States. Without the United States as an open market willing to take Asian goods, intra-Asian trade would collapse tomorrow morning. No country could pay its Japanese import bills and very quickly no one would be creditworthy. East Asians point to rapidly rising intraregional trade, but those statistics are misleading. What looks like South Korean sales to China are dependent upon China's sales to the United States. China's 1995 trade surplus with Japan is similarly misleading since it sells Japanese components that are installed on products that are re-exported to Europe and America. Almost nothing is sold to the Japanese consumer. Without the American trade the intraregional sales would stop.

When the United States has to shift from having a large trade deficit to having a substantial trade surplus to pay interest on its outstanding international debt, east Asian trade will collapse unless Japan is willing to quickly become a large net importer, buying what the United States now buys—something that is possible but highly unlikely. When the end comes, all of the trading patterns (what is exported and what is imported) on the Pacific Rim and in the third world more generally will have to be fundamentally rebuilt.

Yet no one on the Pacific Rim or anywhere else has an interest in helping the United States solve this fundamental problem. As long as the United States runs a larger trade deficit than Japan runs a trade surplus, no one else has an economic problem. The rest of the world's international accounts are balanced and they can pay their Japanese bills (their Japanese trade deficit) with their American earnings (their American trade surplus). This plus an American tradition of dealing with Japan on a bilateral basis turns what should be a multilateral problem into a bilateral problem only of interest to the United States and Japan.

But let no one doubt that this earthquake will happen. No one knows when, but the forces on each side of the fault are enormous.

APPENDIX A
SAVING MORE TO CORRECT TRADE DEFICITS

Since it is so often said that the United States needs to save more to correct its trade deficit and that Japan will continue to have a trade surplus unless it saves less, it is important to understand the aspects of truth and falsity in such statements. There is no doubt that America needs to save more, but the evidence is not a balance of trade deficit. America needs to save more, since it is not investing enough to ensure adequate growth in the future. A trade deficit, if it were made up of investment goods, might be part of the solution, not part of the problem, in curing an investment deficit.

Those who imply that simply saving more would easily or quickly solve the U.S. current account deficit are fundamentally misusing some simple accounting identities. Those identities flow from the way in which the National Income and Product Accounts are constructed. In those accounts, as the name implies, there are two ways of measuring the total output of the economy. Of necessity two different ways of measuring the same thing must come to the same conclusion. On the product side the National Income and Product Accounts measure the production of consumption goods (C), investment goods (I), government goods (G), and exports minus imports (X−M). On the income side they measure personal income, which can be divided into consumption (C), savings (S), and taxes (T).

Because they are measuring the same gross domestic product, GDP, C+I+G+(X−M) must equal C+S+T. Algebraically, the Cs cancel and the resulting equation can be written as X−M must equal (S−I) plus (T−G). If government budgets are balanced, then the T−G term is zero and X−M must equal S−I. If a country (America) has a balance of payments deficit it must therefore be true that its savings are not large enough to cover its investments. Conversely, if a country has a balance of payments surplus (Japan), it must be true that its savings plus tax revenue must exceed its investment and government spending.

It is important to understand that such identities do not imply causation. It is just as true to say that a smaller trade deficit would lead to more savings relative to investment as it is to say that more savings relative to investment would lead to a smaller trade deficit. Suppose that the United States was to save more. More savings (or less consumption, since they are just two different ways of saying the same thing) leads to less demand for goods and services, production falls, people are laid off, there is less investment and the GDP falls. The balance of payments gets better precisely because incomes are down and people cannot afford to buy imported products.

Since consumers will also stop buying domestically produced products as their incomes fall, the cut in incomes required to reduce imports to the level of exports could be very large. As incomes go down, savings also decline because of the lower incomes from which savings can be made, but since investment is falling even faster due to falling output, savings and investment will eventually come into balance and when they do exports must equal imports, but both happen at much reduced levels of output.

Conversely, suppose the United States was to solve its trade imbalance by imposing import quotas. With fewer exports to America, production and incomes fall in the rest of the world. With lower incomes, a country such as Japan saves less, bringing investment and savings back into balance in Japan. In the United States those who have been spending their money on imports must save more or shift to higher-price domestic products. As they buy those products, unemployed resources are employed, incomes rise, and with higher incomes comes more savings. In addition, with more domestic production and higher prices business savings rise. If imports are fixed at the level of exports, some combination of the two must happen until savings and investment come back into balance to match the balance that has been forced using quotas between exports and imports.

The same analysis applies in Japan. It could correct its balance of payments surplus by saving less (consuming more) or by exporting less. Exporting less would in fact cause less savings, since fewer exports would lead to falling production, lower incomes, and hence less savings. If importing was made easier, the same analysis holds; the only difference is where the job losses are located—the import-competing industries versus the exporting industries.

If Japan had excess production capacity, there would be a way to cure the problem that does not imply a lot of pain. Japan would stimulate its economy (lower taxes, more spending) and part of the higher incomes earned by those newly employed workers would go to buy imports. If at the same time Japan made it easier for foreigners to export to Japan so that more of existing incomes were spent on imports, its surpluses would disappear. Workers in import-competing industries would be laid off, but they would find reemployment in the rapidly expanding domestic economy. Unfortunately, the Japanese surpluses are now so large and its propensity to import so small that even with the surplus production capacity that does exist in 1995, a painless structural adjustment is not possible.

While accounting identities always hold, they say nothing about bilateral trade deficits or surpluses. Japan runs trade surpluses with countries that save more than it does (South Korea or Taiwan) and with countries that save less than it does (the United States, the United Kingdom). America has an overall deficit but it has a trade surplus with Europe even though Europe saves more than America. America could have an excess of investment over savings and Japan an excess of savings over investment yet America could run a bilateral trade surplus with Japan.

Chapter 11

Economic Instability

BUSINESS CYCLES

Business cycles are as intrinsic to capitalism as earthquakes are to the earth's geology. Capitalism has always had them and always will have them. In the fifty years from 1945 to 1995, the United States had ten years in which output fell (1946, 1949, 1954, 1958, 1970, 1974, 1975, 1980, 1982, 1991), and in 1960–61 there was a twelve-month period with negative growth although it wasn't deep enough to cause either of those two calendar years to fall into the negative category.

Capitalistic recessions occur for a number of reasons. For sometimes good reasons and sometimes trivial reasons, demand starts to rise or fall rapidly in some sector of the economy. Negative growth in 1946 and 1954 was caused by cutbacks in military procurement following World War II and the Korean War. The 1958 recession followed in the wake of an unsustainable boom in auto sales where people in the preceding years were buying the cars that they had not been able to buy in the 1930s or allowed to buy during World War II and the Korean War. But once that pent-up demand had been satisfied, sales fell back dramatically in 1958. The recessions of the 1970s were all connected to the various oil and food shocks. The 1982 recession was deliberately engineered by the government (the Fed's very high interest rates) to tame inflation. If we were isolating the causes of the 1990–91 recession, our analysis would focus on the earlier crash in real estate prices and the resultant reduction in wealth (and hence purchasing power) caused by that crash.

In addition to exogenous upward or downward shocks, the internal dynamics of economic decisions (what in economics is known as the multiplier-accelerator model) leads to business cycles. Demand rises and factories accelerate their production. Because sales are rising business firms all along the delivery chain decide that they need to add to their inventories of finished goods or goods in the process of being produced. Each firm orders more of the products or components in question. To meet that demand, factories further accelerate production. With rising intermediate and final demands nearing capacity, factory owners place large orders for new equipment to increase capacity. Delivery times lengthen. Hearing about shortages, consumers start to buy ahead of their needs. Panic buying may set in among both consumers and producers who worry that they will not get what they need as delivery times lengthen. For a while such a cycle can feed on itself. Demand rises, factories accelerate production, orders for components rise, more plant and equipment is bought. Demand rises!

Eventually the cycle has to turn. Consumers decide that they have more than enough of the product on hand. Sales stabilize and quit rising. Inventory orders fall; factories reduce production. With production falling, factories stop ordering new equipment. Even a slowdown in the rate of growth can lead to a dramatic reduction in the orders for, and the production of, new equipment. With production falling in both the consumer goods sector and the producer goods sector, workers are laid off, incomes and purchasing power fall. With less consumer income, sales fall. Undesired inventories build up. Firms cut back further on orders. The economy spirals downward.

The gasoline shortages and long lines at filling stations after the first OPEC oil shock in the early 1970s are now thought to have been caused not so much by shortages of gasoline but mostly by consumers fearing gasoline shortages who were continually topping up their tanks rather than driving with them half or mostly empty as they usually did.[1] This desire to fill up what in the industry is known as "secondary storage facilities" created a real shortage in gasoline, soaring gasoline prices, and long lines at the pump. OPEC raised prices but the shortages were made at home—not by OPEC selling less oil to the wealthy industrial world.

In capitalism booms lead to booms and declines feed upon declines. In theory, those who control inventories should moderate cycles. Seeing where the economy is going in the long run, they should use up their stocks of inventories on the inevitable upswings and build up their stocks of inventories on the downswings. And whatever their ability to do this in the past, that ability should be greater now with modern information technologies and the sophisticated mathematics of just-in-time inventories. Inventory cycles should have become weaker. But it is one of the mysteries of economics that all of our improvements in inventory control have not caused them to do so. Inventory cycles are, if anything, worse than they used to be. Those who control inventory investments and disinvestments pile on strong upward or downward trends—making those trends worse rather than better. The volatility of inventories increases as the absolute level of inventories declines relative to production—just as the danger of falling over the edge of a cliff goes up the closer and faster one is running to the edge of the cliff.

Theoretically, capitalism should not have business cycles at all. As demand falls or rises, prices and wages, not output, should fall or rise. Supply and demand should ensure that all of the productive factors that want to be employed are employed. Workers who are laid off should quickly find reemployment by offering to work for lower wages. Employers, if necessary, should fire existing workers who refuse to work for lower wages to make room for those who will. However, markets, especially the labor market, just don't seem to quickly and easily clear by lowering wages or prices. Output adjusts more quickly than either wages or prices—exactly the reverse of what should happen.

As a result, capitalism comes with recessions. They are part of the capitalistic system. They cannot be eliminated. But to say that recessions will exist is not to say how often or how deep they will be, or how speedy the recoveries. Until the 1990s post–World War II recessions have been short, shallow, and infrequent, because governments, the United States in particular, came running to the rescue with easier monetary policies and fiscal policies whenever recessions threatened or occurred.

The 1980–81 recession is a good example. In 1982 and 1983 the United States rushed to the rescue with large cuts in interest rates (three-month Treasury bill rates fell 39 percent from 1981 to 1983) and a huge fiscal stimulus package (with President Reagan's large tax cuts and big increase in defense spending, the government deficit rose 263 percent between 1981 and 1983).[2] Keynesian aggregate demand management policies were alive even in the conservative Reagan administration. Like a Ferrari with the pedal to the metal, economic growth promptly took off at a 10 percent rate in the first twelve months after Paul Volcker announced his dramatic changes in monetary policies. As a result of this aggressive stimulus to demand, the rest of the world escaped from their recessions by exporting more to a rapidly growing American market.

The shift in America's global position has some serious consequences for how severe business cycles will be in the era ahead. Contrast the actions of the early 1980s with what happened a decade later in the aftermath of the 1990–91 recession. For the first time since World War II, there was no American locomotive. The United States did not rush to the rescue with big cuts in interest rates or a huge increase in its fiscal stimulus. Instead it relied on modest cuts in interest rates to engineer a moderate recovery in America. But a moderate American recovery was no longer big enough to pull the rest of the world out of their recessions.

To work well, the global capitalistic system as it was designed after World War II needed a dominant economic locomotive—a country that could act to help others improve their economic conditions since it did not have to worry about its own economic condition.[3] But in the first half of the 1990s, the United States was no longer such a country. U.S. policy makers were notably uninterested in aggressively helping the rest of the world recover from their recessions. During and after the 1990–91 recession, America's antirecessionary interest rate cuts were modest, no fiscal stimulus was applied, and its interest rates were pushed back up long before it was appropriate from the perspective of the rest of the world given their weak to nonexistent recoveries. The change in America's willingness to adopt policies that would help the rest of the world was dramatic, since there were no domestic excuses for its unwillingness to act more aggressively. American inflation was both low and falling. Before, America had always been willing to help end world recessions even at some cost to itself. Now it was unwilling to help even when there were no costs to itself.

Without an American global economic locomotive, recessionary recoveries were very slow in Europe and Japan. Europe's postrecessionary recovery was better than that of Japan but still not strong enough to eliminate persistent, and what increasingly looked like permanent, double-digit unemployment rates. With an anemic 2.1 percent growth rate in 1994, unemployment rates were still rising in most of Europe.[4]

Technically, recessions officially end with two quarters of positive growth, but what might be defined as a real recovery (falling unemployment) was not in sight. Some European countries such as Finland and Sweden were not expected to return to 1990 GDP levels until 1996.

Europe found that it could not use lower interest rates to stimulate growth, since Germany's high interest rate policy (designed to fight inflation flowing from the integration with East Germany and to attract capital investment into East Germany) imprisoned everyone else's monetary policies. Germany essentially became a sea anchor preventing rapid recovery. Eventually Italy and Britain could not hold out and in the summer of 1992 were forced to cut themselves loose from the D-mark zone and substantially devalue. That allowed them to lower their interest rates, and with lower interest rates and lower costs due to devalued currencies, their growth accelerated, but most of Europe hung on to D-mark parity, high interest rates, and slow growth. What the United Kingdom and Italy gained, the rest of Europe probably lost.

The Germans simply were unwilling to replace the American global locomotive with a regional European economic locomotive. Without a global or a regional locomotive, in the mid-1990s Europe suffers from double-digit unemployment, has been operating at or very near those high levels of unemployment for almost a decade, and no one expects to do much better in the foreseeable future.

National countercyclical Keynesian stimulus policies have simply disappeared. In the aftermath of the 1990–91 recession, only Japan and the United States reduced interest rates to stimulate demand and no country even attempted countercyclical fiscal policies—tax cuts or expenditure increases. In the summer of 1992 just when they should have been stimulating their economies, Italy, France, and the United Kingdom were all raising interest rates to defend their currencies.

Inaction can be explained by some combination of fears of inflation, an inability to control structural budget deficits, and the growth of a global economy where one-country Keynesian policies have become impossible. But the bottom line was inaction.

In the 1970s and 1980s inflation did not seem to disappear regardless of how high unemployment went—in Spain unemployment reached 22 percent yet inflation was still close to 5 percent and expected to rise.[5] To prevent inflation from accelerating, national governments seemed always to be braking their economies and the right moment to accelerate seemed never to appear.

If governments are to run countercyclical fiscal policies, they must be able and willing to raise taxes and cut spending in booms in order to have the economic room to cut taxes and raise spending during recessions. Keynesian policies do not call for perpetual large government deficits. If one isn't able to raise taxes or cut spending during booms, one cannot for long lower taxes and increase spending during recessions. In 1981–82 President Reagan cut taxes and raised spending but failed completely when it came time to raise taxes and cut spending in the mid-1980s. Instead he predicted a painless return to balanced budgets (under the doctrine of supply-side economics, growth would be so vigorous that government budgets would come back into balance without taxes having to be raised or spending cut), but it proved not to be true. The fiscal dividends of the 1960s no longer existed. Even in a period of rapid growth, government spending, mostly related to the elderly, was rising more rapidly than government tax revenue.

With everyone running large structural budget deficits that can only grow larger with time, no government feels that it can lower taxes or raise spending during recessionary periods to combat recessions. If they showed any willingness to raise spending during recessions, that willingness would lead to voter demands for permanent, not temporary, increases in spending. This spending would have to be balanced in the long run by higher taxes that are both undesirable economically and unfeasible politically. Since raising taxes after recessions are over has become politically impossible, governments now live in a fiscal prison from which they cannot escape.

Keynesian countercyclical policies are also blocked by the emergence of a global economy that has made one-country national Keynesian economics impossible for all but the world's very largest countries. The world's financial markets can now move so much money around the world so quickly that monetary policies have to be adjusted to their dictates—and not to the domestic needs of the economy. To keep from being hit by an outflow of funds governments often have to raise interest rates when slack domestic demand and unemployed productive resources (both human and physical) would call for precisely the opposite—lower interest rates. To attempt to reflate when others don't simply produces balance of payments problems (imports rise faster than exports), falling currency values that accelerate inflation because of higher import prices, little increase in domestic employment since too much of the extra spending goes to imports, and a rapid retreat to austerity under threat of capital flight.

As a consequence, recessions can only be tolerated—they cannot be fought. New governments facing high unemployment often talk about stimulus but end up adopting austerity measures (higher taxes and cuts in spending) that are just the opposite of what Lord Keynes would have prescribed and what they themselves promised to get elected. Campaigning on a full-employment platform when they came into power in the early 1980s, the French Socialists tried to reflate using classic Keynesian monetary and fiscal policies to move France back toward full employment. They completely failed and were driven to policies of austerity before they even got started. A decade later a new conservative French government also promises action to fight unemployment, but by late 1995 it too was trying to impose austerity policies. France is the fourth largest economy in the world. If it cannot act independently, one-country national monetary and fiscal policies are now clearly impossible for everyone with the possible exception of the Big Three (the United States, Japan, and Germany). In a global economy where a one-country Keynesian stimulus is impossible, there are no local mechanisms for fighting recessions.

In the United States the realities are more complex. While structural budget deficits stopped the Clinton administration from using countercyclical fiscal policies to speed the recovery from the 1990–91 recession (they were proposed but later dropped), experience indicates that the United States could still, if it wished, act alone. In the recession of the early 1990s the United States successfully used lower interest rates to help it recover from a recession. But the United States is unique in that it doesn't care what happens to the value of its currency. Imports are a small fraction of its GDP, Americans don't borrow in foreign currencies, few Americans take foreign vacations, and the American market is so large, so competitive, and so important that exporters tend to price in dollar terms—holding dollar prices constant even though the value of the dollar has declined (essentially lowering American prices if they were evaluated in their home currencies). As a result, the value of the dollar has little impact on either domestic costs of living or the inflation rate. In addition, the rest of the world is willing to lend to America in its own currency and thus America can finance balance of payments deficits far longer than those who have to borrow the funds in someone else's currency. As with everyone else, low interest rates lead to a lower value for the dollar, but unlike everyone else, Americans don't care. But what is true for America is true for no one else.

In Germany and Japan no one knows what would happen if they tried to vigorously reflate. Are they large enough to still have some national economic independence left, or have they too lost their economic independence? In the case of Germany no one knows, since they haven't attempted to do so recently.

While Japan, like the United States, moved to lower interest rates to counteract its recession, lower interest rates did not kick-start the Japanese economy as they did the American economy. The big difference between the two countries was what happened to wealth. In the United States the stock market boomed, creating greater personal wealth and more consumption, while in Japan the stock market crashed, destroying, as we have seen, vast amounts of personal wealth. A 36 percent fall in net worth has to have enormous negative consequences for both consumption and investment spending. In all probability Japan could reflate but only if it was willing to structurally rebuild itself so that it was a domestically pulled rather than export-led economy. As an export-led economy it is simply too dependent on growth in the rest of the world to restart its own economic engines.

The United States, Japan, and Germany (together composing about 50 percent of the world economy) could coordinate their fiscal and monetary policies to become a joint world locomotive. Growth responded rapidly to the coordinated monetary and fiscal policies put in place in the aftermath of the October 1987 stock market crash. In mid-1987, 1988 was expected to be a mediocre year by the economic forecasters.[6] In November 1987 it was expected to be a very bad year. But 1988 was in fact the best year of the decade. Coordinated monetary and fiscal policies put in place to offset the effects of the stock market crash quickly accelerated the global economy. But the necessary coordination is not politically feasible without a clear crisis. The three countries are almost never at exactly the same stage of the business cycle at the same time, and as a result the countries don't need exactly the same medicine at the same time. Coordination also requires each of the three countries from time to time to do things that are good for the global economy but painful at home. The leaders of none of these three countries were elected to help the world at the cost of inflicting economic pain on voters at home. Japan isn't willing to reduce its trade surplus (increasing export demands in the rest of the world), the United States is not willing to shift from being a high-consumption society to being a high-savings and high-investment society (thereby allowing the world's real interest rates to fall), and Germany isn't willing to have low interest rates and take a chance on more inflation.

The difference between a United States that feels its global leadership responsibilities and one that does not, and the effects of noncoordination can be dramatically seen in Chairman Alan Greenspan and the Federal Reserve Board's decision to raise U.S. interest rates seven times in twelve months from early 1994 to early 1995, in contrast with the actions of Chairman Paul Volcker and the Fed in the 1982 recession. The 1982–83 policies made the global recession vanish almost instantly. In contrast, higher U.S. interest rates in the 1994 and 1995 policies made the global recession longer and deeper than it would otherwise have been. From the point of view of European or Japanese cyclical recoveries, Alan Greenspan's rate increases came at exactly the wrong time. Europe was only just beginning to pull out of its very lengthy recession and Japan was still stuck in its recession. Neither needed the United States leading the world to higher interest rates. However weak the recovery would have been, higher American interest rates guaranteed an even weaker recovery.

A decade or two earlier the Fed would have thought about the potential effects of its actions on the "free world" before acting. But without the threat of communism the Fed does not have to worry about the economic health of the free world. Mr. Greenspan could, and would, defend himself by arguing that the world had changed dramatically over the intervening decade. The United States had gone from being the world's largest net creditor nation with trade surpluses and a federal budget balanced at full employment to being the world's largest net debtor nation with persistent structural deficits in both its fiscal and international accounts. It could no longer do what it had done. He is of course right about the circumstances—America's circumstances are very different.

The result, as we have already seen, is 60 percent slower world growth. Governments willing to aggressively fight recessions and stimulate growth were replaced by governments who spent all of their time fighting inflation and protecting currency values.

Yet, citizens still expect their governments to alleviate, if not eliminate, recessions. Incumbent governments lose elections when recessions occur. Citizens don't like to see their governments humiliated by the world's financial markets. They take out their resulting anger, not on amorphous financiers, but on their elected politicians. With governments' ineffectual standing aside in the face of capitalism's inevitable downturns, governments themselves grow weaker as their leaders are thrown out of office for not doing what their citizens want done. Political leaders can argue with some validity that global conditions just don't let them do what earlier leaders did (act vigorously to end recessions and run their economies with very low unemployment rates) and that they should not be punished for not doing the impossible, but this is a hard message to sell to their electorates. If leaders cannot accomplish what citizens want done, why have them?

The consequences are clear. Without an American global economic locomotive, without macroeconomic coordination among the Big Three, without countries willing to be regional economic locomotives, and with national stimulus impossible for all but the very biggest (perhaps only the United States), the world will have more frequent, longer, and deeper recessions with much slower recoveries. This new reality is evident in Europe and Japan and visible in the United States. A short and shallow recession in 1990–91 was followed by an initially weak but gradually accelerating recovery that was aborted in 1995 by the interest rate increases of 1994. This pattern should be seen as the new standard pattern. The infrequent short, shallow recessions of the post–World War II era are over.

STRONGER FINANCIAL SHOCKS

Like recessions, financial shocks are as old as capitalism itself. Tulip mania started in Holland in 1624. The eighteenth century witnessed the South Sea Bubble in Britain (speculation focused on the shares of the South Sea company that had been chartered to slave and fish in the South Seas) and the Mississippi Land Bubble in France (the focus of the attention was land values in France's territory of Louisiana). The nineteenth century was full of financial panics that only look small in comparison with the "big one" of the twentieth century—the stock market crash of 1929 and the banking collapse of 1930 that led to the Great Depression. That quake almost destroyed capitalism—unemployment hit 27 percent.

The last half of the twentieth century has also seen its share of small and large financial panics. The collapse of the American savings and loan industry, a worldwide collapse in property values, the stock market crash of October 1987, one major stock market crash in a small country (Taiwan), and a very big stock market crash in the world's second biggest economy (Japan). Financial instability is to capitalism what succession problems are to medieval kingdoms or dictatorships.[7] Both put their respective systems at risk.

Like unemployment, theoretically, financial crises should not occur in capitalism. Patient, long-run investors who know the true underlying values beneath those financial assets should be buying and selling in the financial markets to offset the instabilities created by the herd mentality of the short-run speculators who jump on upward and downward trends. Unfortunately, patient financial investors with their eyes on the distant future interested in long-run-equilibrium values just don't seem to exist in any number.

If one examines financial crises, the question is not "Why did the markets crash?" but "How could market prices have reached such unsustainable levels in the first place?" Examine the value of tulips in the 1620s in Holland (one tulip bulb bought three homes in Amsterdam), the value of the shares of the South Sea Company in the early eighteenth century, the value of land along the Mississippi in France's Louisiana Territory in the late eighteenth century during the Mississippi Land Bubble, or the values of the American stock market in 1929 (doubling in 1928 and 1929 although the GNP was already falling in those years), the Taiwan stock market in 1988, property values in the mid to late 1980s, and the Japanese stock market in 1990 (100-to-1 price-earnings ratios) and in each case you see assets clearly grossly overvalued by the financial markets. Given absurd overvaluations, it is only a question of when the market falls and whether the fall is slow or rapid.

How could otherwise smart human beings not see that assets were overvalued? The answer is found in greed. Humans know exactly what is going to happen but they cannot resist. As prices rise in a financial bubble, there is a lot of money to be made in the short run on the way up, even if everyone knows that prices are too high and must eventually fall. Everyone jumps into the markets thinking that they will be smart enough to get out before the end comes. If one gets out too soon, one loses a lot of potential income.

But it is impossible to predict the timing of the peak, since some trivial factor that never will be discovered determines the exact timing of the end of the bubble. To this day, for example, no one can tell exactly why the American stock market started to fall on October 29, 1929—as opposed to a few months earlier or a few months later. Some do get out in time before prices start to fall but most don't. When the end is clear, everyone rushes to sell and prices fall before anyone can exit. At the end of every such bubble, everyone declares that it won't happen again, but it always does. Memories fade and those huge profits on the way up to the peak of the bubble are irresistible.

For the first three decades after World War II, the institutions that had been put in place in reaction to the debacle of the 1930s prevented any repetition of these events. It became possible to believe that financial instability was not an inherent part of capitalism. Believing so, the movement toward less regulation of financial markets began in 1971 when the world moved from fixed to flexible exchange rates. By the late 1970s all of the world's principal countries with the exception of Japan had abolished the capital controls adopted at the end of World War II. Over the decades of the 1970s and 1980s, the regulations adopted to prevent a recurrence of the Great Depression were rescinded.

If legal deregulations had not occurred, technological deregulations would have occurred. New technologies make obsolete many of the regulations, such as capital controls, that had previously existed. If the old regulations had not been rescinded, they would simply have ceased to be obeyed. When money had to be loaded into a backpack and walked across the Alps from Italy to Switzerland, it was possible for the Italian government to enforce capital controls. When money can be moved instantly on a personal computer, the whole idea of capital controls melts away. The necessary laws can be passed, but they cannot be enforced. What is true for capital controls is true for most financial regulations. In the aftermath of today's crashes someone always suggests more regulations to stop future crashes (stop program trading was the cry after the 1987 crash), but in today's world regulations cannot be enforced. If regulations are imposed by some government, those financial activities simply move electronically to some spot on the globe where they are not regulated. When the Japanese government made it illegal to trade some of the complicated derivatives that depended on the value of the Japanese stock market, their trading simply moved to the Singapore stock exchange.

Global capital markets and the existence of electronic trading systems have made it possible to move enormous amounts of money around the world very fast. On a normal day the world capital markets move $1.3 trillion, but all of the world's exports amount to only $3 trillion per year.[8] In a little over two days the world's capital markets move as much money as all of the world's economies move in a year. And on an abnormal day the world's capital markets can move much more than $1.3 trillion. A high-school-educated trader for a British investment bank (Barings) located in Singapore places a $29 billion ($7 billion that it would go up and $22 billion that it would go down) bet on the Japanese stock market.[9] What he did was not unusual. We only know his name (Nicholas Leeson), since he lost $1.4 billion and forced his firm into bankruptcy.[10]

Very large, electronically connected, global markets don't change the probabilities of having financial bubbles, but they do make them potentially bigger and they do link national markets together so that markets are more apt to crash together.

In 1971 it was possible to believe, and almost all economists so believed (including this one), that a movement to flexible exchange rates would lead to great financial and economic stability.[11] (Charles Kindleberger, retired from MIT, is the only economist who can honestly say "I told you so.") Currency values cannot be held constant unless the fundamentals (basically the difference between the rate of inflation and the rate of productivity growth) are equivalent between any two countries. Since the fundamentals are almost never equivalent, a world of fixed exchange rates requires periodic exchange rate adjustments. Under a system of fixed exchange rates, these tend to be large since countries resist changing the values of their currencies until the fundamentals are way out of line and until they have exhausted every effort to stop capital outflows. When this point is reached, currency values have to change in a very predictable manner. While governments dither, funds leave those countries with weak currencies and go to those countries with strong currencies. These movements are essentially riskless opportunities to make a lot of money, since everyone knows which currencies have to rise and which currencies have to fall.

In theory, flexible exchange rates should have led to much smaller, more frequent changes in exchange rates—changes that would be less disruptive to both international trade and foreign direct investment than large infrequent, unpredictable changes in exchange rates that are fought by government. Speculative capital movements should also be smaller, because currencies can, in theory, not deviate very far from their real equilibrium values and with many small changes up and down it should be harder to predict where currency values will go in the short run, increasing the possibilities of sustaining short-run capital losses if one bets in the marketplace, hence reducing the desire to bet. Betting against a currency ceases to be a riskless one-way bet—or so the theory says.

In fact, the move to flexible exchange rates did not work as predicted. Currency movements became greater, and the differences between what purchasing power parity theories would have predicted about currency values and actual values in foreign exchange markets became larger. The speculators who were supposed to be looking at long-run real values and offsetting the effects of the short-run, herd-mentality speculators simply did not exist. Once a rush to the door started, everyone jumped on the trends regardless of fundamentals. Currencies roared up and down.

The real-trade-weighted value of the dollar, for example, rose 52 percent between 1979 and 1984 and then promptly fell 29 percent by 1987.[12] At least one of those two movements should not have occurred in a world dominated by the real long-run fundamentals. What was supposedly impossible, rapid large swings in currency values, became an almost everyday event. Knowing where currency values would be in the future—where long-run investments should and should not be made, who should export what—became harder, not easier, to predict.

The Mexican financial crisis in late 1994 and early 1995 nicely illustrates the problems of financial instability. At any moment there is always going to be a weak link in the world financial system—and even if there isn't one, one can be imagined. In late 1994 and early 1995 the weak link was Mexico.[13] But it could just as well have been someone else. *Fortune* magazine published a list of seven other countries (the Philippines, Indonesia, Brazil, Malaysia, Thailand, Argentina, and Chile) that it thought were just as likely as Mexico to get hit.[14] The international debts of Mexico were not out of line with those of many underdeveloped countries and they were far below those of many developed countries. Relative to GDP, Italy, Belgium, and Greece have international debts at least three times as high.[15]

Mexico's economy was doing well, its budget was balanced, but the peso was overvalued and a consumption-dominated balance of payments deficit had to be financed with short-term capital flows rather than long-run direct investments.[16] By December of 1994 foreign exchange reserves had fallen to such low levels that the Mexican government had to be devalued to correct the overvaluation of the peso.[17] Foreign capital poured out of Mexico fearing even greater devaluations in the future.

These fears spread to other third world countries and for a short time there was capital flight right across the third world, including such unlikely places as Hong Kong. Eventually an enormous rescue package (more than $52 billion) was put together for Mexico, but in the process Mexico essentially lost control over its own economy.[18]

The world community in the form of the IMF and the United States began to dictate how Mexico would run its monetary policies.[19] They required 60 percent interest rates for twenty-eight-day peso loans to the Mexican government and 100 percent interest rates for consumer credit in the winter of 1995. These were guaranteed to cause a recession in Mexico in 1995 and 1996, since expenditures financed with consumer credit and investments financed with bank loans had to plunge.[20] The international community demanded fiscal austerity— sharp expenditure cutbacks in an already balanced budget. Revenue from Mexican oil was to be paid directly into an account at the Federal Reserve Bank of New York and would be controlled by the United States to guarantee non-Mexican bondholders that they would be paid what they were owed. Mexico would receive whatever was left over.[21]

In one month the Mexican-U.S. monthly trade deficit swung from a $1 billion deficit to a slight surplus.[22] Outside of Mexico those who made their living selling products or services to Mexicans found that their markets had suddenly vanished.

If one looks at Mexico in 1995, its economic sins were very minor in proportion to the punishment that was required to restore "investor confidence." Just six months earlier, in the summer of 1994, Mexico was being widely cited as the country doing everything right. It had eliminated the large budget deficits of the early 1980s and was in fiscal balance. It was deregulating and privatizing—more than one thousand state-owned firms had been sold. Deregulation was widespread. Putting aside old Mexican urges to protect itself, it had joined NAFTA and was sharply reducing tariffs and quotas. Inflation was running at the rate of only 7 percent per year in 1994.[23] President Salinas was a hero on the cover of every newsmagazine. A year later he was in exile and being accused of almost every crime known to man.[24] Since the markets could not be blamed by those who operate them, corruption (drugs, murder) and devils (the brother of the president) had to be found. [25]

While Mexico had a trade deficit, that deficit was caused by private sector decisions—the public sector was not a net borrower of money at home or abroad. When the borrowing occurred, commentators noted that deficits in its trading accounts paid for with short-term money flows were okay, since they reflected private decisions to lend or borrow on both sides of the market. In addition, Mexico's trading deficits were far from being the world's worst. It is true that Mexico's problems would have been less if it had had a higher savings rate and its firms and banks had had fewer dollar-denominated loans. But at 16 percent, Mexico's savings rate exceeds that of the United States.[26]

The punishments for a country that just six months earlier had been doing everything right were going to be draconian. Because of the fall in the value of the peso, inflation accelerated to an annual rate of almost 60 percent.[27] For thirteen years the standard of living of the average Mexican had been reduced to implement free market reforms, and at the end of that time what looked to the average Mexican like rich foreign masters who want to take their money home forced policies on Mexico that were expected to cut real family purchasing power a further 33 percent.[28] Among the middle class, a group whose income cuts were expected to reach 50 percent, a movement, El Barzon, arose whose motto was Can't pay, won't pay. What is antiseptically described as a program of austerity in the world's financial press has become sharply falling living standards in the reality of Mexico's barrios.[29]

For the outside world the Mexican prescription worked. Macroeconomic stability was quickly reestablished by the late summer of 1995. Individual Mexicans, however, did not fare so well. Unemployment doubled in the official statistics, and the Mexican labor secretary thinks that the real numbers may be much higher. Retail sales are down 40 percent and no resumption of growth is on the horizon in the fall of 1995.[30]

If one wanted to know the fundamental causes of the Mexican crisis, one might better have looked in the United States. Because of low bank interest rates designed to fight the 1990–91 recession, hundreds of billions of dollars flowed out of American savings accounts into higher-return mutual funds. But to pay higher returns, mutual fund managers had to earn higher returns, and they sent some of their money to Mexico to do so. When U.S. interest rates went back up, the same fund managers wanted to rebalance their portfolios and started to bring their money home. With money flowing out and running a current account deficit, it was only a matter of time until Mexico ran out of foreign exchange reserves. In February 1994 it had $30 billion in exchange reserves. By December it was down to $6 billion.[31] Having inside information as to what was happening to its dwindling foreign exchange reserves, Mexican citizens seem to have started the stampede for the financial exits.[32] Once outsiders got wind of what was happening, they also ran for the exits.

If the capital losses of the international investors in Mexico are compared with the real-income losses of Mexican citizens, it is clear that the Mexicans lost much more. If Mexico had simply defaulted and refused to adopt the austerity package forced upon them by the IMF and the United States, it is clear that they would have suffered a reduction in their real incomes—they would have been unable to finance an import deficit and imports would have dropped, cutting real incomes. But that also happened under the IMF-U.S. plan.

If they had not accepted the IMF-U.S. conditions, however, they would not have been forced to endure a harsh domestic recession on top of the necessary cut in imports. The recession forced upon Mexico cost it 500,000 jobs by April 1995 and another 4 million workers had been reduced to working fewer than 15 hours per week.[33] For Mexico it is clear that the short-run costs of the IMF-U.S. bailout package exceeded the short-run benefits. It is true that if Mexico had defaulted, it would have found it harder to get loans in the future, but not many of those loans are going to be made in any case.

For Mexico it may even be true that the long-run costs exceeded the long-run benefits. The long-term benefits are an earlier return to the international lending markets. But international lenders have notoriously short memories and start to lend again remarkably rapidly. It remains to be seen whether lending restarts faster than it would have if Mexico had defaulted.

Such short-run and long-run cost-benefit analysis leads to a very simple conclusion. Sooner or later some country will refuse to practice the prescribed domestic austerity necessary to satisfy the international lenders of last resort. This country will simply let the international investors take their losses (the more they rush to the exits, the bigger those losses) and be willing to pay the price of returning to the international capital markets at a later date. They will simply put the welfare of their citizens ahead of the stability of the world's financial system.

What happens then? The truth is that no one knows. The argument for helping Mexico is not that Mexicans will be better off (as we have seen, they probably will be worse off) but that refusing to help Mexico would cause such a loss of confidence and panic in the world's financial markets that the markets themselves would collapse. No one of course knows, or can know, whether that argument is true or false until the experiment has been run. If the world's financial markets did collapse, the losers, of course, would not be the Mexicans but the big players in world financial markets—the British, the Germans, the Japanese, and the Americans.

The Mexican bailout required more funds than the IMF was allowed to lend to Mexico under its rules and the United States had to come to the rescue—not because it was obligated to do so under the rules of NAFTA but because its pension funds had hundreds of billions at risk in Mexico. If a bailout had not been offered, the mutual funds would have had to bring their money home at a much worse exchange rate between the peso and the dollar. In reality, the $52 billion loan package protected the American mutual funds more than it did Mexico, but the Mexicans were left to repay the loans. Given this reality, why should Mexican citizens pay the costs of what is essentially an insurance policy to stabilize the world's financial system? Let those who use the system pay the necessary insurance premiums. Rather than being the slogan of a middle-class protest group, Can't pay, won't pay might become the Mexican national slogan next time.

Probably the most interesting event in this episode is that when the United States announced its first very large unilateral American rescue package there was a one-day run on the dollar. Even when the United States announced a more international package with less U.S. involvement, the markets fitfully sold dollars in the belief that even the United States was not big enough and did not have enough resources to rescue what is economically a very small neighbor. In the next few months after the Mexican disaster, the dollar would fall 25 percent in value. The capital markets were willing to flirt with a challenge to the U.S. dollar.[34]

Financial crisis and the resulting loss of national economic independence are not limited to the third world. In the summer of 1992 the targets of the financial speculators were not third world countries but Italy, France, and the United Kingdom. All were trying to maintain the value of their currencies vis-à-vis the German mark as they had pledged to do in the European Exchange Rate System (ERS). Italy and Great Britain did not have the right fundamentals. The gap between their inflation rates and their rates of growth of productivity were much higher than those for Germany, and betting against their currencies was a riskless one-way bet. George Soros supposedly made a billion dollars doing so.

But France, the world's fourth largest economy, had its fundamentals correct. Budget deficits, trade deficits, rates of inflation, rates of productivity growth—all were superior to those of Germany in the summer of 1992.[35] But the speculators still attacked the French franc—and won. To stay within the ERS, France was forced to adopt an austerity package (higher interest rates, etc.) much as if it were Mexico. If the world's fourth largest economy can be attacked when its fundamentals are right, everyone with the possible exception of Germany, Japan, and the United States can be attacked at any time regardless of whether they have or have not committed any economic sins.

Since higher interest rates are the only short-run instruments governments have for stemming capital flight, higher interest rates are one of the outcomes of a world where large amounts of capital can quickly move from country to country. Instead of focusing on generating low interest rates to produce full employment and rapid growth, interest rate policies must now focus on controlling highly volatile capital flows. Monetary policies are held hostage to international capital flows and cannot be used to promote domestic prosperity.[36]

If history is any guide, sooner or later the global financial system will experience its equivalent of the Japanese stock market crash of the 1990s or the American stock market crash of the 1930s. At that point what happens isn't at all obvious. The world will probably discover that the global financial system needs some management, much as national governments discovered that their national financial markets needed management in the 1930s, but there is no global equivalent of national governments that can step into the breech with any capacity to manage, to regulate, or to be the lender of last resort. If any single country, even the United States, tries to become the global regulator or manager after the crisis has begun, financial activity will simply instantly move to some other place in the world where financial markets are unregulated. The IMF will certainly come to the rescue, but it is only a lender of last resort with no regulatory authority. Where and when the financial crisis will come and how big it will be, no one knows. That there will at some unknown point in the future be such a crisis is a complete certainty.

The most likely crisis involves a run against the dollar. Those holding their assets in dollars have taken an enormous financial beating— they have lost 43 to 58 percent of their wealth relative to what they would have had if they had kept their assets in marks or yen the last ten years. At some point they have to want to get out. When a run against the dollar starts, there are enormous amounts of money that can, and will, move into appreciating currencies. Sixty percent of official reserves and 50 percent of private reserves are currently held in dollars. Those funds will certainly move, but they will be a small fraction of the total funds avalanching down the slope. Financial speculators will pile on the downward trends in the dollar and the amounts moving will be many times the world's dollar holdings. Financially sophisticated Americans as well as foreigners will be moving their money abroad to make the enormous capital gains that accrue to those who move early.

Those whose debts are denominated in the appreciating currencies (most likely yen and marks) will find that the real value of their debts explodes—evaluated in their own currencies or in dollars. Many will be unable to repay their yen- or mark-denominated loans. Financial institutions in Japan and Germany will take big losses as foreigners default on their loans. At that point world stability would call for the United States to take both the long-run actions (balance its fiscal and international accounts) and short-run actions (raise its interest rates) to protect the value of the dollar so that it will continue to be used as a store of value and as a medium for transactions. But since, as we have seen, a falling dollar causes little pain in the United States, the domestic political support for taking the necessary remedial actions won't be there and the probability that the American government would be able to impose the economic pain on the American public that the Mexican government imposed on the Mexican public is nil. Americans would see no reason why they should sacrifice to maintain the stability of the world's financial system.

Bargaining power would be on the American side. Americans could, if they wished, simply print up the money and pay off the dollar-denominated foreign loans. Doing so would require a smaller reduction in the American standard of living than if the loans were to be paid off the old-fashioned way—by running a trade surplus. But a fear of this result would be precisely one of the reasons that the run on the dollar starts in the first place.

To depend upon America to stop a run on the dollar is to depend upon a preponderance of domestic political interests that simply is not there. Any belief in American actions to stop a run on the dollar that would involve economic pain is a mirage shimmering in the hot desert air. The fault lines of financial instability are real.

Chapter 12

Social Volcanoes: Religious Fundamentalism and Ethnic Separatism

RELIGIOUS FUNDAMENTALISM

The rise of religious fundamentalism is a social volcano in eruption. Its connection to economics is simple. Those who lose out economically or who cannot stand the economic uncertainty of not knowing what it takes to succeed in the new era ahead retreat into religious fundamentalism. In periods of punctuated equilibrium old modes of human behavior don't work. The new modes of behavior that are required, and which will eventually emerge, threaten cherished ancient values. Periods of punctuated equilibrium are periods of extended uncertainty. No one knows exactly what any individual has to do to succeed, how the system will treat them if they engage in different modes of behavior, and in some fundamental sense no one even knows the new definition of success. Or what is moral or immoral.

Despite what humans, especially Americans, often say, "We like to change," all humans hate to change. It doesn't take much of a cynic to recognize that what Americans mean when they say that they like to change is that they are going to enjoy watching others change while they don't themselves intend to change at all. The Chinese curse "May you live in interesting times" (roughly equivalent to the Western curse "May you burn in hell") comes closer to expressing real human views. Interesting times are times of change, and this implies that human behavior will have to change. Being told that one must change to survive is roughly equivalent to being told that one will burn in hell.

Historically, periods of uncertainty have always seen a rise in religious fundamentalism. Human beings don't like uncertainty and many retreat into religious fundamentalism whenever the uncertainties of the physical world become too great. It happened in the Middle Ages and it is happening now.[1] Individuals escape the economic uncertainty of their real world by retreating into the certainty of a religious world where they are told that if they follow the prescribed rules they will certainly be saved.

The Dark Ages were full of Christian religious fundamentalists who kept popes busy stamping them out. Flagellation (using whips to beat oneself into heaven) is the medieval fundamentalist practice probably best remembered today, but in the Middle Ages it was just one of many—the cult of the Virgin, Beguinism, necromancy. Today's Bosnian Muslims once belonged to one of the many fundamentalist sects (a neo-Manichaean sect called the Bogomils, who hungered for a simpler and purer monotheism and were against elaborate religious rites, costly clerical robes, and the corrupting sale of indulgences) that existed during the Middle Ages. They converted to the Muslim religion during the Ottoman Empire's rule in the Balkans to avoid being oppressed by their Roman Catholic or Greek Orthodox neighbors, who belonged to the religious establishments.[2]

Religious fundamentalism (Hindu, Muslim, Jewish, Christian, Buddhist) is on the rise everywhere. Fundamentalists preach that if one follows their rigorously prescribed route, one will be saved. In their world there are no uncertainties. Those not following their prescriptions deserve to be punished.

In Algeria, Islamic fundamentalism means 30,000 to 40,000 civilians dead with a declared war on all foreigners (some of French ancestry who were born in Algeria).[3] In Israel young male Islamic fundamentalists strap bombs to themselves and blow up people at bus stops or in the middle of Tel Aviv. To do so is to go immediately to heaven and enjoy sex with a multitude of beautiful girls. A reward not unlike that promised to the medieval "assassins" in Persia. An American-Jewish fundamentalist sprays bullets into a mosque in Hebron where he kills twenty-nine Muslims at prayer. His burial place becomes a pilgrimage site for similarly minded Jews. A Jewish rabbi issues a death warrant for the leader of his country under the doctrine of the "pursuer's decree."[4] In India, Hindu fundamentalists tear down a Muslim mosque that has been tolerated for four hundred years and ransack

Muslim neighborhoods in Bombay. In Kashmir and Punjab, religious wars seemingly without end rage on. In Japan, Buddhist fundamentalists mix Hinduism and Buddhism to honor the god Shiva, Hindu lord of destruction, so that they can justify releasing a nerve gas in the Tokyo subways injuring 5,500 and killing 12.[5] The end of the world is at hand for everyone, not just them. Yet Buddhist terrorism is almost an oxymoron.

In the United States, Christian fundamentalists shoot abortion doctors, derail trains, demand school prayers for their neighbors' children regardless of whether those neighbors share their religious beliefs (in the name of virtue my neighbor's behavior must be controlled), and blow up the federal building in Oklahoma City killing 167 people, 19 of whom are children. The Presbyterian minister who kills an abortion doctor knows he "did the right thing." He was obligated by God to kill, and is a martyr.[6]

In the Oklahoma City bombing, Americans were quick to use the term "Muslim fundamentalists" when they did not know who did it, but very reluctant to use the term "Christian fundamentalist" when they did know who had done it. Those arrested were connected with a Michigan militia organized by two Christian ministers (one of whom owns a gun shop), calling themselves "God's Army," which had declared war on the federal government because of its persecution of another Christian fundamentalist sect, the Branch Davidians, at Waco, Texas.[7] An allied group is called Covenant, Sword and Arm of the Lord.[8] Interestingly, the Christian "Army of God" and the Iranian Shiite Muslim fundamentalists even use the same terminology and have the same enemy—the U.S. government is the "great Satan"—the embodiment of evil.

Such groups offer survival training involving shooting and wilderness skills, predict civil wars and race riots, see America at risk from foreign intervention by UN troops, but preach that "God will insure that some will survive (their members) to see a better world."[9] One of their militia field manuals even maintains that "Jesus would not have objected to the use of deadly force."[10] The parallels are there with the Islamic, Hindu, and Buddhist fundamentalists even if Americans do not want to see them.[11]

The excuse for not labeling them Christian fundamentalists is that "real Christians" wouldn't have done what they did. So instead Christians describe them as isolated fanatics and are not willing to see them as an organized Christian fundamentalist movement. But good Muslims, Jews, Hindus, and Buddhists would say the same about their fundamentalists. "Real" Muslims, Jews, Hindus, and Buddhists wouldn't have done it either!

Like the Catholic fundamentalists during the Inquisition, all fundamentalists want a social dictatorship where they are the dictators. The American fundamentalists' television preacher Pat Robertson in his 1991 book *The New World Order* sees the uncertainties of secular current events as "nothing less than a new world order for the human race under the domination of Lucifer and his followers."[12] In his Contract with the American Family, America's forty million fundamentalist voters are supposed to "focus on reversing the ruinous moral decay and social breakdown caused by a 30 year war the radical left has waged against the traditional family and America's religious heritage."[13] These are not the views of democratic give-and-take but the views of those who believe they are waging a no-holds-barred war with the devil. If one wins while wrestling with the devil, one must drive a stake into his heart.

As in the Contract with America, in the Contract with the American Family each of the views to be imposed on the rest of the population has been market-tested in opinion polls and focus groups so that they are worded in such a way that 60 to 90 percent of Americans will agree with them when they hear about them.[14] Whether 60 to 90 percent of the population will want to live with them when they are imposed on them is another matter. Cracking down on pornography is something that everyone can agree upon until they hear what the definitions of pornography are to be.

In Iran and Afghanistan, old governments are overthrown by new fundamentalist governments. In the Middle East a promising peace process is slowed. In India religious wars contributed to centrifugal tendencies that may wind up tearing apart the world's second most populous nation. In Turkey a secular state is threatened as its citizens sit watching Muslims being massacred in Bosnia and Chechenya while the Christian world steps aside and in the process ever larger numbers become fundamentalists.

The economic plates are driving an enormous social gap into the system between those who want to return to the ancient virtues, those who want to enjoy new freedoms, and those who understand that the ancient virtues will not be the future verities. In a period of punctuated equilibrium no one knows what new social behavior patterns will allow humans to prosper and survive. But since old patterns don't seem to be working, experiments with different new ones have to be tried.

If they are to last over time, moral values must contribute to successful human survival. The correct moral values (those that have contributed to long-run human survival), about sexual abstinence of unmarried young people, for example, are simply different before and after the invention of the pill. But experimenting with new forms of family formation, many of which will prove not to work, scares the fundamentalists, who want to believe in certainty and eternal truth. But how is one to find the new moral values that will contribute to human survival without a period of experimentation that will be upsetting to many?

All of these pressures are greatly exaggerated in the new lifestyles shown on the electronic media. They are interesting to watch precisely because they let a person think about and mentally experiment with new lifestyles without having to take the risk of actually being the first to practice them and perhaps ruin one's life. At its heart the electronic media is in reality neither left nor right but libertarian. It preaches the doctrine that individuals should be allowed to do anything they wish unfettered by social conventions.

From the point of view of the fundamentalist, however, those new video lifestyles have to be repressed, since they are exhibiting what is immorality by the standards of the old values. They must be denounced as evil. In their hearts religious fundamentalists are social dictators. Because they know the correct route to heaven, coercing others to follow that route is precisely what one ought to be doing. Since it is "right," it isn't dictatorial. The libertarian media ask their neighbor to leave them alone; the religious fundamentalists see it as their religious duty to force their neighbor to "behave."

In the United States, Christian fundamentalists are one of two groups whose votes (the other being white male high-school-educated graduates) powered the 1994 congressional landslide for the Republicans. To a great extent the two groups overlap, and it should come as no surprise that high-school-educated white males have taken the biggest cuts in their current wage rates and their future prospects. Three out of every four Christian fundamentalists voted Republican in 1994 and in the aggregate they provided 29 percent of the votes that Republicans received.[15] No one doubts that Christian fundamentalists will control the nomination of the next Republican candidate for President and Robert Dole jumps to their tune.

In America the political manifestations of this fundamental tension is now most clearly seen within the Republican party—the preferred party both of most libertarians and of most Christian fundamentalists. They are allies when it comes to disliking Democrats, yet when it comes to regulating social behavior no two groups could be further apart.

In the end humans will not adopt libertarian, anything-goes values. They don't work. But they won't end up adopting the current set of religious values either. They also don't work. Only social experimentation can determine what works, and that experimentation is what fundamentalists hate most. As a result, most of the terrorism of religious fundamentalism lies ahead of us and not behind us.

ETHNIC SEPARATISM

Ethnic separatism, like religious fundamentalism, is a common phenomenon in periods of economic uncertainty. Statistically, since real per capita GDPs are continuing to climb, everyone is still playing in a positive-sum game where everyone can win, but if 80 percent of all earners are experiencing real-wage reductions, as they are in the United States, the average worker does not see the positive-sum game. He sees a negative-sum game where there are more losers than winners. There aren't enough good jobs to go around, most of his compatriots are getting real-wage reductions, and he is in a fight with others for his economic survival. Needing both allies who can help him win in those battles and enemies who can be deprived of their good jobs, it is not surprising that the average worker is sympathetic to ethnic separatism in an era of punctuated equilibrium.

Those of us who have come of age during the cold war tend to forget that periods when national borders are moving are much more common than periods when they are frozen into place.[16] With the cold war over, a more normal pattern has been restored. Since the Berlin

Wall has come down, twenty new countries have been created and two countries, East and West Germany, have become one country. What we have seen in border adjustments so far is not the end of a process of adjusting to the disappearance of communism but just the beginnings of new patterns of national geography. Once borders begin to move anywhere in the world, it legitimates the idea that they can move elsewhere.[17]

Nations hold together because of outside challenges or powerful inside ideologies. Communism was such a powerful inside ideology. It persuaded ethnic groups to live together (if not to like, at least to tolerate each other) who had never lived together peacefully before. It is perhaps well to remember that Stalin began his life in postrevolutionary Russia as the Commissioner of Nationalities. He suppressed Russia's ethnic groups with a combination of ideology and force. The *Communist Manifesto* explicitly ruled out the ethnic national state.[18] Today's rulers of Russia and most other countries have neither force nor ideology on their side.

Communism was the powerful outside challenger that held ethnic forces in check elsewhere. If ethnic or regional groups fought each other, they would end up being taken over by the Communists. During the cold war the Northern League, a party that advocates splitting Italy into two countries (from their perspective separating a rich, efficient, honest northern half from a poor, inefficient, dishonest southern half), could not have existed in Italy because to have voted for them would have been to give the election to the Communists. Today northern Italians are free to tell southern Italians what they think of them. Italy is no longer held together by the glue of the cold war.

Occasionally, as in Yugoslavia, communism was both the inside ideology and the outside threat. Tito used Communist ideology and the threat of being absorbed into the USSR's Eastern European empire to persuade his now warring ethnic groups that they had to hang together—or hang separately. Once the inside promises of communism were dead and the outside threat of Soviet envelopment was over, ethnic groups were free to massacre each other—and they did so even when to outsiders they looked like very similar peoples.

But it is also important to understand that ethnic divisions are not the twenty-first century's wars of religions as proposed by Samuel Huntington. The nation-state is a nineteenth or twentieth century phenomenon and in most cases it is difficult to devise common principles explaining why today's nations and not some other grouping of nations exist. Whatever principle of separation is suggested, it is easy to find counterexamples. The Arab world, for example, is divided into many countries despite a common language, a common ethnic inheritance, and a common religion.[19]

What is occurring is not religious wars but the phenomenon of ethnic splintering or of religious splintering where the ethnic or religious fault lines are so minor that outsiders often cannot see them even after they are told that they exist. Blood and belonging are in the mind, not on the ground.[20] The issue is not "who is us" but an "us" who often exists when no one else can see why.

Catalonia and the Basque country don't want to be ruled from Madrid. The Basques plant bombs. All of the Spanish are Roman Catholics. The issue in Canada is language, not religion, but every thinking Quebecer knows that they live in an English-language North America where they cannot avoid learning English if they want to have a first-class career even if they are not part of Canada. In France the Bretons talk of more local power. The Corsicans are more violent, exploding four hundred bombs and killing forty in 1994.[21] Britain's Labor party proposes to give the Welsh and the Scottish local autonomy if it is elected. None are religious problems.

Where homogeneous ethnic groups exist in different parts of the same country, large states are breaking up or threatening to break up—as in Canada and India. In ethnically homogeneous states, such as Germany, open immigration is replaced by ethnic immigration where one has to prove that one's grandmother was German—rather than that one is a legitimate refugee.[22] Ethnic states (Slovenia, Israel, Iran, Armenia, Slovakia, the Czech Republic, Afghanistan, Slovakia, Macedonia) arise like weeds in the spring. Where they cannot arise, wars follow (Bosnia, Croatia, Georgia, Nagorno-Karabakh, Rwanda). The hated neighbor often has the same religion. Where ethnic homogeneity geographically does not exist, demands arise for ethnic cleansing even if that term is not used (the Baltic States, the old Yugoslavia, the Muslim republics of the old USSR, and the Christian republics—Georgia, Armenia—of the old USSR).

In the United States the same demands show up not as geographic separatism but in demands for special ethnic quotas and privileges.

Every American can now claim to belong to some minority group that deserves special treatment. Special groups (such as environmentalists, the handicapped) now dominate the political process. A deaf Miss America is criticized by other deaf Americans for speaking rather than using the sign language that makes her handicap obvious. All want to be distinguished from the white male majority and given a guaranteed legal "minority" position. In response the white male "majority" (an actual minority) wants all of those special privileges cleansed from the land.

In the United States it is not obvious that the old melting pot still works—or even that people want it to work. The white citizens of California pass referendums to punish brown immigrants regardless of whether they are legal or illegal. Group identity is now often defined by who you want to send home or cleanse from the land.[23]

All of this occurs in a world where one might think that global communications would be integrating peoples as everyone absorbs a common electronic culture and where almost everyone wants to give up some of their national sovereignty by joining larger regional economic trading groups such as the European Community.[24] But without a sustaining ideology or an outside threat, living peacefully together has become much harder.

Without a challenger, without a dominant ideology that is being propagated or defended, and with no dominant power, history tells us, nation-states drift into confrontation with their neighbors. Challenges to existing borders have succeeded, are succeeding, and will succeed. Bosnia and the old Yugoslavia are the wave of the future. They have echoes already in Czechoslovakia, Chechenya, Armenia-Azerbaijan, and Georgia. They may have had echoes in many other places (Wales, Quebec, Catalonia, Corsica) and will have echoes many other places (Africa, India) in the years ahead.

The world is not going to intervene to stop such disputes. Outsiders don't like watching such events on their TVs, but they like watching their own soldiers die even less. The politicians of the world have also learned that the public attention span is very short. It wants something done about each new problem but only for a short period of time.

If neither a powerful inside ideology nor a powerful outside threat exists, nations break into warring ethnic, racial, or class groups. People talk about a revival of fascism, not because fascist governments are about to return anywhere, but because fascism was the ultimate expression of ethnic superiority and the need for ethnic "cleansing." Hitler hated America precisely because it was an ethnic melting pot without racially pure characteristics. The termites of ethnic homogeneity are busy gnawing at the social fabric almost everywhere.

Why not break up into tribal ethnic groups and fight it out? Such sentiments are legitimated by today's world economy. Everyone now understands that one does not have to be a big economy with a big internal market to succeed. City-states like Hong Kong or Singapore can succeed. It used to be that everyone thought that breaking up a country into smaller pieces meant a lower standard of living; today everyone knows that isn't true. As a result, one can go it alone and does not have to cooperate with other ethnic groups to have a high standard of living. With this knowledge goes one of the previously existing impediments to ethnic feuding.

Chapter 13

Democracy Versus the Market

Democracy and capitalism have very different beliefs about the proper distribution of power. One believes in a completely equal distribution of political power, "one man, one vote," while the other believes that it is the duty of the economically fit to drive the unfit out of business and into economic extinction. "Survival of the fittest" and inequalities in purchasing power are what capitalistic efficiency is all about. Individuals and firms become efficient to be rich. To put it in its starkest form, capitalism is perfectly compatible with slavery. The American South had such a system for more than two centuries. Democracy is not compatible with slavery.

In an economy with rapidly increasing inequality, this difference in beliefs about the proper distribution of power is a fault line of enormous proportions waiting to slip. In democratic-capitalistic societies power comes from two sources—wealth and political position. Over the past two centuries two factors have allowed these two power systems based on antithetical principles about the right distribution of power to coexist. First, it has always been possible to convert economic power into political power or, conversely, political power into economic power. Few held one without quickly gaining the other. Second, government has been actively used to alter market outcomes and generate a more equal distribution of income than would have been produced in the market if it had been left alone. Those who saw themselves losing out in the market economy saw government as a positive force working to keep them included when it came to harvesting the economic fruits of capitalism. Without these two realities there probably would have been a major quake at the fault line between democratic and capitalistic principles about the distribution of power long ago.

On the distribution side of the equation, capitalism can adjust equally well to a completely egalitarian distribution of purchasing power (everyone with the same income) or a completely inegalitarian distribution (one person has all of a nation's income over and above that necessary for subsistence for the rest of the population). Capitalism would simply produce a different set of goods to satisfy a different pattern of tastes.

On the production side, however, capitalism generates great inequalities of income and wealth. Finding those opportunities in the economy where one can make a lot of money is what drives capitalism's efficiency. Some find them; some don't. Driving others out of the market and forcing their incomes to zero—conquering their earning opportunities—is what competition is all about. Once wealth is acquired, opportunities to make more money multiply, since accumulated wealth leads to income-earning opportunities that are not open to those without wealth.

Looking at the measured distribution of human talents, it is possible to believe that market economies on their own would produce distributions of income and wealth that would be equal enough to be compatible with democracy. One of the mysteries of economic analysis is why market economies produce distributions of income that are so much wider than the distributions of any known human characteristic or talent that can be measured. The IQ distribution, for example, is very compressed compared with the distributions of income or wealth. The top 1 percent of the population have 40 percent of total net worth, but they do not have anything like 40 percent of total IQ. There simply aren't individuals with IQs thousands of times higher than those of other people (one has to be only 36 percent above average to have an IQ in the top 1 percent).[1]

Even starting with egalitarian distributions of purchasing power, market economies quickly convert equalities into inequalities. Whatever distribution of goods and services is initially bought, workers will not be paid the same. People are paid unequal amounts because they have unequal talents, because they have made unequal investments in their skills, because they have unequal interests in devoting their time and attention to earning money, because they start from different positions (rich or poor), because they face unequal opportunities (black versus white, the well connected versus the unconnected), and because, perhaps most important of all, they have unequal amounts of luck.

The income-generating process is not an additive one where a 5 percent advantage in each of two aspects of a person's income-generating potential leads to a 10 percent difference in earnings. It is more multiplicative. An individual who is 10 percent above average on each of two income-generating characteristics earns four times the income (10 times 10 for a total income of 100) of a person who is 5 percent above average on each of these two characteristics (5 times 5 for a total income of 25).

There is also a very nonlinear relationship between talent and pay that can be best seen in sports salaries. Below a talent level that will allow a person to become a professional basketball player in the NBA, earnings are zero. At the right talent level, minimum earnings are $150,000.[2] If talent gaps (how fast they can run, how high they can jump, what percentage of their shots they hit) between marginal players and the stars were measured, the gaps would be very small, but the salary gaps are enormous. Small talent gaps allow the stars to dominate the game.

While earnings differentials can be huge, they are inherently limited, since everyone has the same inherently limited number of hours that they can work. Wealth, however, is not similarly constrained. It has no upper limit. Wealth can generate wealth and that process is not limited by the individual's personal time. Others can be hired to deploy their employer's wealth. Advantages compound. Over time in unfettered markets income inequalities grow. Those who have made money have the money and contacts to invest in the new opportunities to make more money.

Great wealth is also not produced in the patient process of saving and then reinvesting at market rates of return that is described in economics textbooks. An individual who started with $100,000 and was willing to save and reinvest all of his interest payments would still have only $238,801 at the end of forty years given the real rate of interest of the last ten years (2.2 percent).[3]

Bill Gates, America's richest man with $15 billion in wealth, did not get rich by saving his money. He got rich on a combination of luck and talent. Like every other very wealthy person in American history, he got rich by finding a situation or being lucky enough to enjoy a situation where markets were willing to capitalize his current earnings at some very high multiple because of their future potential. Microsoft, his company, was lucky enough to buy an operating system for personal computers from another company that had gone bankrupt at precisely the time that IBM needed such a system for its new personal computers. In what will be recorded as one of the biggest economic mistakes in computer history, instead of writing their own operating system, which would have delayed the IBM personal computer's introduction for a few months but possibly preserved the market for them for a long time, IBM bought the system now known as MS-DOS from Microsoft on a nonexclusive basis. Bill Gates was lucky to be in the right place with the right product, but let it also be said that he was talented and took advantage of the opportunities given to him. Great wealth requires both.

Capitalistic economies are essentially like Alice in Wonderland, where one must run very fast to stand still—just stopping inequality from growing requires constant effort. Historically, since market economies haven't produced enough economic equality to be compatible with democracy, all democracies have found it necessary to "interfere" in the market with a wide variety of programs that are designed to promote equality and stop inequality from rising.[4]

Compulsory publicly financed elementary and secondary education was followed by cheap land-grant universities in the nineteenth century. The Homestead Act gave land to Americans wishing to go west rather than making them pay for it. The railroads were regulated to prevent the owners from using their monopoly power to reduce the incomes of their middle-class customers. Later, antitrust laws were introduced to stop other types of monopolists from exercising their market power. Both were survival-of-the-fittest capitalists who were deliberately hobbled by government. The twentieth century followed with the progressive income tax—the rich should pay more than an equal share of the costs of government; unemployment insurance should be provided to those thrown out of work, social security given to those too old to work, and financial aid to widows and orphans (AFDC). After World War II, the GI Bill of Rights was invented to provide free education for a whole generation of American males. In the 1960s it was civil rights, the war on poverty, and affirmative action for minorities. In the 1970s it was national health insurance for the elderly (Medicare) and for the poor (Medicaid). At the end of all of those efforts, the United States still had a very unequal distribution of income and wealth, but a much more equal distribution of purchasing power than it would have had if these activities had not been undertaken.

Historically, democratic governments, not the market, built the middle class.[5] Programs such as the GI Bill and Medicare were very visible ways for democracies to make a statement to those who at any particular time might be losing out in the market's competition. No matter how badly capitalism is treating you, these programs said, democracy is on your side. Democracy cares about capitalistic economic inequality and is working to reduce it. The combination worked. The potential conflict between capitalistic power and democratic power did not explode.

While there probably have been periods of time when economic inequalities rose slightly since capitalism emerged, they were unmeasured and unknown—or at least debatable. Since accurate data have been kept, there have been no other periods of sharply rising inequality. As a result, the simultaneous existence of the two different power systems has never been tested during a time when rapidly rising economic inequalities were widely known and government was determined to do nothing about them. That test is now under way.

Using political power to reduce market inequalities requires a high-wire balancing act. If too much income is taxed away from those who have earned it under the rules of capitalism and handed out to others who are given income on some basis other than their productive effort, capitalistic incentives cease to function. When the gap grows too large between what they pay and what they receive, business firms simply move to places on the globe where they do not have to pay high social charges. Individual workers similarly disappear into the underground economy where social charges and taxes are not paid. Both activities cause the tax revenue necessary to pay for redistributive activities to melt away. Conservatives are right when they argue that government social welfare activities are antithetical grafts on the root stock of capitalism. Not surprisingly, right-wing political parties have only grudgingly accepted the social welfare state on the basis that it was not as bad as full-blown socialism.

The key question is, of course, how much inequality can government prevent before the too-much limit is reached. To some extent that depends on the types of taxes and expenditures that are used to limit income differences. More taxes can be collected with a system of taxes based on consumption rather than one based on income, since the first exempts the investment activities that are central to capitalism's performance. Similarly, more taxes can be collected to finance skill-training programs without adverse incentive consequences than can be collected to pay for direct income-transfer programs, since the individual receiving training has gotten a gift from government but he or she has had to work to take advantage of that gift. Income transfers, in contrast, allow individuals to effectively opt out of the capitalistic process. They get, but they don't contribute.

Empirically, a lot of income was redistributed in countries like Sweden before incentive problems arose. Probably the social welfare state could have continued growing for a long time in most countries if it were not for the elderly and the "second generation" problem outlined in Chapter 5. But those problems are real and the social welfare state is in retreat. In the future it will not be a mediating force between capitalism and democracy. As the gap between top and bottom widens and the middle shrinks, democratic governments are going to have severe problems dealing with the unequal socioeconomic structure left behind.[6]

Democracy, if one means everyone voting, is a very new social system and has not yet proven that it is the "fittest" political form available. The concept of democracy was born long ago in ancient Athens, but until America arose it was applied very restrictively. In ancient Athens democracy did not apply to women or to a large number of males, perhaps the majority, who were slaves. Ancient Athens was what we might today call an egalitarian aristocracy. It was not what we mean today by democracy.

Even in America, it is clear, the Founding Fathers did not intend to give the vote to everyone. Slaves and women were not allowed to vote and the Founding Fathers expected that states would set wealth requirements for voting that the states never in fact set. Universal democracy needed a civil war to end slavery and a constitutional amendment to let women vote. The French Revolution occurred at about the same time as the American Revolution, but in most of Europe, where land had great value and yielded political power, democracy began much later—often not until the end of the nineteenth century—and universal voting rights are a very recent phenomenon.

LIVING WITH INEQUALITY

Historically, some very successful societies have existed for millennia with enormous inequalities in the distribution of economic resources—ancient Egypt, imperial Rome, classical China, the Incas, the Aztecs. But all of those societies had political and social ideologies that were congruent with their economic realities. None believed in equality in any sense whatsoever—not theoretically, not politically, not socially, not economically. In ancient Egypt and Rome the official ideology called for a very unequal sharing of power and economic rewards. A large fraction of the population were slaves in ancient Rome and the official ideology held that slavery was good for those with a slave mentality.[7] Since fairness is determined in a social process where comparative and normative reference groups are central to feelings of unfairness, ancient environments made slavery seem fair to both great thinkers, such as Aristotle, and the slaves who were brought up in those societies.[8] The political sphere and the economic sphere believed in congruent inequalities.

In contrast, capitalism and democracy are very incongruent when it comes to their assumptions about the right distribution of power. Democracies have a problem with rising economic inequality precisely because they believed in political equality—"one person, one vote." Democracy holds out beliefs and references groups that are not compatible with great inequalities. Capitalism also has a hard time defending the inequalities that it generates with a contrary set of beliefs as to why those inequalities are right and fair.

Capitalism can argue that the economic process is fair, but it has to be agnostic about the "rightness" and "fairness" of any specific outcome. But if anyone believes the outcome of the process is unfair and goes looking for a justification for not accepting the outcome of that process, it is always possible to find some place where the process is not in accordance with the theories of competitive markets. As a result, those who defend capitalism usually assert that capitalism will provide rising real incomes for almost everyone and only sometimes admit inequalities may rise. Unfortunately, as we have seen in Chapter 2, this assertion has not been true for more than twenty years.

For humans, unhappiness results when reality falls short of expectations (falling real wages in a land that expects rising real wages) and when the rules for success are unknown and changing (what does one have to do to raise one's income when real wages are falling for males at all income levels?).[9] Unfortunately, our world is full of such uncertainties and expectational gaps.

The alternative to having government jump into the market on the side of those who are losing out in the market is to drive the economically weak out of society. A nineteenth-century economist, Herbert Spencer, formulated a concept he called survival-of-the-fittest capitalism (a phrase that Darwin eventually borrowed to use in his explanations of evolution).[10] Spencer believed that it was the duty of the economically strong to drive the economically weak into extinction. That drive was in fact the secret of capitalism's strength. It eliminated the weak. Spencer created the eugenics movement to stop the unfit from reproducing, since this was simply the most humane way to do what the economy would do in a more brutal way (starvation) if left to itself. In Spencer's view all remedial social welfare measures simply prolonged and expanded human agony by increasing the population who would eventually die of starvation.

The Contract with America is very Spencerian in tone and offers a return to survival-of-the-fittest capitalism. It is, of course, less honest than Spencer and denies that anyone will starve to death. In its view, no social safety net is necessary since, if the social welfare system is taken away, no one will fall off the economic trapeze. If individuals are forced to face the reality of starvation, everyone will buckle down to work. Fear will make them work so hard (hold on so tight) that they won't fall off. Spencer's view that individual defects lead to economic inadequacies that cannot be corrected by social actions are today mirrored in books such as *The Bell Curve*. Those at the bottom of the economic system both deserve to be there and cannot be helped because of their personal inadequacies.[11]

No one has ever tried survival-of-the-fittest capitalism for any extended period of time in the modern era. Hong Kong is often cited as an example but it doesn't come close. In Hong Kong the government owns all of the land under the city and more than one third of its people live in public housing.[12] When these apartments are sold as condominiums (and two hundred thousand have been over the past sixteen years), only families with incomes below $4,100 per year are allowed to buy and they get to buy at about half market rates for similar private apartments.[13] Highly socialistic actions, but government actions solving a problem that would be explosive if it were left to the market given Hong Kong's population and shortage of space.

History also teaches us that the survival-of-the-fittest versions of capitalism do not work. The free market economies that existed in the 1920s imploded during the Great Depression and had to be reconstructed by government. Maybe survival-of-the-fittest capitalism can be made to work, but no one has yet done so. It is also well to remember that the social welfare state was not implemented by wild-eyed leftists. Its midwives were almost always enlightened aristocratic conservatives (Bismarck, Churchill, Roosevelt) who adopted social welfare policies to save, not destroy, capitalism by protecting the middle class.[14]

In our current social system, the achievement of political power does not assure wealth, and the achievement of wealth does not assure political power. In all long-lasting societies, economic and political power have gone together. If such a disconnect exists, those with economic power have an opportunity to bribe those with political power to give them the rules and regulations they need to get even wealthier, and those with political power have an incentive to coerce those with economic power into making them wealthy so that they can enjoy the same material standards of living enjoyed by their friends who are powerful in the economic sphere.

Capitalism and democracy have lived together peacefully in the twentieth century precisely because what is not permitted theoretically happens in sophisticated ways empirically. Unsophisticated conservatives often argued that votes need to be awarded in proportion to wealth to stop the poor from using the political process to confiscate the material assets of the wealthy. The problem is real but it doesn't need such a "crude" solution. Unequal voting rights are not necessary in democracies to preserve capitalistic inequalities, since while everyone has one vote, everyone does not use it, and political influence depends upon campaign contributions as well as votes.

It is not an accident that capitalist societies have constructed political systems where economic wealth can be translated into political power. Today this reality shows up in campaign contributions that buy special interest groups (those with economic power) political influence and a U.S. Senate where most of the one hundred senators are millionaires. Nor is it an accident that America has built a system where those with political power but without wealth are given "opportunities" to convert their political power into wealth. Think of President Lyndon Johnson—a man who became wealthy despite the fact that he held low-wage public jobs for his entire working lifetime. Or more recently, look at Newt Gingrich's efforts to convert his political power into economic power via books, lectures, and "educational" activities where people were willing to pay huge multimillion-dollar sums for products of untested quality. Book publishing companies don't pay $4.5 million advances to authors without successful writing track records. Gingrich's income-generating activities were so successful prior to his becoming speaker of the House of Representatives that his congressional nickname was Newt, Inc.[15] His only mistake was to become too politically powerful too fast and hence attract scrutiny and visibility, before he had completed the task of becoming economically wealthy.

From the perspective of economic theory a campaign contribution is no different from a cash gift to a politician. Both are sums of money that the person needs to achieve his or her goals. Economic theory doesn't, and shouldn't, recognize the difference. Only the legal system makes a distinction between giving a politician money to run his campaign (legal) and giving him money to buy a fancy house (illegal).

The disconnect is less acute than it might be, since above some level of material possessions the purpose of having more money is not more material consumption (there are many who cannot possibly consume their current wealth in their lifetime yet continue to devote their lives to making more money) but the power to make decisions—economic or political. Power is the ultimate consumption good. Almost alone it is wanted, and can be used, in unlimited quantities. To some extent, but not totally, the politician's power can substitute for his lack of money, and the businessman's economic power can substitute for his lack of political power.

The tendency for voting percentages to decline as incomes go down also reduces the dichotomy between the two systems. If the poor cannot get themselves organized to vote, they obviously cannot get themselves organized to expropriate the wealth of the rich. Effectively, because they don't vote, they don't have equal voting power even if the Constitution says they do. In countries where the poor have been organized to vote in large numbers, not surprisingly, governments have been much more aggressive about pushing incomes up at the bottom and holding wealth down at the top. European social welfare systems are different precisely because what would otherwise be low-income families do vote.

In addition, in parliamentary systems members don't have to be rich to run for office (one does not run as an individual) and members of parliament, especially members from left-wing parties, seldom are rich. They vote for more egalitarian tax and redistribution systems, since they are not voting higher taxes on themselves. The taxes affect others and they personally identify with very different income classes (in most European socialist parties ex-schoolteachers are as numerous as lawyers in the American Congress) than their American counterparts. If one wants to find the income point with the most loopholes in the tax code in America, it would not be a mistake to start looking at the provision affecting those with the incomes typically found in the U.S. Senate and House of Representatives.

For Americans interested in preserving social welfare programs for the poor, the central issue is how does one persuade the poor to actually vote for politicians who support these programs. It should come as no surprise that if the direct beneficiaries of a program do not vote for the politicians who support the programs that benefit them, those programs will be the first cut when conservatives no longer fear socialism or communism.

The American system is also changing. The electronic media are making it much easier for economic power to buy political power. The more money it takes to buy the TV ads necessary to run for public office, the greater the advantage given to the wealthy when it comes to running for public office. No one without Ross Perot's $4 billion could even think of being a third-party presidential candidate. Conversely, however, the media's public scrutiny of the private lives of existing politicians is making it harder and harder to accumulate wealth once one is in office. Sophisticated bribes that are perfectly legal (Gingrich's book advance) become politically impossible. Yet if economic power is seen as overtly buying political power for too long a period of time, cynicism about the validity of the democracy where "one man, one vote" does not really exist has to eventually corrode the system.

In the end democracy rests on consent but does not create it, assumes a degree of compatibility among its citizens but does not work to make it true, and works best where it does not have to make zero-sum or negative-sum choices because it has an expanding pie of resources to distribute.[16] But today democracies have none of those advantages. Income stability is being undercut by the tectonic forces of economics. In an electronically wired village, that surge in inequality is going to be well known and perhaps even exaggerated as those with falling real incomes compare themselves with their TV neighbors who always enjoy rising real incomes.

For more than twenty years earnings gaps have been rising, and for more than ten years that reality has been known with certainty. Yet the political process has yet to adopt its first program to change this reality. The problem is of course that any program that might work would have to involve a radical restructuring of the American economy and American society. More money is required but an aggressive program of reeducation and reskilling the bottom 60 percent of the workforce would require a fundamental painful restructuring of public education and on-the-job training. Without a social competitor, fear will not lead capitalism to include the unincluded. Long-run enlightened self-interest should lead to the same result, but it won't.

To some extent the slippage along this fault line is already visible. In the November 1994 election white, high-school-educated males, precisely the group with the biggest reduction in their real incomes, swung heavily from the Democratic to the Republican column. But whatever one thinks about the Republican Contract with America, it says absolutely nothing about falling real wages and how one might deal with this central problem.[17] One can focus attention for a while on the scapegoats—the unwed welfare mother whom no one likes since no one likes the idea of being the sucker who pays for someone else's children. But what happens when it becomes obvious that killing programs for the welfare mothers and affirmative action programs for minorities won't cause wages to stop falling for white, high-school-educated males? Where does the I'm-mad-as-hell vote go next?

The Contract with America turns the issue of equality versus inequality over to the states. They are to run the welfare and education systems. But the states are precisely the level of government that cannot deal with this issue. Wealthy individuals and corporations who generate good, high-paying jobs but who do not want to pay high taxes simply move to states that do not collect them. State inheritance taxes simply lead to a situation where every wealthy person establishes residency in a state without a state inheritance tax before they die. States know that a lot of their young people will end up working in other states, so that it is a waste of money to give them a world-class education. Educational budget cuts are easier than most others, since nothing happens in the short run when school budgets are reduced. To give the job of generating more equality to the states is to say that the job will not be done.

What happens when democratic governments cannot deliver to a majority of their voters what these voters want, demand, and are used to having—a rising real standard of living? In the 1992 election campaign, candidate Clinton promised to focus on American domestic problems—an implicit promise to do something about rising inequalities and falling real wages. Almost four years later the economy is still delivering rising inequality and falling real wages. In 1994 the new Republican congressional majority similarly promised to forsake American global leadership to focus on domestic problems. But it too had nothing to offer to workers with falling wages.

If an American worker has a falling real standard of living, a government that does nothing about it, and no political parties that even promise to do something about his or her major problem, what then?

THE VISION?

If new inside enemies are not to be created to replace old outside enemies as a unifying force to overcome inside frustration, societies need some overarching goal toward which everyone can be working to create a better world. In the past such visions came to those who believed in socialism or the social welfare state. These systems promised a better life for those who felt, and were, left out. They, not revolution or terrorism, were the route to inclusion in America. But militias now derail passenger trains precisely because they know that there is no route for them that will lead to inclusion. The old route to inclusion is gone. Neither socialism nor the social welfare state points to a road that might be traveled to build a better collective future that will include the unincluded. As a result, just when the social system has an urgent need for political parties with sharp new ideas that can be debated in terms of how to deal with the uncertainties of a period of punctuated equilibrium, it gets debates between parties on the right who want to go back to a mythical past (something not possible no matter how much it may be desired) and parties on the left without agendas.

What does democracy mean when political parties don't have different ideological beliefs—different visions of the nature of the system and of where the promised land lies—so that they can debate alternative roads into the future? Elections become popularity polls swirling around trivial issues and dependent upon who looks best on television. Elections come to be seen as replacement of one set of crooks with another set of crooks. Everyone votes to ensure that their ethnic group rather than someone else's ethnic group gets the spoils of office. I vote my narrow economic self-interest without regard for how much that self-interest hurts you.

If democracy is to work, it can be neither a process of electing my friends and relatives as opposed to your friends and relatives nor a process where every candidate just promises to manage the current system better than his opponent. Elections cannot become a simple choice between just another group of self-serving "outs" who want to become self-serving "ins." Real democracy demands real ideological alternatives at election time or it becomes an exercise in tribalism where some tribe (the low tribe in the pecking order) is selected to be blamed for the country's problems—and then punished.

To work, democracy needs a vision of utopia—a route to a better society—a vision of what it is that transcends narrow sectarian self-interest. Historically, political parties on the right have been society's sea anchor. They sell a glorious past, often one that did not actually exist, but a mythical past that is still important. They stand for the preservation of old values and old modes of operation.

Newt Gingrich loves to focus on the pre-1955 era "long before patterns of counterculture belief deep in the Democratic Party undervalued the family and consistently favored alternative lifestyles."[18] In

fact, his idyllic pre-1955 era set teenage birth rate records not sur-
passed since, one third of marriages ended in divorce, racial segregation
was pervasive and *Rebel Without a Cause* and *Blackboard Jungle* were
the in things to watch. But all of those inconvenient facts can be ne-
glected. Parties on the right have held together, since they love a past
that threatens no one in the present and they don't spend much time
talking about the future since any planning for the future quickly becomes divisive. Conservative parties are not expected to have a vision
of the future. The future is left to the market. What will be, will be.

Parties on the left have a more difficult job. It is their job to have
a utopian vision of the future that provides the locomotive power for
change. Often their visions are unachievable and unworkable, but there
are elements within their visions that can be used to build a better
society. Social engineering often does not work but there is always a
need for a social vision of a better future.[19] Historically, parts of these
left-wing visions have often been used by right-wing conservatives such
as Bismarck with public pensions and health care or Churchill with
unemployment insurance to keep the old system in place and left-wing
revolutionaries out of power.

In the last 150 years parties on the left have sold two visions of
utopia—socialism and the social welfare state. The purpose of socialism (public ownership of the means of production) was to ensure
that everyone (not just the capitalists) was included in the fruits of
economic progress. The purpose of the social welfare state was to
provide an income floor for those whom capitalism did not want
(the old, the sick, the unemployed). In the United States, socialism
never became central to any political party's platform, but inclusion
was. The American variant of inclusion depended upon an ever
wider and deeper access to cheap public education, government regulations, and antitrust laws to limit capitalistic economic power, affirmative action to force the inclusion of the excluded, and
middle-class social welfare benefits.

If one looks at those now being slowly excluded (those whose real
wages are slowing falling), none of the traditional American methods
of inclusion work. Skill training for the noncollege-bound is part of
the answer, but it would have to be put together with growth policies
that created the jobs and tight labor markets where real wages would
once again start rising. Not knowing how to put such policies together,

and perhaps being unwilling to do so even if they did know, the political Left has nothing left to sell.

Left-wing parties still may get elected if conservative parties mis-
manage the political process badly enough, but they have nothing positive to offer. The Left can defend the welfare state politically, but
economically the welfare state cannot continue without major surgery.
Downsizing is not something the Left does well. Mr. Clinton did none
of it in his first term in office when he controlled the system. In any
case, no one wins who plays defense all of the time.

All around the world political parties on the left are demoralized or
out of office. In Germany the Social Democratic party's support is at
the lowest point in thirty-six years, the party is self-destructing with
internal battles and has been described as "little boys playing with their
buckets in the sand box."[20] In the United States, officeholders are
switching parties, Democratic to Republican, in record numbers at all
levels of government. The Democrats had a massive defeat in the fall
of 1994. The defeat undoubtedly had many causes but one was the
lack of a vision for the future. They had neither a road map to the
promised land nor even a description of what it might look like if they
could only find the route.

Successful societies have to unite around a powerful story with a
sustaining ideology. If there is no story to tell, leaders have no
agenda—and no self-confidence in what they are doing. To hold together there has to be a utopian vision that underlies some common
goals that members of society can work together to achieve. All religions as well as communism have such stories to tell. The major part
of the appeal of religious fundamentalism is that it has such a story to
tell.

But what is the story that capitalism tells to the community to hold
the community together when capitalism explicitly denies the need for
community? Capitalism postulates only one goal—an individual interest in maximizing personal consumption. But individual greed simply
isn't a goal that can hold any society together in the long run. In such
an environment there may be things that if people did them together
would make it easier for everyone to raise their standard of living, but
there is no way to recognize the need for, and organize, those outside
social factors in a system that recognizes only individual rights and
admits no social responsibilities.

Without a vision there are a number of ways for societies to hold together. Societies can unite in resisting an outside threat. For sixty years the ideological and military threats of first Nazism and then communism held Western democracies together. Internal problems could be postponed and left undealt with. But there is now no outside threat.

Societies can be united in the desire for conquest—building an empire. Conquest is part of human nature and programs such as the man-on-the-moon project were an indirect form of conquest. But geographical conquest is not worth the cost for major powers in an era of nuclear weapons. No one seems to have the imagination or the selling ability to generate whatever today would be the equivalent of the man-on-the-moon program. And it should be remembered that even the man-on-the-moon program had to be sold as part of the cold war race with the Soviets.

If no vision is available, any society will eventually retreat to ethnicity. The social system will be held together by focusing anger on some different and despised minority that needs to be "cleansed" from the land. Eliminate those with a different religion, a different language, or a different ethnic inheritance, and somehow the world will magically be better. In America these forces show up as Proposition 187 in California, eliminating budgets for welfare mothers, and stopping affirmative action in Washington, and in chasing the homeless off the streets in New York.

Without a compelling vision of a better future, social and economic paralysis sets in. With no grand agenda everyone starts trying to impose their personal microagendas for raising their own personal income or wealth. Without an agenda political parties splinter and political power shifts from those who want to do new things to those who want to stop things from being done. Governments lose their ability to impose costs on particular citizens and to accomplish tasks that would make the average person better off. Prisons, superhighways, neighborhood halfway houses, high-speed railways, electrical power plants, and a host of other public facilities have all become difficult or impossible to site. There is no community vision to overcome localized resistance. There is no community process for sharing the negative side effects of necessary public facilities.

In a democracy any single-issue special interest group not bound by an attachment to the community has power far out of proportion to its numbers. The National Rifle Association is a good example. Its members are a small minority of the population; 90 percent of the public supports gun control in public opinion polls, yet gun control is impossible in America. A 10 percent voting group that is willing to vote for or against a politician on one issue is enough to win or lose most elections.

Such groups have risen in numbers partly in response to the spirit of the times (there is nothing out there important enough to make me forget my narrow self-interest) and partly by using targeted media messages that modern electronic publishing permits. In the past one had to address the entire public, since it was not technically possible to address some small subsection of the public. But now it is easy to send a message only to those who might be sympathetic to your message. Shortly it will be possible to specify your own newspaper, the "Daily Me," by telling the computer what types of news you wish to see so that it can prepare a one-of-a-kind newspaper precisely suited to your tastes.[21] A primitive version of such a paper called *Personal Journal* has already been launched by the *Wall Street Journal*.[22] In the reverse direction, this will allow advertisers to send their messages only to those who have indicated that they are sympathetic to such messages, but it will also allow people to put together single-issue political special interest groups much faster and with much less cost. No one will have to speak to all of humanity or the electorate unless they want to—and few will want to. It is simply too expensive and wastes too much time to talk to those who are not sympathetic with one's political position. Instead of attempting to make oneself into a majority, it is far better to make oneself into a powerful special interest group. But forcing minorities talk to each other is the way to teach them to compromise and the way in which minorities become majorities. An era of political dialogue is at an end and an era marked by those who can mobilize their special interest troops the most effectively is at hand. Minority veto replaces majority vote.

While it won't completely cure the problem, there is something that is economically supposed to be done that is almost never done in our society. When society asks its individual members to accept the costs of activities that help everyone (for example, being willing to live next to a jail), then the rest of society should compensate those individual members for their costs even if those costs are only psychological. In practice most societies are willing to compensate individuals for physical property taken in eminent domain proceedings but not for anything else. The concept of compensation needs to be broadly expanded.

When the conservatives argue for legislation requiring compensation if society passes environmental laws that lower the value of some individual's property, they are half right. If individuals are polluting (effectively, dumping garbage on someone else's property), society has every right to stop them from doing so without compensation. If anything, they should be paying compensation to those they injure. But if society wants something positive to happen, something that adds to net welfare, like open space, then society should pay for that park rather than stopping someone from developing their property and essentially forcing them to provide a public park at private expense.

But the principle of compensation should be applied to everything, not just environmental regulations. Those willing to live next to a nuclear power plant or a jail should get a monthly check with the value of the check falling as the distance from the undesirable public facility increases. While there are those who wouldn't live near these facilities for any amount of money, there are others who are willing to do so for surprisingly little amounts of money. If one looks at the Pilgrim nuclear power station south of Boston, one sees houses surrounding what used to be an isolated nuclear power site. Individuals moved in precisely because that power plant meant that they would have to pay less in property taxes than elsewhere.

Much of the NIMBY (not in my backyard) syndrome could probably be eliminated with modest amounts of compensation. Compensation would of course mean that public projects cost more. But being able to do projects that raise social welfare rather than being bogged down in lengthy public disputes is much more important than minimizing the monetary costs by attempting to force individuals to swallow negative side effects. It isn't fair to essentially tax individuals in this way, and we have learned that it also isn't possible. They will resist so successfully that economic progress simply comes to a halt.

But technical solutions won't solve the central problem of a growing split between democracy's belief in equality of power and the market's growing generation of great inequalities of economic power. That solution has to be found in a common set of goals that are exciting enough that people will want to make sacrifices and forget their narrow self-interest in order to reconstruct the economy to produce different results. But what is that overarching vision and program to be?

SPIRALING DOWN

In the absence of any vision that could generate the enormous restructuring efforts that would be necessary to begin reducing inequality and to cause real wages to rise, what happens? How far can inequality widen and real wages fall before something snaps in a democracy? No one knows, since it has never before happened. The experiment has never been tried.

Social systems can certainly snap. The recent sudden unexpected implosion of the USSR is a good example. But to snap there must be some alternative banner under which the population can quickly regroup. In the case of communism that alternative banner was "the market"—capitalism. But if capitalism does not produce acceptable results, there simply isn't any existing alternative system under which the population can quickly regroup. As a result, a sudden social collapse is highly unlikely.

What is more likely is a vicious cycle of individual disaffection, social disorganization, and a consequent slow downward spiral. Consider the slide from the peak of the Roman Empire to the bottom of the Dark Ages. With the onset of the Dark Ages (476 to 1453), real per capita incomes fell dramatically from their imperial Roman peak. The technologies that allowed the Roman Empire to have much higher levels of productivity did not disappear. No malevolent god forced man to forget during the following eight centuries of uninterrupted decline.[23] The rate of invention was actually up from the Roman era. Output was down despite those new and old inventions.[24] The devil appeared in the form of social disorganization and disintegration. Ideology, not technology, began the long downward slide. Humans gradually threw away what they knew over a relatively short period of time. Once they had thrown it away, they could not recapture their old standard of living for more than twelve hundred years. Although it should be remembered that part of the Roman Empire retreated to Byzantium and lived for another thousand years.

There were those in the Dark Ages who knew everything that the

Romans knew about technologies such as fertilization.[25] What later Europeans lost was the organizational ability to produce and distribute fertilizer. Without fertilization, yields fell to the point that on land that had been the part of the breadbasket of the Roman Empire, for every one seed of grain planted only three would be harvested.[26] Put aside one seed to plant next year, subtract seeds eaten or spoiled by vermin, and there was very little left to feed the population through the winter.[27] In the end there were simply not enough calories to sustain vigorous activity and the quality of life had to decline.[28]

Even the mightiest of the feudal barons had standards of living far below those enjoyed by the average citizens of Rome. Without safety from roving robbers and good transportation systems, many of the goods that had been widely available in Rome became unavailable even to the rich. Feeding large cities such as Rome had simply become impossible.[29] Another European city with the size and standard of living of imperial Rome was not again to emerge in Europe until London in about 1750. At the end of the Dark Ages (1453), the Roman roads were still the best on the Continent even though they had had no maintenance for one thousand years.[30]

There were those alive during the Dark Ages who knew that standards of living had been much higher in the Roman Empire and that something better was possible. They had, or could have had, all of the technologies possessed by Rome, but they did not have the values to generate the organizational abilities that would have been necessary to recreate what had previously existed. Investments in the future had become alien—"reserves accumulated in bed chambers, stores, and wine-cellars were merely provisions laid up for future feasts in which the wealth of the house would be lavishly squandered."[31] Values, not technology, dictated that they sit in the Dark Ages century after century.

If one looks at Europe sliding into the Dark Ages and the growth of feudalism, one notices some disturbing parallels worth pondering.[32] Rome's downward spiral did not begin with an external shock. It began with a period of uncertainty. Further military expansion no longer made sense, since Rome was at its natural geographic limits—steppes, deserts, and dense empty forests surrounded the empire on all sides. With its communications, command, and control systems functioning at their technological limits, expansion no longer led to individual or collective wealth. What was to replace conquest as a unifying social force if there was no one left to conquer? If individual and communal wealth could not be obtained through conquest, why should the citizens of Rome pay taxes to support the large political apparatus and army that were necessary to maintain the empire? What was to be done about the huge numbers of immigrants who wanted to become Romans? Plagues arose disorienting everyone in an era when diseases were believed to be caused not by germs or viruses but by the displeasure of the gods. The certainties of the old pagan religion were on the way out; the certainties of the new Christian religion were not yet in place.

In the political and social flipping and flopping that resulted, the economic infrastructure, human and physical, and the social discipline (think of what it takes to feed a city of more than one million people using horses and carts as the primary form of transportation) that allowed Rome to maintain its standard of living and support its armies were allowed to deteriorate. With public consumption rising and the willingness to pay taxes falling, investments that had been made were no longer made. Eventually an economic decline set in that fed upon itself. Lower output led to even less willingness to make the social investments necessary to support the old system, which led to even lower output and yet another round of cutbacks in the necessary social investments.

Consider the parallels between then and now. Immigrants are flooding into the industrial world but no one is willing to incur the costs that will make them into first-world citizens. Both the Soviet empire and the American alliances have broken apart. Weak nations are succumbing to feudal lords (Somalia, Afghanistan, Yugoslavia, Chechenya) and even strong ones are giving up their powers to local leaders. If one takes the Contract with America seriously, the federal American government will give up all of its powers except defense to local leaders. Over time local leaders will cement these powers into their portfolios and the national government will essentially lose its power to act as governments did during the Dark Ages.

Literacy dropped from being widespread at the time of the Roman Empire to a point where only a few monks could read at the peak of the Dark Ages.[33] Today functional illiteracy is on the rise in the United States and much of the rest of the industrial world even as the standards of what it means to have an education that makes one into a functional, productive human being are rapidly escalating.

In the Middle Ages standards of living fell far below where they had been at the peak of the Roman Empire.[34] Productivity fell. Work was brutish compared with what peasants endured in the Roman Empire. Huts were far more crowded.[35] The process began with falling incomes at the bottom of the social ladder and gradually spread up the social ladder. Today total productivity is still rising but real wages have begun to fall for 80 percent of the population. Eventually the social disruptions and declining productivity of those at the bottom has to affect the living standards of those at the top.

In the Dark Ages the public was squeezed out by the private. Banditry became widespread and was seen as a revenge upon the defenders of the political and social order (hence the legend of Robin Hood).[36] Unwalled cities and free citizens were replaced by walled manor houses and serfs.[37] To be safe in their homes, people could not live on the ground-floor level but climbed to the second floors to sleep using removable ladders.[38] Youth gangs and street violence were one of the principal reasons for this retreat.[39] Graffiti dominated the walls of the early Middle Ages—just as it does walls in modern cities.

In our societies just as in the Dark Ages, the private is gradually squeezing out the public. In 1970 twice as much money was spent on public policemen as on private policemen. By 1990 the reverse was true. Twice as much money was spent on private as on public police. The result is effectively a two-tiered system of public safety. Those who can afford to buy the services of a private police force are safer than those who cannot. One can argue that this leaves the public police free to focus on high-crime areas without private police, but if they do so the privately protected group of citizens loses interest in paying taxes to support the public protection of others. But if a political community cannot offer its citizens the essential element of basic protection as they come and go on its streets, it is not a community. It does not merit support.

Today walled, gated, and guarded communities are once again on the rise. Twenty-eight million Americans live in such communities if one counts privately guarded apartment houses, and the number is expected to double in the next decade.[40] The Disney Corporation is building one such community, Celebration City, for twenty thousand residents just south of Orlando, Florida.[41] There is a community in California with a wall, a moat, a drawbridge, and a device called a bollard that shoots a three-foot metal cylinder into the bottom of unauthorized cars.[42] The very word *bollard* comes from the Dark Ages. While this is extreme, there are thirty thousand communities where individuals, like those in the Middle Ages, separate themselves from the outside world with walls and guards at the gates in their urban or suburban enclaves.[43]

The reasons for retreating into a walled and gated community are many—security, lifestyle, exclusivity, homogeneity—but they all end up producing a group of people with little interest in the public sector.[44] Those in the walled communities often pay very heavy fees for services (they would be called taxes if they were collected by governments) and put up with regulations (house colors, shrubbery heights, no flagpoles or visible clotheslines, no streetside parking, no Girl Scout cookie sellers, no outsiders on community streets or in community parks) that would be unconstitutional if they were enacted in a public town.[45] Effectively, public space is being privatized as it was at the onset of the Middle Ages.

Often walled and gated communities are initially welcomed by local taxpayers since they seem to relieve the local community of the burden of providing public services while at the same time they pay taxes. Very quickly, however, these walled and gated communities start to demand rebates on their taxes since they aren't receiving local services and organize tax rebellions to cut their local taxes—an action that reduces someone else's public services but leaves them with well-supplied private services.[46]

As the Roman Empire slid into the depths of the Dark Ages, the private gradually squeezed out the public until effectively the private sector swallowed everything and the public sector disappeared. The intense devotion of the Romans to the *res publica* was lost.[47] Instead of being a citizen of Rome, every individual was attached to a feudal master who controlled all aspects of his or her life—work, housing, reproductive rights, justice. Almost by definition feudalism is public power in private hands.[48] Those who had been free citizens gradually sold themselves into serfdom to gain safety from roving gangs and essential services that only a feudal master could provide.

The biggest cities were less than one twentieth the size of imperial

Rome and there were very few of them.[49] Only 3 percent of France lived in towns in A.D. 600.[50] Yet, as the French historian Fernand Braudel has remarked, "the difference between a 'culture' and a 'civilization' is undoubtedly the presence or absence of towns."[51] Our cities are similarly in decline.

People quit building and maintaining. With the exception of the cathedrals no stone buildings were built for ten centuries.[52] Investment became alien and wealth was "lavishly squandered" rather than used to promote a better future.[53] Roman water and sewer systems were abandoned and had to be reinvented more than a thousand years later.[54] In our society public infrastructure spending has been cut in half in two decades.

The Middle Ages saw vast numbers of homeless people wandering back and forth across the countryside. Today the homeless are counted in the millions and cutbacks in public housing expenditures promise to substantially increase those numbers. From sympathy to apathy to antipathy characterized the shift in attitudes of those with homes. Instead of solving the homeless problem, the average citizen now wants to drive them out of his neighborhood and into someone else's neighborhood. In the Middle Ages the homeless were similarly driven by force from neighborhood to neighborhood.

In the Middle Ages capital punishment was the answer to any and all problems. In Britain hundreds of crimes could be punished by execution but only one out of one hundred murders was actually solved.[55] Today capital punishment is similarly demanded—and just as infrequently carried out.

Religious fundamentalism arose both then and now.[56] The Crusades, religious warfare, embodied the spirit of the era. People retreated into their religious communities and sought to force others to believe as they believed. Flagellation, monasteries, and the Inquisition were hallmarks of the Dark Ages. In the words of Dostoyevsky's Grand Inquisitor, "miracle, mystery, and authority" were required in human societies and the only legitimate goal was getting into heaven. Those who repented as their bodies were being broken during the Inquisition were being helped to find eternal life.

The men who ruled the Church at the time have been described as the "least Christian of men; the least devout, least scrupulous, least compassionate, and among the least chaste—lechers, almost without exception."[57] They lived at the apex of society with their own legal systems and courts.[58] "They believed that they had God's voice, that they spoke with truth, that anyone who disagreed with them was wrong. They did not tolerate contrary opinion. They damned it."[59] Yet moral behavior declined to the point that then as now family ties dissolved.[60]

Today among Hindu, Muslim, Buddhist, and Christian fundamentalists it is appropriate to murder those who do not believe as they believe. A government building is blown up in Oklahoma City by a militant fundamentalist Christian group, founded by two Christian ministers (one also owning a gun store), who call their militia God's Army. Several months later a group calling itself the Sons of Gestapo destroy a train.

In the Dark Ages as now, there was no vision of how one made a better life.[61] They knew that standards of living had been higher in the past, but they were too disorganized to get back to the past or to organize a march to the future. Today there is a similar lack of vision. Something is going wrong, but no one knows how to reverse it.

The Dark Ages were a period when humans retrogressed politically, socially, and economically far below where they had been. As the historian William Manchester states: "After the extant fragments have been fitted together, the portrait which emerges is a melange of incessant warfare, corruption, lawlessness, obsession with strange myths, and an almost impenetrable mindlessness."[62]

Historians no longer like to use the term Dark Ages for what is now called the Middle Ages, since they have learned a lot about those years (they are no longer "dark") and during that period of time humans developed the two principal values that underlie our current civilization—an interest in systematically developing new technologies and a belief in individual human rights. Neither existed in the ancient world—but without those two fundamental values our modern world could not exist. In the end a period of disorder and decline brought about the most rapid technological and economic advances that mankind had ever seen. A different set of values and a vision of a different future were eventually created. And these new ideologies—the ideologies of rationalism, romanticism, emancipation, utilitarianism, positivism, and collective materialism—created our modern societies far more than the technologies that they use.

It was the Dark Ages and not classical Rome or Greece that led to the industrial revolution and the modern era. Universities were founded and the search for knowledge began, a belief in technology arose, and individualism was invented.[63] Probably because of the idea of a creator God in whose image one was made, men wanted to become creators and they developed a belief in the possibilities of technical progress. It is difficult to know whether the Protestant religion with its belief in individual connections between man and God caused a belief in individuality to arise or whether that belief in individuality caused the Protestant religion to develop, but in any case the belief in individuality did arise. Communities were so poorly developed during the Middle Ages that no one could expect the community to come to their rescue. If individuals were to progress, it would have to be based on their individual initiatives. Eventually a big retreat led to a big advance. But it is well to remember that there were one thousand years in between the two events.

As illustrated by both the inability of China to use its remarkable technological advances to generate the industrial revolution and the inability of the Dark Ages to get back to levels of productivity that had previously existed, the best social systems do not automatically arise even though the necessary technology is present. The message of history is clear. Social institutions do not take care of themselves. The best institutions and beliefs do not automatically pop to the top.

No one can know exactly what will happen in our society if inequality continues to rise and a large majority of our families experience falling real wages. But it is fair to surmise that if capitalism does not deliver rising real wages for a majority of its participants in a period when the total economic pie is expanding, it will not for long hold on to the political allegiance of a majority of the population. Similarly, if the democratic political process cannot remedy whatever is causing this reality to occur within capitalism, democracy will eventually be similarly discredited. A large group of voters with free-floating hostility, not benefiting from the economic system and not believing that government cares, is not a recipe for economic or political success.

In a world where national leaders cannot deliver real-wage increases and cannot prevent real-wage reductions, sooner or later they, or some other newly elected leader, will start pointing the finger of blame at someone else in the hopes that their supporters will see these groups as the cause of the problems. In the United States white high-school-educated males have been led to believe that affirmative action for women and blacks is the source of their real-wage reductions. Affirmative action is to be eliminated. Californians blamed their problems on immigrants. As punishment, both legal and illegal immigrants are to have their public services reduced. In Congress the poor are the enemy and must have their entitlement programs cut to save the entitlement programs for those far wealthier than they.[64]

None of these actions solves the basic problems. All are diversionary attempts to direct public anger at some powerless minority who can be blamed. Affirmative action, for example, is something much more talked about than actually done and none of the researchers into falling real wages for white males has ever uncovered even a shred of evidence that affirmative action explains any of the observed decline in the real wages of white males. Uneducated sick immigrants are neither going to make life in California better nor lead anyone to go home. Treating immigrants badly once they are here is roughly like shooting oneself in the foot. The right answer is to make them into productive citizens who can support themselves rather than forcing them to remain dependent and poor. Congress can cut all of the programs for the poor to zero and it still will have made essentially no progress on eliminating a big and growing structural deficit.

Yet these "falsehoods" are going to have a profound effect on American politics. One can argue that affirmative action programs were not designed to be permanent when they were begun, have been expanded to cover too many "phony" groups, and have not in recent years been enforced in such a way as to make much of a difference anyway—but the efforts to roll back all affirmative action programs let a nasty genie out of the bottle. Black incomes are far below those of whites and now government is not even going to pretend that it intends to do something about this festering problem. Blacks, not surprisingly, see it as a declaration of economic war on their future opportunities. White militias square off against the black Million Man March.

While the manifestations of the emotions that will be released will hopefully be different from those in the old Yugoslavia, the accusations currently being made echo those from the old Yugoslavia. To be real

Serbs, the Serbs have to cleanse their lands of Croatians, Bosnian Muslims, Albanians, and Macedonians. They are protecting the Christian world from the Muslim world yet they fight just as bitterly against their fellow Christians—the Croatians. Similarly, America is to be cleansed of the poor, the single mother, the immigrant, and those who cannot succeed without the aid of affirmative action to make America into the real America that it mythically used to be.

Without a social competitor it will be tempting for capitalism to ignore its intrinsic internal shortcomings. That temptation can already be seen in the industrial world's high unemployment rates. It should come as no surprise that as the threat of socialism dies, the level of unemployment tolerated to fight inflation rises, income and wealth inequalities rapidly widen, and the lumpen proletariat cast off by the economic system grows. These were the problems of capitalism at its birth. They are part of the system. They led to the birth of socialism, communism, and the social welfare state. If these solutions do not function, and they do not, then something else has to be grafted on to the system, but what is it to be?

Internal reform is very difficult in capitalism, since it has a set of beliefs that deny the need for deliberate conscious institutional reforms. Social institutions in the theory of capitalism take care of themselves.[65] Societies with efficient institutions drive those with inefficient institutions out of business since they are more productive. Deliberate social reform isn't necessary. The invisible hand of the market delivers efficient institutions just as it delivers the goods that individuals most want.

The collapse of communism can even be seen as a validation of this principle. The theory works. The fallacy of this perspective emerges in the length of time necessary for efficient institutions to run inefficient institutions out of business. In the case of communism it took seventy-five years. It took almost one thousand years to chase the Dark Ages away. Without the right institutions, the best technologies never were of value to China and the benefits of their brilliant inventions never emerged. The inefficient ultimately do get defeated—but they often stay inefficient for centuries and the efficient emerge in some other part of the world.

THE ROLE OF GOVERNMENT

Historically, government has played an important role in including the unincluded into capitalism. As will be seen in the next chapter, the role of government is going to be central, although very different from that suggested in either socialism or the social welfare state, in restoring an economy that can generate rising real wages for most of its citizens in an era of man-made brainpower industries. Capitalism, however, finds it very difficult to define government's appropriate role. Debates about the proper role of government and whether it should or should not do something to alter the outcome of the market are in fact peculiar to the era of capitalism, since in all other earlier successful systems there was no distinction between the public and the private. In ancient Egypt or Rome no one would have known what anyone was talking about if they had started discussing the limits of government. What we think of as public and private were so intertwined as to make such a distinction useless. Similarly, in feudalism the feudal baron provided both what we would call state services (defense, law, and order) and what we would call private employment. His orders applied in everything that was done within his domain. Only in capitalism is there a private economic sector where capitalism rules and a public state sector to deal with noneconomic problems where other forces rule.[66] Not surprisingly, in this context capitalism wishes to limit the role of the public sector to the lowest possible level consistent with its own survival.

If government is not to be a socialistic owner of the means of production or a provider of social welfare benefits, what is it to be?[67] Capitalism's theoretical answer is that there is almost no need for government or any other form of communal activities. Capitalistic markets can efficiently provide all of the goods and services that humans want or need except those few items known as pure public goods.

Pure public goods have three unique characteristics that defeat the efficiency of private markets, but those same three characteristics are so unique that perhaps there is only one pure public good, national defense—and even that could be debated. The first characteristic of a pure public good is that any one person's consumption of that good, no matter how extensive, does not reduce the quantity of that good available to be consumed by anyone else. Humans are not rivals when it comes to their consumption. If one person enjoys the use of national defense, that does not affect the enjoyment or use of national defense by anyone else. With normal economic goods if one person eats a carrot, another person cannot eat the same carrot. Since pure public goods are not used up by any one person's consumption, how should they be sold in a market economy? Normal goods are bought precisely to give the buyer a monopoly position with respect to the consumption of what he has bought.

The second characteristic of a pure public good is that it is impossible to stop others from enjoying its use. If President Reagan's Star Wars missile defense system had been built, it would have protected everybody or nobody. It is not possible to sell goods on private markets when potential buyers can refuse to pay and still enjoy the free usage of the good in question if it exists at all.

The third characteristic flows from the first two. Because everyone can enjoy the simultaneous usage of these goods, and because no one can be prevented from using them, everyone has an incentive to hide their real economic demands for these pure public goods to avoid having to pay their fair share of the costs. Individuals will not reveal their preferences, since if they pretend that they have no interest in (demand for) national defense, someone else will have to pay for the programs such as Star Wars even though such goods are really valuable to them. With normal goods, individuals reveal their preferences when they buy them. In doing so they publicly signal that those goods are worth to them at least as much as their market price. If they hide their preferences, they don't get what they want.

As a result of these three characteristics, it is necessary to use governments and their abilities to collect involuntary taxes to raise the funds to provide the pure public goods that people actually want. Relative to real wants and demands, free markets would provide too few pure public goods. But if one looks at most of the activities of modern governments, very few of them meet the tests of being pure public goods. Even national defense may not fully qualify (someone could organize a Star Wars defense system for part of the country and not the rest of the country).

Education and health care certainly don't qualify. Individuals do not share their education or health care with anyone else and those who don't pay for education or health care can be excluded from usage. Private markets can and do organize successful education and health care institutions. Public safety is the same. Policemen or firemen can guard one person, but not another. Private policemen are in fact replacing public policemen. Justice could be, and is, being privatized.

In addition to pure public goods, some activities have what economists call positive or negative "externalities." Education may provide positive externalities in that working with other educated people raises my productivity. Therefore, I have an interest in subsidizing their education. Conversely an airport generates negative externalities, since those who live near it have to listen to its noise. But in either case the correct answer is at most a system of public subsidies or public taxes to encourage or discourage such activities. The correct answer is never public provision and never a subsidy so big that it pays the entire costs of some activity. Most of the benefits go to those who are educated— even if some of the spillover helps others.

Consider the post office. One can make the argument that back in colonial America when the American post office was invented by Benjamin Franklin, it was an essential ingredient of communication that held together thirteen quite different colonies. If America was to become America and the citizens of thirteen different colonies were to become Americans, they needed to communicate with each other and there was a governmental role for making this communication cheaper, and more equal in price, than it would have been if a new country had waited for a private mail service to appear. But none of those arguments applies today. There are private postal services that operate more efficiently than the public postal services, and what holds our culture together is the electronic media, a private media, and not the ability to send first-class letters to each other at the equal cost of thirty-two cents. United Parcel or Federal Express would be glad to take over the function of the post office. Private companies would similarly be glad to build and operate toll roads. By putting bar codes on cars and sensors on the streets, we could make every road, including city streets, a toll road. Social security could be replaced with private pension plans.

In a survival-of-the-fittest form of capitalism there is very little role for government. When the Contract with America talks about universal privatization, the Contract with America is talking about a retreat of the public sphere. As the public retreats and less and less effort is devoted to making public activities work, government becomes ever less respected, making further retreats even more likely. Effectively, the public becomes the enemy of the private in political debates—rather than being seen as a complementary factor necessary to the existence of a successful private sector.

In this view economic stability and growth take care of themselves. The goal of economic or social justice is unrecognized. Any attempt to collect taxes, especially progressive taxes, or distribute income on some basis other than market performance interferes with incentives, the efficient working of markets, and leads to the world of the second best. Income redistribution, the major activity of all modern governments, is an activity whose legitimacy is denied. People should be allowed to keep what they earn. To do anything else is to make the market less efficient than it could be. Governments exist to preserve private property—not to take it away.

To play the capitalistic game, the economy must begin with some initial distribution of purchasing power. What is it to be? It is here and only here that there might be a governmental role. After the initial starting point has been determined, the market itself generates the optimal distribution of purchasing power for the next round of economic activity. The game is under way and the differences produced in the market are fair since they are "natural" and the product of a "fair" game.[68] This one-time problem today arises in the formerly Communist countries. To move from a communistic economy to a capitalistic one, private ownership rights must be established over what are now state-owned assets. While there is no theory in capitalism that says one distribution is better or worse than another, some distribution of property rights has to be established. But this starting point was established long ago in the "old" capitalistic world.

Besides providing pure public goods and subsidizing or taxing activities with positive or negative externalities, there is one other role for governments. Capitalism cannot work in a society dominated by theft. It needs a legal system guaranteeing the existence of private property and the enforcement of contracts. But as has been argued by the conservative economists, such as Gary Becker, while it is true that capitalism needs property rights to function, it does not need public prosecutors or public policemen to function.[69] Contracts and private property rights could be enforced by letting everyone sue each other to enforce their legal rights. When it comes to the legal system, capitalism needs something, but that something could be very rudimentary, and much less in the public sector than it is now.

There is of course a weakness in this argument. Consider the issue of theft. It is possible to protect private property rights with locks, burglar alarms, and privately hired guards. But it is costly to do so. It is far more efficient to inculcate social values that lead people not to steal. With such values private property is protected at zero cost. The aggressive individual is socially tamed rather than physically constrained.[70] Societies don't function very well unless most of their members voluntarily behave most of the time.[71] But who is to decide which social values are to be inculcated in the young? For this question capitalism has no answer. Values are just individual preferences. They have no transcendent position. In capitalism the goal of the system is to maximize personal satisfaction by allowing individuals to make personal choices. Individuals are the best judges of the consequences of their actions and individuals can best decide just what raises their own welfare. Individuals optimize, free exchange takes place, markets clear, and there are few social choices to be made.[72] Social ideals such as honesty or equality do not arise.[73]

As a result, from the perspective of capitalism, there are few positives that government can contribute to the economy and many places where it can harmfully interfere. That leads government to be seen as something that frequently wrecks the economy rather than as something necessary for its successful functioning.[74] The conservative view of government sees men in a violent state of nature submitting to central authority in exchange for security and stability. Chaos, the lack of private property rights, essentially leads to the need for government.[75] But historically it wasn't so. Capitalism's conception of government is precisely backward. Groups came long before individuals. Social support and social pressure is what makes humans human.

No significant group of human beings has ever lived in an individualistic state of nature. No set of individual savages ever got together to decide to form a government in their own self-interest. Government or social organization has existed as long as humankind has existed. Instead of existing first and being subordinated to obtain social order, individuality is a direct product of social order. Over time individuals have gradually gained rights vis-à-vis the community rather than giving up some of their individual rights in order to gain the benefits of community. Social values informed individual values and not the reverse.[76] Individuality is a product of community rather than something that must be sacrificed to community.

What is missing in this negative view of government is an understanding that free markets require a supportive physical, social, mental, educational, and organizational infrastructure. More important, they require some form of social glue if individuals are not to be constantly battling each other.

Biologically, some species are solitary animals living alone except when they mate. Other species are herd or pack animals. Man is clearly the latter. Any successful human society has to recognize this reality, but capitalism does not. Successful societies need to keep the two sides of humankind in balance. Yes, individuals are self-interested, but no, they are not just self-interested. Yes, government officials sometimes serve personal ends and not the common good, but no, they are not always so. The issue is not individual choice versus social bonds, but discovering the best mix of individual and communal actions that will allow a society to persist and flourish.

Theoretically, capitalism does not claim that it will arrive at some glorious destination—that it will maximize growth rates or generate the highest incomes. It simply claims that no system can do better when it comes to maximizing individual personal preferences. But it has no theory about how those preferences were, or are to be, formed. It will maximize perverse self-destructive preferences just as fast as it does altruistic humanitarian preferences. Wherever preferences come from, and however they are formed, capitalism exists to satisfy them. As a result, capitalism isn't about abstract efficiency—inculcating values of honesty so that the system runs at a lower cost. It is about letting everyone maximize their utility by exercising their own individual personal preferences. Wanting to be a criminal is just as legitimate as wanting to be a priest.

One can make the argument, as the communitarian movement does, that our societies were more efficient and human in the past and could be more efficient and human in the future if the right social values were inculcated in the young. Those arguments may be true, but no one knows how to get from here to there. Exactly what are the right values and how do we agree upon them? The Christian fundamentalists have a set of values (no abortions, school prayer, creationism) that many others do not want taught to their children. Even if values are agreed upon, what are the legitimate and illegitimate techniques of inculcating those agreed-upon values? Even if both ends and means could be agreed upon, how does one resist the fundamental forces of economic plate tectonics? Values are not, and will not be, inculcated by the family, the Church, or other social institutions in either the present or the future. They are, and will be, inculcated by the electronic and visual media.

The media makes money by selling excitement. It is exciting to break the existing social norms. One can even argue that the media needs to break more and more fundamental norms to generate excitement, since the violation of any code of conduct becomes boring if we have seen it violated often enough. Stealing cars and being chased by the police is exciting the first time, and maybe the one hundredth time, but eventually watching a car chase is not exciting and some more fundamental violation of a social norm has to be committed to generate excitement. Excitement sells. Obeying the existing or new social norms is not exciting and does not sell. Resisting the impulse to steal a car is never exciting. It's just that simple.

PREFERENCES

Values or preferences are the black hole of capitalism. They are what the system exists to serve, but there are no capitalistic theories of good or bad preferences, no capitalistic theories of how values arise, and no capitalistic theories of how values should be altered or controlled. History never repeats itself, since what came before always alters what will come. But history, much like airline accidents, can teach us lessons about building more successful human societies if, like airline accidents, history is carefully analyzed as to what went wrong. To ignore the social aspects of humankind is to design a world for a human species that does not exist. The near extinction of free market capitalism during the Great Depression and one thousand years of human decline during the Dark Ages are both social accidents that must be understood. The long successes yet ultimate failures in Egypt, Rome, and China are monuments to both human achievement and human stupidity.

Chapter 14

A Period of Punctuated Equilibrium

CAPITALISM WITHOUT OWNABLE CAPITAL

To become viable, capitalism needed an ideology of personal income aggrandizement, but it also needed the technology of the steam engine—born in 1795.[1] But in the twenty-first century, brainpower and imagination, invention, and the organization of new technologies are the key strategic ingredients. Physical capital is still necessary but it has become a commodity borrowable in the global capital markets of New York, London, and Tokyo. This leads to a central question. What does capitalism become when it cannot own the strategic sources of its own competitive advantage?[2]

If firms where skills, education, and knowledge are already the dominant source of strategic advantage are examined (consulting firms, law firms, investment banks, accounting firms), they are usually owned and operated quite differently from traditional capitalistic firms.[3] Few are listed on the stock exchanges. They are usually owned by the working partners rather than outside capitalists. Even when they are listed on the stock exchanges, they are managed in very different ways. Employees usually earn a large fraction of their income in bonuses based on performance (a form of ownership) and often have to leave much of those bonuses with the firm until they retire (effectively being forced to become capitalists). CEOs play very different, much less important roles. The partners select the CEO. "Employees" have a lot more freedom to make business decisions than occurs in a traditional hierarchical industrial firm such as General Motors or General Electric.

When these firms try to run as normal capitalistic firms, they sooner or later get into trouble. There is no better example than the investment bank Salomon Brothers. The first generation of partners grows rich listing on the New York Stock Exchange and selling out to capitalistic shareholders. But why should the next generation of partners split their earnings with some absentee capitalist when they can work for other firms and not have to split the profits? When at Salomon Brothers the capitalists insisted on getting their share of the earnings, there was a mass exit of the most talented income-generating partners. In this case the capitalists, led by Warren Buffett, who is often touted as America's shrewdest investor, may end up owning an empty shell.

Since everyone buys the same equipment from the same global suppliers, the technologies that can give a firm a competitive edge are not embedded in unique equipment that competitors cannot afford, but in the minds of the firm's employees who know how to use that equipment in unique or enhanced ways. The firm's only significant asset goes home every night, is an independent decision maker as to where his skills will be employed, controls the effort that she will or will not put into the firm's activities, and cannot be owned in a world without slavery. When a firm's employees leave, the firm's unique ideas and technologies automatically go with that employee to the new employer. Unless the firm can hold on to its employees, proprietary knowledge effectively ceases to exist.

Schumpeter's (the inventor of the concept of entrepreneurship) entrepreneur becomes a very different entrepreneur. He need not be the owner of capital or someone who focuses on putting a supply of capital together. He focuses on, and has the knowledge necessary to put together, the right human brains. With modern communications technologies it is also clear that brainpower does not need to be concentrated en masse. Economies of scale were central to the efficiency of industrial capitalism, but there are not large economies of scale to be reaped from having enough funds to hire a large amount of brainpower at one location. Small brainpower cells can be linked together electronically without anyone having to own all of them. Communication among assets becomes more important than the concentration of assets.

The transition ahead can be verbally minimized by calling skills, education, and knowledge "human capital." Doing so makes it sound as if replacing physical capital with human capital is a minor change at most—but it isn't. While there are similarities, the differences are more important than the similarities when it comes to defining the nature of capitalism when human capital is the dominant factor of production—not just an important adjunct to physical capital.[4]

Human capital differs from physical capital in three important ways. (1) Human capital cannot be owned. Capitalists don't invest in things they cannot own. (2) Human capital investments often require a time horizon far longer than that permitted by capitalism. (3) The knowledge investments that have to be made to generate man-made brainpower industries have to be made in a social context completely foreign to the individualistic orientation of capitalism.

Capitalism is efficient precisely because it harnesses the ruthless competitive forces of greed and the desire to get rich to force profit maximization. The capitalist actively searches for people who can be fired and machines that don't need to be replaced. He quickly adopts new, more efficient, production technologies when they earn above-market rates of return. He is not locked into old ways of "doing it." Firms enter markets and industries with above-average profits and exit markets and industries with below-average profits. In the process they equalize returns and ensure that funds are invested in the places where they yield the greatest payoffs. The profit-maximizing capitalist invests until the rates of return on his investments are equal to the risk-adjusted interest rate. Monetary benefits have to exceed monetary costs.

Capitalistic individuals maximize the only things that give them utility—consumption and leisure. The production side of the economy (giving up consumption to invest and giving up leisure time to work) is a cost that must be incurred to gain the desired consumption goods that are necessary to enjoy life and leisure. To ensure that they are maximizing their lifetime utility, capitalists invest (give up current consumption) using the calculus of discounted net present values.[5] Following this procedure the net present value of the future consumption goods that can be gained by investing must always be higher than the value of the current consumption goods that must be forgone to make those investments.

Future consumption benefits are discounted using an interest rate that reflects the individual's rate of time preference. Rates of time preference measure how much people have to be paid in terms of tomorrow's consumption to give up consumption today. If an individual would trade $100 in consumption privileges today for $105 worth of consumption privileges one year from now, then the individual had a 5 percent rate of time preference. If the rate of return on investment exceeds the rate of time preference, consumers will voluntarily quit consuming and lend their consumption funds to those wishing to invest. By doing so they increase the total net present value of their lifetime consumption. The payments that they get in the future generate consumption that is worth more to them in the present than the consumption that they lose in the present.

Financial markets equalize rates of time preference by borrowing funds from consumers with low rates of time preference and lending funds to consumers with high rates of time preference and investors with high rates of return investment opportunities. As the current consumption of the lenders goes down, their rate of time preference goes up (with less of it, the value of current consumption goes up) and as the current consumption of the borrowers goes up, their rate of time preference goes down (with more of it, the value of current consumption goes down). Similarly, as more investments are made, the rate of return on new investments falls. Eventually an equilibrium market rate of interest is generated where no one, consumer or investor, wants to increase or decrease their lending or borrowing.[6]

Consider a college education as a hard-nosed capitalist might consider it. Sixteen years of expensive investments must be made before the returns begin.[7] Approximately $65,000 must be invested to acquire a K–12 education; depending upon the quality one wants to buy, $80,000 to $120,000 will be necessary to buy a college education, and the sixteen years spent in school will mean forgone earnings of about $68,000. Sixteen years of high-quality education will require a total investment of about $250,000 per child.

The risks that this investment will not pay off are enormous. During the peak earning years of forty-five to fifty-four years of age, 26 percent of all white males with bachelor's degrees will earn less than the median white male high school graduate and 21 percent of all white male high school graduates will earn more than the median white male with a bachelor's degree.[8] Since individuals have some idea of whether they will be in the upper tail of the high school earnings distribution or the lower tail of the college earnings distribution, the risks of failure are not 47 percent, but the probability that the individual buying a college education will not end up with earnings higher than they would have had with just a high school degree is still very high.

There are other risks. The payoff to getting a college degree depends upon the earning differences between university and high school graduates over the future course of their lifetimes, but what are those differences going to be in the future? If male wages are falling at all education levels, as they are, whatever the financial value of an education today, its asset value will be less in the future.

Education is a very lumpy investment where often there is little or no payoff from having a little bit more. If the investor does not complete a degree program at the university level, an extra year of college education has very little effect on her earnings. This problem is compounded by a U-shaped pattern of returns. There are big returns to the first years of education (the education where one gains literacy) and big payoffs to the last years of education (a college or graduate degree where one distinguishes oneself from the pack) but only small payoffs to those years of education that move the individual from somewhat below average to somewhat above average.[9] Those with a lot less education than the average American lose a lot of potential earnings and those with a lot more education than the average American gain a lot, but earnings gains are very small for the years when the investor is essentially moving across the crowded central parts of the education distribution and remains more or less average for a long period of time. If education is viewed marginally, one year at a time, no one can justify investing in those middle years. A local minimum prevents the achievement of a global optimum.[10]

With a 7.2 percent discount rate (the 1994 risk-free government borrowing rate for a sixteen-year financial instrument), $1.00 sixteen years in the future is worth only $0.33 today. Using the risk price rate used in the private economy (12.2 percent), that $1.00 sixteen years into the future is worth only $0.16.[11] Even in a risk-free environment, if one adds up the money that will have to be invested and the length of time until the payoffs occur, it is highly unlikely that an educational investment will pay off for the individual. Adding a risk premium that brings the discount rate up to 30 percent (the rate used by many capitalistic business firms when they make risky investment decisions), $1.00 sixteen years from now is worth only $0.02.

Put bluntly, private capitalistic time horizons are simply too short to accommodate the time constants of education.[12] Capitalists simply don't invest in sectors where they have to commit to a sequence of investments with low returns, high risks, and falling asset values.

The fracturing of the post–World War II social contract and the shift from an inflation-prone to a deflation-prone environment have also, as we have seen earlier, created a world where future productivity gains are more likely to show up as falling prices and less likely to show up as rising wages. In a world of rising wages, those who invest in skills gain most of the rewards from the higher productivity generated by their educational investments. In a world of falling prices the gains go not to those making skills investments but to those buying the cheaper products made with those better skills. Since workers pay the lower prices without investing in their own skills (most of the price decreases are caused by someone else's, and not their own, skill investments), there is no incentive to invest. The risk-reward linkage necessary for capitalism to work is broken. Everyone wants to "free ride" someone else's skill investments.

To compound the problem, the actual owner of the capital, the child, has neither the knowledge, the decision-making capacity, nor the budget to make the necessary investments. Decisions have to be made by investors who cannot legally own their investments.

No hard-nosed capitalistic mother and father would or should invest in sixteen years of education for their children. A good government bond is a better investment. This is of course one of the principal reasons why public education had to be invented. It would be nice to believe that parents would disregard capitalistic self-interest and make the right investments for their children, but they never have.[13] Too many parents are not willing to sacrifice their own immediate economic welfare on the altar of their children's education. Vague concern for the welfare of one's children doesn't offset the harsh realities of market incentives that call for very different expenditure patterns that focus on the short run.

Rationally, the poor should not educate their children. They have more important things to do with their money. The middle class, if given a chance, too often chooses not to educate their children. The rich most of the time will educate their children, but this creates a bipolar society divided between the educated and the illiterate. There is a harsh fact that should be remembered. No country has ever become even semiliterate without a publicly financed compulsory education system.

Yet at the same time the difference in median wages between those with and without education ($28,747 for a white male high school graduate and $42,259 for a white male college graduate) indicates big differences in average productivity and a huge direct social payoff when those educational investments are averaged across millions of workers.

There are also indirect returns (spillovers or externalities), since an educated worker working in an educated society has higher productivity than an educated worker working in an uneducated society. A trivial but not unimportant example: While checking out of a New York hotel, I am behind a delivery man who cannot read and therefore must wait in line for the check-out clerk to read the name on the package he is delivering and tell him the room number to which the package is to be delivered. The illiterate takes longer to do his job than a literate would, but his ignorance also uses up the time of the hotel clerk and the time of those of us waiting in line behind him to check out. All of us become less efficient because of his ignorance.

What are irrational educational investments for individuals can be very rational social investments. No one can predict which individual will get a big payoff from education—but some will. Working with other educated people, everyone's education has a higher payoff. If prices fall because higher skills lead to higher productivity, there are big payoffs for everyone even if there is very little private payoff to the individual making the skill investments.

Twelve years of publicly provided compulsory education violates every principle of capitalism. Something is given away that could be sold. People are forced to buy something they may not want. Educational vouchers are often recommended by conservatives, but they are no more in accordance with capitalistic principles than the public provision of education if they pay the full cost of the education. The issue is not who writes the monthly check to the teacher (a public school district or a private company indirectly hired with government vouchers), but the public subsidy itself. Vouchers can only be justified if they pay part of the costs of education to ensure that the externalities of education are taken into account but the individual is always left with the decision to buy or not to buy. One hundred percent publicly financed compulsory education can only be justified if one recognizes that there are social goals as well as individual goals, social payoffs that do not necessarily accrue to individual investors, and investments that capitalism needs to survive but cannot and will not make for itself.

Every social system has weaknesses and strengths. Capitalism's strength is its ability to cater to different individual preferences. Capitalism's biggest weakness is its myopia. It intrinsically has a short time horizon. Private business firms usually use three- to five-year planning horizons. In the past, long-term government investments have come to the rescue of capitalism. But they are now being cut back—partly because of the spirit of the times, partly because of cutbacks in defense budgets, and partly because of the budgetary pressures created by the elderly. The GI Bill of the 1950s and the National Defense Education Act of the 1960s are both gone—50 percent fewer American Ph.D.s in science and engineering are being trained than two decades ago. In accordance with the spirit of the times, at the undergraduate level state universities are relying less and less on public money and more and more on tuition payments from students. At private universities loans have to a great extent replaced scholarships. If one looks at state and local spending cutbacks in the 1991–92 recession, they were disproportionately concentrated on elementary and secondary education.

Although I came from a family where large educational investments were not possible, after eight years of university education at Williams, Oxford, and Harvard when I received my Ph.D. in economics in 1964, I had no educational debts. A combination of my own earnings, private scholarships, and public funds had paid my educational bills. That would be inconceivable today. To get the education I got, I would have had to be willing to incur huge educational debts—debts that would frighten most individuals (including me), debts that would have almost certainly required an initial job that paid a lot more than a Harvard assistant professorship in economics.

Private investments in education are by their very nature inegalitarian and will always be very narrowly concentrated among those with large incomes. Those with more money find it easier to invest, are more willing to invest since they see the payoff for such investments in the earnings of their friends, and can afford to undertake the high risks that any particular individual's earnings will not rise with more education. Those without funds cannot afford to bet on the possibility that there will be big economic payoffs to more education—and are often scared by the risks of failure.

Private credit markets accentuate these differences. Before government guaranteed student loans, those without funds found it difficult, often impossible, to borrow funds for educational investments. The private market was smart enough to know that too many would default because their individual educational investments would not pay off. And even if the investment did pay off, debt repayment problems would exist. Physical capital can always be repossessed and resold if the borrower simply refuses to pay. Human capital cannot be repossessed and resold.

On-the-job training opportunities are even more unevenly distributed. Profit-maximizing private firms award training opportunities to those who are the cheapest to train. Most of the time this means those who already have the most education and training, since learning is a process whereby it becomes easier and cheaper to learn the more that one has learned. One learns how to learn. As a result, on-the-job skills go to those who have acquired off-the-job skills. And when it comes to investments in on-the-job skills, business firms have even shorter time horizons than parents. They have no paternalistic urges and they worry that workers once trained will leave for higher-paying jobs elsewhere.

Since skills lead to earnings and earnings lead to skills, the net result is a private investment process whereby most skills are acquired by, or given to, those who already have the most skills. Any country that relies on private investment in human skills will quickly find itself with not just too few skills but with a very unequal skill distribution.

Much of the rest of the industrial world has a publicly financed form of education not found in the United States—postsecondary education programs for the non-college-bound (the German apprenticeship training system, the French payroll training tax) or a social system designed to limit individuals' freedom to quit and go to work for another employer after one is trained (the Japanese system of lifetime employment). If one wants to see capitalistic markets fail and undersupply the skills that it needs, one need only look at the supply of the equivalent skills in the United States. The mid-level skills typically acquired in apprenticeship training, which lie at the heart of German and Japanese economic success, are conspicuous by their absence in the United States.

In the nineteenth and twentieth centuries, Communists and socialists wanted to elevate human beings to a more central position than they held under capitalism. That was their appeal. Paradoxically, at exactly the time that socialism and communism have died, technology is elevating humans to a more central position. That is going to force capitalism to invent new forms where human beings, rather than machinery, are central—exactly what the Communists wanted, and failed, to accomplish.

But paradoxically, just as one would think that firms would be building closer relationships with their key knowledge workers to keep them committed to the firm, they are smashing the implicit post–World War II social contract and breaking the bonds that have been established. Knowledge workers, like other workers, are now fired when not needed and have their real wages reduced when alternative cheaper supplies are found. Firms invest less in the on-the-job skills of their employees, since they know that fewer of them will be around in the future. With downsizing, responsibility for investment in on-the-job skills shifts from employer to employee, but since employees don't know where they will be working in the future, they don't step into the gap because they don't want to waste their investment funds on skills that they will not be using.[14] The net result is less skills investment at exactly the time that more skills investment is needed. The system evolves toward less commitment and less investment just as it should be evolving in the opposite direction.

The World Bank has recently started estimating productive wealth per capita. Large, lightly populated but still well-educated countries such as Australia ($835,000 per person) and Canada ($704,000 per person) have the most productive wealth since they have a lot of land and natural resources relative to their populations. In these countries land and natural resources account for most of total productive wealth and human skills account for only about 20 percent of total wealth. In contrast, in a country like Japan (fifth on the list with $565,000 per person), more than 80 percent of productive wealth is held in the form of human skills and knowledge. The United States (twelfth on the World Bank's list with $421,000 per capita) falls in between. Sixty percent of its wealth is human capital.[15] While the numbers are as accurate as such numbers can be, what the World Bank did not say, and should have said, was that in the future the value of wealth held in the form of natural resources is going to be falling and the value of wealth held in the form of human resources is going to be rising. Wealth is the name of the game, but the game is different.

INFRASTRUCTURE AND KNOWLEDGE

Infrastructure can be bought and sold in private markets. With modern electronic sensors, user tolls could be collected on almost everything. By putting bar codes on cars, spreading sensors around the city, drivers could be sent a monthly bill depending upon where they drive, when they drive, and how much they drive. But there is still a reason for public involvement. In many cases to spread and accelerate economic development, infrastructure (transportation, communications, electrification) has to be built ahead of the market—but that means a long period of time before capitalistic profits are earned. Capitalists won't, and shouldn't, wait for those profits to appear. Capitalistic infrastructure can only be built behind, with, or slightly ahead of the market. Historically, private money built America's railroads east of the Mississippi where markets already existed; public money was necessary to build them west of the Mississippi where markets were to be built.

Publicly financed high-speed passenger rail systems now exist in every major industrial country except the United States and Canada. Many lines such as the bullet train line between Tokyo and Ōsaka are very profitable. But no such trains have been built, or ever will be built, entirely with private money in the United States. The length of time until the payoffs occur is too long, the economic risks are too high, and without the right of public domain, the land cannot be acquired for the necessary right-of-ways. If any hard-nosed capitalist has forgotten these realities, the current financial problems of the privately financed (at least on the English side) channel tunnel between England and France will remind them.

The public Rural Electrification Administration (REA) was necessary to bring electricity to rural America. Private utilities would not make the necessary investments since there weren't enough customers. Yet with rural electrification came a revolution in farming that made American agriculture the most productive in the world—less than 2 percent of America's hours of work can feed America and much of the rest of the world. The long-run payoffs were there. Over time electricity usage gradually rose. Now private utilities are anxious to take over many of those REA cooperatives.

Throughout the history of American economic growth, government investments have played a major role. They include but are not limited to the financing of Eli Whitney's invention of interchangeable parts (musket research financed by the War Department and demonstrated to President Jefferson in 1801), the National Road in 1815, the Erie Canal in 1825, cross-continental railroads west of the Mississippi, free land under the Homestead Act, land grant colleges, interstate highways, use of the public mails to subsidize early airlines, public airports, atomic energy, and the exploration of space.[16]

The most dramatic recent example is the Internet—America's, and now the world's, electronic highway—a highway that is doubling in size every year.[17] Initially (1969) the Internet was financed by the Defense Department to link military bases and military researchers in the event of an atomic attack. For more than twenty years it was financed by the Defense Department. The National Science Foundation paid for a major expansion in 1986.[18] Only now are people worrying about constructing some system of tolls that would allow it to be financed privately.[19] Initially it could not have been financed privately—the usage wasn't there, would take twenty years to develop, and could not be foreseen since the widespread usage of cheap personal computers was forecast by no one. A social investment in infrastructure provided the development framework for private growth—the means to deliver and sell both new and old services.

Historically, private productivity growth and public infrastructure development are strongly correlated, but economic studies are mixed about the impact of public infrastructure investments on private sector productivity.[20] Big returns are found in some countries (Germany and the United States) and very small ones in others (the United Kingdom).[21] That is what should be expected, since there is no reason to

think that all countries are equally deficient in infrastructure investments, but such studies also focus on the wrong issue. The issue is not
the current payoffs from past infrastructure investments. Statistical
studies of the past say nothing about whether new infrastructure
should or should not be built. The Internet would have failed this test
for twenty years. Informed judgments have to be made on a project-
by-project basis as to whether a project might lead to the equivalent
of the Internet.

In the United States, public infrastructure investment has been cut
in half over the past twenty-five years and has fallen to the point
where the stock of public capital is now declining relative to the
GDP—falling from 55 to 40 percent of GDP in the last decade.[22] Less
is being invested in public infrastructure in the United States than in
any of the G-7 countries—one third as much as Japan. Whatever one
believes about public infrastructure's role in private economic growth,
it is difficult to make such numbers into positive scenarios for the future.

The infrastructure that is really going to count in the future, however, is not so much the physical infrastructure but the knowledge
infrastructure. Brainpower industries require research and development
investments that require long periods of time to pay off. Biotechnology
is going to change the world and probably change the nature of mankind itself—altering genes to prevent diseases and changing characteristics to build better plants and animals, if not human beings
themselves.[23] One thousand years from now it may be the only thing
that mankind will remember about our era. Yet the research and development funds that produced biotechnology would never have been
advanced by capitalism. In the case of biotechnology, thirty years of
massive governmental investments (billions of dollars per year in today's dollars) were necessary before the first marketable products even
looked possible—much less appeared.

Private industrial laboratories focus on projects that are expected
to pay off in six to seven years or less. The only private labs that have
ever focused on anything other than the short-run results are those
such as the Bell Labs and the IBM Labs that were run by quasi-
monopolies. The minute AT&T (forced by government) and IBM
(forced by the market) joined the normal competitive capitalistic world,
they cut long-term research out of their laboratory budgets.[24] Initially

the seven regional telephone companies set up their own research laboratory, Bellcore, to compete with Bell Labs, but Bellcore is now up for sale and the operating companies are getting out of research to focus on short-run economic development.[25]

Studies of private research show that it has social rates of return 35 to 60 percent above that on ordinary physical capital investments.[26] But to find that too little is being invested is not to say that the underinvestment will disappear with time or be eliminated by the market. Social returns may be high, but the returns to the individual companies paying for the research may not be high. Companies often find that what they have discovered becomes useful to someone else who combines what they have discovered with some other thing that they did not have. The best recent example is the Xerox PARC research center in California—companies such as Apple and Adobe owe their founding to it but they obviously don't contribute to Xerox's profits.[27]

Since long-tailed research and infrastructure investment cannot be justified in the investment calculus of capitalism, America has hidden it in the Defense Department and "justified" it by the necessity of defeating communism. Interstate highways (the National Defense Highway Act) were justified as necessary to move mobile missiles rapidly around the country to avoid Soviet targeting in the 1950s. The Internet was to be a bombproof wartime communication system. The peak production of American Ph.D.s in the late 1960s and early 1970s was heavily subsidized under the National Defense Education Act—including the economics Ph.D. of Republican presidential candidate Senator Phil Gramm of Texas—as a response to the Soviet challenge in science. Even the man-on-the-moon program in the 1960s had to be justified as part of a military race with the Russians.

Many of these activities were connected to national defense only in the sense expressed in the old Prussian nursery rhyme:

> For *want of a nail, the shoe was lost.*
> For *want of a shoe, the horse was lost.*
> For *want of a horse, the rider was lost.*
> For *want of a rider, the battle was lost.*

For want of a battle, the kingdom was lost.
And all for the want of a horseshoe nail.[28]

At some level anything and everything could be justified as necessary for national defense.

In the aggregate almost half of total American R&D flows from the federal government, and for research that could not be expected to pay off in the next five years the percentages approach 100. Yet under the pressures of generating more competitiveness in the private economy and adjusting to the end of the cold war in the Defense Department, American R&D spending as a fraction of GDP has fallen since 1989 and almost all of that decline has been in long-tailed knowledge development.[29] Looking forward based on 1995 budget resolutions and appropriation bills, federal funding of nonmilitary scientific research will fall by one third by 2002.[30]

Rationally, one can talk about how defense research should be the last thing to be cut in the defense budget. If one believes that an enemy may emerge in the future (the only current rationale for U.S. defense spending since there is no current enemy), rational planning would call for maintaining and perhaps even accelerating R&D spending while building few, if any, of the new weapons developed by that research. Keep up with the technologies that the next potential enemy may exploit but don't build weapons that aren't needed now. If built, they will simply become obsolete before they are needed and the country will have wasted its money.[31] The reasoning is good, but the realities of electoral politics call for exactly the opposite. They call for building things that are not needed (those working in defense plants vote) and cutting back on R&D funding (there are not a lot of voters there) and this is precisely what is happening in the U.S. defense budget.[32]

Health has been the other great cover for public R&D spending. When sick, even the hardest of hard-core capitalists, unless he is very rich, does not want the amount or quality of his health care to be determined by his income, effectively becoming a Communist. Health, particularly that of elected politicians who were the first group of Americans to get national health insurance at the government's military hospitals, was too important to be left to the market. This universal interest in finding cures for the diseases that are going to kill each of us led to generous funding for the National Institutes of Health, which in turn generated both the imagination and money to create the biotechnology industry. Although private firms could have made similar investments in biotech, they didn't. Where governments were not equally farsighted, which is essentially everywhere outside of the United States, the private corporations in those countries are now having to play catch-up in biotech.

Capitalistic rationality always calls for free riding the system whenever that is possible at the individual, firm, or national level. Let someone else pay for the costs of the collective investments that raise individual incomes, firm profits, or national output. Studies, for example, show that one quarter to one third of the benefits of American R&D spending accrue to other members of the OECD.[33] Given this reality, why invest? Internationally, every country should let some other country pay for basic research (basic science moves around the world very fast and everyone has it long before it can be embodied in actual processes or products) and concentrate their funds on short-run development activities where one can potentially get a short-run technical edge that might lead to higher national incomes.

Japan is the best example of the rationality of free riding the R&D system. In the post–World War II era it has concentrated its research spending on applied areas and let Americans do the basic research. It won by doing so. Such a "rational" reallocation of R&D funds from the long run to the short run is now under way inside the United States. But if every country rationally attempts to free ride, there is no spending upon basic research and in the long run technical progress stops.

When the issue was military security and not economic competitiveness, no American would have dreamed of attempting to free ride the military R&D system for fear that the Soviets would continue to spend on basic military science and America would eventually be surprised by some new military weapon that was the equivalent of the atomic bomb. Militarily, free riding could get one into a lot of potential trouble. As a result the United States continued to push basic research even though it knew that others were free riding the system. But the incentives are very different with economic free riding. Free riding is very tempting precisely because it works.

By default in an era of man-made brainpower industries, government will have to play a central role in supplying the three inputs—human skills, technology, and infrastructure—that will determine the success or failure of twenty-first century capitalism. Each of the three is needed, yet spending on each is falling. Capitalism isn't getting what it needs for its own long-run success.

In an era of man-made brainpower industries, the purpose of government is clear. It should be representing the interests of the future to the present. It should be making the necessary investments that capitalism cannot make for itself. But it isn't. Instead government is doing exactly the opposite. It is borrowing from the funds that could be used for investments to improve the future to raise today's consumption for today's citizens.

AN ERA OF SHORTER TIME HORIZONS

At precisely the moment that economic success requires longer time horizons, a wide variety of factors are leading to shorter time horizons. The Harvard sociobiologist Edward O. Wilson believes that short time horizons are built into the human genetic behavioral code—"cooperation beyond the family and tribal levels comes hard"; "genes predispose people to plan ahead one or two generations at the most"; "Life was precarious and short. A premium was placed on close attention to the near future and early reproduction and little else"[34]—but whatever one believes about genetics, it is clear from history (witness Egypt, Rome) that humans have for thousands of years been able to sustain a communal interest in the very long run that was stronger than the individual's interest in the short run.

For the OECD as a whole, savings have halved from more than 15 percent in the mid-1970s to about 7 percent in the early 1990s.[35] For Europe and America more than half of this decline can be traced to less savings by government.[36] Outside of the public sector the elderly and consumer credit seem to underlie much of the fall.[37]

Table 14.1
NATIONAL SAVINGS

	1960–69	1990–92
United States		
National savings	11.0	3.0
Government	0.7	−4.7
Private sector	10.3	7.6
Europe		
National savings	17.3	8.3
Government	3.7	−2.1
Private sector	13.5	10.4
Japan		
National savings	22.0	18.5
Governments	5.6	8.2
Private sector	16.4	10.3

SOURCE: Barry Bosworth, *Prospects for Savings and Investment in Industrial Countries,* Brookings Discussion Paper No. 113, May 1995, Appendix, table I.

If countries with high and rising savings rates are analyzed, they have either compulsory savings (Singapore with a 50 percent savings rate) or what financial experts would call "underdeveloped" capital markets that do not lend for consumption purposes (China with a 40 percent savings rate). None of them has allowed a free market in saving behavior.

In the United States both private and public budgets show a sharp shift toward consumption and away from investment. In the private sector, expenditures on research and development, education, and non-residential physical investment have fallen from 14 to 12 percent of the GDP between 1973 and 1993. Over the same twenty years public spending on research and development, infrastructure, and education has fallen from 11 to 6 percent of the GDP.[38]

Government time horizons are rapidly becoming much shorter with the end of the cold war, the budget pressures of the elderly, the impact of the media, and the political furies that have been unleashed by falling real incomes. Technically, many governments have negative time horizons. If governments' budget deficits are bigger than the investment activities contained in those budgets, as they are for the American federal government, governments are net subtractors from the pool of investable funds. Effectively, they are reducing future growth to support current consumption.

In the private sector, time horizons are becoming shorter with a growing elderly population that does not care about the future, a media whose focus is only on present consumption, consumer credit markets that lend vast amounts for consumption purposes, private or public social welfare benefits that discourage savings for the proverbial rainy day, and private business firms that misuse discount rates. (To offset exaggerated benefits or underestimated future risks instead of working on better revenue estimates and better risk analysis, firms often simply raise the interest rates used to evaluate potential investments but this leads to an unwarranted systematic bias against the long run.)

Unfortunately, capitalism does not include a set of social norms that offsets a natural individual human tendency to emphasize the short run. In capitalism no one can say that an individual ought to consume less and invest more. Individuals have a perfect right to consume all of their income or even to consume more than their total income using mortgage or consumer credit loans. If every individual chooses not to save, the whole society cannot grow, but that is still the individual's right. Capitalism is not a doctrine that promises maximum growth. It promises only to cater to individual preferences. If those preferences are perverse with respect to economic growth—so be it.

What is left out of this analysis is the reality that individuals and their preferences are produced by society and social influences.[39] The individual may be the product of an accidental set of social forces or a planned set of social forces, but in either case he is the product of social forces. There is no intrinsic individual set of preferences. But by being unwilling to recognize this social reality, capitalism cannot justify the actions necessary to produce the individuals who would save and invest for the long run even though they are needed for capitalism's own survival.

Conservative economists who argue for more tax incentives for sav-

ings and investment have to do so on the basis that something else in
the tax or regulatory system is discouraging investment and they are
just offsetting some contrary policy elsewhere.[40] Otherwise their rec-
ommendations would be violating the axiom of capitalism that governments should be neutral in their activities, so that the set of private
posttax activities is as close as possible to the set of private activities
that would occur if no taxes were collected.

As the population grows older, one would expect the center of gravity of time preferences to become shorter, since more of the population
is elderly and will not be alive in the future. Studies show that about
two thirds of the observed decline in U.S. personal savings rates (from
8 percent in the 1960s to 4 percent in the early 1990s) can be traced
to a larger proportion of low or negative savings by elder citizens.[41]
There are more elderly, and once elderly they are saving much less,
consuming much more than their parents did at the same age.

Lower savings rates among the elderly partly reflect less interest in
the next generation. Modern living arrangements attenuate the preferences that individuals in the past may have had for saving to explicitly give inheritances to their relatives. As the extended family dissolves
in our modern era of widely scattered living arrangements, there is less
interest in the welfare of relatives whom the elderly only vaguely know
or have lost touch with.[42] The elderly can also argue that with rising
levels of technology those living in the future will be richer than those
living in the present and that as a result gifts from the present to the
future are perverse transfers from the relatively poor (those alive today)
to the relatively rich (those who will be alive tomorrow).

Americans also saved more in the past, not because they used to
have lower rates of time preference, but because they lived in an economy where they had no choice but to save more. Much of the savings
that ended up as inheritances in the next generation, for example,
wasn't saved for that purpose. Since individuals did not know how
long they would live and depended upon their own savings in their old
age, every individual had to prepare (save) for the possibility that they
would be one of the lucky ones who lived to be very old. In such a
world one needed to save a lot before retirement and be very careful
about dissaving once retired. Without public or private pensions it was
necessary to save money for one's old age even if the rate of return on
those savings was negative. (And in fact it was very low—in the fifty

years from 1920 to 1970 the real, inflation-corrected rate of interest on Treasury bills was 1 percent in the United States.)[43] If one did not save, one was going to starve to death in one's old age. When individuals were unlucky and died at a normal life expectancy, their leftover resources not surprisingly went to the next of kin rather than to some stranger. What was rational for each individual (to act as if they were going to live to be one hundred), in the aggregate led individuals to oversave.

With private and public monthly pensions, individuals do not need to save for the unlikely possibility that they will live to be one hundred. Private and public pensions can take advantage of the law of large numbers and actuarial tables to determine how much they should accumulate to meet their obligations to those who will actually live to be one hundred. As a result, smaller sums need to be accumulated. In addition, private pension plans are often underfunded (how much depends upon what one assumes about future interest rates) and public plans are usually not funded at all. Social Security is a system of intergenerational transfers from the young to the old with no net savings—the amount of money coming in is roughly equal to the amount of money going out. As a consequence, what individuals think they are saving (their monthly contribution) doesn't end up as savings that can be used to make investments—it simply funds someone else's monthly pension check.

Public and private health insurance has similar effects. Without health insurance it is necessary to save money to cover the costs of treatment if one gets sick. Being risk-averse, people don't want to take a chance on running out of the money necessary to save their own lives. Each has to act as if he or she will end up with large medical bills. Being unable to average across large numbers of individuals they cannot use the actuarial tables that health insurance funds use to determine how much they need to charge to cover serious illnesses. In the aggregate, operating as individuals they will save more without health insurance than they would with health insurance programs even if those health insurance plans were fully funded. But public plans are not funded at all and private plans are only minimally funded since no one anticipated today's health expenditure levels.

America's public system of national health insurance for the elderly (Medicare) is a system of intergenerational transfers. The young pay for the health care of the elderly, leaving the elderly free to spend their income on other forms of consumption since they know that they will not need their income to keep themselves alive. The net result is much less savings. The young, paying more taxes, have less disposable income from which they can save, and the elderly have less need to save.

All social welfare programs, private or public, that ensure against the risks of life reduce the rational interest in saving for the future. Conservatives are right to argue that getting rid of social welfare programs would restore incentives to save, but doing so would require an enormous cut in current consumption and an enormous willingness to face huge risks that most individuals don't want to face. Getting along without social welfare programs when one has never had them is very different from getting rid of the social welfare programs once they have existed. If one does not think so, just ask the conservative French minister of finance who was forced to resign shortly after he took office for daring to suggest that pension benefits be cut.[44]

Conservatives are wrong, however, to think that private savings rates are intrinsically high if government would just get out of the way. Marginal rates of time preference (would you believe 60 percent?) have always been far above market interest rates, since individuals were institutionally forced to save in the past.[45] Consider credit cards. From the perspective of capitalism consumer credit is like sex between consenting adults. It is no one's business except that of the lender or the borrower. Yet if everyone can get what they want instantly without having to save and unused credit card balances can replace savings for a rainy day (as they have), why should anyone save? The individual goal is to maximize consumption—not savings and investment.

In the past, without consumer credit, car loans, or home mortgages (all three of which didn't really exist until after World War II and in 1950 still only amounted to 52 percent of personal income) if someone wanted to buy a washing machine, a car, or a house, they had to save the money necessary to buy that item or they did not get to enjoy a washing machine, a car, or a house.[46] With the development and widespread availability of consumer and mortgage credit (in 1994 outstanding loans equaled 107 percent of disposable income), anyone can have anything they want while paying for it after they have it rather than before they have it.[47]

Whether the consumer pays before or after he gets what he wants is critical. If consumers accumulate funds before purchasing, their savings can be used to make productive investments until they have saved enough to buy the desired items. If consumers repay loans after purchasing, then other people's savings have to be advanced to them and they effectively subtract from the pool of loanable funds available for investment. Not surprisingly, across countries personal savings rates are closely tied to the availability of generous consumer and mortgage credit with zero or low down payments.[48] A shift from credit cards where one pays after purchasing (the American system) to debit cards where one pays before purchasing (the Japanese system) makes a big difference in savings rates.

From a savings perspective the tax laws permitting home equity loans will probably prove to be one of America's biggest economic mistakes. In the past, middle-class individuals could count on entering their old age with substantial savings because they had been forced to make monthly house payments (a form of compulsory savings) and because the value of their homes had appreciated. With home equity loans individuals don't have to save to live in their house. They can just keep taking their net equity out. If homes appreciate, home equity loans can actually generate negative savings, since appreciating home values look like, and are, extra financial resources for each individual family but are not savings as far as society is concerned because the higher selling price one American receives is what another American buyer has to pay.

There is no question that America's tax and expenditures systems are biased in favor of consumption. Savings are taxed as income, many forms of consumption such as health care are untaxed, and other forms of consumption such as housing are given large tax breaks.[49] Legislators love talking about changing the system to reward saving and investment. Tax cuts are often justified as incentives to save—but in reality they seldom are. Just lowering taxes, as was done under the Reagan administration, for example, simply left people with more after-tax income to spend on consumption—which is what they did and savings rates actually went down. If more savings are desired, the right technique is not tax breaks for income but tax penalties on consumption that rise as consumption rises. Yet serious legislation to shift from a system of taxes on income to a system of progressive consumption taxes is conspicuous by its absence.

The media magnify the short time horizons that are intrinsic in capitalism. It is almost impossible even to imagine an interesting movie or TV program that shows people forgoing consumption and sacrificing for the future. It is fun to see the ads for new consumption goods; it is fun to see those new consumption goods used in movies and TV programs. The purpose of those ads is to persuade people to buy new goods. They work!

To some extent America is a low-savings society, since it is a low-investment society—not the reverse. Individuals and firms save when they want to invest. If the 149 Japanese firms that were on *Fortune*'s list of the world's 500 largest are contrasted with the 151 American firms on that list, the American firms earned seven times as much relative to sales and twelve times as much relative to assets.[50] Demanding rates of return on investments many times as high as those demanded by Japanese firms, there are simply fewer investment projects that pass capitalistic muster in the United States—and therefore there is less need to save to carry out those projects.

This is why national investment is correlated with national savings despite the existence of a global capital market. Some investments will be internationally financed and won't depend upon national savings, but national investment is highly correlated with national savings, since much of savings is not placed into international capital markets to be allocated to wherever returns are highest but saved because the saver wants to make specific investments that he or she will control. The direction of causation is not from more savings to more investment but from the desire to make a specific investment to more savings. American savings rates are low since Americans don't have investments they want to make.[51] Not wanting to invest, they don't save. Countries achieve more investment by stimulating investment, not by attempting to raise saving rates.

Nowhere is capitalism's time horizon problem more acute than in the area of global environmentalism (a problem I have written on elsewhere and will not belabor or repeat here).[52] What should a capitalistic society do about long-run environmental problems such as global warming or ozone depletion? In both cases what is done now affects the environment fifty to one hundred years from now but has no noticeable effect on what happens today. In both cases there is a lot of uncertainty and risk as to what will happen if nothing is done.

Using capitalistic decision rules, the answer to what should be done today to prevent such problems is very clear—do nothing. However large the negative effects fifty to one hundred years from now might be, their current discounted net present value is zero. If the current value of the future negative consequences are zero, then nothing should be spent today to prevent those distant problems from emerging. But if the negative effects are very large fifty to one hundred years from now, by then it will be too late to do anything to make the situation better, since anything done at that time could only improve the situation another fifty to one hundred years into the future. So being good capitalists, those who live in the future, no matter how bad their problems are, will also decide to do nothing. Eventually a generation will arrive who cannot survive in the earth's altered environment, but by then it will be too late for them to do anything to prevent their own extinction. Each generation makes good capitalistic decisions, yet the net effect is collective social suicide.

THE MISSING INGREDIENT—THE FUTURE

In capitalism there is no analysis of the distant future. There is no concept that anyone must invest in the plant and equipment, skills, infrastructure, research and development, or environmental protection that are necessary for national growth and rising individual standards of living. There simply is no social "must" in capitalism. If individuals choose not to save and invest, growth will not occur, but so be it. Individual decisions maximize total welfare even if they lead to stagnant societies.

In the theory of capitalism, technology just appears and the capitalist invests to take advantage of it. This belief is not surprising given the history of the early industrial revolution. Technology did seem to just appear. Organization, institutions, and investments in R&D were not necessary to develop the spinning jenny, Arkwright's loom, the steam engine, or Bessemer's blast furnace. But all of that changed with the Germans' invention of chemical engineering at the beginning of the twentieth century. Organizations, institutions, and large long-run investments are precisely what is necessary to generate rapid technical progress. Technological breakthroughs are man-made, not God-given.

In capitalism the social context of individual preference formation is completely absent. The importance of social organization in determining the complex nature of rationality, self-interest, motivation, and preference formation goes unrecognized.[53] Preference shaping has been identified as a primary or secondary goal of child rearing, education, religion, advertising, public service announcements, legislation, and criminal punishment but it is unrecognized by capitalism.[54] All societies need a mixture of self-control and social control but even self-control is socially installed.[55] Learning is a social, not an individual, activity. Communities are not aggregations of individuals but interactions among individuals—conversations and storytelling are central.[56]

Yet capitalism has no basis for demanding even self-constraint unless individual actions directly harm someone else.[57] Even Adam Smith two hundred years ago saw that something more was needed. "Men could safely be trusted to pursue their own self-interest without undue harm to the community not only because of restrictions imposed by laws, but also because they were subject to built-in restraint derived from morals, religion, custom, and education."[58]

This leaves a simple question. Who is in command of the social system? Since capitalism believes that there is no social system, its answer is no one. Yet that is not an acceptable answer in the twenty-first century.

Communism fell because it could not solve its internal contradictions. Communism's ideology of radical equality and its belief that there was no need for individual incentives proved to be incompatible with the productive realities of modern human beings in an industrial age. Nor could the social welfare state square its internal contradictions. If taxes were too high and too much income was handed out on some basis other than productive inputs, people's investments or work effort was diverted or fell—making it necessary to raise tax rates even higher and intensifying the initial problem.

In some profound sense capitalistic values are also at war with capitalism. Capitalism will succeed or fail based on the investments that it makes, yet it preaches a theology of consumption. Good physical infrastructure (roads, airports, water, sewage, electricity, etc.) and good social infrastructure (public safety, educational opportunities, research and development) are necessary if economic progress is to occur, yet none of these investments is called for in the theology of capitalism.

Historically, capitalism has solved its internal contradictions by using the public sector to make many of the investments in infrastructure, research and development, and education that it would not make. Private capitalism counted on public "spinoffs." Instead of admitting that it needs help to function efficiently, however, capitalism's usual excuse for government activity has been some military threat. But none now exists.

Part of the problem is that any such admission leads almost automatically to something that would have to be considered an industrial policy. To be effective, any R&D system must know what it wants. Where should those directing government R&D spending bet the public's money? The military knew what it wanted—a missile that landed within fifteen feet, a submarine that stayed underwater forever, a fighter aircraft that flew at three thousand miles per hour. Technologies were developed to meet explicit goals. Just giving money to researchers and telling them to do good things does not work. The funder has to know what he wants and be able to set goals so that failure can be distinguished from success.

The capitalism of classical comparative advantages did not need government R&D funding. Economic activity was determined by the location of natural resources and capital-labor ratios. But in the capitalism of man-made brainpower industries, public technology strategies are central. Man-made brainpower industries will be located at the place where someone organizes the brainpower to capture them. They have no natural home. Organizing brainpower means not just building an R&D system that puts a nation on the leading edge of technology, but also organizing a workforce that has the top-to-bottom skills necessary to be masters of new product, production, and distribution technologies. No one will win without world-class communications and transportation infrastructure. All of these investments will take longer and have a more collective component in the epoch ahead.

When government is asked to make these long-run social investments for capitalism, the requests are all ad hoc flying buttresses—essential to hold up the cathedral of capitalism but officially unrecognized. Being unrecognized they are not maintained and supported by capitalism. But when the public sector atrophies beyond some point, the flying buttresses fall, and the private cathedral falls with them.

It is always easier to give advice to others. Looking back, Americans are quick to note that flourishing societies such as the Incas in Peru or the Moors in southern Spain went into rapid decline when the Spanish stopped maintaining the irrigation systems that had allowed them to exist. The greatest builders of them all, the Khmer empire headquartered in Angkor in what is now Cambodia, may have come to its end through a failure to maintain its enormous complex irrigation system.[59]

Without social organization everyone has an incentive to be a free rider—enjoying whatever benefits exist without putting in any effort to preserve the system that makes the benefits exist. Without organization everyone uses as much water as possible and no one puts any effort into repairing the canals. Within a short period of time there is no irrigation system from which water can be taken and everyone's standard of living falls below where it previously had been. Everyone is individually rational but the net result is collective irrationality.

A similar test lies ahead for us. Can capitalism invest in the human capital, infrastructure, and research and development that will allow it to flourish, or will it, like the Christian Spaniards, get rich in the short run and refuse to make the social investments upon which its long-run success depends?

Nowhere is the internal contradiction between what is needed and what is done more evident than in capitalism's treatment of its own labor force. Companies aggressively assert that they have no long-run obligations to their workforces. Workers are forced to learn that they ought to be short-run earnings maximizers moving to a new employer whenever wage offers are even marginally higher. Staying to wait for future success and future wage increases is "dumb," since the firm is apt to fire you in the future no matter how much you have contributed to their success in the past. Yet that long-term strategic advantage essential to business firms can only be captured by precisely those brainpower workers who have been taught that they should have the values of the old western TV series, *Have Gun, Will Travel.* Mutual loyalty is needed precisely when it is in retreat.

While one can argue about how many actually had it, the implicit post–World War II social contract has been shattered. Data on how long the average worker works for any one employer haven't changed that much, since they are dominated by industries such as fast food services with very high turnover rates, but for skilled white-collar workers in the middle and upper-middle salary ranges, a huge psychological seismic shift is under way. These pressures can only increase, since firms searching for faster productivity growth will have to focus on reducing their white-collar workforces because white-collar workers are now much more numerous than their blue-collar workers. They also now have the means to do so, since in many ways computer technologies are better fitted to doing traditional white-collar jobs (paper shuffling) than they are fitted to doing traditional blue-collar jobs.

The breaking of the old social contract is the result of the bumping together of two economic plates. The global economy simultaneously permits, encourages, and forces companies to move their activities to the lowest-cost locations. Since there are large moving costs, it usually pays companies to attempt to force down costs in their current locations to derive the benefits of lower wages without having to pay those moving costs. Simultaneously, new technologies are allowing firms to work with a very different structure of employment. Without the need for as much face-to-face reporting, electronic telecommunications makes possible fewer levels of management and many fewer workers at the corporate headquarters.

The depth and breadth of knowledge necessary for successful economic production requires putting people to work together in skilled teams. Companies such as Chrysler have proved that there are enormous sources of soft productivity gains to be had if a company can really get its employees to work together and think of the team's self-interest rather than their own self-interest. Capitalism, the triumph of individuality, however, cannot officially recognize the need for teamwork. Even as capitalism is organizing itself into teams and one might imagine that loyalty to the team and the willingness to work as part of a team have become more important, the ingredients that hold economic teams together (lifetime employment, real wage increases) are disappearing. Just when the need for employing human skills in unselfish teams would seem to call for attaching that skilled workforce closer to the company and making it more a part of the company team, real companies are moving in precisely the opposite direction.

How these two incompatible objectives are to be put together is not at all clear. In the 1980s and early 1990s some firms experimented with a social contract where there was a core group of permanent workers who enjoy the old arrangement and a peripheral group of temporary workers who enjoy no social contract (the General Motors pattern at Saturn). But this pattern only works if the group outside of the social contract is relatively small. It also assumes that a firm can identify who the core workers are. Looking at the downsizing movement and reductions in real wages that have occurred, an observer would come to the conclusion that there are no core workers except very senior managers. Rising inequality and falling real wages now afflicts a majority, not a minority of the American workforce. Something else will have to be developed.

Perhaps a new social contract could be built on the basis that no firm will guarantee lifetime employment with rising wages but that it will guarantee that while a worker is on the firm's team the employer will work with that individual to invest in his or her lifetime career skills—skills that can raise wages or skills that could be used at another company. Lifetime employment is replaced with lifetime employability. Such a contract would clearly require huge changes in normal human resource policies. Employees would have to be consulted as to what skills they will acquire, would have to be allowed to refuse investments they did not think wise, and would need to be given skills acquisition possibilities that are of no use to their current employers. Who pays for what parts of these investments in skills is not at all obvious. Perhaps lifetime employability is workable, but not one company has yet worked out what such a contract would mean and how it would work.

If capitalism is to work in the long run, it must make investments that are not in any particular individual's immediate self-interest but are in the human community's long-run self-interest. How does a doctrine of radical short-run individualism emphasize long-run communal interests? How can capitalism promote the values that it needs to sustain itself when it denies that it needs to promote any particular set of values at all? Put simply, who represents the interests of the future to the present?

As a result, capitalism is going to be asked to do what it does least well—invest in the distant future and make deliberate adjustments in its institutional structure to encourage individuals, firms, and governments to make long-term decisions. If one asked what must governments do in capitalistic societies to make conditions better, the socialist answer was to own and run business firms. That answer proved to be incorrect. The right answer is to force a high level of private and public investment.

History shows us that very different balances between public and private and between consumption and investment are possible, but it also shows us that it is not possible to run a good society without a balance in both areas. All public, the model of communism, does not work. All private, the model of feudalism, and the implicit model of capitalism, also does not work. Neither all consumption nor all investment can work. In the era ahead, capitalism will have to create new values and new institutions that allow a new strategic balance in each of these areas.

The pressures are building up within the volcano. How is capitalism to function when the important types of capital cannot be owned? Who is going to make the necessary long-run investments in skills, infrastructure, and research and development? How do the skilled teams that are necessary for success get formed? In periods of punctuated equilibrium there are questions without obvious answers that have to be answered.

Chapter 15

Operating in a Period of Punctuated Equilibrium

THE POLITICAL PROCESS

Capitalism has a current advantage in that with the death of communism and socialism, it has no plausible social system as an active competitor. It is impossible to have a revolution against anything unless there is an alternative ideology. But dissatisfaction and free-floating hostility is growing everywhere—not just in the November 1994 American elections. In the first round of the 1994 French elections, Jean-Marie Le Pen on the far right gathered 15 percent of the vote from the same white males who voted for the new Republican majority—those with falling economic prospects whose fears could be focused on immigrants. California's Proposition 187 is alive and well in France. Religious fundamentalists want to seize control of the political process (in Algeria, Israel, Egypt, India, Japan, the United States) and throw out the current governments so that they can install their version of certainty and truth almost everywhere.

Free market conservatives play with fire when they politically ally themselves with the religious fundamentalists, since their goals are congruent only when it comes to getting rid of the current governments. Religious fundamentalists don't believe in free markets in goods and services any more than they believe in free markets in ideas. Fundamentalists know what should be sold and what should not be sold. Iran is the place where religious fundamentalism has succeeded in gaining control of the government. The merchants of the bazaar were instrumental in financing Khomeini's Islamic revolution, since they hated the Shah's economic reforms, which threatened them with new competitors in the form of traditional Western retailing. But once in power the religious fundamentalists turned on those same merchants to re-strict what they could or could not sell. Modesty demanded that women buy the "right" clothes. The definition of pornography sud-denly expanded to include almost everything they didn't like. Today those merchants in the bazaar find their businesses in far worse shape than when the Shah was in control.

Governments are in trouble everywhere in the world, since they have no answers to the real problems and worries facing their citizens. The policies being enacted because of the great Republican victory of 1994 don't even address the problems of falling real wages and rising inequality. Eventually those same voters will again become unhappy voters and chase after whatever demagogue happens to be around at the time. The fury that was directed at the Democrats in late 1994 could easily be directed back at the business community in the years ahead if the "right" (wrong?) leaders emerge. A large group of voters with free-floating hostility, not benefiting from the economic system, is not a recipe for economic or political success.

Democracies react well to crises since crises focus everyone's atten-tion on the same issues and demand action. Without a crisis galvaniz-ing public attention, democracies almost never act. To change, democracies need to persuade large numbers of their average citizens (far more than 51 percent) that change is necessary. Majorities are inherently conservative, since change means that the majority must it-self abandon old ways. Without a crisis it is difficult to persuade a large majority that something has to change. Without a crisis minori-ties hurt by change can always block change. Democracies pay much more than proportional attention to one-issue minority groups, since they often swing close elections and can be made into solid supporters quickly—simply support them on their one hot issue.

But current economic events are not a crisis. The real income of nonsupervisory workers is declining less than 1 percent per year. Changes are dramatic over twenty-five-year periods of time, but not in any one year. A dramatic change has occurred in the distribution of income and wealth over the past twenty-five years and absolutely noth-ing has been done to reverse it. Policies to reverse current trends are not even being debated.

At the same time, these trends are produced by forces so funda-mental that it is clear that they are not going to be reversed by marginal reforms in economic policies. Massive structural changes will be required. That is of course what democracies do least well. When democracies are forced to move, instead of making radical changes and moving to the global optimums, democracies tend to move slowly along the line of least resistance to local optimums. With normal evolution, that is the correct strategy. In a period of punctuated equilibrium it is not. Local optimums, the line of least resistance, often leads away from and not toward global optimums.

For a while, using the titles of two recent books, it is possible to have an Age of Contentment for the upper classes while having an Age of Diminishing Expectations for the middle and lower classes.[1] But such a duality is not forever possible. Social systems float on a molten magma of compatible ideologies and technologies. It is not possible to have an ideology of equality (democracy) and an economy that generates ever larger inequalities with absolute income reductions for a majority of the voting population.

American capitalism has strengths and weaknesses when it comes to dealing with these pressures. Its strength is that it has more fundamental political support than capitalism in Europe. The fact that socialist parties have never been a force in American politics says something important about America. Faith in capitalism's ability to deliver rising standards of living will probably die more slowly in the United States than it will in Europe. American capitalism's prime weakness is that it is the major deliverer of what elsewhere would be social welfare benefits (medical care, pensions) to the working middle class. Economically, to lose one's job, and hence one's company-provided fringe benefits, is much less serious in Europe than it is in the United States. There the social welfare state picks up more of what is lost when unemployment strikes.

As middle-class fringe benefits are cut back, the anger of the middle is rising and will rise rapidly. Eventually the middle class will demand that the political process act to stop its benefits and standards of living from being reduced, and it will have less and less interest in politically protecting capitalism. Just such anger led President Clinton and his wife to make health care their primary issue in the first two years of Clinton's administration. The Clintons fumbled the health care reform process, but the middle-class anger at being deprived of health care will return.

Politically, capitalism stands alone in a way that it has not stood alone since the mid-nineteenth century. Then, capitalism survived politically precisely because it coopted groups of workers—middle- and lower-level managers, white-collar workers, skilled blue-collar workers—into thinking of themselves as part of the capitalistic team. With downsizing, capitalism is in effect telling a lot of its past political supporters that they are no longer part of the "team." Having been thrown off capitalism's economic team, it is only a matter of time until those same workers desert capitalism's political team.

In the short run, capitalism can politically afford to be much tougher economically on its workforce than it used to be when socialism or communism threatened it with an internal revolution and an external threat. But at some point, something will arise to challenge capitalism and capitalism will need the political support of more than those small numbers of individuals who are actually owners of substantial amounts of capital. Where is this support to come from?

The facts are clear. Income and wealth inequalities are rising everywhere. Real wages are falling for a large majority. A lumpen proletariat unwanted by the productive economy is growing. The social contract between the middle class and corporate America has been ripped up. The prime remedy for inequalities in the past one hundred years, the social welfare state, is in retreat. Economic plate tectonics is rapidly changing the economic surface of the earth.

The revival of free market survival-of-the-fittest economics is not surprising in that it fills people's need for some kind of social understanding to guide their actions—a return to mythical ancient virtues.[2] It's what people do when they are confused. But something new is going to have to be invented to cope with the current period of punctuated equilibrium and the very different future that will come out of it.

New productive technologies are raising the importance of social investments in infrastructure, education, and research while values are moving toward more individuality with much less social interest in communal investments. A more rugged version of survival-of-the-fittest capitalism is being preached at precisely the moment that the economic system is discovering the productivity gains that can flow from teamwork. The belief that the capitalistic system is perfect and needs no social support has returned just when a new capitalism without ownable capital has to be invented.

A BUILDER'S IDEOLOGY

At this point it is tempting to outline a long list of public policies that would help capitalism get what it needs. What tax and budgetary policies would lead to more long-term investments? What R&D strategies should be employed? Which are the infrastructure projects with long-run spillovers? What are the right reforms in pension and health care programs for the elderly? How does one generate the most skilled labor force in the world? How should formal education be integrated with on-the-job training? Who should pay for what? Some of these questions have been partially answered in the course of this book, but attempting to definitely answer all of these questions now would be a mistake.

Appropriate public policies aren't the current issue. The current issue is persuading ourselves that the world has changed and that we must change with it. Adopting the right policies once the need for change has been recognized intellectually, and more important emotionally, is the easy part of the task. Many public policy possibilities exist for getting from here to there. What we first have to do is figure out where the "there" is and then create a sense of urgency about getting there.

As a boy growing up in Montana before the era of jet aircraft, my flights of fancy still turned to the railroads. At that time one of the fastest trains in the world was the Great Northern's *Empire Builder* as it powered its way across Montana and North Dakota on its way from Minneapolis to Seattle. The name of that train captures the attitudes that must be generated to succeed in the era ahead. As the name implies, there were no empires on the northern Great Plains to be conquered. There was only empty space where James J. Hill envisioned that he and his trains would be the catalyst for building an empire. In the end he was wrong. No empire was ever built. The gold mines that at one time looked so promising petered out. But the name of his train embodies what has to be done.

Today there are no physical empires worth conquering. Holding more physical territory does not make one a better economic competitor. Those who succeed will build the man-made brainpower industries of the future. They will build something where there is today empty intellectual and economic space. Some possibilities that look like economic gold mines will peter out as they did for Mr. Hill, but other technologies that look like wastelands will prove to be economic bonanzas. But to capture those bonanzas one must be there with a commitment to empire building.[3]

No sensible person has ever set the goal of reducing his or her own consumption. Saving is not fun. But participating in the process of using the funds released by saving to build something can be fun. If it is to succeed, the capitalism of the future will have to shift from a consumption ideology to a builder's ideology. Growth is not an automatic process of quietly moving from one equilibrium point to another. The growth path is a noisy process of disequilibrium where a lot of fun is to be had. Technology is not manna from heaven. It is a social process of human creation and innovation. In this context investment must be seen, not as a cost to be avoided, but as a direct generator of utility to be embraced. The individual who invests in what will probably be the most valuable skills that any individual can have, the ability to operate in a global economy, is not being forced to sacrifice consumption but is building a skill set that will bring more enjoyment than an item of consumption.

The savings habits of the self-employed illustrate the attitudes that must be generated. In the United States at every income level the self-employed are much larger savers and investors than those who work for someone else but make the same income. The self-employed directly see what they are building. Building a better business generates more utility for them than having a bigger home or driving a bigger car. As builders their time horizons are much longer than those of either absentee capitalists or consumers.

In big corporations mostly owned by the pension funds and mutual funds, the shareholders are so distant, so diversified, and so amorphous that none of them can get any enjoyment out of creating or building. They only see dividends. If one looks at large corporations still controlled by a dominant family (Mars, Wal-Mart, Miliken, Microsoft), one sees very different behavior patterns and time horizons than those inside equally large businesses owned by institutions. Their personal goals, their family goals, and their business goals are all consistent with a building mentality.

Everyone cannot be self-employed. The economy does not need them in this role and many individuals who should be small savers don't have the necessary personal aptitudes. While everyone cannot participate directly as builders, everyone can participate in the building process in a social sense when government builds the projects that it will need to build. Most Americans did not work on the man-on-the-moon project in the 1960s. Yet all of us took great pride in what was accomplished and I don't remember hearing anyone at the time saying that "too much" money was being spent. In continental Europe the same feeling exists today about high-speed intercity rail travel. Everyone tells you that their trains are the fastest—or soon will be the fastest. Complaints about taxes and government budgets abound, but never once during a year of living in Europe and traveling widely did I hear someone objecting to that part of their government's budgets.

I suspect that the same feeling probably existed in ancient Egypt when they were building the pyramids. Today we marvel at the proportions of their total incomes and working time that must have effectively been collected in taxes to build the pyramids, but they undoubtedly took great pride in what they were doing. In the jargon of modern economics they got personal utility by building for the infinite future. They did not see what they were doing as depriving themselves of the consumption goods they would need to have a high standard of living in the present.

If individuals are to have a builder's mentality, then government must be active visible builders. Some of the building should be physically visible. Deciding to beat the Japanese and Europeans when it comes to having the best intercity high-speed rail network in the world would be a good place to start. But much of the building will be human. The United States should commit to having the most skilled and best-educated labor force in the world. This means being willing to measure objectively where America stands today, finding out who has the best-educated labor force at every level, being willing to chart our progress or lack of progress in catching up with and then passing whoever is best, and committing to doing whatever is necessary to achieve that goal. If something does not work it should be ruthlessly junked and other means adopted—but nothing will be allowed to stop us from reaching the goal.

The real heroes of the future are neither the capitalists of Adam

Smith nor the small businessmen politicians love to praise, but those who build new industries.[4] They were willing to live the difficult life outside of the boundaries of routine—to overcome the natural human psychic reluctance to try the new in the face of a social environment that is always attached to the past.[5] They have the ability to dream, the will to conquer, the joy of creating, and the psychic drive to build an economic kingdom.[6]

Joseph Schumpeter thought that capitalism would die out because it would be undercut by the bureaucratization of invention and innovation and by the intellectual scribblers who would point to the nobler goals of other systems such as socialism.[7] He actually predicted the disintegration of the family, since children would cease to be economic assets and parents would refuse to undertake the necessary sacrifices to support them when they became cost centers.[8] Historically, he was wrong about R&D, identified the wrong scribblers, and is looking ever more right about the family.

Research and development, especially fundamental R&D, does have to be bureaucratically funded by big companies or big government. The tinkerer-inventors of nineteenth-century British fame no longer stand at the heart of technological progress. But this still leaves plenty of economic niches for small inventors and innovators to use the basic scientific principles whose discovery was funded by big science to build small firms that eventually become big firms. It also does nothing to reduce the fun of invention for those employed who are funded by the big funders. My institution, MIT, lives or dies with the big funders, but those doing the research have an exciting time and MIT is the country's largest incubator of new firms.

The modern equivalent of Schumpeter's scribbler is the TV set. Officially, it sings hymns of praise for capitalism but unofficially it inculcates a set of antiproduction values. Consumption is the name of the game; no one should postpone immediate gratification. In TV land, creators and builders are conspicuous by their absence. Time horizons become ever shorter based on both the ideologies of the programs and the ways in which that content is presented—moving faster and faster from one scene to another. Put a stopwatch on the evening news programs and measure the longest amount of time they are willing to spend on any one topic no matter how important.

Without an outside threat how does TV man force himself to make the investments and reforms that are essential to the future? Neither his explicit capitalistic ideology nor his implicit TV ideology recognizes sacrificing to build the future. He is the ultimate consumer in the present. Where are the values that support necessary investments in education, R&D, and infrastructure to be generated? If they don't get generated what happens?

The modern scribblers, the TV set, was probably one of the major factors lying behind the fall of the Berlin Wall in 1989. East Germans sat there watching West German television knowing what they were missing. The ideology of socialism could not replace the goods of capitalism. In North Korea, TV sets are built so that they cannot receive the signals of South Korea, and the DMZ still stands. The North Koreans simply don't know they are missing anything that anyone else has.

ADJUSTING TO A NEW GAME

Adjusting to new realities is difficult. Countries fundamentally are what they are and often cannot do what they need to do even though they know what they should do. Everyone in America knows that Americans need to save more, yet the United States can do nothing to reduce its consumption. Europe knows that it cannot forever continue without employment growth, but it cannot give up its fight against the ghosts of inflation and isn't willing to deregulate its labor markets to jump-start its economic engines. Japan knows that its current economy does not work and knows that it uniquely has less residential space per person than any other wealthy society, but it cannot restructure to be a domestically led economy focused on improving the housing stock. Each of the major world players rationally knows some of what it needs to do but cannot act rationally.

America

Making the necessary changes will be hard for everyone but especially hard for Americans. They are not unique in believing that their social system is the world's best; many citizens of many countries have similar beliefs, but Americans are unique in believing that their social system is perfect—given by founding fathers who are demigods at the very least. The American political system is also now the world's old-est. Both of these factors lead Americans whenever something goes wrong to find fault not with a system that needs institutional repairs but with "bad" individuals—the devil. In American political theology the bad guys never ultimately win. Vietnam was a bigger shock in America than it would have been almost anywhere else precisely be-cause the good guy, we Americans, did not in the end win. In American theology there are no trade-offs between liberty and equality. Ameri-cans can have both. The right rules (system) will produce deliverance—and once in place, like Moses' Ten Commandments, those rules are written in stone and never need to be altered. America does not need social planning or elite knowledge. The man on the street knows best. Americans don't have to accept the allocation of losses. Free markets will bring forth not just the best that there is to be had, but perfection at no cost.[9]

Americans will also have to cope with losing their position as the world's dominant economic, political, and military power. Rationality would call for Americans to play an active, but a reduced and different role on the world stage. America has immense powers of persuasion and assimilation; it is the world's only country with global interest and a global reach. But emotionally the loss of leadership is more likely to lead to isolationism.[10] Everyone will deny that they are isolationists ("isolationism" is a bad word, much like "Munich"), but Americans are now saying in the legislation working its way through Congress that they don't want to pay for activities such as the United Nations, that they don't want to pay for regional development banks, and they don't want to send American troops abroad under international aus-pices—precisely the activities that allow America to be a world military power and exercise leadership. Whatever Americans say, American "isolationism" is in resurgence.

Europe

The European model, sometimes called the Rhine model to distin-guish it from the Anglo-Saxon model of capitalism, faces quite different problems.[11] Its savings and investment rates are much higher than those in America; it has a more communitarian character and is willing to make much larger social investments. But it believes that social security is the "rightful" outcome of economic progress and that this commitment to nonnegotiable social requirements and the social welfare state cannot work in a global economy.[12] Nowhere is this better illustrated than in the travails of the new conservative French government.[13] Finance ministers get fired for even suggesting cutbacks in pensions, nothing can be done to cut back expenditures, labor market deregulation disappears as strikes appear.

While the U.S. social welfare system is 55 percent publicly financed and 45 percent privately financed, in Europe the public sector carries 80 percent of the burden and the private sector only 20 percent.[14] As a result, the collapse of the social welfare state hits Europe both earlier and harder. As one German accurately put it, we "are a socially oriented nation where the commitment of the strong to the weak is a notion that can no longer be afforded."[15]

Part of the European problem arises precisely because that German observer looks like he is wrong. In Europe's largest economy, Germany, combining capitalism and the social welfare state seems to work better than anywhere else. Germans complain but they enjoy higher wages and twice as many paid days away from work (42 holidays and vacation days plus 19 sick days) as the Americans or Japanese. It works in the sense that Germany still has an economy that can afford to give real-wage increases while running a trade surplus.[16] Germany works precisely because it is highly competitive vis-à-vis other European countries that have the same social welfare system but are less efficient. It would not work if they did not exist. But the German experience leaves the rest of Europe uncertain as to whether they too could make the system work if they could just change something to become more like the Germans. German "success" makes it much harder to build something new.

But in the long run European businesses will avoid paying for the social welfare system by going abroad and European laborers will continue to disappear into the black economy. The current system cannot continue. Official statistics tell us that unemployment is higher and earnings lower relative to what could be gotten elsewhere in Europe in southern Italy or southern Spain in the 1990s than they were in the 1960s. Yet in the 1960s millions and millions of Spaniards and Italians moved north in their own countries or became guest workers in Germany or Switzerland to get jobs. Today no one moves. It is simply more attractive to work in the black economy and collect social welfare benefits than it is to move to a job.

In two decades European unemployment rates have gone from half those of the United States to more than twice those of the United States. Without changes two decades from now that gap will become much larger. Twenty-five years have passed with no growth in European employment. The system will break with another twenty-five years of the same experience.

There is another fundamental place where the Rhine model does not work. Remember that list of the twelve largest firms in America in 1900—eleven of twelve died before the end of the century. To be successful, economies need small companies that grow up to be big companies. Part of Europe (northern Italy, for example) is full of excellent small companies but they never succeed in growing from small to large. As long as a company is small enough to stay under the government's economic radar screens, business regulations (such as those making firing labor very expensive) either don't apply or can be evaded.[17] Not long ago I visited one of those good small companies in northern Italy. Its management spent much of their time thinking of how they could move some of their activities out of Italy so that they could continue to be small and not bothered by government regulations. Those energies could have been better directed.

If a company is already very large, those same regulations can be financed out of quasi-monopoly profits or governments will take special actions to offset existing regulations if they are too burdensome. The big cannot be allowed to fail. When Fiat needed to reduce the size of its labor force, the Italian government paid most of the costs of early retirement for its redundant workers. Watching Fiat collapse because it could not reduce its wage costs was simply too great an economic shock to contemplate. Mid-sized firms are not rescued in the same manner.

It is the dynamic mid-sized firm that is in trouble under the existing regulations and social welfare spending of the Rhine model. That mid-sized firm is too large to be exempted from the regulations and too large to take unnoticed evasive actions to avoid the restrictive regulations. At the same time it is too small for the state to care about it and too small to merit state aid to help pay for the existing regulations. Yet without small firms that become mid-sized firms, and mid-sized firms that become large firms, new technologies cannot be employed and new jobs will not be generated.

If one looks at Europe, one sees that it is very good at what it has traditionally done (in the chemical, auto, and machine tool industries) but very weak in all new high-technology sectors (microelectronics, biotechnology) despite the fact that no one is better when it comes to basic science and engineering. Something fundamental has to change, but no one wants to make those changes.[18]

Japan

With higher savings rates and an even more communitarian spirit than Europe, Japan will have less trouble than anyone else in adjusting to an era where long-term social investments are required. One can even argue that Japan invented human capitalism before the technology demanded it. Human resources have long been considered a Japanese firm's most important strategic asset.[19] Excessive individualism is to be avoided and the whole organization cannot succeed unless each individual understands his duties and obligations.[20] Individuals identify with the firm.[21] Individuals collaborate in teams, compete across groups, profits are shared as bonuses, and old-fashioned capitalists have essentially disappeared with the cross-ownership structure of the Japanese business groups.

But profits have also almost disappeared.[22] In 1994 the 149 Japanese firms that were on *Fortune*'s list of the world's 500 largest earned a 0.7 percent rate of return on revenues and a 0.2 percent rate of return on assets.[23] The Japanese system is not socialism, but a profitless capitalism isn't a capitalism that can thrive.

In many senses Japan is the winner of the post–World War II capitalistic game. It took longer to get organized to play this new game than any other country after World War II, but it eventually learned to play the game better than anyone else. In terms of international purchasing power, it had by far the highest per capita GDP of any major country in early 1995 ($38,000 per person at 100 yen to the dollar versus $25,000 for the United States). But those who play a game well and win are usually the last to be willing to notice that the game has changed and that they will have to learn to play a different game. Japan is no exception to this basic rule.

In the past Japan had a big advantage. Having been defeated in a major war, having unconditionally surrendered, and having had a decade of outside occupation, it was obvious to everyone in Japan that the old Japanese world had been blown up and something new had to replace it. In many ways the changes that will be required in the next two decades are much bigger than those that were made in the two decades after World War II, but this time Japan will have to change without the benefit of a defeat and outside pressure. It will have to change despite the fact that it is a winner. Nothing in recent Japanese behavior even hints that such changes are possible—much less likely.

Since World War II, Japan has depended upon the economic locomotive of America and more exports to save it from recessions. Japan is now so big and the locomotive in America so much weaker that even a much bigger export surplus (almost doubling from 1991 to 1994) won't succeed in ending its recessions. Nor will lower interest rates. Rates near zero (now 0.35 percent on bank savings accounts) have failed to stimulate demand.[24] Japan needs a domestically pulled, rather than export-led, economy not because the rest of the world says so but because Japan is now so big that it cannot be run successfully as an export-led economy. Yet Japan cannot change.[25] It simply sits in an ever-lengthening recession.

History tells us that Japan changes jerkily when confronted with a crisis (the Meiji restoration, the response to the defeat and occupation of World War II), but this time there will be no crisis. The pressures just build up along the fault lines. But if one waits until the earthquake occurs, Japan may be as badly prepared for the coming social and economic earthquake as it was for the physical earthquake in Kōbe. Until then it believed that its structures were more earthquake-proof than those in the rest of the world—but it wasn't true.

As we have seen, the current trading pattern on the Pacific Rim depends upon everyone being able to run large trade surpluses with the United States, which they can then use to pay for their large trade deficits with Japan. The pattern cannot continue. At some point Japan's two biggest export markets, the rest of the Pacific Rim and the United States, are both going to collapse.

Japan sometimes talks about a "flying goose" trading group on the Pacific Rim where Japan would be the lead goose.[26] If such a group were to emerge, wisdom would call for gradually solving the trade imbalances on the Pacific Rim now (importing much more from other countries in the Pacific Rim) rather than waiting for the financial crisis that will bring these trading patterns to a sudden halt. But there is no sign of this wisdom in Japan.

Global leadership in a multiethnic world requires a multiethnic state or at least a society that finds it easy to absorb talented people from different ethnic groups. Yet Japan is the ultimate homogeneous ethnic state where bringing talented non-Japanese into the system (its country, its business firms, its universities) and treating them as equals with equal chances to win is the most difficult thing in the world.[27] Even ethnic Japanese who have lived outside of Japan for any period of time, such as those from Brazil, find it almost impossible to become reintegrated into Japanese society. Children of businessmen stationed abroad have similar problems. Look at the top one hundred executives of any large Japanese business firm and ask how many are not Japanese. Becoming a global leader rather than a global follower will require an enormous change in Japanese culture.

To lead it is also necessary to tap into individuality and fundamental creativity. It is possible to catch up, and even become 20 percent better, by copying. The basic breakthroughs have been made and one simply does the details better than those who made the basic breakthroughs in the first place. But it is not possible to lead without being able to develop the fundamental breakthroughs that lead to entirely new industries. Japan copies the American semiconductor industry, learns to make basic random access memory chips better than the Americans, and gains a dominant market share. But Japan did not invent the microprocessor that became the heart of a new semiconductor industry and quickly lost its once dominant position. It conquered consumer electronics but now faces losing it to lower-cost South Koreans and more technically innovative Americans as the personal computer and the consumer electronics industries merge.

As is seen in the case of China, success requires much more than being able to invent new technologies. One has to have the social attitudes that makes individuals want to use those new technologies to build a new society even when they do not, and cannot, know the precise outlines of those new societies. Japan fell behind economically before Admiral Perry arrived since the kingdom of Japan was closed to the outside world. Today it is the mind of Japan that is closed. The latter is no less of a handicap than the former. No one can succeed with a Middle Kingdom mentality and no one today has more of a Middle Kingdom mentality than the Japanese.

Normally those who are the top-of-the-food-chain, survival-of-the-fittest species have little to worry about. Evolution occurs slowly and makes them into even better, more dominant species. But in periods of punctuated equilibrium the species that has the most to fear is the dominant species. The best adapted have the biggest changes to make when the environment suddenly changes. The Japanese are that survival-of-the-fittest species. Since they have the biggest changes to make, they have the most to worry about.

CONCLUSION

The danger is not that capitalism will implode as communism did. Without a viable competitor to which people can rush if they are disappointed with how capitalism is treating them, capitalism cannot self-destruct. Pharaonic, Roman, medieval, and mandarin economies also had no competitors and they simply stagnated for centuries before they finally disappeared.[28] Stagnation, not collapse, is the danger.

Periods of punctuated equilibrium are periods of great optimism and great pessimism. For those very good at playing the old game, the dinosaurs, they are disasters. Millions of years of supremacy disappear in a flash. Evolution along the old lines is impossible. For those who are good at adjusting to new circumstances and can learn to play new games, the mammals, periods of punctuated equilibrium are periods of enormous opportunity. It is precisely the disappearance of the dinosaurs that made it possible for humans to take control of the system. If the dinosaurs had continued to rule, our ancient ancestors probably would have been eaten and we wouldn't be here. But during the transitions in periods of punctuated equilibrium, no one knows who will be a dinosaur and who will be a mammal. That depends upon who is the best at adjusting to a new world—something that can only be known with certainty looking backward.

The intrinsic problems of capitalism visible at its birth (instability, rising inequality, a lumpen proletariat) are still there waiting to be solved, but so are a new set of problems that flow from capitalism's growing dependence upon human capital and man-made brainpower industries. In an era of man-made brainpower industries those who win will learn to play a new game with new rules requiring new strategies. Tomorrow's winners will have very different characteristics than today's winners.

Technology and ideology are shaking the foundations of twenty-first-century capitalism. Technology is making skills and knowledge the only sources of sustainable strategic advantage. Abetted by the electronic media, ideology is moving toward a radical form of short-run individual consumption maximization at precisely a time when economic success will depend upon the willingness and ability to make long-run social investments in skills, education, knowledge, and infrastructure. When technology and ideology start moving apart, the only question is when will the "big one" (the earthquake that rocks the system) occur. Paradoxically, at precisely the time when capitalism finds itself with no social competitors—its former competitors, socialism or communism, having died—it will have to undergo a profound metamorphosis.

It is easy to get discouraged and become a pessimist if one looks at what must be done and compares it with the seemingly glacial pace of social change. But to do so would be to make a mistake. Social change occurs in much the same manner as waves hitting rocky cliffs on the Maine coast. On each and every day the rocks win. The waves thunder into them and nothing seemingly happens. But we know with absolute certainty that eventually every one of those rocks will be bits of sand. Every day the waves lose, yet in the long run they win.

Given our new understanding of the tectonic forces altering the economic surface of the earth and the period of punctuated equilibrium that they have created, let's return to the problem of constructing a capitalistic ship that will safely take us into an era. Like Columbus and his men, all of us aboard the good ship "capitalism" are sailing into a new uncertain world. Being smart, Columbus knew that the world was round, but he got his mathematics wrong and thought that the diameter of the world was only three quarters as big as it really is. He also overestimated the eastward land distance to Asia and therefore by subtraction grossly underestimated the westward water distance to Asia. That combination of errors made him think that India (the word for Asia then) was about 3,900 miles from the Canary Islands, more or less where America happened to be. Given the amount of water put on board, without the Americas Columbus and all of his men would have died of thirst and been unknown in our history books.[29]

Columbus goes down in history as the world's greatest explorer, perhaps history's most famous man, because he found the completely unexpected, the Americas, and they happened to be full of gold. One moral of the story is that it is important to be smart, but that it is even more important to be lucky. But ultimately Columbus did not succeed because he was lucky. He succeeded because he made the effort to set sail in a direction never before taken despite a lot of resistance from those around him. Without that enormous effort he could not have been in the position to have a colossal piece of good luck.

With similar persistence and willingness to attempt the unknown, let our journey begin!

NOTES

CHAPTER 1: NEW GAME, NEW RULES, NEW STRATEGIES

1. *International Monetary Fund International Financial Statistics,* Washington, D.C., various yearbooks; Stuart Holland, *Toward a New Bretton Woods* (Nottingham, U.K.: Russel Press, 1994), p. 10.
2. Council of Economic Advisers, *Economic Report of the President 1995* (Washington, D.C.: U.S. Government Printing Office), p. 403.
3. Ibid., p. 314; Robert Solow, *Is All That European Unemployment Necessary?* The World Economic Laboratory, MIT Working Paper, No. 94–06.
4. "Labour Pains," *The Economist,* February 12, 1994, p. 74.
5. Richard Holt, *The Reluctant Superpower* (New York: Kodansha International, 1995), p. 246; "Stock Market Indexes," *Asian Wall Street Journal,* January 1, 1990, p. 18, and August 24, 1992, p. 22.
6. "Industrial Growth," *The Economist,* September 16, 1995, p. 122.
7. *Economic Report of the President 1995,* pp. 276, 311, 326; Council of Economic Advisers, *Economic Indicators,* August 1995, pp. 2, 15.
8. Daniel R. Feenberg and James M. Poterba, *Income Inequality and the Incomes of Very High Income Taxpayers,* NBER Working Paper No. 4229, December 1992, p. 31.
9. "Mexico," *International Herald Tribune,* May 2, 1995, p. 1.
10. Kenneth E. Boulding, *Economics as a Science* (New York: McGraw-Hill, 1970), p. 7.
11. John A. Garraty, *Unemployment in History* (New York: Harper and Row, 1978), p. 134.
12. Fred Block, *Post-Industrial Possibilities: A Critique of Economic Discourse* (Berkeley: University of California Press, 1990), p. 194.
13. Richard Holt, *The Reluctant Superpower* (New York: Kodansha International, 1995), p. 79.
14. Martin Carnoy et al., *The New Global Economy in the Information Age* (University Park: Pennsylvania State University Press, 1993), p. 8.

15. John King et al., *Pakistan* (London: Lonely Planet Publications, 1993), p. 28.

16. John M. Gowdy, "New Controversies in Evolutionary Biology: Lessons for Economics," *Methodus,* June 1991, p. 86.

17. Robert T. Bakker, *The Dinosaur Heresies* (New York: Morrow, 1986), p. 16.

18. William J Broad, "New Theory Would Reconcile Rival Views on Dinosaurs' Demise" *New York Times,* December 27, 1994, p. B7; John Noble Wilford, "New Dinosaur Theory: Sulfur Was the Villain" *New York Times,* January 3, 1995, p. B6.

19. "Railway," *Encyclopedia Britannica,* Vol. 18, 1972 edition, p. 1126, plate 1.

20. Michael J. Piore and Charles F. Sabel, *The Second Industrial Divide* (New York: Basic Books, 1984).

21. Robert L. Heilbroner, *The Making of Economic Society* (New York: Prentice-Hall, 1962), p. 39; *The Nature and Logic of Capitalism* (New York: W. W. Norton, 1985), p. 109.

22. Jerome M. Segal, "Alternative Conceptions of the Economic Realm," in *Rationality and Efficiency: New Perspectives on Socio-Economics,* ed. Richard M. Coughlin (London: M. E. Sharpe, 1993), p. 288.

23. Patrice Higonnet, David S. Landes, and Henry Rosovsky, eds., *Favorites of Fortune: Technology, Growth, and Economic Development Since the Industrial Revolution* (Cambridge, Mass.: Harvard University Press, 1991), p. 2.

24. *Encyclopedia Britannica,* Vol. 8, p. 42.

25. Jane Chisholm and Anne Millard, *Early Civilization* (Tulsa, Okla.: Osborne, 1988), p. 14.

26. Chisholm and Millard, *Early Civilization,* p. 17.

27. John Romer, *Ancient Lives: Daily Life in Egypt of the Pharaohs* (New York: Henry Holt & Co., 1984), p. 123.

28. *Encyclopedia Britannica,* Vol. 19, p. 204.

29. Gay Robins, *Women in Ancient Egypt* (Cambridge, Mass.: Harvard University Press, 1993), p. 14.

30. Andrea Giardina, ed., *The Romans* (Chicago: University of Chicago Press, 1993), p. 1.

31. James P. Speer, *Conflict and War: History, Causes, Consequences, Cures* (Fort Bragg, Calif.: QED Press, 1986), p. 9; Edith Hamilton, *The Roman Way* (New York: W. W. Norton, 1993), p. 132.

32. Florence Dupont, *Daily Life in Ancient Rome* (Oxford, U.K.: Blackwell, 1989), p. 23.

33. Jean Paul Morel, "The Craftsmen," in Giardina, ed., *The Romans,*

p. 228; Braudel, *History of Civilization,* p. 19; Frances and Joseph Gies, *Cathedral, Forge, and Waterwheel: Technology and Invention in the Middle Ages* (New York: HarperCollins, 1994), p. 17; M. I. Finley, *Economy and Society in Ancient Greece* (London: Chatto and Windus, 1981), p. 173.

34. Anthony Marks, Graham Tingay, in Giardina, ed., *The Romans,* p. 18.

35. Ibid., p. 32.

36. Edith Hamilton, *The Roman Way* (New York: W. W. Norton, 1993), p. 178.

37. John Matthews, "Roman Life and Society" in *The Oxford History of the Classical World,* ed. John Boardman, Jasper Griffin, and Oswyn Murray (New York: Oxford University Press, 1986), p. 752; J. F. Drinkwater and Andrew Drummond, *The World of the Romans* (New York: Oxford University Press, 1993), p. 63.

38. Florence Dupont, *Daily Life in Ancient Rome,* p. 7.

39. Ibid., p. 27.

40. Robert Parker, "Greek Religion" in *The Oxford History of the Classical World,* p. 261.

41. Jean Paul Morel, "The Craftsmen," in Giardina, ed., *The Romans,* p. 321; Jean Michel Carried, "The Soldier," in Giardina, ed., *The Romans,* p. 228; *Encyclopedia Britannica,* Vol. 19, p. 453.

42. *Encyclopedia Britannica,* Vol. 20, p. 632.

43. Paul Veyne, "The Roman Empire," in *A History of Private Life from Pagan Rome to Byzantium* (Cambridge, Mass.: Belknap Press, 1987), p. 118.

44. Andrea Giardina, "The Merchant," in Giardina, ed., *The Romans,* p. 245; Andrea Giardina, ed. *The Romans* (Chicago: University of Chicago Press, 1993), pp. 30, 245.

45. Paul Veyne, *Bread and Circuses* (London: Penguin, 1990), p. 251.

46. Dupont, *Daily Life in Ancient Rome,* p. 31.

47. Veyne, *Bread and Circuses,* p. xvii.

48. Ibid., p. 16.

49. Ibid., pp. 136, 148.

50. *Encyclopedia Britannica,* Vol. 19, p. 454.

51. Leonardo B. Dal Maso, *Rome of the Caesars* (Florence: Bonechi Edizioni, 1990), p. 1.

52. Giardina, ed., *The Romans,* p. 33.

53. Paul Veyne "The Roman Empire," p. 163.

54. Yvon Thebert, "Private Life and Domestic Architecture in Roman Africa," in *A History of Private Life from Pagan Rome to Byzantium,* p. 351.

55. Veyne, *Bread and Circuses,* p. 251.

56. Alain Peyrefitte, *The Immobile Empire* (New York: Knopf, 1992), p. 420; Braudel, *History of Civilization,* p. 168.

57. Robert J. Thomas, *What Machines Can't Do: Politics and Technology in the Industrial Enterprise* (Berkeley: University of California Press, 1994), pp. xiv, 6, 10.

CHAPTER 2: MAPPING THE ECONOMIC SURFACE OF THE EARTH

1. U.S. Bureau of the Census, *Money Income of Households, Families and Persons in the United States 1992, Current Population Reports, Consumer Income,* Series P-60–184 (Washington, D.C.: U.S. Government Printing Office, 1993), p. 176.

2. Claudia Goldin and Robert A. Margo, "The Great Compression: The Wage Structure of the United States at Mid-Century," *The Quarterly Journal of Economics,* February 1994, p. 4.

3. U.S. Bureau of the Census, *Current Population Reports, Consumer Income, 1992,* Series P-60 (Washington, D.C.: U.S. Government Printing Office, 1993), pp. xvi, xvii, 14; Sheldon Danziger and Peter Gottschalk, eds., *Uneven Tides* (New York: Russell Sage Foundation, 1993), p. 7.

4. Daniel R. Feenberg and James M. Poterba, *Income Inequality and the Incomes of Very High Income Taxpayers,* NBER Working Paper No. 4229, December 1992, p. 31.

5. Ibid., p. 5.

6. Margaret M. Blair, "CEO Pay: Why Such a Contentious Issue?" *The Brookings Review,* Winter 1994, p. 23; Nancy I. Rose, "Executive Compensation" *NBER Reporter,* Winter 1994–95, p. 11.

7. "Nice Work," *The Economist,* December 10, 1994, p. 67.

8. Robert H. Frank, "Talent and the Winner-Take-All Society," *The American Prospect,* Spring 1994, p. 99.

9. Peter Kilborn, "More Women Take Low Wage Jobs Just So Their Families Can Get By," *New York Times,* March 13, 1994, pp. 16, 24.

10. U.S. Bureau of the Census, *Current Population Reports, Consumer Income, 1992,* p. B-6.

11. Ibid., p. 21.

12. Lynn A. Karoly, "Changes in the Distribution of Individual Earnings in the United States, 1967–1986," *Review of Economics and Statistics,* February 1992, pp. 107, A 78; Danziger and Peter, eds., *Uneven*

Tides, pp. 69, 85, 102, 129; Steven J. Davis, *Cross-Country Patterns of Changes in Relative Wages,* Brookings Papers on Economic Activity, p. 273; Karoly, "Changes in the Distribution of Individual Earnings," pp. 107, 113; Frank Levy and Richard J. Murnane, "U.S. Earnings Levels and Earnings Inequality," *Journal of Economic Literature,* September 1992, p. 1333.

13. "Wealth: The Divided States of America," *New York Times,* April 23, 1995, p. F2; Steven Sass, "Passing the Buck," *Regional Review,* Boston Federal Reserve Bank, Summer 1995, p. 16.

14. Barry Bluestone, *Economic Inequality and the Macro-Structuralist Debate,* Eastern Economics Association Meetings, February 1994, p. 8; Lynn A. Karoly, "The Trend in Inequality Among Families, Individuals, and Workers in the United States," Rand Corporation, 1992, pp. 44, 66, A16, 221; Lawrence Mishel and Jared Bernstein, *The State of Working America 1992–1993* (Washington, D.C.: Economic Policy Institute/M. E. Sharpe, 1993), p. 14.; "Male Educated in a Pay Bind," *New York Times,* February 11, 1994, p. D1; Richard D. Reeves, "Cheer Up, Downsizing Is Good for Some," *International Herald Tribune,* December 29, 1994, p. 4.

15. U.S. Bureau of the Census, *Income, Poverty, and Valuation of Noncash Benefits: 1993. Current Population Reports, Consumer Income,* Series P-60-188 (Washington, D.C.: U.S. Government Printing Office, 1995), p. x; Council of Economic Advisers, *Economic Report of the President 1995* (Washington D.C.: U.S. Government Printing Office, 1995), pp. 276, 311.

16. *Economic Report of the President 1995,* p. 310.

17. Kevin Phillips, *Boiling Point: The Decline of Middle Class Prosperity* (New York: Random House, 1993), p. xvii.

18. Keith Bradsher, "American Real Wages Fell 2.3 Percent in 12-Month Period," *New York Times,* June 23, 1995, p. D4.

19. Mishel and Bernstein, *The State of Working America 1992–1993,* p. 36.

20. Jason DeParle, "Sharp Increase Along the Borders of Poverty," *New York Times,* March 31, 1994, p. A18.

21. Center for National Policy, *Job Quality Index,* November 15, 1993.

22. David E. Bloom and Richard B. Freeman, "The Fall of Private Pension Coverage in the United States," *American Economic Review,* May 1992, p. 539; Virgina L. DuRivage, ed., *New Policies for the Part-time and Contingent Work Force* (New York: Economic Policy Institute/M. E. Sharpe, 1992), p. 22.

23. The Urban Institute, *Inequality of Earnings and Benefits,* Winter/Spring, 1994, p. 21.

24. "The Widening Pension Gap," *Fortune,* March 16, 1995, p. 48; Bloom and Freeman, "The Fall of Private Pension Coverage in the United States," p. 540.

25. Karoly, "The Trend in Inequality," pp. 44, 66, A16, 221.

26. Steven Greenhouse, "Clinton Seeks to Narrow a Growing Wage Gap," *New York Times,* December 13, 1993, p. D1.

27. U.S. Bureau of the Census, *Current Population Reports, Consumer Income, 1993,* p. x.

28. Council of Economic Advisers, *Economic Report of the President 1995* (Washington, D.C.: U.S. Government Printing Office), pp. 276, 311, 326.

29. Ibid., pp. 276, 326.

30. Kilborn, "More Women Take Low Wage Jobs," p. 24; Wallace C. Peterson, *Silent Depression* (New York: W. W. Norton, 1994).

31. Keith Bradsher, "Sluggish Income Figures Show Gains for Some," *New York Times,* October 6, 1995, p. A22.

32. U.S. Bureau of Census, *Current Population Reports, Consumer Income, 1993,* p. x.

33. Mishel and Bernstein, *The State of Working America 1992–1993,* p. 72.

34. Tamar Lewin, "Mom Is Providing More Income," *International Herald Tribune,* May 12, 1995, p. 14.

35. Danziger and Gottschalk, eds., *Uneven Tides,* p. 195.

36. "Getting Their Dues," *The Economist,* March 25, 1995, p. 86.

37. Stephen S. Roach, "Announced Staff Cuts of U.S. Corporations," in Morgan Stanley Special Economic Study, *The Perils of America's Productivity-Led Recovery,* 1994.

38. George Church, "The White Collar Layoffs That We're Seeing Are Permanent and Structural," *Time,* November 22, 1993, p. 35.

39. U.S. Department of Labor, *Employment and Earnings,* January 1981 and January 1982, pp. 36, 20.

40. Ibid., pp. 28, 29.

41. Richard E. Caves and Matthew B. Krepps, *Fat: The Displacement of Nonproduction Workers from U.S. Manufacturing Industries,* The Brookings Papers on Economic Activity, No. 2, 1993, p. 231.

42. John A. Byrne, "The Pain of Downsizing," *Business Week,* May 9, 1994, p. 61; Matt Murry, "Amid Record Profits Companies Continue to Lay Off Employees," *Wall Street Journal, Europe,* May 8, 1995, p. 1.

43. Farrell Kramer, "AT&T and Sprint Plan Big Job Cuts," *Boston Globe*, November 16, 1995, p. 46.

44. Dean Baker and Lawrence Mishel, *Profits Up, Wages Down*, Economic Policy Institute Briefing Paper. Washington, D.C.: 1995, p. 1.

45. Caves and Krepps, "Fat," p. 227.

46. Martin Neil Baily, Eric J. Bartelsman, and John Haltiwanger, *Downsizing and Productivity Growth: Myth or Reality*. National Bureau of Economic Research Working Paper No. 4741, May 1994.

47. Martin Orth and Rudiger Edelmann, "Flexible Working Times: Only a Trendy Concept?" *Deutscheland No. 1*, February 1994.

48. "Deutsche Bank Plan to Cut 10,000 Jobs," *New York Times*, September 18, 1995, p. C2.

49. German Information Center, *Unemployment in Germany*, March 1994.

50. Marlise Simons, "In French Factory Town, Culprit Is Automation," *New York Times*, May 12, 1994, p. A3.

51. Mishel and Bernstein, *The State of Working America*, p. 174; Robert E. Scott and Thea M. Lee, *Reconsidering the Benefits and Costs of Trade Protection*, Economic Policy Institute Working Paper No. 105, April 1991, p. 41.

52. William J. Carrington, "Wage Losses for Displaced Workers: Is It Really the Firm That Matters?" *Journal of Human Resources*, Summer 1993, p. 454.

53. Church, "White Collar Layoffs," p. 35.

54. Bruce Butterfield, "Working but Worried," *Boston Globe*, October 10, 1993, p. 1.

55. "Companies Rewrite the Rules on Jobs," *Financial Times*, January 7, 1995, p. 12.

56. Bennett Harrison, *Lean and Mean* (New York: Basic Books, 1994), p. 201; Polly Callaghan and Heidi Hartmann, *Contingent Work* (Washington, D.C.: Economic Policy Institute, 1994).

57. DuRivage, ed., *New Policies*, p. 56.

58. DuRivage, ed., *New Policies*, pp. 3, 21, 22.

59. Jason DeParle, "Report to Clinton Sees Vast Extent of Homelessness," *New York Times*, February 17, 1994, p. 1; Christopher Jencks, "The Homeless," *New York Review of Books*, April 21, 1994, p. 20.

60. "Europe and the Underclass," *The Economist*, July 30, 1994, p. 19.

61. "Homeless in France," *International Herald Tribune*, December 20, 1994, p. 1.

62. Sylvia Nasar, "More Men in Prime of Life Spend Less Time Working," *New York Times*, December 1, 1994, p. 1.

63. Alan Cowell, "Where Juliet Pined Youths Now Kill," *New York Times,* March 22, 1994, p. A4.

64. Nasar, "More Men in Prime of Life," p. 1.

65. Jencks, "The Homeless," p. 23; Robert N. Bellah et al., *The Good Society* (New York: Knopf, 1991), p. 4.

66. A. M. Rosenthal, "Just Walking Past the Broken People," *New York Times,* January 18, 1995, p. 4.

67. Quoted in Peter S. Canellos, "The Outer Class," *Boston Globe,* February 6, 1994.

68. Tamar Lewin, "Families in Upheaval Worldwide," *International Herald Tribune,* May 31, 1995, p. 1.

69. Tamar Lewin, "Family Decay Global, Study Says," *New York Times,* May 30, 1995, p. A5.

70. Urban Institute, *Welfare Reform Brief No. 13,* p. 3 as corrected.

71. "The Family: Home Sweet Home," *The Economist,* September 9, 1995, p. 26.

72. Seth Faison, "In China, Rapid Social Changes Bring a Surge in Divorce Rate," *New York Times,* August 22, 1995, p. 1.

73. Steven A. Holmes, "Low-Wage Fathers and the Welfare Debate," *New York Times,* April 25, 1995, p. A12.

74. Duncan Lindsey, *The Welfare of Children* (New York: Oxford University Press, 1994), p. 69.

75. Robert N. Bellah et al., *The Good Society* (New York: Knopf, 1991), p. 46.

76. Bob Tyrrell and Charlotte Cornish, "Beggar Your Neighbor," *Financial Times,* November 17, 1993, p. 14.

77. David Popenoe, "The Family Condition of America," in *Values and Public Policy,* ed. Henry J. Aaron, Thomas E. Mann, Timothy Taylor (Washington, D.C.: Brookings Institution, 1994), p. 104.

78. Ibid.

79. Ibid., p. 46.

80. Ibid., p. 73.

81. "The Family: Home Sweet Home," p. 26.

82. Faison, "In China, Rapid Social Changes," p. 1.

83. James Q. Wilson, "Culture, Incentives, and the Underclass" in *Values and Public Policy,* p. 46.

84. Fred Block, *Post-Industrial Possibilities: A Critique of Economic Discourse* (Berkeley: University of California Press, 1990), p. 27.

85. "Upon the States' Shoulders Be It," *The Economist,* March 25, 1995, p. 67.

86. "The Future Surveyed," *The Economist*, September 11, 1993, special section.

87. James Q. Wilson, "The 1994 Wriston Lecture," The Manhattan Institute, November 1994.

88. Gunnar Myrdal, *Against the Stream* (New York: Pantheon Books, 1972), p. 175.

89. Peter Drier and John Atlas, "Housing Policies Moment of Truth," *Challenge*, Summer 1995, pp. 8, 70.

90. Jack Beatty, "Who Speaks for the Middle Class?" *The Atlantic*, May 1994, p. 73; Wallace C. Peterson, *Silent Depression* (New York: W. W. Norton, 1994), p. 53.

91. Bellah et al., *The Good Society*, pp. 141, 175.

92. Phillips, *Boiling Point*, p. 175.

93. Ibid.

94. David Fletcher, "Worst-Off Fall Further Behind," *Daily Telegraph*, June 3, 1995, p. 5.

95. Steven Davis, *Cross-Country Patterns of Change in Relative Wages*, NBER Working Paper, 1994.

96. "Inequality," *The Economist*, November 4, 1994, p. 19; "Rich Man, Poor Man," *The Economist*, July 24, 1994, p. 71.

97. "Real Earnings Down for West German Workers, up in East," *The Week in Germany*, March 11, 1994, p. 4.

98. Ibid.

99. *International Herald Tribune*, "French Staff Takes IBM Wage Cut," December 27, 1994, p. 10.

100. Susan N. Houseman and Katharine G. Abraham, *Labor Adjustment Under Different Institutional Structures: A Case Study of Germany and the United States*, Upjohn Institute Staff Working Papers, April 1994, p. 6; R. Dore, *Incurable Unemployment: A Progressive Disease of Modern Societies?* Center for Economic Performance Paper No. 6, August 1994.

101. "Marketing Labour," *The Economist*, April 1, 1995, p. 44.

102. David Marsh, "German Exporters Feeling the Squeeze," *Financial Times*, March 24, 1995, p. 2.

103. Robert Solow, *Is All That European Unemployment Necessary? The World Economic Laboratory*, MIT Working Paper No. 94-06, 1993.

104. "Labour Pains," *The Economist*, February 12, 1994, p. 74.

105. Heino Fassbender and Susan Cooper Hedegaard, "The Ticking Bomb at the Core of Europe," *McKinsey Quarterly*, No. 3, 1993, p. 132.

106. Ibid.
107. "Doleful," *The Economist*, October 9, 1994, p. 17.
108. Richard Donkin, "World Outlook for Jobs Gloomy," *Financial Times*, April 27, 1994, p. 4.
109. Ibid.
110. Frank Riboud, "Army of Invalids," *Worldlink*, May/June 1994, p. 5.
111. Ibid.
112. Council of Economic Advisers, *Economic Report of the President 1995*, p. 314.
113. Oliver J. Blanchard, "European Unemployment," *NBER Reporter*, Winter 1993–94, p. 7.
114. James M. Poterba and Lawrence H. Summers, *Unemployment Benefits, Labor Market Transitions, and Spurious Flows*, NBER Working Paper No. 4434, August 1993.
115. "The 12% Shame," *The Economist*, April 1, 1995, p. 42.
116. Richard Freeman, "The Trouble with Success," *The Economist*, March 12, 1994, p. 51.
117. "How Regulations Kill New Jobs," *The Economist*, November 19, 1994, p. 82.
118. "European Bosses Ask for Cuts in Employee Benefits," *Straits Times*, August 20, 1994, p. 13.
119. Robert J. Gordon, *Back to the Future: European Unemployment Today Viewed from America in 1939*, Brookings Papers on Economic Activity, No. 1, 1988, p. 271.
120. Audren Choi, "Daimler Benz Looks to Flee German Woes," *Asian Wall Street Journal*, March 13, 1995, pp. 1, 2.
121. "Dark Days," *The Economist*, October 9, 1993, p. 59.
122. "Nothing Could Be Finer," *The Economist*, November 19, 1994, p. 77.
123. "Herr Lazarus," *The Economist*, March 18, 1995, p. 68.
124. "Labour Costs," *The Economist*, May 27, 1995, p. 110.
125. Ariane Benillard, "Cost Savings of Relocation Lure German Companies," *Financial Times*, November 9, 1993, p. 1.
126. "New Law Allows Private Employment Agencies," *This Week in Germany*, April 22, 1994, p. 4.
127. "Low Pay Forces Desperate 1 Million to Take Second Jobs," *Guardian*, October 24, 1994, p. 4.
128. Takeuchi Hiroshi, "Reforming Management," *Journal of Japanese Trade and Industry*, No. 2, 1994, p. 12; "Japan: One in Ten?" *The Economist*, July 1, 1995, p. 52.

129. "Inequality," *The Economist*, November 4, 1994, p. 19.
130. "Shoot Out at the Check Out," *The Economist*, June 5, 1993, p. 81.
131. Ed Bark, "CBS Is Joining the TV Youth Movement," *Dallas Morning News*, p. C1.

CHAPTER 3: PLATE ONE: THE END OF COMMUNISM

1. "Oil," *The Economist*, July 15, 1995, p. 88.
2. Clyde Prestowitz, "Good but Not Good Enough," *World Link*, March/April 1994, p. 31.
3. Kenneth Gooding, "Metals Analysts Expect Fall in Russian Nickel Exports," *Financial Times*, May 2, 1995, p. 23.
4. Adi Ignatius, "Former U.S. Executives Advise Russians How to Convert Military Factories," *Wall Street Journal*, June 26, 1992, p. D7.
5. Jenny Luesby, Mikki L. Tait, and Chrystia Freeland, "Australia 'Furious' at Soaring CIS Wool Exports," *Financial Times*, August 24, 1995, p. 5.
6. Craig R. Whitney, "West European Companies Head East for Cheap Labor," *New York Times*, February 9, 1995, p. D1.
7. "Making Shoes in Brazil," *The Economist*, June 24, 1995, p. 61.
8. Richard Eckaus, *The Metamorphosis of Giants: China and India in Transition*, MIT Working Paper, March 1994.
9. "Statistics Cheats Disrupt China's Economic Plans," *South China Morning Business Post*, August 18, 1994, p. 1.
10. "China: Not So Miraculous?" *The Economist*, May 27, 1995, p. 63.
11. "Survey: China," *The Economist*, March 18, 1995, p. 9.
12. Paul R. Gregory and Robert C. Stuart, *Soviet Economic Structure and Performance* (New York: Harper and Row, 1990), p. 356.
13. "Survey: Russia's Emerging Market," *The Economist*, April 8, 1995, p. 4.
14. "Rural Discontent Sparks Alarm," *South China Morning Post*, February 13, 1995, p. 1; "Survey: China," *The Economist*, March 18, 1995, p. 23.
15. United Nations, *Statistical Yearbook for Asia and the Pacific* (New York, 1993), pp. 86, 150.
16. "Fund Reviews China's Economy, It's Big," *New York Times*, May 10, 1993, p. 1.
17. John Gittings, "Chinese Whispers in a Vacuum," *Guardian*, February 3, 1995, p. 26.
18. John D. Friske, *Chinese Facts and Figures Annual Handbook*, Vol. 18, (Beijing: Academic International Press, 1994), p. 114.

19. Alice H. Amsden, Jacek Kochanowicz, and Lance Taylor, *The Market Meets Its Match: Restructuring the Economies of Eastern Europe* (Cambridge, Mass.: Harvard University Press, 1994).

20. Michael W. Bell, Hoe E. E. Khor, and Kalpana Kochhar, *China at the Threshold of a Market Economy*, International Monetary Fund Report No. 107, September 1993, p. 16.

21. Ibid., p. 58.

22. Michael Specter, "Russia's Fall Grain Harvest Seen as the Worst in 30 Years," *New York Times*, October 10, 1995, p. A10.

23. Wanda Tseng et al., *Economic Reform in China*, International Monetary Fund Report No. 114, November 1994.

24. *Dun's Asia/Pacific Key Business Enterprises, 1993/94*, (Sydney, Australia: Dun and Bradstreet Information Series, 1994), p. 223.

25. Jeffrey D. Sachs, *Reforms in Eastern Europe and the Former Soviet Union in Light of East Asian Experience* (Cambridge, Mass.: Harvard Institute for Economic Development, 1995), p. 44.

26. Payroll data from Ford Motor Company archives.

27. "USSR," *The Economist*, July 13, 1991, p. 110.

28. John Maynard Keynes, *The General Theory* (London: Macmillan & Co., 1936), p. 383.

29. "A Survey of Vietnam," *The Economist*, July 8, 1995, p. 4.

30. Keith Bradsher, "Skilled Workers Watch Their Jobs Migrate Overseas," *New York Times*, August 28, 1995, p. 1.

31. Andrew Stark, "Adieu, Liberal Nationalism," *New York Times*, November 2, 1995, p. A27.

CHAPTER 4: PLATE TWO: AN ERA OF MAN-MADE BRAINPOWER INDUSTRIES

1. Paul A. Samuelson and William D. Nordhaus, *Economics* (New York: McGraw-Hill, 1989), pp. 901–910.

2. This list was sent to me by a reader of my *Head to Head* (New York: Morrow, 1992) and supposedly appeared in the *Wall Street Journal* at the turn of the century, but I have been unable to locate the exact citation.

3. B. R. Mitchell, *British Historical Statistics* (New York: Cambridge University Press, 1933), pp. 104, 253.

4. Alfred D. Chandler, Jr., *Scale and Scope: The Dynamics of Industrial Capitalism* (Cambridge, Mass.: Harvard University Press, 1990), pp. 638–43.

5. Lester C. Thurow, *Head to Head* (New York: Morrow, 1992). p. 204.

6. Ibid., p. 45.

7. Eduardo Borenstein et al., *The Behavior of Non-Oil Commodity Prices,* International Monetary Fund, August 1994, p. 1; International Monetary Fund, *Primary Commodities: Market Development and Outlook,* July 1990, p. 26.

8. Professor Boskin denies that he ever made any such remark but it will go down in history as his most famous remark regardless of whether he did or did not actually make it.

9. U.S. Department of Labor, *Employment and Earnings,* March 1993, pp. 93, 99.

10. Lawrence F. Katz and Lawrence H. Summers, *Rents: Evidence and Implications,* Brookings Economic Papers, Microeconomics 1989, pp. 209, 220.

11. Fortune, *The Fortune 500,* April 19, 1993, p. 254.

12. "Put Away Childish Things," *The Economist,* July 8, 1995, p. 14; "Survey: The European Union," *The Economist,* October 22, 1994, p. 1.

13. Brent Schlender, "Why Andy Grove Can't Stop," *Fortune,* July 10, 1995, pp. 90, 94.

14. Lawrence M. Fisher, "Microsoft Net Is Stronger Than Expected," *New York Times,* July 18, 1995, p. D4; Michael A. Cusumano and Richard W. Selby, *Microsoft Secrets* (New York: Free Press, 1995).

15. "Oh What a Difference a Day Makes," *Fortune,* September 4, 1995, p. 21.

16. Office of Technological Assessment of U.S. Congress, *Multinationals and the National Interest,* 103d Congress, Washington, D.C., p. 2.

17. John Holusha, "First to College, Then the Mill," *New York Times,* August 22, 1995, p. D1.

18. William L. O'Neill, *American High: The Years of Confidence, 1945–1960* (New York: Free Press, 1986), pp. 9–10.

19. Peter Applebome, "Study Ties Educational Gains to More Productivity Growth," *New York Times,* May 14, 1995, p. Y13.

20. JoAnne Yates, *Control Through Communications* (Baltimore: Johns Hopkins University Press, 1989).

21. John Koomey, *Report for the Department of Energy on Usage of Computers* (draft).

22. Daniel Yankelovich, "How Changes in the Economy Are Reshaping American Values," *Values and Public Policy,* ed. Henry J. Aaron, Thomas E. Mann, and Timothy Taylor, (Washington, D.C.: Brookings Institution, 1994), p. 46.

23. National Issues Forum, *Kids Who Commit Crimes* (New York: Mc-Graw-Hill, 1994), p. 24.

24. Ibid., p. 26.

25. Suzanne Hamlin, "Time Flies, but Where Does It Go?" *New York Times,* September 6, 1995, p. C1.

26. Elizabeth Kolbert, " Television Gets Closer Look as a Factor in Real Violence," *New York Times,* December 14, 1994, p. 1, D20.

27. Ruben Cataneda, "Homicides in D.C. Fall," *Washington Post,* March 30, 1995, p. B1.

28. Fox Butterfield, "Many Cities in U.S. Show Sharp Drop in Homicide Rate," *New York Times,* August 13, 1995, p. 1.

29. Martin F. Nolan, "California Sees Prisons Filling As Colleges Decline," *Boston Globe,* August 28, 1995, p. 3.

30. "Republic of the Image," *New Perspectives Quarterly,* Summer 1994, p. 25.

31. Richard Bernstein, " 'Jefferson' Turning Rumor into Movie Fact," *International Herald Tribune,* April 13, 1995, p. 20.

32. Bernard Weinraub, "Dole Sharpens Assault on Hollywood," *International Herald Tribune,* June 2, 1995, p. 3.

33. Robert H. Bellah et al., *Habits of the Heart* (New York: Harper and Row, 1985), p. 279.

34. Shlomo Maital, *Minds, Markets, and Money,* (New York: Basic Books, 1982), p. 39.

35. Eric Hobsbawm, *Age of Extremes: The Short Twentieth Century, 1914–1991* (London: Michael Joseph, 1994), p. 3.

36. Robert L. Heilbroner, *The Nature and Logic of Capitalism* (New York: W. W. Norton, 1985), p. 109.

37. "The Future of Democracy," and "Democracy and Technology," *The Economist,* June 17, 1995, pp. 13, 21.

CHAPTER 5: PLATE THREE: DEMOGRAPHY—GROWING, MOVING, GETTING OLDER

1. Paul Kennedy, *Preparing for the Twenty-first Century* (New York: Random House, 1992), p. 23.

2. "India's Long Multiplication," *The Economist,* February 18, 1995, p. 73.

3. "Two Billion More Third World People Predicted by 2030," *Boston Globe,* August 4, 1994, p. 4.

4. Paul Taylor, "AIDS Epidemic Casts Pall over Zimbabwe," *International Herald Tribune,* March 13, 1995, p. 2.

5. Lester R. Brown, Hal Kane, and Ed Ayres, *Vital Signs 1993* (New York: W. W. Norton/World Watch Institute, 1993), p. 106.

6. Barbara Crossette, "Severe Water Crisis Ahead for Poorest Nations in Next 2 Decades," *New York Times*, August 10, 1995, p. A13.

7. Leslie Spencer, "Water: The West's Most Misallocated Resource," *Forbes*, April 27, 1992, pp. 68–74.

8. "India's Long Multiplication," *The Economist*, February 18, 1995, p. 73.

9. "Growing Population," *The Economist*, May 20, 1995, p. 116.

10. Charles A. S. Hall et al., "The Environmental Consequences of Having a Baby in the United States," *Population and Environment*, July 1994, p. 509.

11. Virginia D. Abernethy, *Population Politics: The Choices That Shape Our Future* (New York: Insight Books/Plenum Press, 1993), p. 37.

12. George J. Borjas, "The Economics of Immigration," *Journal of Economic Literature*, December 1994, pp. 1668, 1670.

13. *The New Republic*, January 20, 1995, p. 24.

14. Steven A. Holmes, "A Surge in Immigration Surprises Experts and Intensifies a Debate," *New York Times*, August 30, 1995, p. 1.

15. Paul J. Smith, "East Asia's Immigration Crisis Demands Careful Choices," *International Herald Tribune*, May 22, 1995. p. 8.

16. Hal Kane, "What's Driving Migration?" *World Watch*, January/February 1995, pp. 25, 26.

17. U.S. Bureau of the Census, *Statistical History of the U.S.* (Washington, D.C.: U.S. Government Printing Office, 1970) p. 105.

18. Vernon M. Briggs, Jr. "Immigration and the U.S. Labor Market: Public Policy Gone Awry," Public Policy Brief, Jerome Levy Economics Institute of Bard College, 1994, p. 9.

19. Ben J. Wattenberg and Karl Zinsmeister, "The Case for More Immigration," *Commentary*, April 1990, p. 19.

20. "Immigration: Tuscon or Bust," *The Economist*, May 20, 1995, p. 59.

21. Scott Derk, ed., *The Value of a Dollar* (Detroit: Gale Research, 1994), pp. 52, 53.

22. Suzuki Hiromasa, "Problems with Foreign Workers," *Journal of Japanese Trade and Industry*, November 2, 1994, p. 44.

23. Youssef M. Ibrahim, "Muslim Immigrants in Europe: A Population Apart," *International Herald Tribune*, May 6, 1995, p. 1.

24. National Issues Forum, *Admissions Decisions* (New York: McGraw-Hill, 1995), p. 27; Borjas, "The Economics of Immigration," pp. 1670, 1701.

25. Holmes, "A Surge in Immigration," p. A15.

26. Harriet Orcutt Duleep, *Social Security and the Emigration of Immigrants*, ORS Working Paper No. 60, p. 10.

27. George J. Borjas, *Immigration and Welfare 1970–1990*, NBER Working Paper No. 4872, September 1994.

28. Frederick Rose, "The Growing Backlash Against Immigration Includes Many Myths," *Wall Street Journal*, April 16, 1995, p. 1.

29. Holmes, "A Surge in Immigration," p. A15.

30. Borjas, *Immigration and Welfare 1970–1990*.

31. Ibid., p. 22.

32. John Ridding, "Disaffected Find a Home in the Front," *Financial Times*, May 2, 1995, p. 2; William Drozdiak, "French Gear Up for 2nd Vote on Presidency," *Washington Post*, April 25, 1995, p. A12.

33. Arsen J. Darney, ed., *Statistical Record of Older Americans* (Detroit: Gale Research, 1994), pp. 47, 48, 49, 64.

34. "Ageing Population Puts the Strain on Pensions," *European*, October 28, 1994, p. 20.

35. Aline Sullivan, "Retiring Baby Boomers Dread the End of the Boom Times," *International Herald Tribune*, March 11, 1995, p. 16.

36. U.S. Bureau of the Census, *Statistical Abstract 1994* (Washington, D.C.: U.S. Government Printing Office), p. 16; Keizi Koho Center, *Japan 1995: An International Comparison*, p. 9.

37. Advisory Council on Social Security, *Future Financial Resources of the Elderly: A View of Pensions, Savings, Social Security, and Earnings in the 21st Century*, December 1991, pp. 12, 13.

38. Ibid., p. 39.

39. Elizabeth Kolbert, "Who Will Face the Music?" *New York Times Magazine*, August 27, 1995, p. 57.

40. *Financial Times*, Editorial, December 19, 1994, p. 13.

41. "A Powerful Political Lobby," *Financial Times*, March 28, 1995, p. viii.

42. Ibid.

43. Barry Bosworth, *Prospects for Savings and Investment in Industrial Countries*, Brookings Discussion Paper No. 113, May 1995, pp. 12, 14.

44. Office of Management and Budget, *Budget of the United States Government, Fiscal Year 1996*, Historical Tables (Washington, D.C.: U.S. Government Printing Office, 1995), p. 122.

45. Erik Ipsen, "Europe's Ailing Pensions," *International Herald Tribune*, December 4, 1993, p. 1.

46. U.S. Bureau of the Census, *Income, Poverty and Valuation of Noncash Benefits: 1993, Current Population Reports, Consumer Income*, Series P60-188 (Washington, D.C.: U.S. Government Printing Office), pp. 41, 45.

47. Jean Michel Paul, "Belgium's Debt Crisis Is Europe's Too," *Wall Street Journal Europe,* May 22, 1995, p. C9.
48. Bosworth, "Prospects for Savings and Investment," p. 13.
49. Ibid.
50. Daniel B. Radner, *The Wealth of the Aged and the Nonaged 1984,* Social Security Administration, ORS Working Paper No. 36, 1988.
51. Edward N. Wolff, "Changing Inequality of Wealth," *American Economics Review,* May 1992, p. 554.
52. Ann Reilly Dowd, "Needed: A New War on the Deficit," *Fortune,* November 14, 1994, p. 191.
53. "The Budget Pain Will Come and the Young Will Suffer," *International Herald Tribune,* February 18, 1995, p. 6.
54. "Health Spending," *The Economist,* June 24, 1995, p. 98.
55. Richard W. Stevenson, "A Deficit Reigns in Sweden's Welfare State," *New York Times,* February 2, 1995, p. 1.
56. "Stripping Down the Cycle," *The Economist,* July 3, 1993, p. 61.
57. "House of Debt," *The Economist,* April 1, 1995, p. 14.
58. "Public Sector Finances," *The Economist,* July 8, 1995, p. 115.
59. Paul, "Belgium's Debt Crisis," p. 8.
60. Newt Gingrich, *Contract with America* (New York: Times Books, 1994), p. 115.
61. "French Finance Minister Resigns," *Boston Globe,* August 26, 1995, p. 2.
62. Robert Pear, "Panel on a U.S. Benefits Overhaul Fails to Agree on Proposals," *New York Times,* December 15, 1994, p. A24.
63. "Taking Care of Granny," *The Economist,* June 3, 1995, p. 25.
64. *Health and Wealth,* special issue of *Daedalus,* Journal of the American Academy of Arts and Sciences, Fall 1994.
65. John Pender, "Not Such a Safe Haven," *Financial Times,* December 23, 1994, p. 15.
66. Sylvia Nasar, "Older Americans Cited in Studies of National Savings Rate Slump," *New York Times,* February 21, 1995, p. 1.
67. Wallace C. Peterson, *Silent Depression* (New York: W. W. Norton, 1994), p. 149; David Popenoe, "The Family Condition of America," in *Values and Public Policy,* ed. Henry J. Aaron, Thomas E. Mann and Timothy Taylor (Washington, D.C.: Brookings Institution, 1994), p. 104.
68. Quoted in Alan Riding, "Passions Ignited, French Students Protest Wage Policy Again," *New York Times,* March 26, 1994, p. 3.
69. Dennis Kelly, "Seniors Much Less Likely to Back Local Education Bonds," *USA Today,* June 30, 1993, p. 1.

70. William Celis, "Schools Reopen in Town That Made Them Close," *New York Times*, September 2, 1993, p. A14; Isabel Wilkerson, "Tiring of Cuts, District Plans to Close Schools," *New York Times*, March 21, 1993, p. 20.

71. Mancur Olson, *The Rise and Decline of Nations* (New Haven: Yale University Press, 1982), p. 8; Stephan P. Magee, William A. Brock, and Leslie Young, *Black Hole Tariffs and Endogenous Policy Theory* (New York: Cambridge University Press, 1989), p. xv.

72. U.S. Bureau of the Census, *Money Income of Households, Families, and Persons in the United States, 1992, Current Population Reports*, Series P60-184, pp. 148, 150.

73. John Eatwell, Murray Milgate, and Peter Newman, eds., *The New Palgrave: Social Economics* (New York: W. W. Norton, 1987), p. 10; "Statistisches Budesamt," *Statistisches Jahrbuch 1994*, Federal Republic of Germany, p. 82.

74. Michael V. Leonesio, *The Economics of Retirement: A Nontechnical Guide*, ORS Working Paper No. 66, Social Security Administration, April 1995, pp. 65, 66.

75. Leslie Wayne, "Pension Changes Raising Concerns," *New York Times*, August 29, 1994, p. 1.

76. "Skimpy Savings," *Fortune*, February 20, 1995, p. 38.

77. Ibid.

78. "Why Baby-Boomers Won't Be Able to Retire," *Fortune*, September 4, 1995, p. 48.

79. Ibid.

80. Ibid.

81. "The Economics of Aging," *Business Week*, September 12, 1994, p. 60.

82. Louis Uchitelle, "Retirement? Most Americans Have Grown to Fear It," *International Herald Tribune*, March 27, 1995, p. 3.

83. Scott Lehigh, "Social Security," *Boston Globe*, August 20, 1995, pp. 81, 82.

84. Dean R. Leimer, *A Guide to Social Security Money's Worth Issues*, ORS Working Paper No. 67, Social Security Administration, April 1995, p. 28.

85. Assar Lindbeck, *Uncertainty Under the Welfare State*, Seminar Paper No. 576, Institute for International Economic Studies at University of Stockholm, July 1994, p. 6.

86. Leimer, *A Guide to Social Security Money's Worth Issues*, p. 26.

87. Dowd, "Needed: A New War on the Deficit," p. 191; Internal Revenue

Service, "Form 1040A, 1994" (Washington, D.C.: U.S. Government Printing Office, 1993).

88. "Sweden: Judgement Day," *The Economist*, February 18, 1995, p. 37.

89. "The Enlightened Welfare Seeker's Guide to Europe," *The Economist*, March 12, 1994, p. 57.

90. Assar Lindbeck, *Overshooting, Reform, and Retreat of the Welfare State*, Institute for International Economic Studies at University of Stockholm, No. 499, 1994.

91. Barry P. Bosworth and Alice M. Rivlin, eds., *The Swedish Economy* (Washington, D.C.: Brookings Institution, 1987), pp. 199, 207.

92. "Sweden Shows Effects of Painful Cure," *Financial Times*, November 8, 1993, p. 3.

93. Damon Darlin, "A New Flavor of Pork," *Forbes*, June 5, 1995, p. 146.

94. "Expanded Medicaid Crowded Out Private Insurance," *The NBER Digest*, 1994, p. 1.

95. Yair Aharone, *The No Risk Society* (New Jersey: Chatham House, 1981), pp. 48, 62.

CHAPTER 6: PLATE FOUR: A GLOBAL ECONOMY

1. Richard N. Cooper, *Environmental and Resource Policies for the World Economy* (Washington, D.C.: Brookings Institution, 1994), p. xi.

2. Eric Hobsbawm, *Age of Extremes: The Short Twentieth Century, 1914–1991* (London: Michael Joseph, 1994), p. 56.

3. Ibid., p. 72.

4. International Monetary Fund *International Financial Statistics*, 1980 yearbook, Washington D.C., pp. 62, 63; *Financial Statistics*, 1986 yearbook, pp. 70, 72; U.S. Department of Commerce, *Survey of Current Business*, Washington, D.C., 1989, 1992, p. 61.

5. J. Bradford De Long and Barry Eichengreen, *The Marshall Plan: History's Most Successful Structural Adjustment Program*, NBER Working Paper No. 3899, November 1991.

6. Tom Buerkle, "EU Heads Boldly into a High-Stakes Debate on Expanding Eastward," *International Herald Tribune*, June 2, 1995, p. 1.

7. DRI/McGraw-Hill, *Impact of the Peso Crisis*, February 1995, p. 1.

8. Ibid., p. 6.

9. "Canada's Endangered Bacon," *Fortune*, March 10, 1995, p. 75.

10. "Financial Indicators," *The Economist*, February 25, 1995, p. 109.

11. "The Americas Drift Toward Free Trade," *The Economist,* July 8, 1995, p. 45.
12. Noel Malcolm, "The Case Against 'Europe,' " *Foreign Affairs* March/April 1995, p. 68.
13. "No Cannes Do," *The Economist,* July 1, 1995, p. 23.
14. Tom Buerkle, "Seven European Nations Drop Border Controls," *International Herald Tribune,* March 25, 1995, p. 1.
15. Malcolm, "The Case Against 'Europe,'" pp. 54, 59.
16. World Bank, *World Tables for 1994* (Baltimore: Johns Hopkins University Press, 1995), p. 27, 29.
17. Michael Richardson, "APEC's Crisis of (No) Consensus," *International Herald Tribune,* March 17, 1995, p. 17.
18. Steven Brull, "Waves in Pacific Trade: APEC Struggles to Tie Down Specifics," *International Herald Tribune,* July 6, 1995, p. 11.
19. Kevin Murphy, "Building Blocs: A Rising Yen Challenges the Dollar," *International Herald Tribune,* March 27, 1995, p. 11.
20. Commission of the European Communities, *Towards a New Bretton Woods: Alternatives for the Global Economy,* European University Institute, May 1993.
21. International Labor Organization, *World Employment Report,* Geneva, 1995, p. 35; Warwick J. McKibbin and Dominick Salvatore, *The Global Economic Consequences of the Uruguay Round,* Brookings Discussion Papers No. 110, February 1995, p. 3.
22. David Buchan, "GATT Deal May Enrich World by $270 Billion," *Financial Times,* November 10, 1993, p. 7; McKibbin and Salvatore, *The Global Economic Consequences of the Uruguay Round,* p. 5.
23. Elmer Hankiss, "European Paradigms: East and West 1945–1994," *After Communism, What?* special issue of *Daedalus,* Summer 1994, p. 115.
24. Philip R. Schlesinger, "Europe's Contradictory Communicative Space," *Europe Through a Glass Darkly,* special issue of *Daedalus,* Spring 1994, p. 27.
25. "You're Not in Kansas Anymore," *The Economist,* February 4, 1995, p. 57; Schlesinger, "Europe's Contradictory Communicative Space," p. 33.
26. "La Regle du Jeu," *The Economist,* March 18, 1995, p. 18.
27. Office of Technology Assessment, *Multinationals and the U.S. Technology Base* (Washington, D.C.: U.S. Government Printing Office, 1994), p. 7.
28. David Shribman, "GATT: Vilifying the Inscrutable," *Boston Globe,* July 22, 1994, p. 3.

29. Zanny Minton-Beddoes, "Why the IMF Needs Reform," *Foreign Affairs,* May/June 1995, p. 123.

CHAPTER 7: PLATE FIVE: A MULTIPOLAR WORLD WITH NO DOMINANT POWER

1. Eric Hobsbawm, *Age of Extremes: The Short Twentieth Century, 1914–1991* (London: Michael Joseph, 1994), pp. 258, 275.

2. J. Bradford De Long and Barry Eichengreen, *The Marshall Plan: History's Most Successful Structural Adjustment Program,* NBER Working Paper No. 3899, November 1991.

3. Richard Holt, *The Reluctant Superpower* (Toyko: Kodansha International, 1995), p. 117.

4. De Long and Eichengreen, *The Marshall Plan,* p. 14; U.S. Bureau of the Census, *Historical Statistics of the United States, Colonial Times to 1970, Vol. 1* (Washington, D.C.: U.S. Government Printing Office, 1975), p. 228.

5. *Budget of the United States Government, Fiscal Year 1996* (Washington, D.C.: U.S. Government Printing Office, 1995), p. 115.

6. Newt Gingrich, *Contract with America* (New York: Times Books, 1994); *New Republic,* March 25, 1995, p. 21.

7. Robert W. Tucker and David C. Hendrickson, *The Imperial Temptation: The New World Order and America's Purpose* (New York: Council on Foreign Relations), 1992.

8. Samuel Brittan, "Time to Bury Those League Tables," *Financial Times,* May 25, 1995, p. 10.

9. Steven Brull, *International Herald Tribune,* March 8, 1995, p. 1.

10. "Japan's GDP Rivals That of the U.S.," *International Herald Tribune,* May 10, 1995, p. 19.

11. Charles Wolf, Jr., "The Fine Art of the False Alarm," *Wall Street Journal,* November 1, 1994, p. A20; World Bank, *World Tables 1994* (Baltimore: Johns Hopkins Unversity Press, 1994).

12. "Russians Don't Like Dead in Chechen on TV," *International Herald Tribune,* December 22, 1994, p. 6.

13. Russell Watson, "Russia's TV War," *Newsweek,* February 6, 1995, p. 8.

14. DRI/McGraw-Hill, *Review of the U.S. Economy,* p. 87.

15. "OECD Chides the U.S. Over Foreign Aid Cuts," *International Herald Tribune,* March 8, 1995, p. 2.

16. Johsen Takanashi, "Dollar Being Eclipsed as Global Standard," *Nikkei Weekly,* June 5, 1995, p. 6.

17. *Economic Report of the President 1995* (Washington, D.C.: U.S. Government Printing Office), pp. 278, 279.

18. International Monetary Fund, *International Trade Policies: The Uruguay Round and Beyond,* Vols. I, II, Washington 1994.

19. David Halberstam, *The Next Century* (New York: Morrow, 1991), p. 52.

20. "U.S. House Votes to Cut UN Peacekeeping Funds," *The Japan Times,* February 18, 1995, p. 2.

21. "House Votes to Curb Role in UN," *International Herald Tribune,* February 17, 1995, p. 1.

22. Gingrich, *Contract with America,* p. 17.

23. Ibid.

24. Quoted in Richard L. Berke, "Pat Buchanan Is Driving the '96 Race Rightward," *International Herald Tribune,* May 31, 1995, p. 1.

25. Michael Dobbs, "NATO Expansion Popular But Don't Look at the Price," *International Herald Tribune,* July 8, 1995, p. 1.

26. Clyde Haberman, "Israel Warns U.S. Not to Cut Aid to Nations in Peace Talks," *New York Times,* March 4, 1995, p. 4.

27. Michel Albert, *Capitalism Against Capitalism* (London: Whurr Publishers, 1993), p. 35.

28. Tan Kim Song, "Money Market Chaos a Threat to APEC's Aims," *The Sunday Straits Times,* April 16, 1995, p. 1.

29. Laura Keeton, "Legal Beat: More Legal Aliens Seeking Citizenship to Keep Benefits," *Wall Street Journal,* March 6, 1995, p. B1.

30. Jerry Gray, "Budget Axes Land on Items Big and Small," *New York Times,* February 28, 1995, p. A14.

31. "Mexico Crisis and Stable Rates Cause Dollar Malaise," *International Herald Tribune,* February 17, 1995, p. 11.

32. Anthony Robinson, "Warning on 'Malady' of Weak Leadership," *Financial Times,* May 4, 1995, p. 4.

33. Steve Farka, *Mixed Messages: A Survey of Foreign Policy Views of American Leaders* (Washington, D.C.: Public Agenda Foundation, 1995), p. 28.

34. Quoted in Craig Lambert, "Leadership in a New Key," *Harvard Magazine,* March/April 1995, p. 31.

35. Ibid.

36. Major Garrett, "Beyond the Contract," *Mother Jones,* March/April 1995, p. 54.

37. Newt Gingrich, "Only America Can Lead," *New Perspectives Quarterly,* Spring 1995, p. 4.

CHAPTER 8: THE FORCES REMAKING THE ECONOMIC
SURFACE OF THE EARTH

1. International Monetary Fund, *International Financial Statistics*, Washington, D.C., various yearbooks; Stuart Holland, *Toward a New Bretton Woods* (Nottingham, U.K.: Russel Press, 1994), P. 10; Council of Economic Advisers, *Economic Report of the President 1995* (Washington, D.C.: U.S. Government Printing Office), p. 403.

2. Sylvia Nasar, "More Men in Prime of Life Spend Less Time Working," *New York Times*, December 1, 1994, p. 1.

3. Robert D. Hershey, Jr., "Survey Finds 6 Million, Fewer Than Thought, in Impermanent Jobs," *New York Times*, August 19, 1995, p. 31.

4. Polly Callaghan and Heidi Hartmann, *Contingent Work* (Washington, D.C.: Economic Policy Institute, 1991), p. 2.

5. Lenore Schiff, "Why Inflation Will Keep Falling," *Fortune*, October 2, 1995, p. 60.

6. George J. Borjas, "The Economics of Migration," *Journal of Economic Literature*, December 1994, p. 1668.

7. Reported by Nicholas Fiore, *Carpenter Technology*, at Conference on *Leveraging Taiwanese Resources*, MIT-EPOCH Foundation, October 12–14, 1995, Taipei.

8. Economic Policy Institute, *Declining American Incomes and Living Standards*, 1994.

9. Craig R. Whitney, "West European Companies Head East for Cheap Labor," *New York Times*, February 9, 1995, p. D1.

10. Richard J. Murnane, John B. Willet, and Frank Levy, "The Growing Importance of Cognitive Skills in Wage Determination," *Review of Economics and Statistics*, May 1995, p. 258.

11. Neal Templin, "Dr. Goodwrench, Auto Plants Are Demanding Higher Skilled Labor," *Wall Street Journal*, March 11, 1994, p. 1.

12. U.S. Department of Commerce, *Survey of Current Business* (Washington, D.C.: U.S. Government Printing Office, 1994), pp. 82, 84.

13. Paul Krugman, *Peddling Prosperity* (New York: W. W. Norton, 1994), p. 231.

14. Eli Berman, John Bound, and Svi Griliches, "Changes in the Demand for Skilled Labor in U.S. Manufacturing," *Quarterly Journal of Economics*, May 1994, p. 367.

15. Robert Z. Lawrence and Matthew J. Slaughter, "Trade and U.S. Wages: Great Sucking Sound or Small Hiccup?" *Micro-BPEA Meet-*

ings, Washington, D.C., June 1993; Paul Krugman and Robert Lawrence, *Trade, Jobs, and Wages,* MIT Working Paper, 1994.

16. George J. Borjas and Valerie A. Ramey, "Time Series Evidence on the Sources of Trends in Wage Inequality," *AEA Papers and Proceedings,* May 1994, p. 10.

17. Farhad Rassekh, "The Role of International Trade in the Convergence of Per Capita GDP in the OECD, 1950–1980," *International Economics Journal,* Vol. 6, No. 4 (Winter 1992), p. 1; Manouchehr Mokhtari and Farhad Rassekh, "The Tendency Toward Factor Price Equalization Among OECD Countries," *Review of Economics and Statistics,* November 1989, p. 636; Dan Ben-David, "Equalizing Exchange, Trade, Liberalization and Convergence," *Quarterly Journal of Economics,* August 1993, p. 653; Ana L. Revenga, "Exporting Jobs," *Quarterly Journal of Economics,* February 1992, p. 255; David L. Dollar and Edward N. Wolff, "Convergence of Industrial Labor Productivity Among Advanced Economies, 1963–1982," *Review of Economics and Statistics,* November 1988, p. 549.

18. Jeffrey D. Sachs and Howard J. Shatz, *Trade and Jobs in U.S. Manufacturing,* Brookings Papers on Economic Activity, No. 1, 1994, p. 1.

19. Derek Bok, *The Cost of Talent* (New York: Free Press, 1993), p. 223.

20. Ibid.

21. Rassekh, "The Role of International Trade," p. 1.

22. *Economic Report of the President, 1995,* p. 279.

23. Economic Policy Institute, *Declining American Incomes and Living Standards* (Washington, D.C.: U.S. Government Printing Office, 1994), p. 12.

24. Laura D'Andrea Tyson, William T. Dickens, and John Zysman, *The Dynamics of Trade and Employment* (Cambridge, Mass.: Ballinger, 1988), p. 102.

25. U.S. Bureau of the Census, *Current Population Reports, Consumer Income,* Series P-60 (Washington, D.C.: U.S. Government Printing Office, 1973, 1993), pp. 119, 144.

26. Robert H. Topel, "Regional Labor Markets and the Determination of Wage Inequality," *American Economic Review,* May 1994, p. 17.

27. Harold Lydall, *A Theory of Income Distribution* (Oxford, U.K.: Clarendon Press, 1979).

28. Lester C. Thurow, *Generating Inequality* (New York: Basic Books, 1974).

29. Michael Sattinger, "Assignment Models of the Distribution of Earnings," *Journal of Economic Literature,* June 1993, p. 833.

30. Thurow, *Generating Inequality.*

31. Ibid.

32. Robert H. Frank, "Talent and the Winner-Take-All Society," *American Prospect,* Spring 1994, p. 99.

33. Robert Taylor, "Decline in Worker Organization," *Financial Times,* June 2, 1995, p. 8.

34. "Trade Unions: Adapt or Die," *The Economist,* July 1, 1995, p. 60.

35. George J. Borjas and Valerie A Ramey, *Foreign Competition, Market Power and Wage Inequality: Theory and Evidence,* Working Paper No. 4556 NBER, December 1993; Lawrence M. Kahn and Michael Curme, "Unions and Nonunion Wage Dispersion," *Review of Economics and Statistics,* November 1987, p. 600.

36. Economic Policy Institute, *Paying the Toll* (Washington, D.C., 1994), p. 1.

37. "Nothing Could Be Finer," *The Economist,* November 19, 1994, p. 77.

38. Ibid.

39. Economic Policy Institute, *Paying the Toll,* p. 1.

CHAPTER 9: INFLATION: AN EXTINCT VOLCANO

1. Jeffrey C. Fuhrer, ed., *Goals, Guidelines, and Constraints Facing Monetary Policymakers* (Boston: Federal Reserve Bank of Boston, June 1994).

2. Robert Hershey, Jr., "Federal Reserve Raises Its Rates 7th Time in a Year," *New York Times,* February 2, 1995, p. 1.

3. "Economy Expanded As Inflation Fell," *New York Times,* October 23, 1995, p. 34.

4. Louis Uchitelle, "Labor Costs Show Small Increase," *New York Times,* January 2, 1995, p. D1; "Core U.S. Inflation Lowest Since 1965," *International Herald Tribune,* January 12, 1995, p. 5; "OECD: No Inflation Problem Seen in 1995," *International Herald Tribune,* December 21, 1994, p. 1.

5. Joshua Ogawa, "Wholesale Prices Estimated to Have Kept Falling," *Nikkei Weekly,* June 12, 1995, p. 3.

6. Robert D. Herse, Jr., "Statistics Never Lie, but They Increasingly Mislead in America," *International Herald Tribune,* January 17, 1995, p. 17.

7. Mark K. Sherwood, "Difficulties in the Measurement of Service Outputs," *Monthly Labor Review,* March 1994, p. 1.

8. "Who's Afraid of the Big Bad Deficit?" *The Economist,* September 30, 1995, p. 39.

9. Zvi Griliches, "Productivity R&D, and the Data Constraint," *American Economic Review,* March 1994, p. 1.

10. James Aley, "Medical Inflation Lives," *Fortune,* March 20, 1995, p. 24.

11. Robert Barro, in the Bank of England's Quarterly Bulletin as reported in "The Costs of Inflation," *The Economist,* May 13, 1995, p. 90.

12. Samuel Brittan, "Elusive Case for Stable Prices," *Financial Times,* May 18, 1995, p. 9.

13. Samuel Brittan, *The Role and Limits of Government* (Minneapolis: University of Minnesota Press, 1983), p. 113.

14. "What's Happening to Inflation?" *The Economist,* September 16, 1995, p. 85.

15. Lenore Schiff, "Why Inflation Will Keep Falling," *Fortune,* October 2, 1995, p. 59.

16. Jeff Faux, "A National Embarrassment," *Challenge,* January-February 1995, p. 6.

17. Ibid., p. 11.

18. Stephen S. Roach, *The Next Leg of Disinflation,* Morgan Stanley Special Economic Study, June 1994.

19. Anne Romanis Braun, *Wage Determination and Income Policy in Open Economies* (Washington, D.C.: International Monetary Fund, 1986), p. 100.

20. John Kenneth Galbraith, *The Great Crash of 1929* (New York: Houghton Mifflin, 1954; reprint, 1988), p. 184; U.S. Department of Commerce, *Long Term Economic Growth 1860–1970* (Washington, D.C.: U.S. Government Printing Office, 1973), p. 222.

21. Louis Uchitelle, "Manufacturers Challenge Economic Policy," *New York Times,* September 24, 1995. p. 38.

22. Robert Heilbroner and William Milberg, *The Crisis of Vision in Modern Economic Thought* (New York: Cambridge University Press, 1995), p. 120.

23. OECD, *Quarterly National Accounts,* No. 2, Paris, 1995, p. 145.

CHAPTER 10: JAPAN: THE MAJOR FAULT LINE ACROSS WORLD TRADE AND THE PACIFIC RIM

1. Deizai Koho Center, *Japan 1995: An International Comparison* (Toyko: 1995), pp. 34, 35; U.S. Department of Commerce, *Survey*

of *Current Business,* December 1993, pp. 71, 72.

2. U.S. Department of Commerce, *Survey of Current Business,* pp. 38, 42.

3. Richard Holt, *The Reluctant Superpower* (New York: Kodansha International, 1995), p. 246; "Stock Market Indexes," *Asian Wall Street Journal,* January 1, 1990, p. 18; August 24, 1992, p. 22.

4. Nikko Research Center, *The Nikko Chartroom* (Tokyo: July 1995), p. 8; "Japanese Property Crumbling," *The Economist,* July 8, 1995, p. 83; "Slow Crisis in Japan," *Financial Times,* July 1, 1995, p. 8.

5. "Japanese Property Crumbling," p. 83; Akira Ikeya, "Falling Land Prices Spur Call for Tax Reform," *Nikkei Weekly,* August 28, 1995, p. 2; Sheryl WuDunn, "Erosion in Japan's Foundation," *New York Times,* October 4, 1995, p. D1.

6. Robert E. Scott, "A Trade Strategy for the 21st Century," in T. Schafer, ed., *Foundations for a New Century* (Washington, D.C.: Economic Policy Institute, M. E. Sharpe, forthcoming), p. 2.

7. *Car and Driver: The Catalog,* Japan ed., Buyers Guide (Tokyo: Diamond, 1995), p. 17.

8. "OK Mickey, Let's Say You Won," *The Economist,* July 1, 1995, pp. 65–66.

9. Ibid., p. 75.

10. Guy de Jonquieres, "Japanese Quietly Celebrate World Trade Victory," *Financial Times,* March 20, 1995, p. 4.

11. Gerard Barker, "Driven Off the Oriental Highway: Japan Is Crowing over Its Victory in the U.S. Car Clash," *Financial Times,* July 2, 1995, p. 9.

12. Steven Brull, "Another Seoul Pothole for Automakers," *International Herald Tribune,* August 20, 1994, p. 7.

13. Sheryl WuDunn, "Protectionism Without Quotas," *International Herald Tribune,* March 21, 1995, p. 17.

14. Clay Chandler, "Kodak Strives for Japan Exposure," *International Herald Tribune,* June 27, 1995, p. 17.

15. "Top 300 Foreign Owned Companies in Japan, 1990," *Toyko Business Today,* August 1991, p. 54.

16. William Dawkins, "Pressure on Japanese Rates as GDP Falls," *Financial Times,* March 19, 1995, p. 3.

17. "Industrial Growth," *The Economist,* September 16, 1995, p. 122.

18. Mihoko Ida, "For Savers, Lower Interest Rates Not Enriching," *Nikkei Weekly,* September 18, 1995.

19. "Borrowing," *The Economist,* October 28, 1995, p. 123.

20. The Japan Research Institute Economics Department, "Escaping the

Deflationary Spiral," *Japan Research Quarterly,* Autumn 1995, p. 35.

21. Seymour Martin Lipset, "Pacific Divide: American Exceptionalism—Japanese Uniqueness," *International Journal of Public Opinion,* Vol. 5, No. 2 (Spring, 1994), p. 121.

22. *Economic Report of the President 1995,* p. 402.

23. Richard Covington, "Ignoring Copyright Pact, China Reopens Factories That Pirated U.S. CDs," *International Herald Tribune,* June 2, 1995, p. 1; "That Damned Dollar," *The Economist,* February 25, 1995, p. 17.

CHAPTER 11: ECONOMIC INSTABILITY

1. Daniel Yergin, *The Prize: The Epic Quest for Oil, Money, and Power* (New York: Simon and Schuster, 1991), pp. 615–17.

2. Council of Economic Advisers, *Economic Report of the President 1995* (Washington, D.C.: U.S. Government Printing Office), pp. 358, 366.

3. Benjamin C. Schwarz, "Is Capitalism Doomed?" *New York Times,* May 23, 1994, pp. 1, 15.

4. *Economic Report of the President 1995* pp. 401, 403.

5. "Economic and Financial Indicators," *The Economist,* June 5, 1993, p. 131.

6. "Slow Growth Seen for '88," *Pensions and Investment Age,* Vol. 15, (December 28, 1987), pp. 3, 46.

7. Robert L. Heilbroner, *Behind the Veil of Economics* (New York: W. W. Norton, 1988), p. 29.

8. Morris Goldstein et al., *International Capital Markets,* International Monetary Fund, Washington D.C., April 1993, p. 4; "A Survey of The World Economy," *The Economist,* October 7, 1995, p. 10.

9. Saul Hansell, "The Collapse of Barings: For Rogue Traders Yet Another Victim," *New York Times,* February 28, 1995, p. D1.

10. "Gone Dutch," *The Economist,* March 11, 1995, p. 83.

11. Peter Clark et al., *Exchange Rates and Economic Fundamentals,* International Monetary Fund, December 1994.

12. Ibid., p. 401.

13. DRI/McGraw-Hill, *Impact of the Peso Crisis,* February 1995, p. 1.

14. "After Mexico, Who's Next?" *Fortune,* March 6, 1995, p. 14.

15. "Submerging Europe," *The Economist,* March 18, 1995, p. 78.

16. "Symposium: The Changing Structure of Mexico," *Challenge,* March/April 1995, p. 12–63.

17. R. Dornbusch and A. Werner, "Mexico: Stabilization, Reform, and No

Growth," *The World Economic Laboratory* MIT Working Paper No. 94-08, 1994; "Survey Mexico—Another Day, Another Dive," *The Economist,* October 28, 1995, p. 6.

18. Geri Smith and Stephen Baker, "The Fall of Carlos Salinas," *Business Week,* March 27, 1995, p. 52.

19. Anthony DePalma, "Turmoil Grips Mexico over Shock Plan for Economy," *International Herald Tribune,* March 13, 1995, p. 1.

20. "Mexican Package Gets Short Shrift," *Financial Times,* February 23, 1995, p. 6.

21. David E. Sanger, "Mexico Is Facing New Restrictions to Get U.S. Help," *New York Times,* February 20, 1995, p. 1; David E. Sanger, "Peso Rescue Sets New Limits on Mexico," *New York Times,* February 22, 1995, p. 1.

22. Lawrence Malkin, "Trade Deficit Expands as Mexico Crisis Takes Its Toll," *International Herald Tribune,* March 13, 1995, p. 1.

23. Leslie Crawford, "Inflation in Mexico Accelerated in March," *Financial Times,* March 25, 1995, p. 4.

24. Harry Hurt III, "It's Time to Get Real About Mexico," *Fortune,* September 4, 1995, p. 99.

25. A. M. Rosenthal, "Cover-up Chronology," *New York Times,* April 4, 1995, p. A25.

26. "Of Politics, Pensions, and Piggy Banks," *The Economist,* July 1, 1995, p. 82.

27. Ibid.

28. DePalma, "Turmoil Grips Mexico," p. 6; Leslie Crawford, "Anger on the Streets As Mexico Swallows the Economic Medicine," *Financial Times,* March 11, 1995, p. 4.

29. Douglas Farah, "First the Peso, Then the Mexican Dream," *International Herald Tribune,* March 18, 1995, p. 1.

30. Anthony DePalma, "After the Fall: Two Faces of Mexico's Economy," *New York Times,* July 16, 1995, p. F1.

31. "Sorry, Gringos," *The Economist,* August 26, 1995, p. 65.

32. Ibid.

33. Leslie Crawford, "Mexico's Vigil of Woe," *Financial Times,* June 2, 1995, p. 12.

34. "Mexico Crisis and Stable Rates Cause Dollar Malaise," *International Herald Tribune,* February 17, 1995, p. 11.

35. International Monetary Fund, *International Financial Statistics Yearbook, 1994,* Washington, D.C., 1995, p. 23.

36. Michael Mussa et al., *Improving the International Monetary System* (Washington, D.C.: International Monetary Fund, 1994).

CHAPTER 12: SOCIAL VOLCANOES:
RELIGIOUS FUNDAMENTALISM AND ETHNIC
SEPARATISM

1. Adrian H. Bredero, *Christendom and Christianity in the Middle Ages,* trans. by Reinder Bruinsma (Grand Rapids, Mich.: William B. Eerdmans, 1986), pp. 358–369; Jonathan Sumption, *Pilgrimages* (New Jersey: Rowman and Littlefield: 1975), pp. 270–279.

2. Karl E. Meyer, "Editorial Notebook: The Roots of Bosnia's Anguish," *New York Times,* February 28, 1993, sec. 4, p. 14.

3. "Time to Help Algeria," *The Economist,* February 18, 1995, p. 13.

4. Serge Schmemann, "Police Say Rabin Killer Led Sect That Also Targeted Palestinians," *New York Times,* November 11, 1995, p. 1; John Kifner, "Zeal of Rabin's Assassin Springs from Rabbis of Religious Right," *New York Times,* November 12, 1995, p. 1.

5. Nicholas D. Kristof, "New Chemical Cache Spreads Fear," *International Herald Tribune,* March 25–26, 1995, p. 1.

6. Tom Kuntz, "From Thought to Deed: In the Mind of a Killer Who Says He Served God," *New York Times,* September 24, 1995, p. E7.

7. Jack Lessenberry, "Michigan Group United by Guns, Anger," *Boston Globe,* April 22, 1995, p. 1.

8. John Kifner, "Despite Oklahoma Charges, the Case is Far from Closed," *New York Times,* August 12, 1995, pp. 1, 24.

9. Gustave Niebuhr, "A Vision of Apocalypse: The Religion of the Far Right," *New York Times,* May 22, 1995, p. A8.

10. Gustav Niebuhr, "Assault on Waco Sect Fuels Extremists' Rage," *New York Times,* April 26, 1995, p. A12.

11. Bruce Hoffman, "In America, Too, Violence All the Worse for Its Religious Pretenses," *International Herald Tribune,* April 27, 1995, p. 8.

12. William Pfaff, "No Excusing Those Who Brook the Reverend's Nonsense," *International Herald Tribune,* March 11, 1995, p. 6.

13. Frank Rich, "Gingrich Family Values," *New York Times,* May 14, 1995, p. E15.

14. "The Tablets of Ralph," *The Economist,* May 20, 1995, p. 60.

15. "The Counter-attack of God," *The Economist,* July 8, 1995, p. 25.

16. Tom Nairn, "Internationalism and the Second Coming," *Reconstructing Nations and States,* special issue of *Daedalus,* Summer 1993, p. 168.

17. Charles F. Doran and Ellen Reisman Babby, eds., *Being and Becoming*

Canada, The Annals of the American Academy of Political and Social Science, March 1995.

18. Tony Judt, "1988: The End of Which European Era?" *After Communism, What? Daedalus,* Summer 1994, p. 24.

19. Martin Kramer, "Arab Nationalism: Mistaken Identity," *Reconstructing Nations and States,* special issue of *Daedalus,* Summer 1993, p. 171.

20. Francis Fukuyama, "Blood and Belonging," *New York Times Book Review,* April 10, 1994, p. 7.

21. Marlise Simons, "Corsican Separatists Separate," *International Herald Tribune,* June 3, 1995, p. 2.

22. Douglas B. Klusmeyer, "Aliens, Immigrants, and Citizens," *Reconstructing Nations and States,* special issue of *Daedalus,* Summer, 1993, p. 102.

23. Eric Hobsbawm, *Age of Extremes: The Short Twentieth Century, 1914–1991* (London: Michael Joseph, 1994), p. 11.

24. Ralph C. Bryant, "Increasing Economic Integration and Eroding Political Sovereignty," *The Brookings Review,* Fall 1994, p. 42.

CHAPTER 13: DEMOCRACY VERSUS THE MARKET

1. Arthur R. Jensen, *Straight Talk About Mental Tests* (New York: Free Press, 1981), p. 6.

2. Richard Sandomir, "Pro Basketball: Players Sue to Raise NBA Salary Cap," *New York Times,* November 10, 1994, p. B4.

3. Council of Economic Advisers, *Economic Report of the President 1995* (Washington, D.C.: U.S. Government Printing Office), pp. 280, 358.

4. Martin Baily, Gary Burtless, Robert E. Litan, *Growth with Equity* (Washington, D.C.: Brookings Institution, 1993).

5. Jennifer L. Hochschild, *What's Fair? American Beliefs About Distributive Justice* (Cambridge, Mass.: Harvard University Press, 1981), p. 9.

6. Francis Fukuyama, *The End of History and the Last Man* (New York: Avon Books, 1992), pp. 242, 291.

7. *Encyclopedia Britannica,* Vol. 20, 1972 edition, p. 631.

8. J. L. Baxter, *Behavioral Foundations of Economics* (New York: St. Martin's Press, 1993), pp. 28, 35.

9. Ibid., p. 53.; Tibor Scitovsky, *The Joyless Economy* (New York: Oxford University Press, 1978), p. 109.

10. Jonathan H. Turner, *Herbert Spencer: A Renewed Appreciation* (Beverly Hills, Calif.: Sage Publishers, 1985), p. 11; J.D.Y. Peel, *Herbert*

Spencer, The Evolution of a Sociologist (New York: Basic Books, 1971); Herbert Spencer, *The Principles of Biology,* Vol. 1 (New York: Appleton & Co., 1866), p. 530.

11. Richard J. Herrnstein and Charles Murray, *The Bell Curve: Intelligence and Class Structure in American Life* (New York: Free Press, 1994).

12. Census and Statistics Department, *Hong Kong Annual Digest of Statistics, 1994 Edition* (Hong Kong: Government Printer), p. 198.

13. Ng Kang-Chung, "Resale Reform to Free Flats for Needy," *South China Morning Post,* Sept 16, 1995, p. 1.

14. John A. Garraty, *Unemployment in History* (New York: Harper and Row, 1978), p. 134.

15. Peter Applebome, "In Gingrich's College Course, Critics Find a Wealth of Ethical Concerns," *New York Times,* February 20, 1995, p. C7.

16. Eric Hobsbawm, *Age of Extremes: The Short Twentieth Century, 1914–1991* (London: Michael Joseph, 1994), p. 138.

17. Newt Gingrich, *Contract with America* (New York: Times Books, 1994).

18. Ibid.

19. Nordal Akerman, ed., *The Necessity of Friction* (Heidelberg: Physica-Verlag, 1993), p. 12.

20. Alan Cowell, "Socialists Are Sinking in Germany," *New York Times,* September 24, 1995, p. 4.

21. Michael Thompson-Noel, "A Daily Dose of Pick and Mix News," *Financial Times,* March 13, 1995, p. 10.

22. Richard Tomkins, "Enter the Bespoken Newspaper," *Financial Times,* March 13, 1995, p. 11.

23. Fernand Braudel, *The Identity of France,* Vol. II, *People and Production* (New York: Fontana Press, 1991), p. 102.

24. Frances Gies and Joseph Gies, *Forge and Waterwheel: Technology and Innovation in the Middle Ages* (New York: HarperCollins), 1994, pp. 1, 3.

25. Braudel, *The Identity of France,* p. 102.

26. Georges Duby, ed., *A History of Private Life: Revelations of the Medieval World* (Cambridge, Mass.: Harvard University Press/Belknap Press, 1988), p. 123.

27. Gies and Gies, *Forge and Waterwheel,* pp. 37, 43.

28. Fernand Braudel, *The Structures of Everyday Life: The Limits of the Possible,* Vol. 1, (New York: Harper and Row, 1981), p. 123.

29. William Manchester, *A World Lit Only by Fire: The Medieval Mind and the Renaissance* (Boston: Little, Brown, 1992), p. 47.

30. Ibid. p. 5.

31. Ibid. p. 69.

32. Braudel, *The Identity of France,* p. 102.

33. Manchester, *A World Lit Only by Fire,* p. 96.

34. Ibid., p. 51.

35. Ibid.; Georges Duby, Dominique B. Arthelemy, and Charles De La-Ronciere, "Portraits," in Georges Duby, ed., *A History of Private Life: Revelations of the Medieval World* (Cambridge, Mass.: Harvard University Press/Belknap Press, 1988), p. 170.

36. Fernand Braudel, *The Mediterranean and the Mediterranean World in the Age of Phillip II* (New York: Harper and Row, 1973), p. 745.

37. Duby, ed., *A History of Private Life,* p. 23.

38. Ibid. p. 397.

39. Duby, Arthelemy, and De LaRonciere, "Portraits," pp. 116, 165; Norman F. Cantor, *The Civilization of the Middle Ages* (New York: HarperCollins, 1993), p. 197.

40. Timothy Egan, "Many Seek Security in Private Communities," *New York Times,* September 3, 1995, p. 1.

41. Ibid. p. 22.

42. Adam Pertman, "Home Safe Home: Closed Communities Grow," *Boston Globe,* March 14, 1994, p. 1.

43. Dale Mahadridge, "Walled Off," *Mother Jones,* November/December 1994, p. 27.

44. Ibid.

45. Egan, "Many Seek Security," p. 22.

46. Edward J. Blakely and Marach Gail Snyder, *Fortress America: Gated and Walled Communities in the United States,* Lincoln Institute of Land Policy, June 10, 1994, p. 11.

47. Ibid. p. 9.

48. Cantor, *The Civilization of the Middle Ages,* p. 195.

49. Manchester, *A World Lit Only by Fire,* p. 47.

50. Cantor, *The Civilization of the Middle Ages,* p. 119.

51. Fernand Braudel, *A History of Civilization* (New York: Penguin Press, 1963), p. 17.

52. Manchester, *A World Lit Only by Fire,* p. 5.

53. Duby, ed., *A History of Private Life,* p. 69.

54. Cantor, *The Civilization of the Middle Ages,* p. 187; Gies and Gies, *Forge and Waterwheel,* p. 178.

55. Manchester, *A World Lit Only by Fire,* pp. 6, 7.

56. Ibid. p. 11.

57. Ibid. p. 37.

58. Malcolm Barber, *The Two Cities: Medieval Europe 1050–1320* (New York: Routledge, 1992), p. 27.

59. Cantor, *The Civilization of the Middle Ages*, p. 27.

60. Manchester, *A World Lit Only by Fire*, p. 73.

61. Susan Strange, "The Defective State," *Daedalus*, Spring 1995, p. 56.

62. Manchester, *A World Lit Only by Fire*, p. 3.

63. Ibid. pp. 86, 90, 102, 121.

64. Jerry Gray, "Budget Axes Land on Items Big and Small," *New York Times*, February 24, 1995, p. A14.

65. Gunnar Myrdal, *Against the Stream* (New York: Pantheon, 1972).

66. Robert Heilbroner and William Milberg, *The Crisis of Vision in Modern Economic Thought* (New York: Cambridge University Press, 1995), p. 108.

67. Richard Holt, *The Reluctant Superpower* (New York: Kodansha International, 1995), p. 1.

68. R. C. Lewontin, Steven Rose and Leon J. Kamin, *Not in Our Genes: Biology, Ideology, and Human Nature* (New York: Pantheon Books, 1984), p. 69.

69. Gary S. Becker and William M. Landes, *Essays in the Economics of Crime and Punishment* (New York: Columbia University Press/National Bureau of Economic Research, 1974), p. 18.

70. Lewontin, Rose, and Kamin, *Not in Our Genes*, p. 5.

71. Amitai Etzioni, *The Spirit of Community: Rights, Responsibility, and the Communitarian Agenda* (New York: Crown Publishers, 1993), p. 30.

72. Daniel Bell and Irving Kristol, eds., *The Crisis in Economic Theory* (New York: Basic Books, 1981); Samuel Brittan, *The Role and Limits of Government* (Minneapolis: University of Minnesota Press, 1983), p. 26.

73. Myrdal, *Against the Stream*.

74. Fred Block, *Post-Industrial Possibilities: A Critique of Economic Discourse* (Berkeley: University of California Press, 1990), p. 39.

75. James M. Buchanan and Robert D. Tollison, *Theory of Public Choice: Political Applications of Economics* (Ann Arbor: University of Michigan Press, 1972).

76. Mark A. Lutz and Kenneth Lux, *Humanistic Economics* (New York: Bootstrap Press, 1988).

CHAPTER 14: A PERIOD OF PUNCTUATED EQUILIBRIUM

1. Joseph Nathan Kane, *Famous First Facts* (New York: H. W. Wilson, 1981), p. 611.
2. Peter F. Drucker, "The Age of Social Transformation," *Atlantic Monthly*, November 1994, p. 53.
3. "It's People, Stupid," *The Economist*, May 27, 1995, p. 67; U.S. Department of Commerce, *1987 Census of Service Industries* (Washington, D.C.: U.S. Government Printing Office, 1990); American Bar Foundation, *Lawyers' Statistical Report* (Chicago: 1994), p. 6.
4. Lester C. Thurow, *Investment in Human Capital* (Belmont Calif.: Wadsworth, 1970).
5. $NPV = \sum_{t=0}^{\infty} \frac{(R - C)_t}{(l + r)^t}$

   Where NPV = Net Present Value
   r = discount rate
   t = time
   R = returns
   C = costs

6. Within capitalism the tension between consumption and investment is harmonized by bringing each individual's rate of time preferences into balance with the market's rate of interest. If the market rate of interest is 10 percent, then any individual with a rate of time preference less than 10 percent can raise the discounted net present value of their lifetime consumption by saving more, not consuming today, and enjoying 10 percent more consumption one year from now. Each such individual continues saving more until their current consumption is low enough relative to their expected future consumption to raise their rate of time preference to 10 percent—the market rate of interest. At this point they will have maximized the net discounted value of their lifetime consumption and they have no further interest in cutting current consumption to raise future consumption.

   Conversely, if rates of return on new investments are below rates of time preference for some consumers, they will increase their consumption (cut back on savings and borrow to increase their consumption), to once again maximize the net present value of their lifetime consumption. The consumption that they get in the present is worth more to them than the consumption that they will have to give up in the future when they have to repay their loans. If the market interest rate is 10 percent, any individual with a rate of time preference above 10 percent will rationally borrow funds to raise their current consumption. They will do so until their current consumption is so large relative to their future consumption that their rate of time preference has fallen to 10 percent. Here again, at this point they will have maximized the net discounted value of their lifetime consumption.

If there are a lot of people with rates of time preference below 10 percent, then their additional savings will drive market interest rates down. Conversely, if there are a lot of people with rates of time preference above 10 percent, their extra consumption will drive market rates of interest up. The same is true for investors. Investors needing funds to finance projects earning more than 10 percent will drive market interest rates up; investors liquidating investments that earn less than 10 percent will drive interest rates down. Capitalistic investments are optimal when market rates of interest are such that no one has an incentive to further adjust their consumption or investment spending.

7. U.S. Department of Commerce, Bureau of the Census, *Money Income of Households, Families, and Persons in the United States, 1992, Current Population Reports, Consumer Income,* Series P-60 (Washington, D.C.: U.S. Government Printing Office, 1993), pp. 144, 146.

8. Ibid. p. 121.

9. George Psacharopoulos, "Returns to Education: A Further International Update and Implications," *Journal of Human Resources,* 1985, p. 583.

10. James M. Poterba, *Government Intervention in the Markets for Education and Health Care: How and Why?* NBER Working Paper No. 4916, 1995.

11. James M. Poterba and Lawrence H. Summers, "A CEO Survey of U.S. Companies' Time Horizons and Hurdle Rates," *Sloan Management Review,* Fall 1995, p. 145.

12. Poterba, *Government Intervention in the Markets for Education and Health Care.*

13. Michael Prowse, "Time to Separate School and State," *Financial Times,* March 13, 1995, p. 15.

14. Michael J. Piore, *Beyond Individualism* (Cambridge, Mass.: Harvard University Press, 1995), p. 77.

15. Peter Passel, "The Wealth of Nations: A 'Greener' Approach Turns List Upside Down," *New York Times,* September 19, 1995, p. C12.

16. Richard D. Bartel, "Editorial Perspective," *Challenge,* January-February 1995, p. 3.

17. "Size of the Internet," *The Economist,* April 15, 1995, p. 102.

18. Computer Science and Telecommunications Board and National Research Council, *Realizing the Information Future: The Internet and Beyond* (Washington, D.C.: National Academy Press, 1994), p. 2.

19. "A Survey of the Internet: The Accidental Superhighway," *The Economist,* July 1, 1995, p. 13.

20. M. Ishaq Nadiri and Theofanis P. Mamuneas, *Infrastructure and Public R&D Investments and the Growth of Factor Productivity in U.S. Manufacturing Industries,* NBER Working Paper No. 4845, August 1994; Douglas Holtz-Eakin and Amy Ellen Schwartz, *Infrastructure in a Structural Model of Growth,* NBER Working Paper No. 4824, August 1994; Dean Baker and Todd Schafer, *The Case for Public Investment* (Washington, D.C.: Economic Policy Institute, 1995), pp. 4, 6, 9.

21. Robert Ford and Pierre Poret, *Infrastructure and Private Sector Productivity,* OECD Economic Studies No. 17, Autumn 1991, p. 63.

22. Baker and Schafer, *The Case for Public Investment,* pp. 4, 6, 9; Council of Competitiveness, "Charting Competitiveness," *Challenges.* October 1995, p. 3.

23. Natalie Angier, "Science Mimics the Movies: Frankensteinian Fruit Fly Experiments Point to Master Gene for Eye Formation," *International Herald Tribune,* March 25–26, 1995, p. 1.

24. John Holusha, "The Risks for High Tech When Non-Techies Take Over," *New York Times,* September 5, 1993, p. F7; Gautam Naik, "Corporate Research: How Much Is It Worth? Top Labs Shift Research Goals to Fast Payoffs," *Wall Street Journal,* May 22, 1995, p. B1.

25. Malcolm W. Browne, "Prized Labs Shift to More Mundane Tasks," *New York Times,* June 20, 1995, p. C1.

26. Laura D'Andrea Tyson, *Who's Bashing Whom? Trade Conflict in High-Technology Industries* (Washington, D.C.: Institute for International Economics, 1992), p. 32.

27. Karen Southwick, "How Far Can Serendipity Carry Adobe?" *Upside,* September 1995, p. 48.

28. Marguerite de Angeli, *Book of Nursery and Mother Goose Rhymes* (New York: Doubleday and Co., 1953), p. 137.

29. Ann Markusen and Michael Oden, "Investing in the Peace Dividend," in T. Schafer, ed., *Foundations for a New Century* (Washington, D.C.: Economic Policy Institute/M. E. Sharpe, forthcoming), p. 17.

30. Malcolm W. Browne, "Budget Cuts Seen by Science Group as Very Harmful for U.S. Research," *New York Times,* August 29, 1995, p. C1.

31. Philip J. Hilts, "U.S. Intends to Raise Science and Technology Spending, Gore Says," *New York Times,* August 4, 1994, p. 19.

32. "Survey Defense Technology," *The Economist,* June 10, 1995, p. 8; Carol Lessure, *Defense Budget Project,* President Clinton's Defense Transition Program, May 10, 1994, p. 8.

33. "Of Strategies, Subsidies, and Spillovers," *The Economist,* March 18, 1995, p. 84.

34. Edward O. Wilson, "Is Humanity Suicidal?" *New York Times Magazine,* May 30, 1993, p. 25–26.

35. Barry Bosworth, *Prospects for Saving and Investment in Industrial Countries,* Brookings Discussion Papers No. 113, May 1995, p. 2.

36. Ibid. p. 4; Martin Wolf, "The Costs of Low Savings," *Financial Times,* May 2, 1995, p. 20.

37. Bosworth, "Prospects for Saving and Investment," pp. 8–9.

38. Ibid. appendix, table 1.

39. *Budget of the United States Government, Fiscal Year 1996,* Historical Tables (Washington, D.C.: U.S. Government Printing Office, 1995), p. 122; Council of Economic Advisers, *Economic Report of the President 1995* (Washington, D.C.: U.S. Government Printing Office, 1995), p. 274; U.S. Department of Commerce, *Statistical Abstract of the United States 1994* (Washington, D.C.: U.S. Government Printing Office), pp. 372, 607; *Statistical Abstract 1979,* p. 285; U.S. Department of Commerce, *National Income and Product Accounts of the United States, 1959–1988* (Washington, D.C.: U.S. Government Printing Office, 1992), p. 64; Richard Ruggles, "Accounting for Savings and Capital Formation in the United States, 1947–1991," *Journal of Economic Perspectives,* Spring 1993, p. 11.

40. Robert Heilbroner and William Milberg, *The Crisis of Vision in Modern Economic Thought* (New York: Cambridge University Press, 1995), p. 86.

41. Federal Reserve Bank of Kansas City, *Policies for Long-Run Growth,* 1992, p. 186.

42. Sylvia Nasar, "Older Americans Cited in Studies of National Savings Rate Slump," *New York Times,* February 21, 1995, p. 1.

43. Edward C. Banfield, *The Unheavenly City Revisited* (Boston: Little, Brown, 1968), p. 53.

44. U.S. Department of Commerce, *Long-Term Economic Growth 1960–1970* (Washington, D.C.: U.S. Government Printing Office, 1973), pp. 222–25.

45. "French Finance Minister Resigns," *Boston Globe,* August 26, 1995, p. 2.

46. Shlomo Maital and Sharone L. Maital, "Is the Future What It Used to Be? A Behavioral Theory of the Decline of Savings in the West," *Journal of Socio-Economics,* Vol. 23, No. 1/2 1994, p. 10.

47. *Economic Report of the President 1986,* pp. 282, 336, 338.

48. *Economic Report of the President 1995,* pp. 306, 362–363.

49. Council on Competitiveness, "Can Credit-Happy America Be Saved?" *Challenges,* February 1995, p. 1.

50. "How Washington Can Stop Its War on Savings," *Fortune,* March 6, 1995, p. 133.

51. "Global 500," *Fortune,* August 7, 1995, p. F1.

52. Martin Feldstein, "Too Little, Not Too Much," *The Economist,* June 24, 1995, p. 72.

53. Lester C. Thurow, *The Zero-Sum Society,* Chapter 5, "Environmental Problems" (New York: Basic Books, 1980), pp. 103–122; Lester C. Thurow, *Head to Head,* Chapter 7, "Festering Problems: Global Environmentalism" (New York: Morrow, 1992), p. 219.

54. Richard M. Coughlin, ed., *Morality, Rationality, and Efficiency: New Perspectives in Socio-Economics* (London: M. E. Sharpe, 1991), p. 5.

55. Ibid. p. 46.

56. Richard Thaler, *Quasi Rational Economics* (New York: Russell Sage Foundation, 1991), p. 77.

57. Piore, *Beyond Individualism,* pp. 137–138.

58. Fred Hirsh, *Social Limits to Growth* (Cambridge, Mass.: Harvard University Press, 1976), pp. 143, 156.

59. Ibid. p. 137.

60. Bruno Dagens, *Angkor: Heart of an Asian Empire* (New York: Harry N. Abrams, 1995); Dawn F. Rooney, *Angkor* (Chicago: Passport Books, 1994), p. 32.

CHAPTER 15: OPERATING IN A PERIOD OF PUNCTUATED EQUILIBRIUM

1. Paul Krugman, *The Age of Diminishing Expectations* (Cambridge, Mass.: MIT Press, 1990).

2. Fred Block, *Post-Industrial Possibilities: A Critique of Economic Discourse* (Berkeley: University of California Press, 1990), pp. 2–4.

3. J. L. Baxter, *Social and Psychological Foundations of Economic Analysis* (New York: Harvester Wheatsheaf, 1988).

4. Joseph A. Schumpeter, *The Theory of Economic Development* (New York: Oxford University Press, 1961), p. 92.

5. Ibid. p. 84.

6. Ibid. p. 223.

7. Joseph A. Schumpeter, *Capitalism, Socialism, and Democracy* (New York: Harper Colophon Books, 1975), pp. 132, 139, 143.

8. Ibid. p. 157.

9. Mona Harrington, *The Dream of Deliverance in American Politics* (New York: Alfred A. Knopf, 1986).

10. Fernand Braudel, *A History of Civilization* (New York: Penguin Press, 1994), p. 475.

11. Michel Albert, *Capitalism Against Capitalism* (London: Whurr Publishers, 1993).

12. Ibid. p. 8.

13. "France Strikes Against Chirac," *The Economist,* October 14, 1995, p. 57.

14. Heino Fassbender and Susan Cooper-Hedegaard, "The Ticking Bomb at the Core of Europe," *The McKinsey Quarterly,* No. 3, 1993, p. 130.

15. Amity Shlaes, "Germany's Chained Economy," *Foreign Affairs,* September/October 1994, p. 109.

16. David Goodhard, "There's Still Life in the Old Model," *Financial Times,* April 12, 1994, p. 17; Fassbender and Cooper-Hedegaard, "The Ticking Bomb at the Core of Europe," p. 135.

17. Alessandra Del Boca and Paola Rota, "How Much Does Hiring and Firing Cost: Survey Evidence from Italy," University College Discussion Paper No. 95-15, 1994.

18. Richard Stevenson, "Swedes Ask Reluctantly Is Welfare Too Generous," *International Herald Tribune,* February 3, 1995, p. 1.

19. John E. Rehfeld, "In Japan Personnel Has the Corner Office," *New York Times,* May 1, 1994, p. F9.

20. James Fallows, *Looking at the Sun* (New York: Pantheon Books, 1994), pp. 85, 113.

21. Robert Ozaki, *Human Capitalism: The Japanese Enterprise System as World Model* (New York: Penguin Books, 1991).

22. "Japan Survey," *The Economist,* July 9, 1994, p. 13.

23. "Global 500," *Fortune,* August 7, 1995, p. F1.

24. Mihoko Ida, "For Savers, Lower Interest Rate Not Enriching," *Nikkei Weekly,* September 18, 1995, p. 17.

25. William Dawkins, "Cloud over Rising Sun," *Financial Times,* May 20, 1995, p. 9.

26. Takishi Inogushi, "Shaping and Sharing Pacific Dynamism," *Annals of*

the American Academy of Political and Social Science, September 1989, p. 47.

27. Lauren Fredman, "Foreigners Lament: We're Going Nowhere," *Nikkei Weekly,* April 4, 1994, p. 16.

28. George Brockway, *The End of Economic Man* (New York: W. W. Norton, 1993), p. 253.

29. *Encyclopaedia Britannica,* Vol. 16 (Chicago: 1972), p. 111.

Index